SLOW TRAVEL

South Devon & Dartmoor

Local, characterful guides to Britain's special places

Hilary Brad

EDITION 2

Bradt Travel Guides Ltd, UK
The Globe Pequot Press Inc, USA

Bradt

South Devon & Dartmoor

*Devon's combination of moor, river and sea is an
invitation to travel slowly, whether on foot, bicycle,
horseback or in a canoe. The less energetic can watch
the scenery gently unfold from the comfort of a
steam train or riverboat, or potter around
a quintessential English village.*

1 Salcombe from its estuary. 2 Some of Dartmoor's clapper bridges date back to medieval times. 3 Happy Devon canoeists on the Dart. 4 South Devon abounds in farmers' markets. 5 The steam train approaching Paignton on the Dartmouth line.

A TASTE OF SOUTH DEVON

From cream teas to cheeses and from seafood to wine and cider, South Devon has treats for everyone. Almost every town has a market selling the freshest of lip-smacking local produce.

1 Sharpham Vineyard. Devon's south-facing slopes are perfect for wine production. 2 The Market Plaice, Plymouth. 3 Powderham Castle hosts the vibrant Powderham Food Festival in October. 4 Mushroom specialists at Totnes Food Market. 5 Few visitors can resist a traditional Devon cream tea – in Devon the jam usually goes on top of the cream. 6 The Zero Waste Shop in Totnes does what it says: sells food with no packaging. You bring your own container.

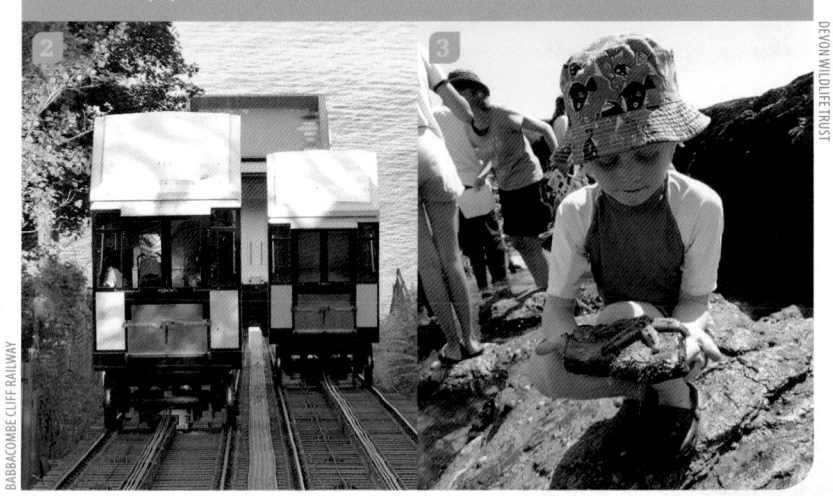

DEVON ON THE WATER

South Devon is the place for messing about in boats, whether on the sea, estuary or the River Dart. Swimmers have a choice of secluded coves or wild swimming in rivers and lakes, as well as broad sandy beaches.

1 Brixham, the hub of Devon's fishing industry. 2 Babbacombe Cliff Railway carries visitors down a steep cliff to Oddicombe Beach. 3 South Devon's rocky coastline is perfect for rock-pooling. This child has found a spiny starfish. 4 Boats moored on the River Dart.

5 Blackpool Sands, south of Dartmouth. 6 At high tide the sea tractor is the only way to reach Burgh Island. 7 Dippers are often seen on the rivers of Dartmoor. 8 Gammon Head in winter. The South West Coast Path can be enjoyed at any time of year.

AUTHOR

Hilary Bradt co-founded Bradt Travel Guides in 1974, and now lives in semi-retirement in Seaton, East Devon. After 40 years of writing guidebooks to Africa and South America, she has embraced her chosen home to the extent of insisting that such a large, varied and beautiful county deserved three Slow guides, not just one. A keen walker, she has hiked many miles of the South West Coast Path and inland footpaths, as well as enjoying Dartmoor on someone else's legs – on a horse. Most Saturdays see her taking part in one of Devon's parkruns (5k, but she's appropriately slow) and during the summer a swim in the sea, just a few minutes away, is always a pleasure. She is a productive member of the South West Sculptors' Association and lectures regularly on travel-related topics at libraries and literary festivals, both in Devon and further afield.

CO-AUTHOR

Janice Booth settled in Devon in 2002 and considers it her 'home county', after many decades in other parts of Britain. During the war she lived briefly in Colyton, and her mother took her 'to the seaside' at nearby Seaton (where she now lives) via a branch of the old Southern Railway. On family holidays she tasted her first clotted cream in Sidmouth aged eight, rode on the Burgh Island tractor aged ten, and rock-hopped along the shore near Wembury in her early teens. She's fascinated by Devon folklore, has co-written (with Hilary) Bradt's *Slow Travel East Devon & the Jurassic Coast*, and is co-author of the Bradt guide to Rwanda, a country she loves. In Seaton she enjoys the shingly beach, uses her Senior Bus Pass enthusiastically, and struggles to resist pasties and clotted cream.

Authors' note

The two authors researched this book both together and apart, so the 'I' could be either Janice or Hilary. Just so you know …

Second edition published April 2018
First published April 2014

Bradt Travel Guides Ltd
IDC House, The Vale, Chalfont St Peter, Bucks SL9 9RZ, England
www.bradtguides.com
Print edition published in the USA by The Globe Pequot Press Inc,
PO Box 480, Guilford, Connecticut 06437-0480

Text copyright © 2018 Hilary Bradt
Maps copyright © 2018 Bradt Travel Guides Ltd (includes map data © OpenStreetMap
contributors)
Photographs copyright © 2018 Individual photographers (see below)
Project Manager: Maisie Fitzpatrick
Series Design: Pepi Bluck, Perfect Picture
Cover: Pepi Bluck, Perfect Picture

ISBN: 978 1 78477 077 8 (print)
e-ISBN: 978 1 78477 542 1 (e-pub)
e-ISBN: 978 1 78477 443 1 (mobi)

British Library Cataloguing in Publication Data
A catalogue record for this book is available from the British Library

Photographers
Photos © individual photographers and organisations credited beside images & also from
picture libraries credited as follows: Alamy.com (A), Dreamstime.com (D), Shutterstock.com
(S), Superstock.com (SS), Visit Dartmoor – Official Dartmoor Tourism Organisation
www.visitdartmoor.co.uk (VD)

Front cover Bonehill Rocks on Dartmoor (Adam Burton Photography)
Back cover Anstey's Cove, near Torquay (Unique Devon Tours)
Title page Forest by the River Dart (VD)

Maps David McCutcheon FBCart. S

Typeset by Pepi Bluck, Perfect Picture
Production managed by Jellyfish Print Solutions; printed in India
Digital conversion by www.dataworks.co.in

CONTRIBUTORS

Alex Graeme runs Unique Devon Tours (⟁ uniquedevontours. co.uk), which offers tailor-made, small group guided tours of Devon (see ad in fourth colour section). We have unashamedly used his knowledge and expertise for boxes (pages 10 and 268–9) and tips on accommodation.

Joanna Griffin won Bradt's 'Perfect Day' competition for East Devon with her evocative description of wild swimming and was a finalist in Bradt's 2018 New Travel Writer of the Year award. She has since researched wild swimming throughout the region; her suggestions can be found on pages 81, 173 , 214 and 240.

ACKNOWLEDGEMENTS

Two people living in East Devon can't pretend to know everything about another region of the county. But through friends, acquaintances, and chance meetings at bus stops or shops, they can end a summer of research knowing a heck of a lot.

Author and ornithologist Tony Soper provided local information and the box on birdwatching (pages 162–3) retained from the last edition. Likewise Philip Knowling gave prompt answers just when we needed them, and permission for some of his boxes on follies to be reused, while Dave Clegg brought us up to date on the Dartmoor Railway.

Hilary is particularly grateful to her old friends Bridget and Jerry Gurney, who provided exceptional accommodation and local knowledge in East Portlemouth, and her colleagues in the South West Sculptors' Association, who chipped in with warm recommendations for their home areas: Derek Cadle, Jenny Distin, Rose Ellis, Angela Holmes, Jean Lock, David Newman, Verity Newman, Luke Shepherd and Pippa Unwin with an extra thank you to Pippa who introduced me to so much in the Aveton Gifford area, and Jenny and Jean, whose enthusiasm and way with words provided quotes from 'locals' around Galmpton and Kingsbridge.

Finally we would like to thank Imogen Vignoles and the Mais Estate for kind permission to use extracts from *Glorious Devon* by S P B Mais.

Suggested places to base yourself

These bases make ideal starting points for exploring localities the Slow way.

OKEHAMPTON pages 212–15
Its dramatic 11th-century castle overlooks the Okement River. Nearby are unspoilt villages and the nostalgic Dartmoor Railway.

CHAGFORD pages 234–7
The perfect base for exploring northern Dartmoor, with its rich prehistory and scenic mix of wooded valleys and high moor.

Cornwall

TAVISTOCK pages 264–6
This gracious town with its historic market is at one end of Drake's Trail for cyclists (Plymouth is the other end) and is the western gateway to Dartmoor.

WEMBURY pages 164–6
Handy for Plymouth but very unspoilt, this is one of the best beaches in the region; it has excellent rock pools as well as sand, good coastal walks and surfing.

KINGSBRIDGE pages 131–2
This very pleasant small town, only a short ferry trip from Salcombe, has a wide selection of inland footpaths and easy access to the coast path.

BIGBURY BAY pages 143–5
The best combination of sandy beach, pretty villages and the coast path. You can surf at nearby Bantham, or take the 'sea tractor' to Burgh Island.

CHAPTER 7
page 204

Okehampton

A3072

A30

A382

Chag...

Moretonhampste...

DARTMOOR

A386

Tavy

B3212 Widecombe-
the-Moo...

A30

A3079

A30

NATIONAL

B3357

Tavistock

Princetown

CHAPTER 6
page 182

Ashburton

CHAPTER 8
page 222

PARK

Tamar

Plym

Buckfastleigh

CHAPTER 5
page 150

A386

PLYMOUTH

A

A38

A379

Avon

CHAPTER 4
page 118

Wembury

Kingsbridge

A3

Bigbury
Bay

A37

Salcombe

BOVEY TRACEY pages 250–2
If you´re into crafts this is the perfect centre. Apart from the craft gallery there are some unusual independent shops, and Dartmoor is on your doorstep.

THE EXE ESTUARY pages 25–34
Its tidal flats, marshes and nature reserves are a haven for waterbirds, particularly winter migrants, and other wildlife.

SHALDON pages 42–3
Top choice if you want to escape the more commercial aspect of the beach scene. The excellent Shaldon Wildlife Trust is nearby and there´s boating on the Teign estuary.

TORQUAY pages 54–61
The place for grand hotels, with some surprisingly quick escapes into the countryside and coastal walks. Don´t miss Living Coasts.

TOTNES pages 82–8
A unique town, full of character, with a variety of accommodation and eateries; the many nearby attractions include Dartington Hall.

THE RIVER DART pages 98–100
The Dart river valley caters for adventurous visitors of all ages, with crabbing for kids, boating or kayaking for teenagers and adults, and walking for everyone. Or enjoy its tranquil hideaways and picture-perfect views.

DARTMOUTH pages 107–14
To the east and west of this appealing town with its rich maritime heritage are some of the coast path´s finest stretches.

A377

M5

A30

EXETER

A3052

Topsham

Teign

Exe

A379

Exmouth

Bovey Tracey

CHAPTER 1
page 22

A38

A380

Dawlish

Teignmouth

Newton Abbot

Shaldon

CHAPTER 2
page 48

Torquay

Paignton

Dart

CHAPTER 3
page 78

Brixham

Totnes

Dartmouth

0   5 miles
0   5 km

N

CONTENTS

GOING SLOW IN SOUTH DEVON & DARTMOOR.... 7
A taste of South Devon & Dartmoor **7**, Getting there & around **11**,
Some favourite visits **14**, Books & media **18**, How to use this book **19**

1 THE EXE & TEIGN ESTUARIES 23
Getting there & around **23**, Essential Exeter **24**, The Exe Estuary **25**, Dawlish Warren &
Dawlish **34**, The Teign Valley **39**, South of the Teign **44**

2 THE ENGLISH RIVIERA: TORBAY 49
Getting there & around **50**, North of Torbay **51**, Torquay & around **54**,
Paignton to Brixham **63**, Brixham **72**

3 TOTNES & THE RIVER DART 79
Getting there & around **80**, Totnes **82**, Dartington & around **89**, The middle &
lower River Dart **98**, Riverside villages **100**, Dartmouth & around **107**, Kingswear &
the coast toward Brixham **116**

**4 THE SOUTH HAMS
& DEVON'S FAR SOUTH** 119
Getting there & around **120**, The Slapton area **122**, Approaching the South Hams from
Dartmoor **126**, Devon's far south **129**, The southern beaches **139**, River Avon, Bigbury-on-Sea
& Burgh Island **142**, Ayrmer Cove, Westcombe Beach & Ringmore **145**, Modbury & area **146**

**5 PLYMOUTH, THE TAMAR VALLEY
& SOUTHERN DARTMOOR** 151
Getting there & around **152**, Plymouth **153**, South & southeast of Plymouth **164**,
The Yealm Estuary **166**, The Tamar Valley **168**, East of the Tavy **172**,
Southern Dartmoor **177**

6 THE EASTERN FRINGE OF DARTMOOR 183
Getting there & around **184**, The northern Teign Valley **184**, Newton Abbot &
area **188**, Ashburton **193**, Buckfastleigh & area **195**

**7 THE NORTHWESTERN FRINGE
OF DARTMOOR** 205
Getting there & around **205**, The Beacon Villages **207**, Okehampton & around **212**,
Lydford & around **216**

8 DARTMOOR NATIONAL PARK 223
Dartmoor: the hand of man **224**, Dartmoor tin & the stannary towns **226**, Getting there &
around **227**, Chagford, Castle Drogo & the north **234**, The east **243**, Bovey Tracey **250**,
The high moor **252**, Southwest Dartmoor **259**, The western moor **264**, Off the B3357 **267**

ACCOMMODATION 274
INDEX 283

SOUTH DEVON & DARTMOOR

> [The holidaymaker] comes to Devon for what he cannot get anywhere else, clotted cream the colour of cowslips for breakfast, lunch, tea and dinner, scenery as rich as the cream, contact with a glorious past history and a very pleasant type of modern people. The way, and I think the only way, to see Devon, is to go slowly in and about her, to keep moving, but to keep moving at snail's pace.
>
> S P B Mais, 1928

One thing that has been a constant pleasure when researching our three Slow guides to Devon is the way that early guidebook writers like S P B Mais anticipated our current appreciation of the Slow movement. Indeed, there's nothing new in Slow; it's a rediscovery of the perfect way to enjoy the most beautiful and intriguing parts of our country. It's about taking the time to visit a church, or watch the scenery unfold from a bus window, or observe a peacock butterfly fluttering from flower to flower, or sit gazing out to sea from the coastal path, or plunging from the moor into one of those deep, wooded valleys we call combes. Indeed, that's where the county gets its name: Dyfnaint was the Celtic name for Devon, and means 'dark and deep valleys'.

A TASTE OF SOUTH DEVON & DARTMOOR

Cream teas and cider are the treats most associated with Devon, and indeed they're a big part of any holiday here. But foodwise there's so much more.

With Devon's high rainfall (shh!) and rich and varied grazing, **meat** is of exceptional quality, and restaurants take pride in sourcing it from named local farms, so that what you're eating comes directly or indirectly from our fertile soil. **Seafood** also is superb, as you might expect in the only English county with two separate sea coasts. Restaurants often have

THE SLOW MINDSET

Hilary Bradt, Founder, Bradt Travel Guides

We shall not cease from exploration
And the end of all our exploring
Will be to arrive where we started
And know the place for the first time.

T S Eliot, 'Little Gidding', *Four Quartets*

This series evolved, slowly, from a Bradt editorial meeting when we started to explore ideas for guides to our favourite country – Great Britain. We wanted to get away from the usual 'top sights' formula and encourage our authors to bring out the nuances and local differences that make up a sense of place – such things as food, building styles, nature, geology, or local people and what makes them tick. Our aim was to create a series that celebrates the present, focusing on sustainable tourism, rather than taking a nostalgic wallow in the past.

So without our realising it at the time, we had defined 'Slow Travel', or at least our concept of it. For the beauty of the Slow movement is that there is no fixed definition;

we adapt the philosophy to fit our individual needs and aspirations. Thus Carl Honoré, author of *In Praise of Slow*, writes: 'The Slow Movement is a cultural revolution against the notion that faster is always better. It's not about doing everything at a snail's pace, it's about seeking to do everything at the right speed. Savouring the hours and minutes rather than just counting them. Doing everything as well as possible, instead of as fast as possible. It's about quality over quantity in everything from work to food to parenting.' And travel.

So take time to explore. Don't rush it, get to know an area – and the people who live there – and you'll be as delighted as the authors by what you find.

their own suppliers, who rush the catch to them straight from their boat. If you're self-catering look in fishmongers for the 'catch of the day'.

Local dairies offer more calorific delights. The very best **clotted cream**, thick, velvety and yellow, comes from Devon and Cornwall, and its taste is quite unlike that of thinner creams. It can vary according to the breed of cow and the preparation (milk is heated very slowly and then cooled, so that the cream rises to the top and can be skimmed off). A recent transatlantic visitor expected her 'Devon cream tea' to be a cup of tea with cream in it, so was surprised to receive freshly baked scones spread thickly with clotted cream and jam, accompanied by a generous pot of tea. In Devon, the jam usually goes on top of the cream, in Cornwall underneath. And to sample the cream tea nominated as the best in Devon, you'll need to visit an unpretentious outdoor eatery in Dartmouth (page 113).

The **cheeses** range from hard and nutty to soft and squashy, and from raspingly strong to gently creamy; you'll find them on sale locally. They're enriched with all manner of herbs and flavours; different dairies have their own specialities, some dating back several centuries. For instance, Quicke's traditional mature cheddar comes from land near Exeter that has been farmed by the same family for over 450 years (∂ quickes. co.uk); and Curworthy Farm near Okehampton (∂ curworthycheese. co.uk) uses a 17th-century recipe.

Pasties are another temptation, and both their fillings (a mix of meat and vegetables) and their pastry vary according to the maker. You'll just have to sample a few to find your favourite! The aroma as they're taken from the baker's oven is hard to resist. In Devon, the crimp (closure) traditionally arches over the top; in Cornwall it's along the edge of the base.

CHEERS!

The mild climate and south-facing slopes are also conducive to wine-making, with the **Sharpham Vineyard** (pages 102–3) leading the way with its wine tastings, vineyard tours, and café. At **Old Walls Vineyard** (page 41) near Teignmouth you can 'rent' an area of vines and receive the fruits of its harvest once bottled.

South Devon also has some internationally famous **gin** distilleries: Salcombe Gin (page 135) has won many awards, as has Plymouth Gin (page 155), made traditionally by one man in one Victorian copper still. Devon's first single malt **whisky** distillery is just getting under way in Bovey Tracey (∂ dartmoorwhiskydistillery.co.uk), and planning permission for one in Princetown was granted in 2017. Several breweries around the county, small and larger, have their own ranges of ales: you'll find them in shops and pubs, together with plentiful local advice as to which you should try.

Cider

Two types of cider are brewed in the UK – in eastern counties, Kent and East Anglia, and in the west in Devon and Somerset. We in the West Country have a valid claim that ours is the best. True cider apples are only grown here, and most cider producers use varieties that date back hundreds of years with evocative names such as Fair Maids of Devon, Pig's Snout, Tail Sweet, Devon Crimson and Slack-Ma-Girdle. The distinctive cloudy cider, which is unfiltered and unpasteurised, is produced in Devon, as is the famous high-alcohol scrumpy.

WASSAILING

Alex Graeme

Imagine leaving your house after dark and walking by night along lanes and across fields, with the distant beat of drums drifting through the still air. Then from down in the valley ahead you start to hear other sounds – stringed instruments, laughter, bellows of excitement, and the clacking of wood hitting wood. 'Old apple tree, old apple tree, we wassail thee …' reaches your ears, and there's no doubt as to where you're heading. It's the ancient, pagan festival of wassailing, and it doesn't get much more atmospheric than in the depths of Devon.

The tradition began a very long time ago, somewhere in the dark ages. A wassail is a ceremony where offerings are made to the apple trees, in the hope their next harvest will be large enough to make plenty of cider. Wassails traditionally take place in January, on the old 12th night (either the 5th or 16th of the month), although nowadays different wassails are held on different nights around Devon. To appeal to the spirits of the apple trees and deter evil spirits, singing, dancing, chanting and toasts are the order of the night – I've experienced Mummers' plays, shotguns being fired, and sometimes the trees being doused in cider. Thankfully I haven't as yet observed any sacrifices, although I suspect

they may have taken place once upon a time. Anything to protect the apple harvest!

Wassails are held throughout Devon, although they are fairly scarce these days. My favourite is at The Old Church House in Torbryan. Here the Beltane Border Morris Dancers defy many of the traditional stereotypes, with their blackened faces, fast and hard dancing, and seemingly vicious swinging of their wooden sticks! There is something quite primeval about the whole experience; as the spectators wander together into the orchards to address the trees, a collective warmth spreads among the crowd, and the wassail songs and blessings begin. By this stage the sticks have become flaming torches, and the flickering light catches eyes that are both wary and cheerful: slightly unnerved by the strangeness, but joyous at attending such a timeless ritual.

Do try to experience at least one wassail. It's so special, and the memory will stay with you for a very long time. Drinking the cider that the very same trees you are blessing helped create the year before is part of the cycle of life. Each year we take our children, and often their friends, and it really is one of the highlights of our winter.

Cider enthusiasts can fuel their interest through the website ⊘ real-cider.co.uk. A few of the region's cider producers are below.

Ashridge Cider Staverton ⊘ ashridgecider.co.uk. Best known for their sparkling ciders using the traditional champagne method, they also make organic vintage ciders.
Heron Valley Drinks Loddiswell ⊘ heronvalley.co.uk. One of the largest of the region's producers, with their own mobile bar, they make a variety of juices and cider vinegar as well as a range of ciders either bottled or bagged.
Hunts Cider Stoke Gabriel ⊘ huntscider.co.uk (page 75)
Luscombe Organic Drinks Buckfastleigh ⊘ luscombe.co.uk. Well known for their range of organic fruit juices and soft drinks, Luscombe also make a medium dry cider.
Ron Barter Dunsford ⊘ 01647 252783 ⊠ lowleyfarm@aol.com. Here is something completely different. Ron is part of the Dartmoor Artisan Trail (page 229), producing cider using one of the UK's oldest working cider presses in a barn that dates back to Saxon times, full of antique cider-making tools and equipment. Tours can be arranged, including cider tasting.
Sampford Courtenay Cider ⊘ devoncider.com. Make a good variety of ciders which can be bought online or at their shop at Solland Farm, EX20 3QT ⊘ 10.00–18.00 Tue–Sun.
Yarde Cider Stoke Gabriel ⊘ yardecider.co.uk. A small family business producing organic craft cider and apple juice. They also hold a wassail (see box, opposite) in January.

GETTING THERE & AROUND

It goes without saying that Slow Travel favours public transport above the car, and in Devon this isn't just because it's better for the environment. Although Devon actually has more miles of road than the whole of Belgium, many of these are car-unfriendly single-track lanes with high banks and hedges where you rely on intuition rather than eyesight to deal with oncoming cars. S P B Mais recognised the problem for drivers: 'If you keep to the road you will not see Devon at all, only a succession of whitewashed thatched cottages red with fuchsia clustered round a tall grey granite church tower at three- or five-mile intervals as you bore your way through green tunnel after green tunnel.'

It is entirely possible to enjoy a holiday in Devon without a car. Transport to the area is good, and there are usually local buses to get you to the places of interest. Each chapter has specific information on public transport. A useful organisation for **planning journeys by bus and/or train** is Traveline (⊘ 0871 200 2233 ⊘ traveline.info).

If you are stuck at a bus stop with no bus and only an unsmart mobile phone, you can phone the number (which is also shown on most bus stops) for help and advice. Another excellent **website** for all forms of travel – bus, train, cycle, walking – is ⊘ traveldevon.info. Its interactive bus map is particularly useful.

Local buses are a boon for bus-pass holders, but even for paying passengers there are often special deals such as the DevonDay bus ticket which gives unlimited bus travel throughout Devon. Praiseworthy community-run buses such as Tavistock Country Buses (page 227) are an extra bonus. Devon County Council publishes a series of regional bus timetables as well as a bus map of the county. We list relevant ones in each chapter and they can be picked up in most tourist information centres and some shops or newsagents.

CYCLING & WALKING

These are now combined in each chapter under the heading **Self-powered travel**.

This part of Devon has a good range of dedicated **cycle paths** as well as the 99-mile Coast-to-Coast Route 27 from Ilfracombe to Plymouth. A Croydecycle map (see opposite) covers the whole route. Others are being developed by Sustrans (⊘ sustrans.org.uk). See also ⊘ traveldevon.info.

Among the most popular **cycle trails** are Drake's Trail, the Dart Valley Cycle Way, the Granite Way, the Stover Trail, and the Dartmoor Way. These, and others, are listed in the relevant chapters.

For **walkers**, there's the **South West Coast Path** from Starcross to Plymouth, a distance of almost exactly 100 miles. Some of the best walks in all of Devon are here, with the most rewarding short stretches described in each relevant chapter. Those tackling the whole trail, or planning to walk for several days, would do well to use the services of a luggage transfer company so they can walk unencumbered. **Luggage Transfers** (⊘ luggagetransfers.co.uk) will also arrange walker-friendly accommodation for you. Likewise, Dartmoor is the starting/finishing point for the **Two Moors Way**, a stiff but hugely rewarding challenge linking Dartmoor and Exmoor, which can now be extended to Wembury to make coast-to-coast trail.

If you fancy the idea of letting someone else do all the planning and organisation and luggage transfer, the tour operator **On Foot Holidays** (⊘ onfootholidays.co.uk), which specialises in self-guided walking

SINGLE-TRACK ROADS

You can get to all sizeable towns in Devon on good main roads, but if you visit more remote areas you may well have to drive on single-track roads with passing places. They're perfectly manageable if you remember three things.

- As you drive past passing places, make a mental note of where they are, so that you know how far you've got to go if you need to reverse.
- When you're reversing, rather than pulling sideways into the passing place as you reach it, you may find it easier to continue reversing straight back on the crown of the road until you've passed it and then drive forward into it. Visibility is often better.
- Whether you're reversing or driving forward, and whichever side the passing place is on, keep to the left so that the oncoming driver passes on your right. And remember to use your indicators.

holidays in Europe, has an appealing six-day inn-to-inn walk, *A tale of two rivers*, taking you from Dunsford on the River Teign to Dartmouth. The longest days are about 20km but these can usually be shortened.

Walking (& cycling) guides & maps

There are plenty of **guidebooks** for walkers. Some are listed in the relevant chapters; Pathfinder's *South Devon and Dartmoor* by Sue Viccars is particularly useful, covering as it does the same area as this book. The best guide to the South West Coast Path is Trailblazer's *Dorset and South Devon Coast Path*, by Henry Stedman and Joel Newton, which has detailed maps and suggestions for accommodation.

The 1:25,000 Ordnance Survey Explorer **maps** covering Dartmoor and South Devon are huge, double-sided affairs, prefixed OL (the scale means they are great for detail but very unwieldy – we dubbed them 'the table cloth'). Much more useful are the series produced by Mike Harrison under his Croydecycle imprint (Croydecycle.co.uk) at a scale of 1:12,500 (about five inches to a mile). Personal (he walks or cycles every road and path), idiosyncratic (plenty of observations to help the walker, such as the condition of the footpath or little nuggets of history) and small-pocket-sized, these cover all of the coastal areas in this book and some popular inland places such as Totnes and Kingsbridge but not Dartmoor. The relevant maps are listed in each chapter and are widely available from TICs and gift shops. Mike is also the brains behind the excellent *South Devon* map at 1:100,000 which despite its relatively small scale is my map of choice for finding my way around the region. It almost exactly corresponds with the area covered in this book and manages to pack in more detail, including town plans, than any other map.

SOME FAVOURITE VISITS

EXCEPTIONAL CHURCHES

S P B Mais wrote: 'We are now beginning to discover in a quickly-changing England that almost our only link with the past lies in our churches … [They] bring back memories of our ancient stock. I make no more apology for turning aside into every church than I do for exploring every stream and river.'

We have turned aside into many churches and described them with enthusiasm for the same reason that so moved Mr Mais. From their monuments and tombstones to the present day's flower rota and village-life kneelers, they represent an unbroken link with the past. Churches are also repositories for important art (just how important is illustrated by the theft in 2013 of Torbryan's treasures). Devon's intricately carved wooden screens with their panels of painted saints are exceptional; there are more complete ones here than in any other county, so we can be forgiven for describing them with such affection. Likewise, carved bench ends and stained-glass windows which show us the mindset of a medieval craftsman whose life was dominated by the twin fears of God and the law, as well as his deep understanding of the rural life he was familiar with. And when asked to portray an animal he had never seen, he did his best.

Some of our favourites are Combeinteignhead and Haccombe (pages 44–6), Bere Ferrers (pages 169–70), Doddiscombsleigh (pages 185–6) and Higher Ashton (page 186), as well as the unique Victorian St Raphael's chapel in Dartmoor (page 260).

BEACHES

When I say I live in Devon, the response is often 'Oh lovely! We used to go there every year for our holidays,' and indeed Devon's beaches rival any in England. Unlike sandy North Devon, many in the south are

GOOD TIDINGS

Devon's beautiful stretches of coastline are particularly tempting for visitors fascinated by cliffs, beaches and the seashore. However, lifeboats all too often have to rescue people trapped by the incoming tide. These call-outs can be dangerous, costly, and are avoidable by checking the **tide tables** (available in local shops and TICs) before any seashore wander.

Non-seawise visitors don't always realise how much the extent and times of tidal ebb and flow vary with the moon's phases. The fact that you could walk past those rocks yesterday at midday and return safely doesn't mean you can do the same tomorrow: the tide may not ebb so far, or may rise higher, and you'll be trapped. (If this happens, don't try wading; there can be dangerously deep pools close to rocks.) These differences vary from place to place and from day to day, throughout the year, so – better safe than sorry!

shingle or a mixture of shingle and sand, but any slight disadvantage is offset by their setting, tucked into coves and framed by greenery. Some (such as Wembury) have rock pools to explore; others (for example Anstey's Cove) have exceptionally beautiful pebbles. We describe South Devon's best Slow beaches in the relevant chapters, but for an overview the excellent website ⊘ devonbeachguide.co.uk locates and describes every beach in the county, illustrating them with photos.

ANIMALS & WILDLIFE

Some visitors are bored by birds but adore zoos, while others abhor zoos but would happily spend all day in a hide. We love both, so have catered for both types of enthusiast.

Exceptional spots for **birdwatching** include the Exe Estuary (page 29), Dawlish Warren (pages 35–6), Berry Head (page 77), Slapton Ley (pages 122–3), Charlton Marsh (pages 132–3) and the Tamar Estuary (pages 162–3).

Birdwatchers and other wildlife enthusiasts should check out the **Devon Wildlife Trust** (✆ 01392 279244 ⊘ devonwildlifetrust.org), an active, 50-year-old charity with wildlife reserves and other conservation projects throughout Devon. The **RSPB** (⊘ rspb.org.uk) also manages several reserves here and organises birdwatching events.

Foremost among the area's **zoos**, **aquariums** and **farm attractions** are: Shaldon Wildlife Trust (page 42), Torquay's Living Coasts (pages 59–60), Paignton Zoo (pages 67–8), Totnes Rare Breeds Farm (pages 88–9), the National Marine Aquarium, Plymouth (page 156),

DOG-FRIENDLY DEVON

One of the biggest changes since the last edition is that some places (beaches, parks, restaurants …) have become fussier about welcoming dogs, so their owners need to know where they are or are not allowed. Claire Doyle has come to the rescue with her excellent little booklet *The Doggy Devon Guide to dog-friendly Devon* (doggydevon.co.uk), which is packed with helpful facts about travelling with your dog: pubs and restaurants, accommodation – and especially beaches. Over 100 Devon beaches are listed, with easy tell-at-a-glance coding showing whether and when your pet can accompany you.

The booklet is available from some TICs and direct from Claire via her website.

Dartmoor Zoo (page 178), Buckfastleigh's Otters & Butterflies (pages 198–9), Pennywell Farm (pages 202–3) and the Miniature Pony Centre near Moretonhampstead, Dartmoor (page 245).

NATIONAL GARDEN SCHEME (NGS) & OPEN STUDIOS

The NGS (ngs.org.uk) started in 1927: householders across England and Wales open their gardens to the public on various dates each year to raise money for nursing charities. This offers visitors the perfect way to get under the skin of Devon and to understand Devonians or – if you are visiting from overseas – the English. We consider ourselves the most passionate gardeners in the world and Devon, with its rich soil and mild climate, makes enthusiasts out of even reluctant horticulturists. There are now more than 3,700 participants with homes of every size, from manor houses to semi-detached cottages. And it's not just their gardens you'll enjoy. Almost every householder taking part in the scheme adds to the money raised by providing coffee and tea with a wonderful array of home-baked cakes. There are gardens opening at different times throughout the year, from January to December, although more, of course, in spring and summer. Some open only for one weekend so you need to plan ahead. The NGS annual publication, the *Garden Visitor's Handbook* (known as 'the yellow book'), gives a complete countrywide list and can be bought via the NGS website, but there are separate county lists too. The Devon one can usually be picked up free at tourist offices and other local outlets.

One NGS participant in South Devon is Heather Jansch. Using curved or chunky pieces of driftwood collected from Devon's estuaries and beaches, she creates horses that prance and leap through her acres of meadow and woodland near Newton Abbot. She is just one example of the county's artists who invite visitors to see them at work and to buy their art at lower prices than in a gallery. She also has a small part-time shop in Ashburton. Her studio, at Sedgewell Coach House, is open to the public during both the NGS scheme and the **Devon Open Studios** fortnight which takes place annually in September. This is an initiative of the Devon Artist Network (⌒ devonartistnetwork.co.uk), a non-profit organisation set up in 2004 to promote the visual arts and create opportunities for local artists; participating studios around the county are listed on its website.

FAIRS & FESTIVALS

These are very much a part of Devon life, some of them deeply traditional and others with a modern touch. You'll come across far more than we've listed here, particularly during the summer months.

Ashburton Medieval Fair ⊙ Jul; **Ashburton Food Festival** ⊙ Sep (pages 193–4)

Blackawton Festival of Wormcharming Nr Totnes ⌒ wormcharming.co.uk ⊙ Apr

Bovey Tracey Contemporary Craft Festival ⌒ craftsatboveytracey.co.uk ⊙ Jun

Brixham Pirate Festival ⌒ brixhampirates.com ⊙ May

Chagstock Music Festival ⌒ chagstock.info ⊙ Jul

Dart Music Festival Dartmouth ⌒ dartmusicfestival.co.uk ⊙ May

Dartmoor Folk Festival South Zeal ⌒ dartmoorfolkfestival.org.uk ⊙ Aug

Dartmouth Food Festival ⌒ dartmouthfoodfestival.com ⊙ Oct

Dawlish Carnival ⌒ dawlishcelebratescarnival.co.uk ⊙ Aug

Galmpton Gooseberry Pie Fair ⌒ galmptontorbay.org.uk ⊙ Jul (page 71)

Kingsbridge Fair Week ⌒ kingsbridgefairweek.co.uk ⊙ Jul

Marldon Apple Pie Fair ⌒ marldonhistory.co.uk ⊙ Jul

Okehampton Baring-Gould Folk Weekend ⌒ wrenmusic.co.uk ⊙ Oct

Plymouth International Firework Championship ⌒ britishfireworks.co.uk ⊙ Aug

Powderham Garden Festival ⊙ Apr; **Food Festival** ⊙ Oct (pages 30–3)

Salcombe Regatta ⌒ salcombeinformation.co.uk ⊙ May

Salcombe Town Regatta & Crabbers' Race ⌒ salcombeinformation.co.uk ⊙ Aug

Shaldon Water Carnival ⌒ shaldonwatercarnival.co.uk ⊙ Aug

Teignmouth Folk Festival ⌒ visitsouthdevon.co.uk ⊙ Jun

Totnes Carnival & Orange Race ⌒ visittotnes.co.uk ⊙ Aug (page 87)

Widecombe Fair ⌒ widecombefair.com ⊙ Sep (page 254)

BOOKS & MEDIA

NEWSPAPERS & LOCAL RADIO

The *Western Morning News* (⊘ westernmorningnews.co.uk) has been published six days a week since 1860 and is an excellent paper for Devon-based visitors, with lots of information and reports on local events as well as politically unbiased international news. Taking the longer view is the monthly magazine *Devon Life* (⊘ devonlife.co.uk) with in-depth articles on a range of town and country issues. The *Devonshire Magazine* (⊘ devonshiremagazine.co.uk), with a lively range of articles promoting the county, is distributed free at numerous locations or is available by subscription – see its website.

 Radio Devon (103.4MHz FM), broadcast since 1983 from the BBC studios in Plymouth, is one of the most listened-to of the BBC's local radio stations. Tune in to hear traffic news as well as local-interest stories and interviews.

BOOKS

The books below have been particularly useful for our research – and the list is church-oriented because Devon's little village churches are such an integral part of its history. A good website for finding out-of-print editions is ⊘ abebooks.co.uk.

IN PRINT

A Cloud of Witnesses (2011 & 2013) and *Showing the Path to Heaven* (2014) Wilks, Diane. Azure Publications. Descriptions of medieval panel paintings of saints in Devon churches.
Crossing's Guide to Dartmoor Crossing, William, 1909. A 1990 paperback edition (Peninsula Press) is currently available. Practical, authoritative and informative, with a good index.
Devon Hoskins, W G Collins, 1954; reprints 2003 & 2011. Phillimore & Co. Hoskins is *the* authority on Devon and his gazetteer is comprehensive.
Devon's Fifty Best Churches Gray, Todd. The Mint Press, 2011. Some fine photos of the churches and their carvings, accompanied by location maps and informative text.
England's Thousand Best Churches Jenkins, Simon. Penguin, 1999. The essential companion for any churchophile; 33 of Jenkins' choices are in Devon.
The Pilgrim's Guide to Devon Churches Cloister Books, 2008. A practical and sturdy little handbook, systematically listing and describing all of Devon's Anglican churches.
The South Devon Coast Harper, Charles G Chapman & Hall, 1907; reprint 2013, Hardpress Publishing. A lengthy and often entertaining look at Devon a hundred years ago.

OUT OF PRINT

Devon: A Shell Guide Jellicoe, Ann & Mayne, Roger. Faber & Faber, 1975. The erudite research and literary style that you would expect in a Shell Guide.

Early Tours in Devon and Cornwall Pearse Chope, R (ed). James G Commin, 1918; reprint 1967, David & Charles. Fascinating reports from early travellers in Devon, including John Leland (travelling 1534–43), Celia Fiennes (1695), Daniel Defoe (1724) and Robert Southey (1802).

Glorious Devon Mais, S P B. Great Western Railway Company, 1932. In his very readable style, Mais brings the scenery and people affectionately and enjoyably to life.

Some Old Devon Churches Stabb, John. Simpkin, Marshall, Hamilton, Kent & Co, 3 vols, 1908–16. Careful descriptions of many of Devon's finest churches, with grainy old black-and-white photos.

The King's England: Devon Mee, Arthur. Hodder & Stoughton, 1928 and later. Arranged alphabetically as a gazetteer, Mee's descriptions include some unusual details and a sprinkling of old tales and legends.

The Worthies of Devon Prince, John. 1701, reprinted 1810. In quaintly archaic English Prince chattily describes eminent Devonians and their families from the 11th century onwards. Copies are scarce but it has been scanned to CD, available from ⊘ parishchest.com.

HOW TO USE THIS BOOK

If you look at a map of Devon, you'll see that you can extract an Africa-shaped chunk from the Exe estuary and the A30 and A386 roads that run around the northern perimeter of Dartmoor to Plymouth. This is what we have (mostly) done in *South Devon and Dartmoor*, though some villages north and west of the main road have been described – because they deserve to be. Chapter divisions are relatively arbitrary; the largest (final) chapter covers Dartmoor National Park and some villages beyond its perimeter. We have put the villages and attractions around the western and eastern sections of the national park – some still technically inside the park but with a different character – in separate chapters. Divisions in the south of the county are dictated by water, either the sea or rivers.

MAPS

Each chapter begins with a map with **numbered stopping points** that correspond to numbered headings in the text, and the relevant regional maps – large scale maps for cyclists and walkers – are listed under the *Self-powered travel* headings.

FOOD, DRINK & ACCOMMODATION

We've listed some of our, and local people's, favourite pubs, cafés, restaurants and farm shops – anywhere supplying particularly good or unusual food or drink or because they're in a convenient location. Just be aware that such places close or change ownership frequently so check before setting out for that special meal.

The last chapter of this book lists a few recommended places to stay – or camp – out of the many hundred in South Devon & Dartmoor. The hotels and B&Bs featured in this section are indicated by 🏠 under the

THE BELL RINGERS OF DEVON

If you're a 'church crawler' like us, you start to notice unusual features. I was struck, for instance, by the floor-level bell ropes in some churches, including Lustleigh, and wondered if they were a rarity. Usually, I thought, the bell ringers climb up to the tower. The opportunity to learn more about this and bell ringing in general came when I met David Trist in the pub at Lustleigh. 'There are a lot of ground floor rings in Devon,' he said. 'This arose because the fashion in Devon was for relatively short solid towers as opposed to Somerset which liked tall towers. The Devon fashion may well have sprung from the local building materials, in this case granite, being both difficult to work and very heavy.' I joked that I knew everything about bell ringing because of a storyline in *The Archers*. 'You're thinking of method ringing,' said David. 'That's not what we do. In Devon we do call-change ringing.'

'What's the difference?'

'Call-changes are a repeated pattern of ringing which then introduces a slight change. Method ringing does not repeat its patterns and is constantly changing its sound on every stroke of the bell. Our tradition of call-changes is probably what all churches used to ring.' David went on to explain that the tradition was passed down through families and communities but because ringing the old bells was hard work, it used to be the 'working' community that did it. Old rules that survive on tower boards state that it was an offence to swear, curse, fight, and draw knives or pistols in church. This says a lot about the bell-ringing community. The gentry and clergy decided to take up bell ringing in order to introduce a more sophisticated style, better suited to people with an education. This was a blatant attempt to exclude the rougher element.

Devon was barely affected by the changes of population brought about by the agricultural and industrial revolutions in other counties, so a strong tradition of ringing continued to be handed down through families – something that continues to this day with the Trouts, Sharlands, Pascoes and Adams dynasties. 'As a result,' said David, 'we maintained our tradition, which is now recognised throughout the country as being uniquely skilful.'

ⓘ FURTHER INFORMATION ON SOUTH DEVON & DARTMOOR

Visit Devon ⊘ visitdevon.co.uk; see ad, 4th colour section. Provides detailed information for visitors, with regional ones focusing on the most popular areas.
Visit South Devon ⊘ visitsouthdevon.co.uk
Visit Dartmoor ⊘ visitdartmoor.co.uk
The English Riviera ⊘ englishriviera.co.uk
Visit Plymouth ⊘ visitplymouth.co.uk
Visit Exeter ⊘ visitexeter.com

---

heading for the town or village in which they are located. Self-catering is indicated by 🏠 and campsites by ⛺. For full descriptions of these listings visit ⊘ bradtguides.com/southdevonsleeps.

OPENING TIMES

Where they are useful, we have given the opening times of pubs, restaurants, tourist offices and attractions. They're correct at the time of writing but some may well change during the life of this book, so if they're important for your planning, do double-check before visiting. The same applies to the times of public transport.

FEEDBACK REQUEST & UPDATES WEBSITE

At Bradt Travel Guides we're aware that guidebooks start to go out of date on the day they're published – and that you, our readers, are out there in the field doing research of your own. You'll find out before us when a fine new family-run hotel opens or a favourite restaurant changes hands and goes downhill. So why not write and tell us about your experiences? Contact us on ✆ 01753 893444 or ✉ info@bradtguides.com. We will forward emails to the author who may post updates on the Bradt website at ⊘ bradtupdates.com/sdevon. Alternatively, you can add a review of the book to ⊘ bradtguides.com or Amazon.

THE EXE &
TEIGN ESTUARIES

1

THE EXE & TEIGN ESTUARIES

This area may not often hit the touristic headlines but it has some of South Devon's loveliest views and best birdwatching. Flatter than much of the county, it is friendly to walkers and cyclists, and its lack of main roads and large 'attractions' makes it well and truly Slow. Into a smallish space it packs rivers, thatched cottages, small ancient churches, beaches, cliffs and coastal views; while local museums and heritage centres offer glimpses of a fascinating rural past. The Exe and Teign estuaries host an exceptional variety of birdlife, and the rail journey southward from Exeter includes one of Britain's most scenic stretches.

WET-WEATHER ACTIVITIES

Exeter Cathedral and **Royal Albert Memorial Museum** (pages 24–5)
Powderham Castle (pages 30–3)
Dawlish Museum (page 38)
Teign Heritage Centre and **art galleries** (page 39)

GETTING THERE & AROUND

The obvious gateway town is Exeter, with its airport, M5 motorway and rail links to London, Bristol and the north, but if you're travelling northward from Cornwall the area is equally accessible from Plymouth. Coming by car the area lies between the fast A380 and the slower A379, so everywhere mentioned here is easily accessible – and with not too many single-track roads, unless you take cross-country short cuts. Views while driving are pleasant but without the drama of Dartmoor.

Slow trains from Exeter to Plymouth stop at Starcross, Dawlish Warren, Dawlish, Teignmouth and Newton Abbot (expresses go direct to Newton Abbot), and offer wonderful estuary views. Leaving from Exeter, sit on the left-hand side. **Buses** B from Exeter High Street and

2 from Exeter Bus Station between them serve all of the above as well as Exminster and Kenton (for Powderham Castle); the number 22 runs between Dawlish Warren and Paignton daily via Shaldon. On Wednesday and Friday the 886 links Shaldon and Newton Abbot twice daily each way via Stokeinteignhead and Combeinteignhead, while the 366 runs once each way Monday–Saturday between Exeter and Kenn. The Devon bus timetable that you need is *Teignbridge*; timetables and routes are available from ⬀ traveldevon.info, as is information about rail travel and cycling. Small **foot ferries** will carry you and your cycle across the Exe (between Exmouth and Starcross, pages 26 and 34) and the Teign (between Teignmouth and Shaldon, page 40).

SELF-POWERED TRAVEL

The recently completed, award-winning **Exe Estuary Trail**, a part of National Cycle Route 2, is the cherry on this chapter's cake, offering some fabulous views and birdwatching across the water. The 26-mile cycleway/walkway, much of it off-road, follows the edge of the estuary from Exmouth on the east bank round to Dawlish on the west bank, past nature reserves and waterside towns. For an excellent downloadable map and details, see ⬀ devon.gov.uk/exeexplorer07.pdf. The South West Coast Path and the Starcross/Exeter stretch of the Exe Valley Way also pass through this chapter's area, which is covered by OS Explorer map 110 and OS Landranger 192.

ESSENTIAL EXETER

Tourist information: Dix's Field (near bus station) ✆ 01392 665700 ⏱ year-round Mon–Sat, variable hours

Strictly speaking this guide starts just south of Exeter, but we're including the city briefly in case you pass through. For fuller coverage see our companion guide to this one, *Slow Travel East Devon & the Jurassic Coast*.

The two must-sees are the **Cathedral** (about five minutes' walk from the central railway station) and the **Royal Albert Memorial Museum** (only about two minutes). From St David's Rail Station they're a stiffish walk uphill (20–25 minutes) but there are buses from the station to the city centre. From the central bus station both are about ten minutes' walk, and on the way you can visit the Tourist Information Centre.

The **Royal Albert Memorial Museum** (Queen St ✐ 01392 265858 ⊘ rammuseum.org.uk ◯ 10.00–17.00 Tue–Sun; free entry) is an imposing gothic building, completed in 1868 and extensively redeveloped in 2010–11. In 2012 it was named the UK's Museum of the Year by Art Fund, the national fundraising charity for art, and described as 'quite simply a magical place'. It claims to be 'home to a million thoughts', and indeed its million-odd exhibits do cover a massive range. As you might imagine, it's strong on the history of Devon and Exeter, from the prehistoric to the present; but also includes international cultures (with some rare West African art), ceramics, natural history (various birds, bugs, mammals and seashells), the 18th- and 19th-century global explorers and many other changing exhibits. Wonderful for a browse – but allow plenty of time.

The great crouching bulk of **St Peter's Cathedral** (✐ 01392 285983 ⊘ exeter-cathedral.org.uk), with its massive carved frontage, was started by the Normans in 1114 and remodelled in decorated Gothic style in 1270–1369. It's hunkered solidly on the Cathedral Green, the weight of centuries pressing it into Exeter's earth; yet when you step inside your eye swings instantly up to the space and grace of its amazing roof: the longest unbroken stretch of Gothic vaulting in the world. When you've recovered from the impact of the building's size and splendour, you can focus on small, intimate details: animals on the choir stalls, sweet-faced angels playing musical instruments, sad swans with entwined necks, intricate roof bosses and the centuries-old hole in the door of the north tower to allow access for the Cathedral cat.

You may want simply to gaze and absorb the atmosphere, but, if you'd like to learn more, the Cathedral shop has guidebooks. The entrance fee helps to maintain this treasure-house of Exeter's history.

THE EXE ESTUARY

This broad stretch of water tethering Exeter to the sea is a haven of birdlife, with nature reserves, easy trails for cyclists and walkers, and exceptional views. The eastern side is outside the range of this book, but we're including some practicalities about it to help you with overall planning. Buses and trains serve towns along both banks. Seasonal foot ferries criss-cross between Exeter, Exmouth, Topsham, Starcross and Old Topsham Lock: see listing on pages 26–7. Different operators offer different concessions, so ask when you're booking. For some routes, Exe Estuary Circular tickets allow a linked trip on all three systems.

From Exeter, two train journeys either side of the Exe estuary are far more scenic than the same routes done by road. Both have sections running very close to the water. On the eastern bank, the short stretch to Exmouth is known as the Avocet Line (avocetline.org.uk) – and with good reason. In winter, thousands of waders and waterbirds come to the estuary, and the train windows offer a tremendous view. During the 30-minute journey you're likely to spot a variety of species – including avocets if you're very lucky – and even the occasional peregrine as it seeks out its prey. Numbers dwindle in summer, but the view is wonderful anyway. The little two-coach train takes up to two cycles if there's room but can be jam-packed with Exeter commuters at peak times, so travel off-peak if possible. From the Paignton/Plymouth train on the western side, you'll see the wetlands taking over from Exeter's urban compactness, Lympstone nestling between its red cliffs, colourful yachts scattered against the distant backdrop of Exmouth, Dawlish Warren's ancient sand dunes and the estuary gradually widening into the open sea of the English Channel. Starcross and Dawlish stations are so close to the water that at high tide it laps just below the platforms. After Teignmouth (pronounced Tin-mth) the train turns away from the sea to travel along the northern bank of the river Teign (pronounced Teen) to Newton Abbot, with peaceful views across to the southern bank.

Running from Exeter's historic quayside to Turf Lock (by the Turf Inn) is the four-mile **Exeter Ship Canal**, opened in 1566 on behalf of Exeter traders to improve access for shipping which had been blocked by weirs. It was the first canal to be built in Britain since Roman times. The big trading vessels have long since departed and now it's a peaceful spot for walkers, cyclists and boaters; the Exe Estuary Trail follows its bank, and bikes, canoes or kayaks can be hired on the quayside (see opposite).

FERRIES & BOAT TRIPS

Exeter Cruises 07984 368442 exetercruises.com Jun–Aug daily, Apr, May & Sep weekends only. Scenic 45min round-trip on canal from Exeter Quay to Double Locks Inn. Also private hire.

Exmouth/Starcross Ferry 07779 157280 & 07974 022536 exe2sea.co.uk & Facebook Apr–late Oct hourly daily, timetable on website; carries cycles (including tandems). Also coastline cruises, cruises on the Exe including RSPB birdwatching, and mackerel fishing.

RSPB ✎ 01392 432691 ⬀ rspb.org.uk/exeestuary. Runs special birdwatching cruises to see avocets, plus nature walks from its HQ at Dart's Farm just outside Topsham.

Stuart Line ✎ 01395 222144 ⬀ stuartlinecruises.co.uk. Birdwatching and other cruises, including wildlife on the Exe estuary, a coastal trip from Exmouth to Torquay and Brixham, and guided winter bird cruises which benefit the Devon Wildlife Trust (page 15).

Topsham Ferry ✎ 07801 203338 ⊙ Apr–Sep Wed–Mon, weekends & bank holidays in winter. Times depend on tide; phone for details. Runs from Ferry Rd in Topsham to Old Topsham Lock on the Exeter Canal/Exe Valley Way (for Exminster Marshes and The Turf Inn).

Topsham to Turf Ferry (*Sea Dream II*) ✎ 07778 370582 ⬀ topshamtoturfferry.co.uk ⊙ late May–mid Sep daily, Easter & Apr weekends only, times on website. From Topsham to Turf Locks for Turf Inn; takes cycles. Also winter birdwatching cruises (book via RSPB) and private hire for river cruises.

CYCLE HIRE

Braking Wind Cycles 2 Park Rd, Dawlish EX7 9LQ ✎ 01626 865161 ⊙ 10.00–16.00 Mon & Wed–Sat; phone to check off-season closure.

Saddles & Paddles Exeter Quay ✎ 01392 424241 ⬀ sadpad.com ⊙ 09.00–18.00 daily (check for off-season changes). Canoe and kayak hire (for Exeter canal) plus bike hire, sales and repairs.

1 EXMINSTER

⌂ & ⛺ **The Turf** (pages 28 and 275)

The avian attractions here are the RSPB's Exminster Marshes Nature Reserve (on the Estuary Trail) and Powderham Marshes. You can also walk or cycle to The Turf, one of the few pubs in the country that can't be reached by car, which has been providing refreshment to lock keepers and passing vessels since 1827.

Powderham Marshes are accessed (courtesy of Palmers Ales) via a track from the car park of the convenient Swan's Nest Inn just south of Exminster; the left turn from the A379 to the Swan's Nest is clearly signposted, at a roundabout. The one-mile trail leads through arable fields managed for farmland birds, including the rare cirl bunting. Brent geese gather there, and finches, including goldfinches and linnets, flock to feed in the stubble in winter. The viewing platform at the end of the trail gives views across the estuary; bring binoculars.

Exminster Marshes are on the cycle trail; by car continue along the Swan's Nest turning until the narrow road crosses the railway, then almost immediately there's a sharp turn right to the free RSPB car park.

It's at the start of a 2½-mile circular trail that takes you through fields alongside the railway – occasional trains whoosh by unnervingly – to the Turf pub on the edge of the Exeter Ship Canal. After pausing here for a drink and to admire the estuary view, follow the cycle trail northward for a peaceful, train-free return alongside the canal, the silence broken only by fish sploshing to the surface, coots scuttling through the reeds and an occasional bird-call. Watch out for kingfishers and, in spring and early summer, hairy dragonflies (*Brachytron pratense*). An observation platform part-way along gives you a view inland; binoculars are helpful here, to identify birds in the fields and ponds, possibly lapwings, kestrels, buzzards, herons, egrets, brent geese, finches and more. After almost a mile, at a small private car park on your left (visitors' parking is allowed, in the marked bays), you can either turn left and return up the lane that led past the RSPB car park or else continue a little further to the Topsham ferry.

Next to the Swan's Nest, on the site of the old Exminster railway station, is **Toby's Reclamation Yard** (✆ 01392 833499), a cornucopia of a place with rooms full of interior and exterior furniture, statuary, building materials, antiques, doors, fireplaces, objets d'art … Happy browsing!

¶¶ FOOD & DRINK

The Turf Exeter Canal, Exminster ✆ 01392 833128 ⌕ turfpub.net ◯ roughly Apr–late Nov. The sign on its wall says The Turf Hotel, but this popular pub, on the edge of the estuary and looking straight across the water to Exmouth, is known locally as The Turf or the Turf Inn. It's a rambling old place, with thick walls and a feel of the sea about it, accessible to visitors only by kayak, boat or ferry (pages 26–7) or by foot and/or cycle – from the RSPB car park or private car park mentioned above, or along the footpath from Powderham Church (about 25 minutes). Despite its isolation, The Turf bustles in summer and at weekends. Camping, B&B and a yurt are also available (page 275).

2 KENTON

The car park in the centre of this pleasant but not especially picturesque village is handily near the 14th-century Church of All Saints, described by John Leland (c1540) as 'a right goodly church': an impressive listed building of red sandstone whose 120-foot tower is the second tallest in Devon. (St Nectan's in Hartland, north Devon, beats it by eight feet.) Don't be put off by the modern entrance; the interior includes a fine rood screen (mentioned in Simon Jenkins' *England's Thousand*

Best Churches), some attractive carving and an unusual wooden 15th-century pulpit that in 1882 was rescued from a cupboard, in pieces, by the ubiquitous Sabine Baring-Gould (page 211) and reassembled. From the outside this church is strikingly similar to St Andrew's in Kenn, only a few miles' drive away.

3 KENN

Tucked away in a green landscape only five miles from Exeter, and perhaps a mile from the busy A38, Kenn presents itself as the perfect Devon village. Well, almost perfect; there's no village shop, but the library, housed in the old phone box, makes up for this. Villagers are invited to borrow a book, read it and return it, and to add more.

BIRD RESERVES AROUND THE EXE ESTUARY

Walking or cycling round the estuary will take you past some of the best mudflats and wetland habitats in Devon. In spring you can see lapwings and redshanks and – if you're seriously dedicated – listen for the rare Cetti's warbler; but autumn is the most rewarding time, when thousands of waterbirds, including dark-bellied brent geese, fly from the freezing Arctic to overwinter there. As winter approaches other wildfowl crowd into the estuary to feed – look out for huge flocks of widgeon and graceful pintail ducks, as well as black-tailed godwits and shoveler ducks.

The ace in the pack, however, is the avocet and you have a good chance of seeing some in the winter (in spring they go to East Anglia and the Netherlands to breed), especially on the special birdwatching cruises run by the RSPB and the Stuart Line from Topsham, Exmouth or Starcross (pages 26–7).

The RSPB (rspb.org.uk/exeestuary) has four reserves along the estuary. On the eastern side is **Bowling Green Marsh**, in the pocket of wetlands south of Topsham between the River Clyst and the Exe; in summer, Topsham Ferry connects it to **Exminster Marshes and Powderham Marshes** on the western side. The smaller **Matford Marsh** is close to the A379 in the surprisingly green outskirts of Exeter, on the edge of the floodplain. On the edge of Exmouth is the extensive and accessible **Exmouth Local Nature Reserve**, one of Devon's largest, with its constantly changing tidal mudflats and sands; and on the western side the **Dawlish Warren National Nature Reserve** (pages 35–6) is centred on a 1½-mile sand-spit at the estuary's mouth. The **Exe Estuary Management Partnership** (01392 382236 www.exe-estuary.org) produces a series of leaflets: *Exe Wildlife*, *Exe Explorer* and *Exe Activities*, available online and from tourist information centres. These are excellent, providing maps and useful details of walks, birds and ferries.

A little brook runs past thatched cottages ending with The Ley Arms, also thatched. Opposite the pub a mature chestnut tree, speckled with red 'candles' or dropping conkers, depending on the time of year, shares a grassy circle with a white wooden signpost. Up on a hill, and framed by trees, is the tall tower of the red sandstone church. An illustrated board by the graveyard points out the flora and fauna found there, and its ancient yew tree is splendid: huge and cathedral-like with its pillars of surviving trunk around a hollow centre.

The church smells right – and that's important – with the indescribable scent of old oak, flowers and mildew that defines our country churches. Part of the font comes from Oberammergau, there's a fine barrel roof with painted bosses, some hand-hewn dark-oak benches and pew shelves, and a finely carved alabaster pulpit with a portrait of St Andrew with his distinctive cross. But the glory of this church is the wooden screen. Lavishly carved with entwining foliage, the niches contain some of the best-preserved painted saints in the county. There's St Sebastian, so cluttered with arrows that it's hard to make out his body; St Apollonia, patron saint of dentists and toothache (page 187); and the four evangelists, who are so holy even the animals at their feet have halos, including a very cute lion. Most unusual is St Mary of Egypt, one of only two depictions in the country (the other is in Norfolk). Mary had a colourful life in the fleshpots of Alexandria, but repented her sins and wandered off into the desert with only three loaves of bread to sustain her and her long hair to keep her warm.

If you visit the church expressly to look at the painted niches, a torch is useful to pick out the details.

4 POWDERHAM CASTLE

Kenton EX6 8JQ 01626 890243 powderham.co.uk castle & grounds Apr–Oct 11.00–16.30 Sun–Fri plus occasional Sat; 50% discount on admission for National Trust & English Heritage members

Entered from the A379 in Kenton, Powderham Castle, dating back to 1391, has been the home of the Earl and Countess of Devon for over 600 years. The present Earl (the 19th, and the 28th generation of Courtenays to live in the castle) inherited the title when his father died in 2015. The castle was besieged during the Wars of the Roses and badly damaged by Parliamentary forces in the Civil War, and, as all good castles should, has its share of ghost stories, notably of a 'grey lady' on the landing and shutters which were mysteriously screwed back into place after being opened to provide blackout during World War II.

Like so many stately homes, it now earns its keep by opening to the public for part of the year, but remains very much a family home, with the Earl's two young children sometimes mingling with visitors. Guided tours of the interior (its beautifully proportioned rooms from a variety of architectural periods include some opulent furnishings and fine 18th-century rococo-style plasterwork) are held throughout the day and prove very popular in summer; one of the enthusiastic guides told me that he barely has time to draw breath. No wonder, when they tell so many anecdotes! The kitchen, as old as the house itself, has been restored, with lots of gleaming copper utensils, to reflect its condition in Victorian times. In 2017 the medieval solar (the old family room, focus of home life through many generations) was also restored.

"A medievally clad storyteller had a string of children trailing, pied-piper-like, behind him."

Among the ancient oaks, chestnut, lime and cedar trees that surround Powderham, an unexpected find is a Wollemi pine, planted by the Earl's father; this prehistoric tree became world-famous following its rediscovery in Australia in 1994. The well-kept grounds offer peaceful strolls, beautiful views and various family-friendly attractions (pets' corner, birds of prey, nature trails), while on some days (check the website for the current programme) a tractor-trailer carries groups on 'safari' to the surrounding deer park with its 600-odd fallow deer and other wildlife. When I was last there a medievally clad storyteller had a string of children trailing, pied-piper-like, behind him. The licensed (dog-friendly) **Courtyard Café** offers snacks, light lunches and diet-busting cream teas; or visitors can use the picnic tables set up in the grounds. Also in the courtyard, the **gift shop** has imaginative souvenirs and crafts, and leads to the **Courtenay Gallery** with ancient treasures from the castle's archives and an interactive digital display exploring 1,000 years of history, as well as a copy of the Courtenay family Bible which, published in 1626, is one of the earliest editions of the King James Version.

The peaceful and appealing little **chapel** was originally built around 1450 as a 'grange' or accommodation for visitors to the medieval castle. Its 16th-century carved pew ends come from St Andrew's Church in South Huish near Kingsbridge, which is now a ruin looked after by (this sounds so sad) the Friends of Friendless Churches. In 1866, when parts of it were already 500 years old, the parishioners of St Andrew's decided that the repairs it needed were far beyond their means (a window had just been blown in by a storm during Divine Service) and it was abandoned. However, some of its 'organs' were transplanted to give new life elsewhere: the 14th-century font went to a new church being built in Galmpton (page 71), near South Huish, and the pew ends were given to the 11th Earl of Devon, who converted the Powderham grange into the present chapel in 1874. Outside the chapel is a large mulberry tree with a notice warning visitors that the fallen fruit underfoot can be messy – and also saying 'help yourself', which I did and they were delicious. Manna from Heaven?

Various events throughout the year (fairs, festivals, music …) include, in April, the popular Toby's GardenFest, run by Devon-born gardener, TV presenter and author Toby Buckland; and in October the Powderham Food Festival with a mass of local contributors. The castle can be busy in summer, so for Slow visitors off-season visits are recommended.

At the top of the castle grounds next to Kenton's main street is a small group of shops, open year-round. The huge **General Trading Company**,

THE ATMOSPHERIC RAILWAY IN DEVON

The possibility of using air pressure to provide propulsion for a vehicle or train came to life early in the 19th century, although Thomas Newcomen (page 110) had pointed the way with his atmospheric pumping engine 100 years earlier. In 1812 George Medhurst of London proposed somehow blowing passenger carriages through a tunnel but unsurprisingly the idea didn't catch on. In 1838 gas engineer Samuel Clegg and marine engineers Jacob and Joseph Samuda jointly took out a patent for a new improvement in valves and at this point atmospheric propulsion with pumping engines became feasible. They set up a working model in Southwark in 1839, and ran a half-mile demonstration track at Wormwood Scrubs from 1840 to 1843. Things were moving fast, with many top-level railway technicians expressing both interest and criticism; the first atmospheric railway opened in Ireland in 1844, followed by one on the outskirts of Paris. Another was started in 1846 on five miles of the London and Croydon Railway, but it encountered too many problems and in 1847 was scrapped.

Among experts keeping a close eye on progress was Isambard Kingdom Brunel, who had been appointed engineer to the South Devon Railway in 1844; he recommended using the system on a much longer stretch, from Exeter to Torre and Totnes. The trains run by Bovey Tracey's House of Marbles (page 251), stocks old-fashioned toys and games (including, of course, numerous and multi-coloured marbles), wonderfully soft alpaca knitwear and other stylish clothing, books, jewellery, toiletries, furnishings, bags and souvenirs. The **Orangery Restaurant** (✆ 01626 891639, also run by House of Marbles) covers the range from breakfasts through lunches to cream teas and is popular locally. When I called in for coffee, the venison sausages and homemade fishcakes looked (and smelt) tempting. **Urban and Rural Plants** (✆ 01626 891133) is a well-stocked garden centre, with plants helpfully classified according to their favoured conditions (wet, dry, sunny, etc). Finally, **Powderham Farm Shop** (✆ 01626 891883) has a great range of locally produced goodies – cheeses, preserves, pâtés, wine, baking, meat, organic fruit and vegetables – and treats from further afield too, depending on season and availability. It also has a small café.

5 STARCROSS

The Exe Estuary Trail from Powderham church (from the A379 the signpost indicates the church and the 'SYC', which is the Starcross Yacht Club) to Starcross is a tarmac road, so if you're driving it's a peaceful

literally ran on air, with a combination of partial vacuum and atmospheric pressure; they were practically silent, and with no nuisance caused by steam or smuts. At stations along the route, including Exeter, Turf, Starcross and Dawlish, pumping houses were built and steam-driven pumping engines were installed in them. The first train ran in September 1847, between Exeter and Teignmouth.

There were always difficulties. Among others, the pumping engines used far more coal than expected, communication between pumping houses was poor, and the leather flap valves sealing the traction pipes deteriorated from use and the salty atmosphere. Treated with oil to prevent this, they then attracted hungry rats and mice, which got sucked in to the tube and thus jammed the piston – at which point third-class passengers might have to dismount and push the train to the next station. At the system's peak, nine trains a day ran between Exeter and Teignmouth at up to 70mph; but the cost and the many operational problems proved insurmountable. The last train ran in September 1848, gradually the machinery was removed, and the pumping houses were closed and dismantled. The one at Starcross is the only one that has survived in situ, although its machinery was stripped out long since.

alternative to the A379. There's a speed limit of 20mph and local residents get extremely fed up with visitors (and other locals) who don't respect it. It's just inland of the railway, which runs along the very edge of the estuary; on its other side is the Powderham deer park, so you could pause for some stag-spotting.

Starcross is an unassuming little place, clinging so closely to the edge of the estuary that from the platform of the railway station, at high tide, you can look straight down into the water. Its value for visitors is the Exmouth–Starcross Ferry (page 26) which docks just a stone's throw from the station; walk down the platform and along a pier and you're there. Combining this with the good bus and rail services (pages 23–4), plus cycling and/or walking, offers you a variety of circular trips around the two shores of the estuary.

The reddish building with a tower, opposite the garage, was the old pumping station of Isambard Kingdom Brunel's atmospheric railway (see box, pages 32–3). The chimney was once much taller, but was damaged in a storm in the 1890s. The Atmospheric Railway Inn has – appropriately – some related memorabilia around the walls: old photos, newspaper cuttings, lamps, models and so forth.

¶¶ FOOD & DRINK

The **Atmospheric Railway Inn** (✆ 01626 890335) and the **Galleon Inn** (✆ 01626 890412 ◯ closed Monday) are both on the main street near the railway station and ferry; both open at noon (hours vary) and serve food Tuesday to Sunday. Opposite the old pumping station the **Westbank Charity Shop Café** (◯ 09.00–16.00 Mon–Fri, 09.00–noon Sat) serves snacks and light meals, and has some leaflets and information about the area. A mile or so south of Starcross, on the edge of Cockwood's tiny harbour, the deservedly popular 17th-century **Anchor Inn** (✆ 01626 890203 ♨ anchorinncockwood.com ◯ 11.00–23.30 daily) specialises in seafood – in fact I counted 18 mussel dishes on its menu!

DAWLISH WARREN & DAWLISH

Here the estuary opens out into the English Channel. Bustlingly busy in the summer, with some very un-Slow 'amusement' areas and tourist paraphernalia, these two small resorts, just a couple of miles apart, retain a flavour of old-time seaside, with long, windswept beaches, ice creams, beach huts and promenades. They're far more peaceful out of season. Below the tideline (gritty sand at Dawlish, finer at Dawlish Warren) you can beach-comb for shells, bleached driftwood, cuttlefish 'bone', sea-smoothed glass and other salty treasures, and swimming is safe. The flat walk between them along the sea wall and cliff path is a constant pleasure – beware of waves in stormy weather – and you can do part of it on the beach at low tide. The waterside rail journey from Exeter is the most memorably scenic in this book, and at its most dramatic during winter storms when trains can get thoroughly soaked. As you approach Dawlish, you can see the repairs to the sea wall made after storm damage in February 2014 left the rails dangling precariously above the waves. Buses B and/or number 2 from Exeter serve both towns between them.

6 DAWLISH WARREN

🏠 **Brunel Holiday Park** (pages 36 and 275)

Tourist information: No tourist office, but info from Dawlish TIC (✆ 01626 215665) plus ⊘ dawlishwarren.info

Apart from its Blue Flag beach, the attraction of Dawlish Warren is its 500-acre **National Nature Reserve** (⊘ dawlishwarren.info, follow links), an area of grassland, sand dunes and mudflats centred on a 1½-mile sandspit/beach stretching across the mouth of the Exe Estuary. It's a wild, peaceful and windswept place where (out of season) you can wander without spotting another soul. Parking is outside, near the entrance, and is free before 09.00 and after 18.00.

The long, sandy, dune-edged shoreline is superb and an internationally important area for wildlife: the main roosting site for the huge numbers of wading birds and wildfowl (dunlin, grey plover, bar tailed godwit, oystercatcher, brent geese, widgeon and teal, among others) that spend the autumn and winter on the estuary. Other habitats include salt marsh, freshwater ponds, wet meadows and woodland.

"In spring the ancient dunes blossom with wildflowers, including the spectacular blue sea holly."

The reserve is also designated a Special Area of Conservation (SAC) for its dune grassland, humid dune slacks and the tiny, rare 'petalwort' that grows there. In spring the ancient dunes blossom with wildflowers, including the spectacular blue sea holly and the yellow evening primrose with its large crinkled petals. With luck and sharp eyes you might also spot the little lilac-coloured sand crocus (*Romulea columnae*), whose only other known location on the British mainland is at Polruan in Cornwall. A small visitor centre ($\mathscr{D}$ 01626 863980) with information and displays is open most weekends from October to March, and most days (irregularly) from April to September. Rangers run guided walks from there. About a mile beyond the visitor centre is a bird hide, excellent for watching the waders and wildfowl in winter. Viewing is best two hours either side of medium-high tides. Dogs must be kept on a lead and are not allowed in some areas.

To get to the reserve from the centre of Dawlish Warren, go through the little railway tunnel by the station, turn left past the amusement area with its arcades and razzmatazz, and continue through the car park to the gate at the far end. The last public toilets are near the tunnel; there's nothing in the reserve. You'll need to return the same way as there is no exit at the far end.

The amusement area does have a useful shop, Warren Trading Co, selling some good outdoor and indoor clothing, and there's an open-air market in the town on Wednesdays. For rail buffs there's some unusual self-catering accommodation at the Brunel Holiday Park (page 275) – in old railway carriages, facing seaward across the line where the atmospheric railway once ran and information panels now tell its story. It's being completely refurbished over the 2017/18 winter so you'll need to check the website for current details.

7 DAWLISH

🏠 **Lammas Park House** (page 275)

Tourist information: The Lawn (next to the public toilets) $\mathscr{D}$ 01626 215665 ○ summer 10.00–17.00 Mon–Sat, winter 10.00–16.00 Thu–Sat, closed 13.30–14.00. Also covers Dawlish Warren & Teignmouth.

> Half village, half town, it is – pleasant but smallish,
> And known, where it happens to be known, as Dawlish;
> A place I'd suggest
> As one of the best
> For a man breaking down who needs absolute rest,
> Especially too, if he's weak in the chest.
>
> R H D Barham, 1867

I wish I could, as local residents seem to, come to terms with the garish amusement complex dominating the main square, because without it Dawlish could be a pretty town. A brook flanked by gardens,

Dawlish Water, runs through the centre, there are some pleasingly twisty streets and attractive buildings, the beach is long and mostly sandy between red sandstone cliffs and there's a friendly feeling of bustle. Oddities are appealing: Dawlish Community Transport runs a little red minibus called Rosie, black swans and various other exotic waterbirds display themselves on Dawlish Water, and the busy railway station café, improbably named Geronimo's Diner, is decorated with Wild West artefacts.

Bus-assisted walk: Holcombe or Teignmouth to Torquay

❋ OS Explorer map 110; start: near Holcombe or in Teignmouth ♀ SX 955748; about 10 miles from Holcombe, 8 from Teignmouth and less if you finish in Babbacombe instead of Torquay; steep ups & downs.

This is one of my favourite sections of the South West Coast Path. The length can be varied and there's a good bus service for transport at each end. It combines the paved stretch that runs between the sea and the railway north of Teignmouth with the ups and downs, woodland, meadow and beaches which characterise the more remote section to Babbacombe or Torquay.

Take the number 2 bus from Exeter towards Teignmouth and get off just past Holcombe, a mile or so south of Dawlish, where a steep and narrow signposted lane (Smugglers' Lane) connects the road with the coastal path, just south of Hole Head. At the bottom, the **Salty Dog Kiosk** has drinks and hot snacks if you need pre-walk fuel. Then it's an easy two-mile stroll partly along the sea wall to Teignmouth, passing the entrance to Eastcliff Park (page 39) towards the end. Follow the promenade to Teignmouth's Back Beach where a ferry (page 40) will take you across the Teign estuary to Shaldon. That's where the energetic part begins. Although you are rarely walking on the level, the variety and beauty of the scenery, with views of the sea and little coves at the bottom of the indented cliffs, help you forget your tired muscles. It may feel isolated but you are never far from the main road and bus services to Torquay or Teignmouth. About an hour out of Shaldon you'll come to Labrador Bay, an RSPB nature reserve, where you may spot cirl bunting, skylarks, or, out to sea, gannets and seals. There's sometimes an ice-cream van in the car park. Continuing towards Teignmouth, if you've got your swimsuit you could have a dip – and a snack – on the idyllic Maidencombe beach and isolated Watcombe beach (pages 51–2).

The trail is well marked, but you should carry a map for reassurance and in case you want to leave it early.

In the early 20th century, Dawlish became famous for the popular perfume Devon Violets, and hundreds of varieties of violet were raised in market gardens – you may still spot them growing wild in the area.

"Anything from a penny-farthing bicycle to bagpipes, 19th-century bridal wear and an ancient mousetrap."

Jane Austen holidayed here in 1802 and complained about the 'particularly pitiful and wretched library'. Today she could enjoy **Dawlish Museum** (✆ 01626 888557 ⊙ May–Sep variable hours Wed–Sun & daily in Aug), with its three floors of wonderfully miscellaneous memorabilia linked to Dawlish and Devon: anything from a penny-farthing bicycle to bagpipes, 19th-century bridal wear and an ancient mousetrap. The Queen's 90th birthday is featured, as is the great storm of 2014 which demolished the local rail line, and there are plenty of activities for children.

South of the main beach (which you enter via a tunnel under the railway) is the smaller Coryton Cove, sheltered and pleasant for swimming. In the days of segregated bathing this was the gentlemen's beach; the ladies had their bathing pavilion towards the other end. At the cove, information boards describe the area's geology and history, including the development of the railway and Brunel's involvement. But at holiday time the beaches and indeed the whole town can become uncomfortably busy.

¶¶ FOOD & DRINK

Daisy's Tea Room 25 The Strand ✆ 07793 209045 ⊙ 10.00–16.00 daily. A friendly traditional place with cream teas, wonderful homemade cakes, salads, snacks and light meals.

Gay's Creamery and Pie Shop 20 Brunswick Place ✆ 01626 863341 ⊙ 07.30–17.00 Mon–Sat, 08.30–17.30 Sun. Pies, pasties, top-class ice creams, homemade cakes, cream teas, salads, hot snacks. Takeaway service but there are benches and tables nearby where you can sit and watch the black swans. Also a good range of local preserves, confectionery, cider and souvenirs.

Reflections Bistro 33 the Strand ✆ 01626 866899 ⊙ 09.00–16.00 Sun–Thu, 09.00–21.00 Fri & Sat (seasonal variations). Relaxed and friendly; busy in summer. Breakfast, snacks, main meals (meat, seafood, vegetarian, gluten-free), cream teas.

The Smugglers Inn 27 Teignmouth Rd (1.2 miles from Dawlish on A379) ✆ 01626 862301 ⊙ 11.00–23.00 daily, main menu available noon–21.00. Spacious restaurant and bar with outside terrace and panoramic coastal views. Daily carvery with meat from award-winning local butcher.

THE TEIGN VALLEY

For there's Bishop's teign
And King's teign
And Coomb at the clear Teign head –
Where close by the stream
You may have your cream
All spread upon barley bread . . .

John Keats, 1818

8 TEIGNMOUTH

Tourist information: New Pavilions building, Den Crescent ☉ variable days/times, year-round. Leaflets are available & volunteer staff may be on duty, but for phone enquiries contact the Dawlish TIC (✆ 01626 215665).

Teignmouth was granted its market charter in 1253 and in the early 14th century was Devon's second-largest port, smaller only than Dartmouth. It has known smuggling and shipwrecks, and in 1690 was left in ruins by a French raid, recalled on a panel at the corner of French Street:

On the 26th day of this instant July 1690 by foure of the clocke in the morning your poor petitioners were invaded by the French to the number of 1,000 or thereabouts, who in the space of three hours tyme, burnt down to the ground the dwelling houses of 240 persons of our parish.

The arrival of Brunel's railway in 1846 brought a huge increase in tourism, and Teignmouth today is a well-laid-out and organised seaside resort with a range of attractions: Victorian pier (now given over to 'amusements'), gardens, clean sandy beach, heated lido and the excellent **Teign Heritage Centre** (✆ 01626 777041 ☉ teignheritage. org.uk ☉ Mar–Oct 10.00–16.30 or 17.00 Tue–Sat), opened in an eye-catching modern building in 2011. Its extensive displays run from prehistory to the present, and include an Edwardian bathing machine, relics from a 16th-century shipwreck, old pier slot machines and other local memorabilia. History walks are organised from here and it's a good source of local information. On the northern edge of town, accessed from the promenade just past the lido, **Eastcliff Park** offers some pleasant clifftop strolls, beautiful sea views, carefully tended lawns, a walled garden dating back to around 1825, and a subtropical valley garden, the Dell, created some 100 years ago.

For me, Teignmouth doesn't have the endearing quirkinesses of some smaller resorts, but its classic Georgian crescents are attractive and visitors return year after year. The back streets are fun, with twisting little alleys and some original small shops. The area around Northumberland Place, where Keats is said to have lived in 1818, is becoming known as an **arts quarter**, with various galleries, of which TAAG (Teignmouth Arts Action Group ✆ 01626 779251 ⬙ teignmoutharts.org ⊙ year-round 10.00–17.00 daily) at No 4/5 is particularly worth visiting, with a constantly changing programme of exhibitions. At No 43 is the independent, family-run Quayside Bookshop (✆ 01626 775436), with new, secondhand and rare books. It's particularly strong on transport.

Teignmouth holds an International Folk Festival in June and its Regatta in July/August. Walks are varied and plentiful, whether along the coast or up into the countryside; and the 18-mile Templer Way to Haytor on Dartmoor starts here.

The **Teignmouth-to-Shaldon foot ferry** (✆ 07896 711822) has been running in various forms since at least the 13th century and is said to be Britain's oldest such service. It carries cycles and dogs, starts from Back Beach near the lifeboat station and runs year-round except over Christmas; times vary seasonally. Also based on Back Beach, **Riviera Cruises** (✆ 07921 761224 ⊙ seasonal) take passengers on bay cruises, River Teign cruises and mackerel fishing trips. Their boat *The Restless* was the Teignmouth auxiliary lifeboat for many years. An alternative to the ferry is to walk to Shaldon across the A379 bridge; when the first – a wooden one – was built in 1827 it had 34 arches and was said to be the longest in the country. A span at the Teignmouth end could be raised to let tall vessels pass through. The centre collapsed in 1838 having been eaten by ship-worm and again in 1893. The bridge was completely rebuilt in 1927–31, using steel for the piers and main girders and concrete for most of the deck, and allowing for subsequent repairs that's the one you see today. It occasionally whistles when winds catch it from a certain direction.

A couple of miles from Teignmouth, tucked away among fields, is the little ruined 13th-century **Chapel of St Mary**, protected by a rusty iron railing with a sign saying Lidwell Chapel. I'm reminded of Tennyson's 'a chapel near the field, a broken chancel with a broken cross' from *Morte d'Arthur*, but this old story is far grizzlier: of a medieval monk living there who murdered visiting travellers and threw their bodies down a well. R H D Barham, son of the author of the *Ingoldsby Legends*, wrote a light-hearted poem about it (*The Monk of Haldon*) in 1867, by which time it was already the stuff of legend, so who knows what's true. Drive out of Teignmouth up the B3912 and, just after the golf course (on your left), a steepish footpath on the right leads down to it. The ground can be very muddy. It's marked on OS Explorer map 110, near Lidwell Farm (♀ SX924762). There's not much to see – only the west wall is still standing and the rest has crumbled – but it's a pretty and peaceful place and a listed monument. Beyond is private land, so you need to return the same way.

"The Romans are thought to have planted vines on the same south-facing slopes and made wine there 2,000 years ago."

Just outside Bishopsteignton on Old Walls Hill is **Old Walls Vineyard** (✆ 01626 770877 ⟶ oldwallsvineyard.co.uk ⊙ 09.00–17.00 daily). It's surprisingly historic: the Romans are thought to have planted vines on the same south-facing slopes and made wine there 2,000 years ago, and the name refers to the nearby remnants of old walls which are all that's left of the 13th-century bishop's palace (*Bishop's-teign-ton*, you see?). There's a shop where you can buy the products, and a pleasant café with light lunches, cream teas – and wine. Tours (booked in advance) are available, showing the whole winemaking process, and an innovative idea is that you can 'rent' vines in a specific area and, after the harvest, receive the wine they produced.

⊪ FOOD & DRINK

Elizabethan Inn Luton TQ13 0BL ✆ 01626 775425 ⟶ elizabethaninn.co.uk ⊙ food served noon–14.00 & 18.00–21.30 Mon–Sat, noon–20.30 Sun. About 3 miles NW of Bishopsteignton in the little village of Luton, this historic inn offers traditional food with an extra touch of class. Pies are highly recommended; veg and herbs come from their own garden.

The Crab Shack 3 Queen St (near Back Beach) ✆ 01626 777956 ⟶ crabshackonthebeach. co.uk ⊙ noon–23.00 Wed–Sun. Very strong on seafood, locally and sustainably caught, from luxury to relatively inexpensive. Pleasant and efficient staff. It's a light and bright place but not large, and it gets busy, so booking is advised at popular times.

Twentysix Café & Bistro 26 Regent St ✆ 01626 879000 ⊙ 10.00–16.00 daily. You're never far from sustenance in Teignmouth but this is a terrific place – food with a French flair, but from top local suppliers, and its cream teas have been voted among the best five in Devon. 'Light' lunches include coq au vin, quiche, a fish & seafood selection, soup & salads. Same management as The Strand Café in Shaldon (page 43).

9 SHALDON

Tourist information: Ness Drive (in the car park) ✆ 01626 873723 ○ May–Sep 10.30–16.30.
The very helpful staff are volunteers so times may vary. Useful websites are
⌂ shaldon-village.co.uk & ⌂ shaldon-devon.co.uk.

This appealing village has a superb location, perched between the Teign
estuary and the sea, and a surprising number of **events** for such a small
place: an international music festival in June, a horticultural show
in July, a water carnival and popular nine-day 200-year-old regatta
(⌂ shaldonregatta.com) in August, various watersports on the Teign
estuary and other local activities to suit the season. On summer
Wednesdays a Craft Fair is held, with craftspeople in medieval costume.
There's a pleasant beach of sand plus shingle (covered at high tide) which
you approach through a tunnel – lots of fun for children – often called
the Smugglers' Tunnel though it seems a little too well built for that. The
beach also has rock pools.

Towering over the shore is a red headland, Ness Point, and tucked
neatly on it is a delightful little zoo, the **Shaldon Wildlife Trust**
(✆ 01626 872234 ⌂ shaldonwildlifetrust.org.uk), which specialises in
small animals such as marmosets and tamarins from South America,
meerkats from Africa and lemurs from Madagascar. There is also a small
collection of reptiles and invertebrates, and
a tropical house with poison dart frogs, tiny
geckos, and an eye-catching blue-spotted
tree monitor. The spacious enclosures are
cleverly designed to maximise space, and
the animals are well cared for.

*"There's a substantial
'summer house', designed
to look like a castle, where
Mrs Homeyard used to
entertain guests to tea."*

The **Homeyards Botanical Gardens** (a
stiffish climb up from the waterfront) were created by the energetic Maria
Laetitia Kempe Homeyard with the money made from the invention
by her husband, William Newcombe Homeyard, of Liqufruta, a garlic-
based cough remedy that was revered as a cure-all in the early part of the
20th century. They're free of charge, natural rather than manicured and
pleasant for strolling, with some unusual shrubs and trees and an Italianate
garden. There's a substantial 'summer house' (now roofless), designed to
look like a castle, where Mrs Homeyard used to entertain guests to tea –
not to be confused with the limestone grotto where the local witch Old
Mother Gum is said to come at dusk for a furtive cuppa. The disused
gardener's hut is now a roost for swallows and lesser horseshoe bats.

Volunteers have been working hard to improve and develop the gardens, and arrange various activities; you can follow the work on their website (⊘ shaldonbotanicals.wordpress.com).

If you take the road to the west along the estuary, about half a mile from Shaldon village centre you'll come to a tiny **church** – St Nicholas – dozing at the end of an alley with its back to the Teign. The writer W H Hoskins dismisses it as containing 'nothing of note', although the font is thought to be Saxon. We visited in early evening, well after closing time, but two parishioners were busy hoovering. And Hoskins was right, there's nothing of much note inside the church, but one of the ladies couldn't wait to show us a special gravestone outside: to William Newcombe Homeyard (of Liqufruta fame, see opposite). When he died in 1927 his widow Maria Laetitia wanted the brand name of his great achievement to be put on his gravestone, but it was vetoed by the vicar as inappropriate advertising. She then asked if she could put a Latin inscription instead and that was approved. So forget the Saxon font and seek out the three-tier commemorative cross with Gothic letters proudly spelling out ATURFUQIL on the top stone, in the 'unfading' memory of its creator. No, it's not Latin, just Liqufruta spelt backwards!

⫼ FOOD & DRINK

Café ODE In the top car park near the tourist centre, Ness Drive ⊘ 01626 873427 ⊘ odetruefood.com ◷ 09.00–17.00 daily plus some evenings. A thoroughly organic place (their motto is 'Good food that doesn't cost the Earth' and even the cutlery is compostable), and the manager told us 'If we're sent vegetables that weren't grown locally we just send them back'. A good range of hot and cold meals and snacks with indoor and outdoor seating. The **ODE Restaurant** at 21 Fore Street (⊘ 01626 873977 ◷ 19.00–21.00 Fri & Sat) offers very fine dining with extensive tasting menus.

Strand Café The Strand (near the ferry) ⊘ 01626 872624 ◷ 10.00–16.00 daily. Breakfasts, popular brunches (including homemade pancakes and waffles with various toppings), cream teas and good baking. Under the same management as the Twentysix Café in Teignmouth.

The Ferry Boat Inn The Strand ⊘ 01626 872340 ◷ noon–23.00 daily. Run by two sisters, close to the ferry and with a beautiful view over the estuary. Its reasonably priced menu is strong on fish.

The London Inn The Green ⊘ 01626 872453 ◷ 11.30–23.00 daily. A relaxed, family-run place with generous helpings of good old-fashioned food. Great value for money. The Sail Loft Boutique behind the pub has some attractive women's clothing, jewellery and accessories.

SOUTH OF THE TEIGN

This smallish strip of countryside manages to contain three exceptional little churches and extremely pretty traditional villages. The lanes between them may be twisty but they're well worth the effort.

10 STOKEINTEIGNHEAD & COMBEINTEIGNHEAD

The alternative spellings, Stoke-in-Teignhead and Combe-in-Teignhead, give a clue to the pronunciation of these two attractive villages. The 'in-teign-head' part is said to come from 'in ten hide', *hide* being an Anglo-Saxon measurement of area. Deep in the countryside yet a stone's throw from Teignmouth and Newton Abbot, they have good pubs, thatched cottages, and interesting churches. Arch Brook, which runs into **Stokeinteignhead**, gives the village some extra charm, which it has in bucketfuls anyway. There's a particularly attractive row of white houses lined up along the combe, and St Andrew's Church has allegedly the oldest screen in the country. Certainly it seems to be a simpler design than usually seen, and there's a brass dated 1375 which makes it the oldest in Devon. On the other side of the main street a community shop, rescued by the villagers from closure, has a good supply of home baking, local vegetables and other necessities.

Combeinteignhead also has an absolute treasure in its 13th-century church of All Saints, which you'd never guess when approaching its shocking pink door and seeing the even more inappropriate pink wall-tiles inside which make it look like a municipal swimming pool. It's only when you get to the north transept (to the left of the altar) that you see the carved bench ends, just a few of them, hiding their light under a bushel of hymn-books and other paraphernalia. The wooden pews in the rest of the church are plain and relatively modern but these date from Elizabethan times, and are fascinating in their subjects as well as the bold carving and beautiful dark oak. There are saints galore, including St Catherine with a big crown and her wheel, a very serious St Peter with exuberant flowing locks and a giant key, St George in full armour spearing a tiny, dog-like dragon, and one of those really obscure saints that turn up in Devon churches from time to time: St Genesius, dressed in a fool's costume of cap and bells. Two strange men, side-by-side, seem at first glance to be dressed in densely pleated costumes, but it's much more likely to be fur (the lion's mane is done the same way).

Each is holding a club, or escutcheon, and has a mop of unruly hair. These are probably 'wild men' or wodwo (woodwose), which appear quite frequently in old church carvings, perhaps representing untamed nature. There is a recognisable lion, but what are we to make of the 'poppy-head' carving (upright on the top of the pew rather than in a panel) which looks like a lion until you notice its long back legs and huge feet clutching a branch? Could it be a baboon? An animal the carver had never seen but had described to him? It has the deep shine of old wood that has been caressed by many hands. There is also an utterly indefinable animal, or possibly it's a fox, carrying off a goose flung over its shoulder – an image that is quite often seen in churches. They make it well worth braving the pink.

Near the church are traditional almshouses built of red sandstone, given to the village by William Bouchier, Earl of Bath, in 1620; also Fowlers Cottage and The Old Bakery, recalling former trades, and the 17th-century cottage that is home to the Wild Goose Inn (page 47).

11 HACCOMBE

This is a very worthwhile diversion but only on a Wednesday in April to September, when the little, peach-coloured **church of St Blaise** is generally open from 14.00 to 16.00, or for a 09.00 service on Sunday mornings. It's awkward to find; set your satnav to postcode TQ12 4SJ rather than to Haccombe, or look at the helpful aerial view on *ð* shaldonchurches. org.uk. Since medieval times the church has been associated with the adjacent manor, originally lived in by the Haccombe family and later by the Carews. The present Georgian building (now converted to flats) replaced the original mansion at the end of the 18th century.

The horseshoes on the church door – only one and a half of them now, although there used to be four – are said to be relics of an ancient wager made between a George Carew, Earl of Totnes, and Sir Arthur Champernowne of Dartington, as to who could ride furthest out into the sea at Torbay. Carew won the gruelling challenge and, on returning to Haccombe, removed his horse's shoes and nailed them to the door, declaring that the brave beast should work no more but live out its days in pasture. So the story goes. Or possibly they were fixed to the door to deter witches, as happened in other churches? Believe what you will!

The church's tiny interior is a treasure-trove of memorials and other ecclesiastical goodies. To put you in the right frame of mind, there's a 'wool-comb' with fearsome nails; St Blaise was martyred by being flayed with a carding comb used to process wool, and then beheaded. Despite this, as a physician he managed to dislodge a fishbone from a child's throat, so is now patron saint of the wool trade and of throat ailments. He is also the patron saint of Dubrovnik, where a reliquary supposedly contains some of the saint's body parts – and a fish bone.

The biggest memorial is for Sir Hugh Courtney who died in 1425 and his wife Philippa; the miniature alabaster memorial nearby is possibly of their son, Edward, who died while a student at Oxford. His feet rest on an appealing dog but sadly his hands are missing. The size suggests that this was a 'heart burial' and that the rest of the body was interred elsewhere. Sir Stephen de Haccombe, the knight who built the church in gratitude for his safe return from the Crusades in 1233, is also there along with his wife Margaret. A rather cute lion cushions his crossed feet. Beneath the carpet by the altar is a fine set of Carew brasses. There's some good medieval stained glass; the east window is 17th-century Flemish. Note, too, the lovely uneven medieval floor tiles.

Unusually, rather than a vicar the church has an archpriest, who reports to the Archbishop of Canterbury rather than a bishop and is entitled to wear a fur stole. This dates from the founding of a college of six chantry priests, with an archpriest at their head, in 1335. At the time of writing, St Blaise has its first female archpriest. Former incumbents included the renowned botanical artist, the Reverend W Keble Martin, appointed to the church when it was little more than an ivy-covered ruin, with only visiting birds to listen to his services. One such was a wren that nested in the pulpit; if you poke your finger into the obvious hole in the stone carving, and wiggle it to the right, you can still feel its nest. No one would dream of removing it! Keble found Haccombe slow after the busy industrial parish he'd just left, and apparently upset his parishioners by visiting all of them twice in one week. His great work, Concise British Flora in Colour, published in 1965 when he was 88, was in fact anything but concise, containing 1,400 meticulous watercolours.

St Blaise's processional cross contains wood from the ancient flagship Mary Rose. After she was raised in 1982, two small pieces of her timber were given to the church in memory of her final captain, Sir George Carew, who drowned when she sank in 1545.

Church Farm (see also *Accommodation*, page 275), signposted as you approach the church and set back among woods and fields, was formerly the manor's Georgian coach house. Now it's the home of BBC TV wildlife producer and author Andrew Cooper and has – with its array of surrounding wildlife (buzzards, barn owls, sparrowhawks, deer, glow-worms, badgers, bluebells …) – featured in the BBC's *Autumnwatch* and *The One Show*. It's not open or visible to the passing public but the Coopers offer (pre-booked) group talks and guided walks (⌕ www.wildlink.org). Andrew also runs wildlife video and photography courses, or you can opt for luxury B&B complete with badger-watching in comfort.

12 PLANT WORLD

St Marychurch Rd, TQ12 4SE ✆ 01803 872939 ⌕ plant-world-gardens.co.uk ◷ Apr–Sep 09.30–17.30 daily

In the 1980s Ray and Linda Brown sold their nursery in the Scottish Highlands and moved in their Cortina Estate to Devon, towing a horsebox full of their plants behind them. Initially they grew strawberries and fuchsia to bring in an income, then in 1986 laid out the garden, the first in the country to be arranged as a world map. Now they have a nursery with a great selection of unusual plants for gardening enthusiasts, and a four-acre garden carved out of a steep hillside showcasing a cottage garden and the flora of four continents in Gardens of the World. Apart from on-site sales, their catalogue contains a wide selection and attracts orders from across the globe. Well laid out and clearly labelled, the gardens are worth the small charge to visit. There's also a café.

Plant World is signposted at the Penn Inn junction on the A380 from Newton Abbot to Torquay, and good directions are on the website.

FOOD & DRINK

Church House Inn Stokeinteignhead TQ12 4QA ✆ 01626 872475 ◷ 11.00–15.00 & 17.30–23.00 Mon–Sat, noon–22.30 Sun. In the spacious dining room of this 13th-century inn, you'll find a strong emphasis on locally sourced food: fish from Torbay, meat products from Shaldon. Good menu, loads of atmosphere.

Plant World TQ12 4SE (see above). The café serves light lunches, homemade cakes and cream teas, with beautiful views over the Teign estuary.

Wild Goose Inn Combeinteignhead TQ12 4RA ✆ 01626 865161 ⌕ wildgoosedevon.com ◷ bar open 7 days (variable times), food served Tue–Sun. A welcoming, family-run pub next to All Saints' Church, with an innovative British menu. Run as a pub since 1840, its current name refers to the geese of a 1960s landlord which tended to chase the customers.

THE ENGLISH RIVIERA:
TORBAY

2
THE ENGLISH RIVIERA: TORBAY

The wide, curved deepwater harbour of Tor Bay has played a regular part in history, as well as attracting more recent visitors to its mild climate and sandy beaches. W G Maton, writing in 1794, reported: 'The bay appears to be about twelve miles in compass [four miles as the gull flies], and is reckoned one of the finest … for ships our coast can boast of.' The Napoleonic Wars (1799–1815) elevated the area still further, partly because the Channel Fleet was anchored in Tor Bay for a while, with Napoleon aboard en route to exile on St Helena, and partly because the war in Europe prevented the nobility from doing the Grand Tour abroad so some used the Devon coast as a substitute. Indeed, Napoleon may have inadvertently promoted the area as a holiday destination. On seeing the bay for the first time he is said to have exclaimed: 'Enfin, voilà un beau pays!' Suddenly, **Torquay** was fashionable and once the Great and the Good started coming here, they never really stopped.

The bay area with its linked towns is officially known as Torbay, but the marketing people prefer 'The English Riviera'. Torquay has its downside – big department stores and traffic jams – and Slow visitors may find **Paignton** hard to love, but if you know where to go and what to see there are all sorts of pleasures to be found: excellent art exhibitions, the spookily fascinating **Kents Cavern** (Torbay is one of UNESCO's Geoparks – the term given to areas of exceptional geological interest), and surprisingly rural lanes folded into the hills behind the town. Tucked behind the craggy projections of **Berry Point** and **Hope's Nose** which contain the bay are quiet beaches and small, pebble-and-sand coves, with more secluded beaches further north towards Teignmouth.

 WET-WEATHER ACTIVITIES
Torquay Museum (pages 58–9)
Bygones (pages 52–3)

Poppins Painting Studio (page 52)
Kents Cavern (pages 55–8)
Living Coasts (page 59)
Torre Abbey (pages 60–1)
Paignton Zoo (pages 67–8)
The *Golden Hind* (pages 75–6)

GETTING THERE & AROUND

The recently completed South Devon Highway (A380) has shortened the driving time from Exeter to a handy 40 minutes. Once in Torquay you would do well to leave your car in a long-term car park and use public transport to avoid the traffic jams.

The **bus** service into the town and along the coast is excellent, particularly the Hop 12, which runs between Newton Abbot and Brixham every ten minutes until late at night. Paignton and Torquay are also accessible by **rail** via a branch line from Newton Abbot. Coming from the River Dart, there's the wonderfully picturesque **steam train** which runs between Kingswear and Paignton, a perfect route for window gazing and a stunning introduction to the beauty of Torbay when approached from the south. A 'Round Robin' ticket enables you to include a cruise on the River Dart to Totnes, and return to Paignton by double-decker bus.

Ferries run regularly between Torquay and Brixham, also from Torquay to Dartmouth and from both Brixham and Torquay to Dittisham and Greenway on the River Dart.

SELF-POWERED TRAVEL

In Torbay itself a bicycle is an efficient means of transport rather than a source of enjoyment; it's ideal for covering the long, bleak stretch of waterfront between Torquay and Paignton, and gives you quick access to Cockington or Marldon. Bicycles can be rented from **Grumpy's Bike Hire** in Wellswood, near Hope's Nose (5 Bishops Rise, TQ1 2PJ ✆ 07724 509038). Once you leave the towns, however, there are all the back lanes to enjoy and easy access to a range of out-of-town attractions.

For such a populated area there is a good selection of **long-distance walking trails**. Wending its way round the area for 35 miles, the **John Musgrave Heritage Trail** starts at Maidencombe, north of Torquay, heads inland following paths and lanes to Cockington, then continues to Totnes. The most rewarding section of the **South West Coast Path** is round Berry Head to Kingswear and the stretch north of Torquay.

NORTH OF TORBAY

Heading north from Torquay (or south from Teignmouth) you'll find a lovely stretch of coast path, giving sudden views of this deeply indented coastline (see box, page 37) and access to the region's hidden beaches, and quite near Torquay are quieter alternatives to the wide Torbay stretch of sand. For organised enjoyment the satellite towns of St Marychurch and Babbacombe have plenty to see and do.

1 MAIDENCOMBE & WATCOMBE

🏠 **Orestone Manor** (page 275)

Best known for its beach, Maidencombe feels a world away from the hustle of Torquay. Its oldest building, the Court House, dates from the 14th century and the primrose-yellow pub, the Thatched Tavern, is picture-postcard pretty. It has links with literary history as well: Rudyard Kipling lived here for a couple of years at Rock House, a spacious mansion with superb views. So why no longer than two years? Because he and his wife were afflicted with 'a gathering blackness of mind and sorrow of the heart' whenever they entered the house. 'It was the Feng-shui – the Spirit of the house itself – that darkened the sunshine and fell upon us every time we entered, checking the very words on our lips.' You can see his point, *"The sand is the colour of a roan pony, mixed with a sprinkling of shingle, with large sedimentary rocks below the red sandstone cliffs and a good supply of tide pools."* actually. The house has a grey, glowering exterior, in contrast with the welcoming **Orestone Manor** hotel next door.

The beach is perhaps the most appealing in the whole region – at least for lovers of Slow. The sand is the colour of a roan pony, mixed with a sprinkling of shingle, with large sedimentary rocks below the red sandstone cliffs and a good supply of tide pools. And the café, the **Beach Box**, is a treat. Hugo is a great cook, turning out hamburgers and hot rolls with finesse, and he cooks a Portuguese-style barbecue on summer weekends (📞 07802 652622).

Watcombe Beach, a mile further south, is even prettier. If coming by car be warned that it is a very steep walk down from the (free) car park, but it's a lovely, more-or-less level walk from Maidencombe along the South West Coast Path. There is a café there too, open only at peak times. These two beaches are perfect for lingering on school holidays when the other Torbay beaches get crowded.

2 ST MARYCHURCH & BABBACOMBE VILLAGE

St Marychurch is notable for its pedestrianised centre, giving visitors the chance to browse at leisure in the small, independent shops. On Fore Street there's a bookshop, Fables, a paint-your-own-pottery place, Poppins, and, for a touch of luxury, Truffles, purveyors of fine chocolates. Almost hidden among the shop fronts is **Bygones** (see below), a chance to slip back into the past. In St Marychurch, despite its name, is **Babbacombe Model Village**, while the Tessier Gardens off Manor Road are a peaceful haven full of flowers and closed to children. When I was there, each bench was occupied by a person quietly sitting listening to the birdsong. Balm for the soul.

East of St Marychurch, towards Torquay, is Babbacombe, where the **church of All Saints** gets a mention in Simon Jenkins's *England's Thousand Best Churches* for its Victorian aplomb. It is flamboyantly in keeping with the English Riviera surroundings. Jenkins points out that the church interior is built of 'no fewer than 50 varieties of Devon marble, in addition to marbles from Belgium and Sicily.'

Bygones

Fore St, St Marychurch TQ1 4PR ✆ 01803 326108 ✆ bygones.co.uk ◷ 10.00–16.00 or 18.00 depending on the time of year, daily except Christmas Day. See ad, 4th colour section.

The modest frontage of this delightful exhibition is easy to overlook as you walk down Fore Street, but it's well worth a visit, especially on a wet day. The cliché 'transported back to the past' is hard to avoid as you stroll down a Victorian street with Queen Vic herself glaring unamusedly down at you. Even those of us who grew up in the 1950s will recognise the authenticity of the sweet shop with its tempting goodies in large glass jars (and we have our own dollop of nostalgia in the Fabulous Fifties exhibition). There's a cobbler and a

"You stroll down a Victorian street with Queen Vic herself glaring unamusedly down at you."

tobacco shop with a range of cigarettes and pipes (remember them?), an ironmonger and an apothecary amongst other businesses. Each shop is stuffed with authentic items bringing memories to anyone over 60 and curiosity for the youngsters. Upstairs the displays are themed: a nursery, bathroom, parlour and kitchen; and a dentist showing sadistic delight in extracting a rotten tooth. Doors lead to a reconstruction of a WWI trench, and an almost whole locomotive snugly contained in the railway room. Bygones was created in 1987, and a recording by the founder is played in the background to put everything into context.

3 ODDICOMBE & BABBACOMBE BEACHES

⌂ Cary Arms and Spa (page 275)

Charles Harper in 1907 found the walk down to the beach too challenging for comfort: 'There are winding walks down to Babbacombe, but for all their circumbendibility they are so steep that by far the easiest way to descend would be to get down on to your hinder parts and slide … the walking down jolts the internal machinery most confoundedly.' Now, fortunately for those worried about their internal machinery, there is a funicular railway to transport visitors up and down the steep cliff – at least in summertime (it is usually closed from early October to Easter). Built in 1926, it is now owned by a community interest company and has its own visitor centre on Oddicombe Beach.

"'The walking down jolts the internal machinery most confoundedly.'"

The name Babbacombe Cliff Railway is misleading since it actually deposits you on Oddicombe Beach. Compared with its quieter neighbour this is a 'happening' beach with a fast-food outlet, watersports and occasional live music festivals. Ideal for families, there's enough red sand for sandcastles and good swimming off the pebble-and-sand shore. Winding, jungly paths take the energetic up to the road or to Babbacombe beach. The shorter, surfaced walkway to this more upmarket beach hugs the cliff, with access to slipways and rocks for adrenalin-fuelled jumps into the sea. The Cary Arms (☏ 01803 327110 ⬭ caryarms.co.uk) has been there for several hundred years and is now a boutique hotel with an excellent restaurant.

From Babbacombe beach you can walk 'over the downs' to Anstey's Cove (page 55), a beautiful leafy stroll of about two miles.

4 TORQUAY & AROUND

🏠 **The 25 Boutique B&B** (page 275)

Tourist information: 5 Vaughan Parade, Torquay ✆ 01803 211211 🖳 englishriviera.co.uk
🕙 10.00–17.00 Mon–Sat, 10.00–15.00 Sun

Visitors have been holidaying in Torquay for hundreds of years. Dr W G Maton wrote happily in 1794: 'Torquay far exceeded our expectation in every respect. Instead of the poor, uncomfortable village that we had imagined, how great was our surprise at seeing a pretty range of neat, new buildings, fitted up for summer visitors, who may certainly here enjoy convenient bathing, retirement, and a most romantic situation.' A visitor burbled to Bishop Phillpotts that Torquay was like Switzerland, to which he replied: 'Yes, only there you have mountains and no sea, and here we have sea and no mountains.' There are, however, hills which give the upper town its attractive, layered look, and some splendid mansions overlooking the bay. The seafront and marina are attractive, and there is a sandy beach – at least until the high tide chases the sunbathers on to the esplanade.

Perhaps the gloss came off with the arrival of the trams, as predicted by Charles Harper in 1905. 'Presently there will be electric tramways at Torquay! Conceive it, all ye who know the town. Could there be anything

BEACHES

There are beaches galore in this region, but it is the secluded coves that are the most rewarding for those looking for beauty as well as swimming. They can be divided into the mostly sandy stretches at the southern, Brixham, end of the bay, and the pebble and sand coves north of Hope's Nose.

In the south, apart from the large and popular sandy beaches at Paignton and Goodrington, the most accessible smallish one is Broadsands, with reddish sand and rewarding rock pools at the southern end at low tide. But it's the little coves, sheltered by red cliffs, that can only be reached on foot which most appeal to me. Accessible from the South West Coast Path as you head south from Teignmouth, there's Maidencombe, Watcombe, Petit Tor, then the popular Oddicombe and Babbacombe beaches.

Beyond Paignton, heading towards Brixham is Elberry Cove (about 15 minutes' walk), a quiet pebble beach, and then Churston Cove, a delightfully secluded sand-and-shingle beach tucked into the wooded hillside. Fishcombe Cove is tiny, equally scenic and secluded, only 15 minutes from Brixham, with the added advantage of a café in summer (page 71).

more suicidal than to introduce such hustling methods into Lotus-land?' The hustling methods of the modern motor car have anyway done for Lotus-land, but stick with it because there are plenty of escapes.

Take the advice of S P B Mais, writing in the 1920s: 'At the back of the inner harbour is the shopping centre. There will be time for this on a wet day. The wise tourist will cling to the coast to explore the outer edges before venturing inland.' I agree, and would add that the most attractive and interesting area of Torquay is the knob that includes Hope's Nose, north of the excellent marine zoo, Living Coasts. The number 32 bus runs to, or near, all the places in this area.

5 ANSTEY'S COVE

This tiny bay is an unexpected delight so close to Torquay. If you miss the sign off Babbacombe Road, head for the huge Palace Hotel (TQ1 3TG); the narrow road to the beach car park goes past it. A steep path runs down from the (free) car park to a broad concrete esplanade with its modest but very good café and a few tables overlooking the pebble-and-rock 'beach' which pretty much disappears at high tide. The pebbles here are the most beautiful in South Devon and the joy of this peaceful place is poking around to find the most perfect one. They are as colourful as marbles, red and white mixed with greens. In summer there are deckchairs for hire and also sit-on-top sea kayaks in the peak holiday months. People come here to sit dreamily looking out to sea and at the view of high red-and-green cliffs with the dramatic spike of Long Quarry Point at its northern end. This is man-made, the result of quarrying in Victorian times for the high-quality limestone, similar to marble, which was used to build some of Torquay's finest houses.

Beyond Anstey's Cove is the much more spacious Redgate Beach, once connected to Anstey's by a wooden bridge but now closed because of the danger of rock falls. Mind you, adventurous souls can still get round at low tide, or swim round at high tide, to enjoy an empty beach.

6 KENTS CAVERN

89 Ilsham Rd, TQ1 2JF ✆ 01803 215136 ⌂ kents-cavern.co.uk. See ad, 4th colour section.

I've had quite a few depressingly commercial and dumbed-down cave experiences and feared that Kents Cavern would be all entertainment and no education. Well, I was wrong. It's wonderful! We were lucky to be on the last tour of the day, with only one enthusiastic family, so our excellent guide was able to match his commentary to our interests. He told us that they can have as many as 30 people, which would not only make it hard to hear the explanations but also diminish the genuine feeling of awe at being in a place inhabited by our human ancestors and animals for around 350,000 years, and where modern man, *Homo sapiens*, sheltered some 30,000 years ago. The prize find at the cavern was a fragment of *Homo sapiens* jawbone, dated to almost 40,000 years ago, making it the oldest fossil of modern man found in Britain. We learned about William Pengelly, the first cave scientist, and his work excavating and identifying the bones found here. There's a model of the great man, frock coat and all, which highlights the difficulty of maintaining Victorian decorum in these conditions. Among the animal remains found in the cave were the teeth of woolly mammoth and scimitar-toothed cat, as well as a large number of hyena bones. Recent evidence suggests that the humans using the cave may have been cannibals: marks from flints used to butcher animals were found on human bones.

The stalactites and stalagmites make Kents Cavern visually superior to the caves at Buckfastleigh (pages 199—200) and knowing that it took them 60,000 years to get that way adds to one's appreciation. There was once an almost complete pillar of stalagmite and stalactite. Now it's just a stub next to its taller companion. Charles Harper, in 1905, describes how this happened: 'It began to be formed when the world was young. It grew and grew with the drops of water, charged with lime, percolating from the roof, and being met by its fellow stalagmite with equal slowness rising from the floor. And stalactite and stalagmite had nearly met, and only wanted another three or four centuries to bridge the remaining interval of an eighth of an inch, when a visitor, falling accidentally against them, broke them off! "What did you say?" one asks the guide. "What *could* you say?" says he.'

The explorers of Kents Cavern

There's nothing secret about Kents Cavern (except, perhaps, when and why the apostrophe was dropped). Humans have been living there, on and off, for nearly 40,000 years, and tourists have been visiting the caves since at least 1571. We know that because William Petre carved his name and the date into the soft limestone walls, and other visitors followed suit in 1615 and 1688.

A walk to Daddy Hole & Anstey's Cove via Hope's Nose

❋ OS Explorer map 110; start: Imperial Hotel, ♀ SX927632; distance: 2½ miles round trip or 4 miles to Anstey's; difficulty: easy to Daddy Hole; moderate to Anstey's Cove.

A quick escape from Torquay is provided by taking the footpath to Daddy Plain and, if you have time, to Hope's Nose, the rocky headland that forms the northern limit of Tor Bay. The path starts at the Imperial Hotel, on Park Hill Road, uphill from Living Coasts. Go through the hotel gate and you'll see the path on the left. It's a most agreeable walk, with good sea views including 'London Bridge', an eroded rock arch, benches to rest on, plenty of wild flowers, and peeps into the gardens of the millionaires' homes that overlook the sea.

Above the curiously named Daddy Hole (Daddy was a colloquial name for Devil or Demon who was allegedly responsible for the landslip which created the hole) is Daddy Plain, an expanse of flat grass, popular with families and their dogs, backed by a row of picturesque houses. It's a shortish walk back down St Mark's Road to Torquay, or there's a bus.

From Daddy Hole the path continues round Hope's Nose, briefly joining Meadfoot Sea Road, before climbing above it to pass through Lincombe Wood on the South West Coast Path. This is a proper walk, with ups and downs, and gorgeous sea views. Soon it splinters off to take you to the tip of the Nose where you have a fine view across to the other horn of the bay, Berry Head. On the rocky shore below there are fossils, but it's strictly forbidden to damage or remove any; this is a Site of Special Scientific Interest, managed by Torbay Coast and Countryside Trust.

Rather than go back the way you came, it's more rewarding to continue to Anstey's Cove, from where you can head for Babbacombe Road and a regular bus service to Torquay.

By the time Dr W G Maton paid a visit in 1794 there was a guardian to prevent such abuses. Maton describes 'Kent's Hole' as 'the greatest curiosity in this part of the country'. He was guided by two women with candles and tinderboxes. 'The lights, when viewed at a distance, gleaming through the gloomy vaults, and reflected by the pendant crystals, had a most singular effect. We began to imagine ourselves in the abode of some magician, or (as our companions were two ancient females, and not the most comely of their years) in the clutches of some mischievous old witches ...'

Although William Pengelly is the name associated with scientific excavation of the caves, he wasn't the first to take an educated look. In 1824 a Mr Northmoore broke through the lime deposits on the floor to the clay below and recognised the bones of extinct animals. The following year the chaplain of Tor Abbey, the Reverend J MacEnery, finding himself with time on his hands, started three years of excavation and discovered 'the finest fossil teeth I had ever seen!' He also collected many bones and some flint implements. Both these men paved the way for William Pengelly's scientific exploration of Kents Cavern between 1865 and 1880, and his conclusion that 'man was, in Devonshire, the contemporary of the mammoth and other extinct cave-mammals; and that, therefore, his advent was at a much earlier period than has commonly been supposed; or that his extinct brute contemporaries lived much nearer to the present day than has been generally believed; or that both propositions are true.' After Pengelly had enlarged the caves and sparked worldwide interest, more people wanted to make a visit. Charles Harper took a look in 1905 or thereabouts. 'A limestone bluff, shaggy with bushes, trees and ivy, rises abruptly to the right of the road, and in the side of it is a locked wooden door, upon which you bang and kick for the guide, who is guide, proprietor, and explorer in one. When he is not guiding, he is engaged in digging … The freehold of the famous cavern which ever since 1824 has been the theme of more or less learned geological treatises was recently sold at auction for a trifling sum; not to an institution or a scientific society but to the guide, who has conducted many geological pundits over it, and by consequence has acquired an air of greater omniscience than the most completely all-knowing of those not remarkably modest men of science.'

"After Pengelly had enlarged the caves and sparked worldwide interest, more people wanted to make a visit."

TORQUAY MUSEUM
529 Babbacombe Rd, TQ1 1HG ✆ 01803 293975 ⌂ torquaymuseum.org ◷ 10.00–16.00 Mon–Sat

There's a miscellany of permanent and temporary exhibits here, including a reconstructed Devon farmhouse, some artefacts excavated from Kents Cavern and unusual fossils, and an Agatha Christie gallery. In fact it's a great little museum, and repays the time spent reading the information boards and getting to grips with Torbay's prehistoric world. Here are remains of woolly rhino and mammoth, an explanation of the Ice Age and descriptions and fossils of the wolves and cave lions that inhabited south Devon. An Explorers' Gallery shows eminent Victorian explorers including Colonel Fawcett, and mineral lovers will learn a lot about Devon marble, quarried at Petit Tor, which was valued for its variety of colours nationwide.

The number 32 bus stops outside the museum, but there are usually parking spaces at the roadside.

7 LIVING COASTS

Beacon Quay, TQ1 2BG ✆ 01803 202470 🖉 livingcoasts.org.uk

The surprise here is not that there should be such a good marine wildlife collection in a seaside resort but that it hasn't been done elsewhere. Living Coasts admirably achieves what it set out to do when it was first opened in 2003: conservation and education. One of the world's rarest species of seabird is here, the bank cormorant from Robben Island. Compared with the puffins and penguins it's pretty boring to look at, but that's not the point; the influx of tourist development on Nelson Mandela's former prison home is pushing its endemic wildlife towards extinction, and Living Coasts has teamed up with the South African conservation group SANCCOB to save these birds and other endangered species.

The place is full of surprises. The puffins are not the usual ones seen in Britain but exotic tufted puffins from the Pacific, and in addition to the familiar African penguins often seen in zoos there are flamboyant macaroni penguins which, with their golden headdresses, live up to their name (macaroni has nothing to do with pasta, it means 'dandy'). There are eider ducks, not your standard ones but beautiful and bizarre spectacled eider ducks; the males look as though they're wearing an apple-green balaclava. Perhaps this gives them added confidence – one was mixing sociably with the penguins when I was there. 'He'll flirt with anyone!' the keeper told me.

The high netted roof gives other birds a chance to do what they're best at – fly. Inca terns sail overhead, and razorbills and kittiwakes snooze on ledges. Avocets and other waders explore the shallows, while filtered sea water is pumped in from the ocean. Mammals are represented by South American fur seals and Asian short-clawed otters, which can be viewed both above and below water. Look out also for the sea horses and octopus. 'Very clever creatures,' commented a member of staff as I watched Octavia the octopus. 'If they weren't so short-lived they'd probably run the planet.' Octavia is a TV celebrity, showing off her skill at problem solving in front of the cameras. She can unscrew a jam jar and work out how to get at food hidden in a series of tubes and boxes.

In the mangrove swamp you can see one of the marvels of evolution, the four-eyed fish, and it's worth describing what is so special about Anableps anableps in some detail. This little fish hails from Central and South America where it spends much of its time floating near the surface of the water, making it vulnerable to predators from both above and below. Evolution has come up with a neat solution: eyes that can see both above and below water at the same time. Each eye has two lenses and two retinas, to give perfect vision whether through water or air, and the fish is as happy breathing air for short periods as it is in the water. But that's just the start of its peculiarity. Whereas most fish have pretty unexciting sex lives, releasing eggs which are fertilised outside the female's body, the four-eyed male fish has an impressive reproductive organ called a gonopodium. But this can only move in one direction – sideways. The female has an appropriate genital opening, but with a sort of hinged lid to it, so she can only be penetrated from one side. Thus for a successful coupling to take place, the fish has to find a compatible mate, either right-sided or left-sided. That accomplished, she pulls off a final trick: the birth of live young rather than the laying of eggs.

Beacon Quay itself is an attractive row of marine-focused shops and restaurants facing the harbour.

8 TORRE ABBEY

The King's Drive, TQ2 5JE ☎ 01803 293593 ⌨ torre-abbey.org.uk ⊙ Wed–Sun

A great deal of thought, time and effort have gone into the restoration of Torre Abbey, with admirable success. The abbey was founded in 1196 and at the time of the dissolution of the monasteries was the wealthiest Premonstratensian house in England. Some of the ancient monastic buildings remain, including an early 14th-century gatehouse and a tithe barn, now known as the Spanish Barn because it rather improbably played a part in the Spanish Armada. In 1588 Sir Francis Drake, on board the *Revenge*, captured the 1,000-tonne Spanish man-of-war *Nuestra Señora del Rosario*. An oil painting of the Spanish captain surrendering to Drake is in Buckland Abbey (pages 174–5). The crippled Rosario was towed into Torbay, where almost 400 of her crew were held prisoner in the tithe barn while she was repaired enough to be used as a floating prison. These prisoners are said to have included a young woman who had disguised herself as a sailor so that she could go to sea with her beloved husband. During their two weeks of imprisonment in the barn she caught a chill and died; it's claimed that her ghost is sometimes seen and heard there, lamenting her fate.

After the dissolution, the abbey passed through many hands before being bought by Sir George Cary in 1653. It remained in the hands of this Catholic family until 1930 when it was bought by Torquay Corporation to be used as a museum and art gallery.

Most of Torre Abbey is now a museum, housing a very good collection of art, including ceramics. There is something here to appeal to everyone, well displayed and free from crowds. Treasures include William Blake's engravings for the *Illustrations to the Book of Job*, and paintings by Holman Hunt and Burne-Jones. Other rooms are preserved as they were when it was the Carys' private residence, with some of their loaned furniture. You can also see the secret chapel, used regularly through the times when Catholicism was banned.

Take time, too, to visit the peaceful and immaculately kept gardens and their palm and cactus houses, and have a snack in the café.

9 COCKINGTON

Initially we were a bit suspicious of Cockington. With all the spontaneously charming villages in Devon this seemed to be more or less manufactured for tourists. However, we were wrong. Yes, Cockington is chocolate-box pretty, yes, it's packed with coach parties and tourists, but Cockington Court is also full of interest and to be able to escape Torquay within minutes and walk through spacious parkland beside a brook is not to be sneered at.

Although you can drive here there are much better alternatives: the Cockington Tripper bus (number 62) runs every 30 minutes or so from Torquay Strand (Harbourside). It's also a very enjoyable 20-minute walk up Cockington Lane, opposite Livermead Beach; the lane crosses the railway line and Old Mill Road, then you'll see the Watermeadow Walk on the right, running parallel to the lane almost all the way to the village less than a mile away.

In 1935, Torquay Corporation bought Cockington and the town has owned it ever since, preserving the traditional thatched cottages and forge as in a time warp. Even the Drum Inn, designed by Sir Edwin

Lutyens in 1934, is perfectly in keeping. The historic house and church are on the edge of the village, in a peaceful area of the old deer park. A long stretch of lawn in front of the house is shaded by trees and village cricket matches are still played there; spectators can enjoy the thwack of ball on willow in idyllic surroundings. But the main interest here is Cockington Court and its church. This elegant mansion was once owned by the Cary family, but is now a centre for crafts, and very good ones too. In the galleries upstairs are some seriously fine jewellery and other 'light' crafts, while in the old stable yard there are seven workshops including glass-blowing. They were giving a demonstration while I was there, and turning out impressively good stuff in front of the clicking cameras.

When you've finished with the crafts and the gardens, there's the church to visit. S P B Mais commented in the 1920s: 'I do not know quite what draws such multitudes to see a church which is surpassed in beauty by many others in the neighbourhood. It must be its accessibility. It is at any rate good that one survival of the feudal system should be visited and appreciated by multitudes who do not ordinarily take the trouble to investigate the insides of churches.' He may say that. I couldn't possibly comment. The ornate and unusual pulpit is said to include decorated timbers taken from the Spanish flagship *Nuestra Señora del Rosario*, which was captured by Sir Francis Drake during the Armada (page 60). It consists of various pieces of screenwork, some from the 15th century, others possibly from the early 16th, and the bookrest from still later. Parts may be from the front of a rood gallery. The whole effect is colourful and a little bizarre. There seem to be cherubs with wings sprouting from the sides of their heads, bringing the disconcerting mental image of heads flapping around the Devon countryside. It is said that the originals may have been portraits of captains or clergymen with huge ears to show that they 'heard all', but were converted to something more appropriate for their new home. Maybe.

FOOD & DRINK IN BABBACOMBE & TORQUAY

As you would expect in the English Riviera, there are plenty of excellent places to eat in and around Torquay. This is just a selection of local favourites to suit all palates and budgets.

Angels Tea Room Babbacombe Downs Rd, Babbacombe TQ1 3LP ✐ 01803 324477. A very popular (so often crowded) traditional tea room with some of the best coastal views in the southwest. The jam and scones are excellent, and there is a good selection of teas.

Blue Walnut Café Walnut Rd, Torquay TQ2 6HS ✐ 01803 605995 ⚲ bluewalnuttorquay. co.uk. What makes this place special is that it is an arts café, with live music and performance poetry, and is also home to an original 25-seat nickelodeon, making it one of the smallest functioning cinemas in the world. There are occasional Friday-night film shows. They also host regular art shows.

Hanbury's Fish Restaurant 24 Princes St, Babbacombe TQ1 3LW ✐ 01803 314616. Highly rated fish and chips; eat in or take away.

Harbour Kitchen 16 Victoria Parade, Torquay TQ1 2BB ✐ 01803 211075. Splendid location on the seafront.

Le Bistrot Pierre Abbey Crescent, Torbay Rd, Torquay TQ2 5FB ✐ 01803 221 213. Normally we'd avoid chains, but this newly opened French restaurant with views across the bay is excellent. The fixed-price lunches are great value, and with seating for nearly 200 people, you'll always find a table even on the busiest days.

Number 7 Beacon Hill, Torquay TQ1 2BH ✐ 01803 295055 ⚲ no7-fish.com. An unpretentious seafood restaurant overlooking the harbour. Daily specials.

The Elephant 3–4 Beacon Terrace, Harbourside, Torquay TQ1 2BH ✐ 01803 200044. This Michelin-starred restaurant is probably the best in Torquay, with two areas: The Room, which is the first-floor 'gracious dining' part (closed in winter), and the ground-floor Brasserie which is slightly less formal and open all year round. Dishes are scrumptious and prices high.

The Orange Tree Restaurant 14–16 Park Hill Rd, Torquay TQ1 2AL ✐ 01803 213936. With prices on the high side this is not a place to rush; true Slow Food of the highest quality, and the wine list is very well chosen. The favourite restaurant of one resident who recommends it 'for a romantic evening and to sample the best Torbay has to offer'.

Wellies 21 Ilsham Rd, Torquay TQ1 2JG ✐ 01803 200307 ⚲ welliesofwellswood.co.uk. A bistro in Wellswood, not far from Kents Cavern. Nearby, at no 39, is Naughty but Nice, a French patisserie which is actually owned by a Frenchman.

PAIGNTON TO BRIXHAM

10 PAIGNTON

🏠 **Redcliffe Hotel** (page 275 for listing; see also box, page 64)

Once upon a time Paignton was a small fishing village surrounded by huge apple orchards. It was the centre of Devon's cider industry, and the harbour, built in 1837 to enable the export of cider all over the country and beyond, kick-started the town's development; the arrival of the railway in 1859 completed the job. I learned about the cider industry from Roger Hunt (see box, page 75); his family has been making cider for eight generations, so he should know.

REDCLIFFE HOTEL

Philip Knowling

On the seafront where Paignton ends and Preston begins, the Redcliffe Hotel was built as a private residence in 1856 by Colonel Robert Smith. He had found success in India, and to mark the fact he built in the Indian style – or a fantasy version of it, known as Hindoo. It's a great grey confection of Eastern arches, exotic turrets, pointed windows and Arabesque crenellations. The Hindoo style stems from the Mughals of central Asia, descendants of Ghengis Khan who founded a golden age of science, arts and architecture; one of their greatest achievements was the Taj Mahal. Mughal architecture uses columns and courtyards, marbles and mosaics, arches, domes and turrets. To the Western eye it is romantic, evocative and elegant but in Torquay Smith's creation must have shocked and bemused the locals. When Robert Smith started work on his grand design in the 1850s Paignton was a small fishing village. He took an early 19th-century coastal defence tower set on an outcrop of red sandstone among the dunes and marshes and turned it into a sumptuous new home, Redcliffe Towers, with 23 bedrooms and five acres of gardens.

After Smith died aged 86 in 1873 the property changed hands; it was owned for a time by Paris Singer, whose father built nearby Oldway Mansion, and it took in troops during the Boer War. Smith lived an exotic life and left us an exotic legacy. A Torquay amusement arcade is perhaps the only other local example of the Hindoo style. Its proximity is surely no coincidence.

For the casual visitor Paignton is a long stretch of sand hemmed in by the traffic-clogged main road and holiday complexes. Even its pier, erected in 1879, now glitters with slot machines and 'amusements'. However, to look no further than the seafront does Paignton a disservice. Like Torquay, it has its quiet attractions tucked away inland where the old town still has some good shops, Victorian houses, a thriving theatre and a historic cinema currently being lovingly brought back to its former glory, and the extraordinary Oldway Mansion.

For family outings **Paignton Zoo** is one of the country's finest, and the **steam railway** to Dartmouth (pages 108–9) is a dollop of nostalgia and a chance to watch some of the best scenery in Torbay passing slowly before your eyes.

A symbol of ancient Paignton survives in the Bishop's Tower, a fragment of the palace of the Bishops of Exeter, 'Lords of the Manor of Peintona' (1050–1549). The last to live here was Myles Coverdale, who was made a bishop in 1551. Coverdale's name lives on as the first translator of the

Bible into English, a predecessor to the King James version. There is no evidence to support the local belief that he worked on the translation while living in the Palace, but the Bishop's Tower was formerly known as the Coverdale Tower. In 1549, during the Prayer Book Rebellion in Devon and Cornwall (page 215), Coverdale played a prominent part in attempts at pacification.

The **church of St John** finds itself in *England's Thousand Best Churches* on the strength of the Kirkham Chantry Screen, though Simon Jenkins also commends the 'jolly use of red piers and white plaster. The effect is appropriately seaside.' Jenkins describes the Kirkham screen as one of the most remarkable monuments to survive in any church in England, but I must admit that I was underwhelmed by this austere church and the jumble of decapitated stone apostles, angels and other holy folk which comprise the screen. Cromwell's men laid about them with their hammers with disastrous effect. Indeed, hammers weren't their only weapons: three Cromwellian cannonballs are on display. Created in the late 15th century as a screen for the tombs of the Kirkham family, the carvings deserve a close examination; some are intact and the detail is extraordinary. The Norman font here is the oldest in Devon, and there is an exceptionally horrible 15th-century stone depiction of a cadaver, a memento mori, carved in unsparing detail. When living, he was an Irish bishop. History buffs will find the Paignton Heritage Society (⌂ paigntonsociety.webs.com) useful.

"The carvings deserve a close examination; some are intact and the detail is extraordinary."

One of Paignton's most important historic buildings is the old **Picture House**. Back in 1915 this was described as 'The coolest house in Paignton' due to having air conditioning. One of the earliest cinemas in the country, it closed its doors in 1999 but is now set again to become the coolest house in Paignton, but in the modern sense. The Paignton Picture House Trust (⌂ paigntonpicturehouse.org) is bringing the building back to its former glory of red plush chairs and intricate stained glass. The place is steeped in history and was a favourite with Agatha Christie. The plan is to use it for a wide range of entertainments while remaining faithful to its original purpose. During the renovation cinema enthusiasts can book a tour through the Picture House Trust.

Oldway Mansion

This once splendid building was the creation of sewing machine magnate Isaac Merrit Singer and modelled on the Palace of Versailles by his architect son, Paris. In 1909 he invited his American lover, the dancer Isadora Duncan, to Oldway, making much of its splendour. She went expecting, she said, 'a glorious time'. It didn't happen. She wrote to a friend: 'I had not reckoned on the rain. In an English summer it rains all day long. The English people do not seem to mind at all. They rise and have an early breakfast of eggs and bacon and ham and kidneys and porridge. Then they don mackintoshes and go forth into the humid country until lunch, when they eat many courses, ending with Devonshire cream.'

THE PUDDEN' EATERS OF PAIGNTON

When King John granted the town's charter in the early 13th century, Paignton's residents offered a giant suet pudding in part payment – and thus became nicknamed 'pudden' eaters' by other folk in the area. For a while a pudding was made annually, but eventually only every 50 years or so. It was boiled in a cloth, with a recipe of flour, suet, raisins and eggs.

One made in 1819 for the annual show took 64 hours to boil and was paraded around the town on a wagon drawn by eight oxen. The largest – weighing one and a half tons – was the centrepiece of a great feast to celebrate the coming of the railway to Paignton, in August 1859. It was shaped like a giant pyramid, 13ft 6in at the base and 5ft around the apex. An uninvited crowd of almost 18,000 people turned up and fights broke out as they surged forward, many of them fuelled by the two wagon-loads of cider that the 'feast' also included. The police tried valiantly to protect the pudding but were outnumbered: soon only the crumbs remained. Post-office workers reported that a number of squashy, greasy little parcels were dispatched the following day.

Smaller commemorative puddings are still occasionally made. One in 1968 marked the original granting of the town's charter, with almost 1,550 portions sold for charity in small souvenir dishes; another, in 2006, celebrated the 200th anniversary of Isambard Kingdom Brunel's birth. For the Paignton regatta in August 2009, a solid, suety, seven-tiered pyramid weighing 70 kilos was chuffed into the town by the Paignton and Dartmouth Steam Railway, then paraded in a 1947 Bedford lorry as the town crier called on the inhabitants to come and eat.

Finally, in August 2014, some 900 years after its creation, came arguably the pudding's finest hour. Sue Perkins explored its origins (and an 11-tier replica was baked) for no less a television programme than *The Great British Bake-Off*. Fame had come at last for this chunky lump of calories whose recipe probably pre-dated the Magna Carta!

Meanwhile Paris had suffered a stroke; under the care of a doctor and nurses, he spent most of his time in his room on an invalid's diet of rice, pasta and water. Isadora was banished to the opposite end of the building for fear of 'disturbing' him. Isolated from her lover, she practised her dancing and entertained herself as best she could, soon ending up in the arms of the conductor and composer André Caplet. Shortly afterwards she returned to France, with very few happy memories of Paignton.

The house, described in the Shell Guide as 'a rollicking extravaganza in hundreds of thousands of tons of pale pink stone' was for years used as council offices and a wedding venue but is now, sadly, closed and its fate uncertain. The grounds, however, are free, open to the public, well tended and magnificent.

11 Paignton Zoo

Totnes Rd, TQ4 7EU ✐ 01803 697500 ⊘ paigntonzoo.org.uk

This distinguished zoo, which celebrates its centennial in 2023, is one of England's best. It is the big sister of Living Coasts in Torquay (pages 59–60) and is a constant pleasure; however often you visit it, there is always something new to see, and a feeling of space and greenery. It was the country's first combined botanical and zoological garden, not always an easy relationship: 'I hate animals,' the former curator of plants once said cheerfully, 'they eat all my plants.' This hasn't changed. Communications Manager Philip Knowling describes it as a 'constant dynamic between gardeners, animal keepers and the public.' The former are enraged when the free-range peafowl eat the seedlings (although when we were there they spent their time displaying sexily to visitors), animals need the privacy that large trees and high vegetation give them, and the public want as clear a view as possible. And, for their own safety, to be kept away from the dangerous animals.'

Paignton Zoo has solid conservation credentials, helping projects in Nigeria, Zimbabwe, Tanzania, Indonesia and the UK. It has some impressive African primates, including Hamadryas baboons and lowland gorillas. 'They're all males,' I was told. 'Because gorillas live in complex social groups, these chaps need to learn how to be gorillas here, before going to other zoos where they can breed. They arrive as youngsters and develop with just what a growing male gorilla needs – tough love.'

Our favourite place was the Reptile House. Not only was it lovely and cosy on a chilly spring day and reminiscent of the Eden Project with its rainforest flitting with free-range tropical birds, but it houses some of my favourite animals such as poison dart frogs, a leaf-tailed gecko from Madagascar, a giant parson's chameleon and the smaller, more colourful panther chameleon. And a simply enormous anaconda. The Crocodile Swamp is also as attractive to humans on a cold day as it is to warmth-loving crocs, and in future you will be able to book ahead to enjoy an after-hours demonstration of crocodile feeding, showing how these normally immobile animals can leap from the water.

The zoo is constantly evolving. Among other plans for the future, which may be the present by the time you visit, is the revamp of the Savannah area, taking away the obvious fences and creating a watering-hole feel for the resident giraffes, zebras and elephants. A vulture aviary is also on the cards.

PAIGNTON'S BEACHES

All the beaches between Paignton and Brixham are shingle and red sand, disliked by some visitors since it can stain your clothes. Perhaps for this reason **Preston Sands** and **Paignton Sands**, which together make up the long stretch of beach next to the B3201, are never crowded. They offer all the requirements for a family outing: car parking close by, toilets, fast food, and amusements. **Hollicombe Beach** to their north ticks most of the boxes for a Slow beach, being a small cove enclosed by red cliffs, and you have to walk here through Hollicombe Park or at low tide from Preston Sands. And it's open all year round to dogs.

"For lovers of undeveloped beaches, it starts to get exciting."

To the south **Goodrington Sands**, between the promontories of Roundham Head and Three Beaches Headland, is also quiet and has the advantage that the steam-train station of Goodrington is nearby.

Then, for lovers of undeveloped beaches, it starts to get exciting with the coves that give Three Beaches its name. First, and really the only accessible one, is **Saltern Cove**, a designated SSSI (Site of Special Scientific Interest) within the Geopark. It's a nature reserve which extends underwater to a depth of 376m. The cove can only be reached from the South West Coast Path, down steep steps. Come at low tide when there are rock pools and a larger area of sand.

Continuing south you'll come to **Broadsands** with its line of multicoloured beach huts. Unlike the busier beaches to the north, there is no main road nearby (though parking is conveniently close) so it's relatively peaceful, though the narrow strip of sand above a seaweedy expanse of pebble-mix belies its name. It has two cafés, toilets and so on, safe swimming for children since it shelves very gradually, and lots of rockpools for them to explore. Little Elberry Cove is further from the car park, so even quieter. And that's it until the approach to Brixham.

FOOD & DRINK

The Old Manor 10 Old Torquay Rd, Paignton TQ3 2QZ ✆ 01803 551157 ⌂ theoldmanorpaignton.co.uk ◷ 11.00–midnight. It comes as something of a surprise to find a Grade II listed pub in Paignton, but the 17th-century thatched inn has been pleasing visitors for many years, winning the Devon Pub of the Year in 2016. The food is classic pub food, nothing fancy but well cooked, and there's a beer garden for the summer and log fires in winter.

MARLDON

🏰 **Brownscombe Tabernacle** (page 275)

Marldon merits a mention because of the welcome speed with which you can lose yourself in the little lanes leading to it, also for Occombe Farm and for Compton Castle, a splendid fortified manor house. The village celebrates an **Apple Pie Fair** each July.

Occombe Farm

TQ3 1RN ✆ 01803 520022 ⌂ countryside-trust.org.uk/occombe ◷ 09.00–16.30

This is a working, organic farm which is open to the public for no charge. It is a wonderfully relaxed place where you can wander around admiring the vegetables and animals, including alpacas, chickens, ducks and some cheerful pigs, or take the 2km nature trail and see what wildlife you can spot. There are plenty of informative signs about food production and no human hassle – you are free to do your own thing. The farm runs events such as cookery courses and a beer and music festival, as well as its café and farm shop (◷ from 10.00) and award-winning **Gribbles Butchery**, with all profits going to the Torbay Coast and Countryside Trust which protects Torbay's wild places including Berry Head. The **café** (◷ 09.00–15.00) is particularly popular for its substantial cooked breakfasts.

12 Compton Castle

TQ3 1TA ✐ 01803 661906 ⊙ Apr–Oct 10.30–16.30 Tue–Thu; National Trust

This medieval fortress is sometimes cited as the finest building of its kind in Devon. It certainly makes a dramatic impression when you round a corner and suddenly see it, its huge castellated walls towering above you in an appropriately threatening way. The house belonged to the Gilbert family from the 1300s to 1800, and again in 1930 when the run-down estate was purchased by a descendant of the original Gilberts and painstakingly restored before being handed over to the National Trust. The estate has strong connections with America: in 1583 Sir Humphrey Gilbert proclaimed Newfoundland a colony in the name of Queen Elizabeth and in the same decade his half-brother, Sir Walter Raleigh, started planning the Roanoke Colony in North Carolina. The family has named their eldest son Walter Raleigh ever since.

There is plenty of interest in the house and garden. Visitors are given an informative guide to take them through the attractive walled Rose Garden and the ornamental Knot Garden as well as the orchard, full of laden apple trees.

Only a few rooms in the house are open to the public, but wherever you're allowed to go, there are squirrels: carved in wood, as stuffed animals lurking in odd corners, and on the Gilbert coat of arms. The reason? Sir Humphrey's ship when he sailed to Newfoundland was called *The Squirrel*. The family motto is *Semper sciurus*, 'always provident', a squirrely characteristic. One item that particularly caught my eye was a magnificent silver centrepiece depicting General Gilbert taking the surrender of the Sikhs in the Anglo-Sikh War of 1839. It shows some splendidly turbaned and bearded mounted Sikhs throwing down their weapons in front of the rather bored-looking general. It was presented to Sir Walter Gilbert, an officer in the British East India Company, by the officers who served under him in the war; it must have cost them a pretty penny.

Don't miss the kitchen, standing separate from the house because of the fire risk, with its enormous range, vast cooking pots, and high barrel ceiling to help disperse any smoke which escaped the chimney.

Children are well catered for, with Tudor games such as croquet and quoits, and costumes to try on. During the school holidays you are likely to be greeted by ladies in Tudor costume giving a gratifyingly deep curtsy.

GALMPTON

Jenny Distin, a resident, says: 'I chose to move to Galmpton because I worked out it has the finest public transport service of any place in Devon not on a bus or train timetable!' The reason is that the station and the bus stops are all called Churston not Galmpton. Even the locals can't work out where Churston ends and Galmpton starts; in my mind the two communities divide roughly into Golfers and Gardeners.

'The highlight of the village year is **Gooseberry Pie Fair** (usually the first Sunday in July) when a specially baked giant gooseberry pie arrives by steam train with a military escort from Dartmouth Royal Naval College. It is paraded through the village followed by pre-school children dressed as gooseberries, blessed by the vicar, then cut by a naval officer with a ceremonial sword before being dished out with clotted cream to the villagers and visitors – who are then entertained with various village fête events. It's been going on since 1873 and is hosted by the **Manor Inn** (⌂ manorinngalmpton.co.uk), which is the hub of the village'.

The Hop 12 bus between Brixham and Newton Abbot runs via Galmpton every 10 minutes or so until late at night.

ON FOOT OR BUS
FROM PAIGNTON TO BRIXHAM

If you have time, an alternative to driving into Brixham is to park at Broadsands car park, and either walk up to the bus stop on the Dartmouth Road or follow the coast path for a bit over two miles to Brixham. To go by bus, take the coastal path north from the far end of the beach and under the viaduct to Broadsands Park Road. Follow this uphill to Dartmouth Road and you'll see the bus stop on the left.

Walkers will follow the coast path through woodland to **Elberry Cove**. This is a popular beach for waterskiing and powerboats so can be noisy. Now comes about a mile of attractive woodland, with steep ups and downs as well as level stretches until you come to one of the nicest beaches (or rather two beaches) of southern Torbay. **Churston Cove** and **Fishcombe Cove** are curves of shingle separated by a headland and enclosed by steep cliffs. Swimmers will need beach shoes to protect their feet although there's access to deep water from rocks and steps. Being only accessible on foot down a very steep path makes them particularly appealing to Slow enthusiasts. Fishcombe has a café and toilets, and dogs are allowed.

Directly above Fishcombe Cove is the **Brixham Battery Heritage Centre** (brixhambattery.net 14.00–16.00 Sun, Mon & Fri). Renovated in 2016 and run by an enthusiastic and dedicated band of volunteers, this is for WWII enthusiasts. The museum houses displays of uniforms, weapons, posters and other items such as the Mickey Mouse gas mask that I remember from my childhood, and a lady's gas mask handbag. Visitors are allowed to handle the weapons, and invited to share their memories and interests. As well as the museum, there's the Battery Observation Post and the main gun emplacement.

The path continues to Brixham, skirting the yacht harbour and passing David Walker and Son to emerge at The Quay.

13 BRIXHAM

 Faithful (page 275)
Tourist information: Hobb Nobs Gift Shop, The Quay (unmanned)

Brixham pushes out towards Berry Head, the southern prong of Tor Bay, and the start of one of the South West Coast Path's most spectacular sections: to Kingswear. In the mid 1500s John Leland described it as 'a praty Towne of Fischar Men, caullid Brixham'. It's still pretty – at least its setting is – and it still has a flourishing fishing trade.

On my last visit I met two Scottish visitors who used to know Brixham a decade or so ago. The elderly man shook his head: 'So much has changed.' Indeed, so visitors need to be prepared for the extensive building and renovation needed to bring Brixham up to the standard that the fishing industry requires and visitors to the English Riviera expect. A new state-of-the-art **fish market** keeps the catch fresh, and **David Walker and Son** (01803 882097 09.00–15.00 Mon–Fri, 08.00–13.00 Sat), who justifiably claim to 'offer the finest fresh fish in the world', provide a range of take-home fish to satisfy your inner Rick Stein. There are also amusement arcades, fish-and-chip shops galore, and all the offerings that help separate visitors from their money.

There is also a quiet, reflective side to Brixham. Walk down the west side of the harbour and you will find a row of benches facing the afternoon sun, where you can watch the harbour activities and observe the busy little turnstones competing with the gulls for scraps. Further along the walkway are lobster traps stacked neatly against the wall and other paraphernalia associated with the fishing trade. Here trawlers set out to catch the fish that end up in so many of the country's best restaurants. Indeed, Brixham has the highest-value catch in the country. If you want to see the real Brixham, unchanged for hundreds of years, you need to be an early riser. The fish auction begins at 06.00 with around 40 different kinds of fish on offer. The **Fish Market Tour** currently takes place every Wednesday in July and August, and fortnightly in September. Its price includes a fish breakfast at Rockfish (page 76) and the tour must be booked in advance by emailing ✉ bfmt2014@gmail.com.

Among Brixham's visitor attractions is a replica of Sir Francis Drake's *Golden Hind* (pages 75–6) and a statue of William of Orange, who landed here in 1688 and changed the course of history (see box, below). A plaque on the harbour wall reproduces a wonderfully grovelling message from the humble folk of Brixham to Prince William Henry, Duke of Clarence and recently appointed Lord High Admiral, on the occasion of his visit in 1828. They obviously had high hopes that his new

WILLIAM OF ORANGE

In 1688 England was in a bit of a mess, with Protestants hating Catholics and Catholics fearing Protestants, and the Protestant monarchy established by Henry VIII looking decidedly shaky. After the Civil War and Republican rule by Oliver Cromwell, Charles II restored the monarchy and the Stuarts, but had too many Catholic sympathies to ensure stability; religious tolerance was not popular in 1660. It didn't help matters that Charles signed a secret treaty with Louis XIV of France, a Catholic monarch who was starting to throw his weight around, on the promise that he would convert to Catholicism – which he did on his deathbed. To strengthen his Protestant credentials he arranged for his niece Mary to marry William of Orange (William III of the Netherlands), grandson of Charles I. Childless (at least by his wife) Charles was succeeded by his brother, the Catholic James II, which threw everyone into a tizzy of paranoia. An openly Catholic monarch would not do. So most of the country welcomed the arrival of William and his invading army. He had a legitimate claim to the throne and impeccable Protestant credentials (he had chased Louis XIV out of Holland). His wife Mary was herself a Protestant and the daughter of King James, who was persuaded to give up the throne. When he changed his mind a few years later he was soundly defeated, with his Catholic followers, in Ireland at the Battle of the Boyne. The Orange Order has been stirring up trouble there ever since. James fled to France while William and Mary ruled together, with reduced powers through parliament's new Bill of Rights. The constitutional change that their rule brought about is known in history as The Glorious Revolution.

position would benefit Brixham, and felt that they'd better get in quick with their praise: 'We felicitate ourselves on having this opportunity of expressing our Respect and Attachment' with a gift of an 800-year-old oak chest containing – gasp – part of the stone on which King William III placed his foot on his arrival at Brixham 140 years earlier. The prince was ecstatic, commending 'this Beautiful and Magnificent bay' and promising to preserve the stone as a 'precious Relick', a reminder of the 'benefit conferred on this TRULY HAPPY ISLAND' by the arrival of his ancestor from the Netherlands.

Set back from the tourist-busy Quay are quieter streets with uncrowded shops and restaurants. Hidden along King Street is the surprisingly shaped blue building known as the Coffin House. It gets its name from its shape: that of a coffin standing on its end. The story goes that a young lady of the town had set her fancy on a young man who in no way met with her father's approval; in fact, he had told the suitor that he'd sooner see him in his coffin than married to his daughter.

"Hidden along King Street is the surprisingly shaped blue building known as the Coffin House. It gets its name from its shape: that of a coffin standing on its end."

So the young man bought the 'coffin house' and showed it to his sweetheart's father – who apparently relented in the face of such ingenuity and gave his blessing to their marriage. A little plaque gives its former name and date (1736), but the building is now occupied by the Destiny Mystical Shop, which seems to have escaped from Totnes, offering tarot reading, crystals, faeries, angels and a yoga and juice bar.

Tucked away in the old police station in New Road is the **Brixham Heritage Museum** (℘ 01803 856267 ☉ summer 10.00–16.00 Tue–Fri, 10.00–13.00 Sat), which houses an eclectic mixture of items mostly illustrating the town's maritime and railway history. There's also a Victorian parlour and nursery, and archaeological exhibits.

One of the pleasures of Brixham is the variety of transport options. It's much nicer to visit without a car, and there is a frequent bus service from Paignton and Kingswear, allowing you to combine a visit here with the steam train from Kingswear. Ferries also run from Brixham to Paignton and Torquay. If you do drive into town, I'd recommend parking at the Oxen Cove car park with access to the coast path leading into Brixham past the yacht harbour. It's a lovely approach to the town.

HUNTS CIDER

You can tour the orchards and cider-making operation (✆ 01803 782422) with prior booking, usually at 14.00 on Wednesdays. The farm also has a caravan park, **Broadleigh Farm Park** (page 275).

Devon is known for its cider so, en route to visit a friend in Aish, on the road to Stoke Gabriel, it was easy for me to give in to temptation and follow a sign to Grove Orchard and its cider sales. I was greeted by Roger Hunt who told me that the Hunts had been making cider for eight generations and that he himself had been involved in the business for 40 years. Clearly I wasn't just going to buy a bottle and leave; as I was shown round the new, state-of-the-art cider barn, I learned a lot about cider. The Hunts have been farmers and part of Paignton's cider industry since 1805 when the family was based at Crabbs Park, Paignton, although they were making cider in a small way from 1771. Orchards were bought and sold, but the family remained in South Devon before moving to their present place with 400 acres, 16 of those given over to apple orchards, on the fringes of the Paignton district. Only traditional Devon varieties of apples are used, with evocative names such as Paignton Marigold, young trees flourishing beside the mature ones planted by Roger's grandfather. Up to 80 tons

of apples are harvested or bought in (but only from Devon) each year to make the six varieties of cider, from a lowish-alcohol one, Clinker (3.8%), for people like me who want a lunchtime tipple without falling asleep, to the more traditional 6% ones like Wobbler (medium-sweet) and Thrasher (dry, 6.2%). The latter, along with Andsome Bay (4.8%), won Gold in the 2017 Taste of the West Awards. A pink one caught my eye – this is Red Head, with strawberry syrup added. Bull Walloper is a rather alarming 7.2% alcohol.

A tour of the orchards and cider-making building shows what a high-tech business this is these days. The old wooden presses straining the juice through straw are now in museums; it's all computerised now, although the basic technique is the same: pick, wash, press, store, remove sediment, ferment, pasteurise, bottle.

Roger and his son Richard are particularly pleased with the new pouches with a tap at the bottom, allowing you to drink small quantities without the cider losing its freshness since air is never introduced.

THE GOLDEN HIND

✆ 01803 856223 ⊘ goldenhind.co.uk

Prominent in the harbour is this replica of Sir Francis Drake's original ship in which he circumnavigated the globe, a feat which brought him lasting fame. The fact that his mission was to rob ships carrying treasure (in other words, he was a pirate) is rather glossed over, with the excuse that half of his booty was given to Queen Elizabeth, enabling her to pay off the national debt and earning him his knighthood as well as enough wealth to buy 40 properties including Buckland Abbey. His crew – the ones that survived the voyage – were well rewarded too. The value of the treasure which was off-loaded in the West Country in 1580 was a mind-boggling £478 million in today's money, and comprised not only Spanish silver and gold, but three tons of cloves from the Spice Islands (Indonesia). Originally he had taken on board six tons but was forced to jettison half this cargo when the *Golden Hind* was caught on a reef. Geographical exploration was never the purpose of the voyage, but when Drake failed to find the Northwest Passage in Alaska he had no choice but to sail west across the Pacific to avoid the Spanish lying in wait for him in South America.

Barely 100ft long, the ship is packed with interest, particularly for children who can collect stamps to show what they've seen, and be awarded a poster giving them honorary pirate status. And they can walk the plank, although sadly for desperate grandparents, it is only a safe simulation.

Adults will marvel at the cramped space that could house 70 men, ten of them officers. Only Drake had a cabin; the rest bedded down wherever they could. Among the well-labelled displays are weaponry, entertainments (the ship carried a band for part of the voyage), cooking facilities, and little nuggets of information such as why birds were kept captive: if the ship was lost they would be released to fly to the nearest land. It's a rewarding visit and worth the quite high admission price.

FOOD & DRINK

Beamers Seafood Restaurant 19 The Quay ✎ 01803 854777. In an enticing location overlooking the harbour and above Hobb Nobs souvenir shop and the tourist information centre, this has an extensive seafood menu as well as steaks, hamburgers and suchlike.

Rockfish Restaurant & Takeaway Brixham Fish Market ✎ 01803 850872 ◷ noon–21.30 daily. Their slogan is 'Tomorrow's fish is still in the sea', a claim that won't be challenged, not in Brixham. With the best location in town and the best range of seafood, this is the place for a special treat. They also serve a great selection of craft beers and cider.

The Curious Kitchen 14–16 Middle St, TQ5 8ER ✎ 01803 854816 ◷ 09.00–16.00 daily, plus 19.00–21.00 Fri & Sat. In a quiet street away from the tourist bustle of the Quay, this is a lovely restaurant of scrubbed wooden tables serving 'real food', mostly vegetarian, and excellent coffee. The portions are huge, but they do kid's portions (half size, half price) which are still enough for smaller appetites.

14 BERRY HEAD NATIONAL NATURE RESERVE

Gillard Rd TQ5 9AP ✆ 01803 882619 🖥 countryside-trust.org.uk/berryhead ☉ year round, although the visitor centre closes during quiet times

This is a blissful oasis where nature and history are the focus, not commerce. The story of Berry Head begins 400 million years ago, when the tropical reef around this chunk of land started its slow progress from seashells to Devonian limestone. Heaved up by geological forces and further sculpted by ice and storms through millions of years, its exposed position left it free from human settlement until man had developed the means to blast his enemies with cannon fire. It is the two fortresses from the time of the Napoleonic Wars that the visitor sees first, with picture-book crenellations and cannons peeping through the gaps. More blasting, this time for the quarrying of valuable limestone, left caves beneath the cliffs.

The combination of the work of man and nature has made this a perfect environment for birds and rare limestone-loving plants and their accompanying wildlife. Twenty-eight species of butterfly have been recorded here, but it is the bird population that is the main draw, with around 200 species seen. A huge colony of guillemots nest on the cliffs; visitors can follow their everyday lives on the CCTV cameras at the visitor centre, or from the bird hide which has posters to help with identification and recent sightings. In the small auditorium in the visitor centre an excellent slideshow describes the geological and human history of the site as well as the wildlife.

A path runs from the fort to the lighthouse at the end of Berry Head where you can admire the 360-degree view. The caves below are also an important roost for greater horseshoe bats. Finally, the licensed **Guardhouse Café** is something special, a favourite with locals as well as visitors: 'You can watch all this wildlife sitting at a picnic table (or inside if it's windy) eating a delicious breakfast, coffee, lunch or tea. Everything is freshly made, imaginative and served with a smile. and it is dog-friendly in a popular walking area. They also do quirky one-off events like a 05.00 breakfast to watch the sunrise at the summer solstice,' says a friend who lives nearby.

There's no public transport here but it's a very rewarding walk from Brixham along the South West Coast Path, which takes you through woods and out to the cliffs with a gorgeous view of the bay before you arrive at the fort. There is a closer (paying) car park, however.

TOTNES &
THE RIVER DART

3

TOTNES &
THE RIVER DART

The **Dart** is one of the loveliest rivers in England and, like Devon's three
other great rivers, the Exe, the Plym and the Taw, has played an important
part in shaping the county's history. It rises in Dartmoor and meanders
down to Dartmouth for 42 miles, with the lower 11 miles tidal. **Totnes**,
at the upper navigable end, has been a prosperous town since at least the
10th century, and continues the trend thanks to the energy and creativity
of its inhabitants. Of all the larger towns in Devon, this is perhaps the
most rewarding to visit, so provides a perfect starting or finishing point
for a walk or cruise down/up the Dart. Although Totnes is as far inland
as you can go by passenger boat, the Dart is still a significant presence
north of the town, and **Dartington Hall**, with its focus on sustainability
and the arts, perfectly complements the spirit of Totnes. The **South
Devon Railway** follows the river upstream as far as Buckfastleigh.

As the river snakes its way south, it passes small villages or grand
houses which flourished as a result of their location and then subsided
into tranquillity when water transport ceased to be viable. Now they
are an ideal base for exploring this exceptionally scenic part of Devon,
and for refreshment while walking the **Dart Valley Trail**. At the river
mouth is **Dartmouth**, and its twin town **Kingswear**, which have been
enchanting travellers for centuries, and to the east and west stretches the
South West Coast Path.

 ## WET-WEATHER ACTIVITIES

Totnes museums (pages 84–5)
China Blue Totnes (page 84)
The Dartington Shops (page 91)
Greenway (pages 106–7)
Dartmouth Museum (page 111)
Coleton Fishacre (pages 116–17)

GETTING THERE & AROUND

Of all the regions in this book, this is the one where you really can leave your car behind and enjoy the variety of public transport on offer. For those with strong legs there are footpaths galore and one of the best short(ish) walking and cycling trails in the county.

Totnes is served by frequent **buses** from all parts of the county, and is on the mainline **railway** from Exeter to Plymouth. The region is blessed with **two steam train** lines: the South Devon Railway between Totnes and Buckfastleigh, with a stop at Staverton, and the Dartmouth Steam Railway between Kingswear and Paignton. (The original trains on this line lost money so regularly that it was closed in 1958 even before Dr Beeching axed his way through all the little unprofitable railways of Britain. It was reopened as a preserved steam line by Beeching himself in 1960.)

By far the most enjoyable way of getting between Dartmouth and Totnes is the **river ferry** (page 98) and there are other vessels and **river boats** calling at villages along the Dart.

In short, bring your car if you must, but you may regret it. Many of the lanes are single-track.

SELF-POWERED TRAVEL

Totnes is full of enthusiastic cyclists, and using the **bicycle** as a means of transport is accepted practice. For recreational cycling, the **River Dart cycle path**, part of the NCN 2 Coast-to-Coast route, provides outstanding river views along largely traffic-free paths. The Totnes–Dartington stretch is 3½ miles in total, going to Dartington and on to Hood Barton in the direction of Staverton and Buckfastleigh. The three-mile ride from Totnes to Ashprington is largely traffic free, but quite hilly. Much of it runs along the old Sharpham carriage drive, and crosses the estate (pages 101–2) on the way to Ashprington. Cycles can be hired at Hot Pursuit (26 The Stables, Ford Rd, Totnes Industrial Estate ✆ 01803 865174 ◯ closed Sun).

There's a wonderful variety of **walks** here, mostly with views of water: either river or sea. **The Dart Valley Trail** is described on page 99, and there are various **South West Coast Path** options. You can also walk the **John Musgrave Heritage Trail** from Totnes to Torbay. The newly established **Franklin Totnes Trail** is a seven-mile circuit of

WILD SWIMMING IN THE RIVER DART

Joanna Griffin

The River Dart is one of Devon's most popular rivers for swimming. Its clear waters, stained the colour of dark red amber by the peaty soil, rush down from the high moor, cascading over large, smooth stones and widening towards Totnes where the river becomes tidal. A popular stretch on Dartmoor itself is around Newbridge. From here, the beautiful **Sharrah Pools** are a 40-minute walk upstream through the National Trust's Holne Woods (page 261). Closer to Newbridge itself, the river is shallow and turbulent, thrust into small waterfalls as it courses over large boulders, but there are still some lovely deep, calm parts to be found on the left bank, perfect for a swim between the banks of birch and ancient oaks.

Once the Dart has left Dartmoor, there are numerous swimming spots en route to Totnes. A favourite along this stretch is **Still Pool**: a wide, calm and reasonably deep section outside the village of Staverton (pages 93–4), just below the weir. Parking is in the old station car park and it is a lovely 10–15-minute riverside walk through the woods to the pool, where there is access from the riverbank or a small beach. This can be a popular spot in the warm weather and you might find you're not alone in the water, but it is pretty and easily accessible.

Totnes, taking in most of the places of interest in the area as well as the lovely riverside path.

A look at the OS Explorer map OL20 will inspire other ideas, although by far the best maps for walkers are the Croydecycle ones (pages 13–14) at a scale of 1:12,500 (five inches to a mile). For this area: Totnes includes Berry Pomeroy and Ashprington, and there are two versions of the Dartmouth map. Each has Dartmouth and Kingswear on one side, including the confusing streets of Dartmouth itself; *Dartmouth & Slapton* covers the region south, and *Dartmouth, Dittisham & Coast to Brixham* is for the north. *Dittisham & Cornworthy* continues up the river as far as Totnes, including the cycle route. As in all these maps, not only is every geographical detail covered but there are helpful notes such as 'stone base' or 'grazed fields'.

The **South Devon Area of Outstanding Natural Beauty** (⊘ southdevonaonb.org.uk) has details of many local walks which can be downloaded.

There are plenty of opportunities for **canoeists and kayakers** on the River Dart (pages 98–100), with the option of renting or bringing your own canoe/kayak.

1 TOTNES

🏠 **Ashley's Shack**, between Totnes & Dartmouth (page 276) ⛺ **Kilbury Manor**, between Buckfastleigh & Totnes (page 276)

Tourist information: The Guildhall, Totnes (but check before visiting – it may move)
📞 07398 018448 🖰 visittotnes.co.uk

A few years ago a hand-painted addition to the town sign summed up the image of Totnes perfectly: 'Totnes, twinned with Narnia.' But Totnes is no fairy tale. Its success in creating a genuine alternative to 'clone towns' is built on the knowledge that the world's supply of oil is dwindling, and that a different, less consumerist lifestyle is not only inevitable but enjoyable. Transition Town Totnes, or TTT, is the result, outlined in *The Transition Handbook* by Rob Hopkins.

Totnes is blessed with a perfect position. Its location at the navigable limit of the River Dart ensured its place in early history, with Brutus of Troy (see box, page 86) allegedly making a rather giant leap for Britain here. Even the Totnes Pound, launched in 2007 as a means of boosting the local economy and still circulating locally, isn't a new idea – the town

CHARLES BABBAGE, INVENTOR EXTRAORDINARY

Charles Babbage hated music, and was tormented by the barrel organs, buskers, fiddlers and other rough-cast musicians who enlivened London's 19th-century streets. He bombarded *The Times* with angry letters, and engineered a parliamentary bill to curb the noise. The objects of his fury retaliated by playing for hours outside his house; in his obituary in 1871 *The Times* commented that he had 'reached an age, [in] spite of organ-grinding persecutors, little short of 80 years'.

Street musicians apart, his interests were wide-ranging. Statistics fascinated him. His writings covered such subjects as how to lay the guns of a battery without exposing men to enemy fire, the causes of breaking plate-glass windows, and the boracic acid works of Tuscany. For all that, he is best known for the **Difference Engine** he invented in the 1820s: a massive calculating machine, designed to produce accurate results for logarithmic and other mathematical tables. For lack of funds it was never built in his lifetime, but a version built in 1991 from his plans by London's Science Museum (where half of his brain is also preserved – the other half is in the Hunterian Museum at London's Royal College of Surgeons) worked as he had forecast. In the 1830s he followed it with his **Analytical Engine**, based on a punched-card system and the precursor of today's computers.

minted its own coins in the 10th century. It grew rich on the cloth trade and in Tudor times was second only to Exeter in the wealth of its citizens. Daniel Defoe described it as having 'more gentlemen in it than tradesmen of note' and an 18th-century visitor wrote approval that Totnes 'abounds in good shops.' There are said to be more listed buildings per head of population here than in any other town in England. This has helped ensure that it still has plenty of good shops, since large chains look for large premises. Among the more unusual shops (both at the upper end of High Street) are the **Devon Harp Centre** and the **Zero Waste Shop** (thezerowasteshop.co.uk), which aims to cut waste by eliminating unnecessary packaging. The shop is owned and run by former footballer Richard Eckersley and sells only vegan and organic produce. Bring your own container, or buy a reusable one in the shop, and serve yourself from a huge range of products. You decide how much you want, rather than the producer deciding for you, and you can even grind your own peanut or almond butter. It's a great idea and very Totnes. Look out also for **Belouche**, at the back of Market Square, which sells high-quality and beautiful rugs, carpets and weavings from around the world.

Born in 1791, Charles was from an old Totnes family, and Totnes claims him as one of its 'sons'. The Elizabethan House Museum (page 85) has a room devoted to him.

Apart from his 'engines', his many inventions included a prototype submarine, an Occulting Light, a system for deciphering codes, and more prosaically the cow catcher on the front of American trains. In 1831 he founded the British Association for the Advancement of Science, and was also instrumental in founding the Royal Astronomical Society and the London Statistical Society.

In 1833 he met Ada Byron (Lord Byron's daughter, sometimes described as the first computer programmer), later to become Countess of Lovelace; she was fascinated by his 'engines' and contributed to his work on them – but died in 1852. In 1864, the ageing and increasingly grumpy Charles wrote his obsessive *Observations of Street Nuisances*, recording 165 of them in less than three months, but achieved little else before his death. However, his name lives on in several university buildings and the Babbage crater on the moon, and there's a commemorative blue plaque on the wall of his former home in the London Borough of Southwark. Since he loved trains, he might be happy that in the 1990s British Rail named a locomotive after him; also perhaps that his lunar crater is well out of reach of noisy street musicians ...

Apart from shopping – and eating in the many cafés and restaurants – there is plenty to engage visitors. The circular, crenellated **Norman castle** sits, like a child's drawing, on a hill and the 15th-century red sandstone **church of St Mary** competes for attention. The rood screen here was carved from Beer stone, rather than the more usual wood, at the command of the town corporation who wanted it to rival Exeter Cathedral. The **Guildhall**, behind the church, started life as the refectory of the Benedictine priory, but was rebuilt during the height of the town's wealth in the mid 16th century for the Guild of Merchants. It has been the home of the town council ever since, currently houses the tourist information centre, and is open to visitors in the summer (○ 11.00–15.00 Mon–Fri, 10.00–16.00 Sat).

About halfway down the High Street on the left-hand side a flattish, rough stone is set into the pavement; this is the so-called 'Brutus Stone' (see box, page 86). Legend apart, another possibility is that it was the *bruiter's* stone (to *bruit* meaning to report or proclaim, often by rumour) where news was announced by the town crier or equivalent.

At the north end of town, across the Town Bridge in Bridgetown, is the **Steamer Quay** (TQ6 9PS) from where you can catch the river ferry to Dartmouth (page 98). It's a lovely walk of about a mile on a leafy footpath alongside the river from the mainline train station (TQ9 5JR). Close to the station is **China Blue** (✐ 01803 860908 ⌂ china-blue.co.uk ○ 09.00–17.30 Mon–Sat, 10.00–17.00 Sun). Here you can paint your own pottery, browse a huge selection of ceramics in the shop, or enjoy a good meal in the café. It's a great place.

MUSEUMS, MARKETS & SPECIAL EVENTS
Museums
Totnes has four unusual and excellent museums, so there's plenty to keep you interested on a wet day.

Starting at the top, opposite Market Square is the **Fashion & Textiles Museum** (43 High St ✐ 01803 862857 ○ mid May–end Sep 11.00–17.00 Tue–Fri). It houses the Devonshire Collection of Period Costume and as such is extraordinarily complete, with clothing ranging from 1650 to the present day. On the first floor is a temporary exhibition which changes each year.

The **Timehouse** (69 Fore St, just below the Eastgate Arch ✐ 01803 862109 ○ 11.00–17.00 Tue–Sat) is unique and gloriously Slow.

It really does need time, ideally over an hour, to appreciate the 'individually themed installations designed to stimulate all the senses and film presentation areas to stimulate the mind'. You enter, appropriately enough, through a shop called Narnia Totnes, but the museum is more Tardis than Narnia, being a complete immersion in 20th-century England, with a few sorties abroad. The colonisation of Australia is put under the lens with a disturbing slideshow showing the fate of Aboriginal Australian from Cook's arrival to the present day (in the room called Cloud 9). Each room is full of the items typical of an era or subject, arranged seemingly haphazardly but with great artistry. Films include life as a child during the war, a look at environmental disasters, and a mini Odeon cinema. There's a Beatles room, a 20th-century room, and a Moroccan bazaar where you can drink mint tea. The museum is the result of the enthusiasm and dedication of artist Julie Lafferty, who put her life savings into the project. It's a great achievement.

One of the Tudor houses on Fore Street contains the **Elizabethan House Museum** (70 Fore St ✐ 01803 863821 ◈ totnesmuseum.org ○ Mar–Sep 10.30–16.00 Mon–Fri), whose 13 little rooms overflow with an eclectic mix of furniture, local history and childhood. Charles Babbage, credited with the invention of the first computer (see box, pages 82–3), has his own room here.

The **Totnes Image Bank** (Town Mill, Coronation Rd, next to Morrisons supermarket car park ○ 10.00–16.00 Tue & Fri) is housed in the restored old water mill. An exhibition of panels shows the history of Totnes from Saxon times to the present day, and upstairs in a separate gallery are displays of some of the 45,000 or so photos documenting the more recent history of the town which have been collected, scanned and catalogued by their team of volunteers. Computers are provided for research and photographic prints are for sale.

Markets

The excellent **weekly market** is held on Fridays and Saturdays in Market Square, spilling over to Civic Square. The large range of stalls include bric-a-brac, old tools, fruit and vegetables, plants, crafts, books, and clothing. Jonas Fishmonger's van is there, selling fish fresh from Brixham, and there's a reasonable choice of hot food – but no drink. For this you need to visit the farmers' market (**Totnes Food Market**), on the third Sunday of the month. It is the variety, rather than the size,

BRUTUS OF TROY & TOTNES:
A NEW TAKE ON AN ANCIENT TALE

As one version of the legend goes, the grandson of Aeneas (hero of Troy and of Virgil's Aeneid) struck up an illicit affair with the niece of a princess. The local soothsayer foretold that any child born to them would cause the death of both its parents and would then wander through many lands before gaining great honour. The mother did indeed die in childbirth, and the boy, Brutus, later killed his father with an accidental arrow while out hunting, having rather improbably mistaken him for a stag.

Consequently Brutus was exiled to Greece, whence, as an adult, he set sail with a group of other Trojans to seek new lands. After two days and one night they came to an island where they found a shrine to the goddess Diana, at which they offered libations and prayed for guidance. That night, the goddess appeared to Brutus in a dream. She told him of an empty island far away beyond the sunset, once peopled by giants, where he and his group could settle. He would breed a race of kings there, whose power would spread around the earth. Onward the group sailed, westward and then north, passing strange and savage shores.

After many months they came to a coastline of ragged grey cliffs, rising from sandy bays. It was the coast of Cornwall, in the land then known as Albion. Easing their ships carefully up a sheltered river, they reached a bay overlooked by a wooded hill. Brutus set off instantly to survey the area, which is now Totnes. A boulder – the Brutus Stone – on which he stepped as he sprang ashore can be seen to this day, in Fore Street. Satisfied, he called his people to inhabit their new home.

Later Brutus set out to seek a site for the capital of his domain. Finally selecting the Thames, he built on its banks the rough wooden settlement that became today's London. It's said he was buried there when he died, 23 years after reaching Devon, in around 1100BC, no doubt with due ceremony and pomp. His three sons divided Britain between them, creating their own kingdoms of England, Scotland and Wales. And thus – as happens in all good legends – the early prophecies were fulfilled.

(Main source: Geoffrey of Monmouth's *The History of the Kings of Britain (Historia Regum Britanniae)*, c.1136)

that makes this market special. You can buy cider and apple juice from Devon orchards and stock up on the local beers. Gin connoisseurs can sample Plymouth's Barbican Botanist, and Love2taste vinegar sells a bewildering variety of related products, inviting you to 'find happiness on the tip of your tongue'. At both the weekly markets and the farmers' market is the innovative **Shrooms on the Road** where Dave Weymouth will proudly show you his chunky king oyster mushrooms, shiitake and girolles, just some of the unusual varieties that he grows or forages, and serve you a delicious mushroom stroganoff.

In the summer Totnes holds an **Elizabethan Market** every Tuesday, when the stallholders dress up in Tudor costumes. It's organised by the Totnes Elizabethan Society, which runs a series of special events. The tourist office has leaflets, or ring ✆ 01803 863043 if this is your special interest.

Special events

The **Totnes & District Show**, on the last Sunday in July, is one of the biggest one-day agricultural shows in the county, dating back 100 years and highlighting the region's farming roots. **Totnes Carnival** is held in mid August, with parades, children's fancy-dress competitions and so on. Unique to the town, however, is the **Orange Race** which follows the carnival. Locals pursue the fruit down the hill, the speed (and danger) of the pursuit dictated by the age of the contestant; there are races for all age groups, from four to over 60. If you want to see the true definition of breakneck speed, watch the adult men's group. Apparently Sir Francis Drake started the ball rolling, so to speak. The **Sea Change Festival** of 'music, culture and high times' takes place at the end of August. Contact the Totnes information centre (page 82) for more information.

🍴 FOOD & DRINK

Some of the most famous food places in the Totnes area are **Ben's Farm Shops**. They were formerly under the umbrella of **Riverford Kitchen**, but changed their name in 2017 since not all products are strictly organic (remember *The Archers*? They had the same problem). But the produce is still locally grown, fresh, varied and irresistible.

There are two outlets in Totnes, **Ben's Wine & Tapas** (50 High St ✆ 01803 840853 ◷ 10.00–22.00 Mon–Thu, 10.00–23.00 Fri & Sat) and the smaller farm shop at 33 High St which sells produce and light lunches.

As you would expect in such a buzzy town, there are plenty of good places to eat.

Pie Street 26 High St ✆ 01803 868674 ◷ from 11.30 daily, various closing times. A perennial favourite for its excellent pies (of course!), chips and other substantial meals. Pie takeaway service available.

Rumour 30 High St ✆ 01803 864682 ◷ 10.00–23.30 Mon–Sat, 18.00–22.00 Sun. For many years this has been the place to go for a treat: all scrubbed wooden tables and cheery diners. The menu is varied and imaginative, with steak and pizza a speciality.

Seeds 2 38 High St, just below Market Square next to Totnes Bookshop. Advertising themselves as 'healthy fast food', this is just what this vegetarian/vegan restaurant does. A choice of tasty self-service dishes ensures that there's no waiting for your order to be taken. Very good value: you can eat well for under £10.

The Curator 2A The Plains TQ9 5DR ✆ 01803 865570 ⊙ 07.30–21.15 Mon–Fri, 09.00–21.15 Sat, 09.00–17.00 Sun. This Italian restaurant is winning plaudits for its morning coffee and the quality of the meals. A small menu but cooked to perfection.

Totnes Brewing Company 59a Castle St, just off the High St 🖥 thetotnesbrewingco.co.uk ⊙ 17.00–midnight Mon–Thu, noon–midnight Fri–Sun. A local microbrewery with lovely premises which suggests 'You bring the food, we'll bring the drinks'.

Willow 87 High St ✆ 01803 862605 ⊙ 10.00–17.00 Mon, Tue & Thu, 10.00–22.00 Wed, Fri & Sat. Willow has been serving vegetarian and vegan meals for many years with no drop in quality. Probably the best option for vegetarians in Totnes, enhanced by its gentle live music.

THE TOTNES LITTLEHEMPSTON STEAM RAILWAY STATION & RARE BREEDS FARM

The charmingly nostalgic station and this appealing little animal centre (✆ 01803 840387 🖥 totnesrarebreeds.co.uk ⊙ Easter–Nov 10.00–17.00; see ad, 4th colour section) are opposite each other across the railway tracks. With its limited space the centre doesn't try to do too much, it just does it small-scale and very well. There are domestic animals such as angora goats which look like gone-wrong sheep with floppy ears and stuck-on horns, plump pygmy goats, Soay sheep and Berkshire pigs. Wild animals include chipmunks and red squirrels with runways so they can exercise safely. Some 'red' squirrels are almost black and I learned from Sam, the owner, that European red squirrels are darker the further south they live. Like us, really. Some remarkably relaxed guinea pigs await a cuddle from children and, at Easter, orphan lambs arrive for them to bottle feed.

It is birds, however, that make this place special. Not only the rare breeds of chicken such as the Light Sussex hens, which are as snazzy as a Japanese painting, and Silkies with feathery feet and topknots, but a unique collection of nine species of owl. Most were hatched from eggs so have only known captivity, and vary from Lady Jane, the magnificent great grey owl who arrived in 2012, to Flitwick the little owl who hatched in 2005 and is so accustomed to people she came over to have her head feathers ruffled. The rarest in the collection is Merlin, the East Siberian eagle owl. There are only 12 of this species in the UK, all his relatives.

You get the chance to gently stroke the feathers of the owls and feel their density (one reason they can fly so silently), and learn their stories and some surprising facts from their handler. I learned, for instance, that the body weight of the biggest owl, Lady Jane, is half that of the smaller European eagle owl; she's all feathers.

I chatted over coffee to Sam Adams, the impossibly young-looking owner who bought the farm in 2015 from Jacquie Tolley who, with her husband, had created it out of 'two acres of jungly land' in 1999.

Sam had worked there as manager before Jacquie retired, and before that at Berry Head Nature Reserve, so she has all the right experience to continue its success. Her plans for the future? 'I'm working closely with the Rare Breeds Survival Trust,' she told me. 'I'd like to get a name on the map for rare breeds, but it's also important for children from cities to get the chance to meet animals they may never have seen before.'

There is no car park at this steam railway station; the mainline station is your best option or, if that's full, there's more parking at the Pavilion (follow signs from the A385 roundabout at the northern end of town) though it's quite a long walk along the pleasant footpath to the steam train station and Rare Breeds Farm. If you are taking the steam train – and it's a lovely journey – it's better to start from Buckfastleigh (pages 196–8), where parking is free.

DARTINGTON & AROUND

🏠 **The Cott Inn** (page 275) & **Dartington Hall** (page 276)

Although the road signs ask you to drive slowly through the village, you would be hard put to find it. Dartington is Dartington Hall, and apart from the village stores and petrol station and a few houses, that's it. But what a special place this is!

2 DARTINGTON HALL

TQ9 6EL ✐ 01803 847147 ⬧ dartingtonhall.com

Dartington Hall has been a significant part of this corner of Devon for at least a thousand years. The FitzMartin family owned it in the 12th century and probably built the church, now ruined apart from the tower. By the mid 14th century it had reverted to the Crown and Richard II granted it to his half-brother John Holland who built the first great country house here.

In 1559 a prominent Devon family, the Champernownes, bought the estate. By the beginning of the 20th century, however, their family fortunes, and the buildings, were in ruins. Leonard and Dorothy Elmhirst saw Dartington's potential and bought it in 1925. He the son of a Yorkshire clergyman and she an American heiress, they shared a vision of rural regeneration through the arts. Leonard had done missionary work in India and studied agriculture in order to improve farming methods there. Returning to India later he became secretary to Rabindranath Tagore, the Nobel-prize-winning writer and social reformer, an appointment that sowed the seed for establishing Dartington Hall as a place of 'experiment and new creation' and restoring it to its former glory. He and his wife (who shared his enthusiasm for radical causes) aimed to bring 'economic and social vitality back into the countryside' as well as creating one of the finest gardens in Devon. They also founded the progressive Dartington Hall School (now closed) and their interest in the arts made their house a magnet for artists and musicians from around the world.

"He and his wife aimed to bring 'economic and social vitality back into the countryside'."

The Dartington Hall Trust (⌀ dartington.org) continues the work done by the Elmhirsts, supporting various projects and the Schumacher school, under the umbrella of sustainability and social justice.

The **Old Parsonage Farm** is just one typically Dartington business, bringing sustainability and innovation to modern farming methods. They have a milking herd of goats (which you can learn to milk yourself) and produce ice cream and yogurt (⌀ dartingtondairy.com). You'll see the ice-cream sign to the left of the drive as you enter the estate. Shortly after it, a modest notice advertising fresh vegetables with a daily selection and an honesty box is the visible sign of one of Dartington's success stories: **Landworks** (⌀ landworks.org.uk). This prisoner resettlement scheme gives prisoners and ex-prisoners the opportunity to learn about working the land, or with the produce of the land (including woodworking). One statistic says it all: nationwide, 46% of prisoners reoffend within one year of release; the comparable reoffending rate for Landworks trainees is 4%.

Dartington is also a centre for **agroforestry**, where Martin Crawford runs the Agroforestry Research Trust to tap into the edible or medicinal products of trees and plants and how best to manage them.

An annual **Summer School and Festival** is held, based around music and poetry, and a continuous programme of craft courses, lectures, films and theatre. This is also a venue for the ten-day **Ways with Words** literary festival in July, and as a frequent visitor I can hardly imagine a more enjoyable occasion. The combination of top-notch speakers and the spacious grounds (equipped with deckchairs) brings an atmosphere of indolence mixed with intellectual stimulation which is completely addictive. There is always plenty else going on too – a sculpture exhibition, informal talks, book sales, and food.

Even when there are no events, Dartington is a wonderfully gentle, peaceful place to visit, just to stroll around the superb gardens, take a look at the Great Hall and any other buildings which are not being used, and eat at one of the restaurants. Perhaps also watch a film at their independent cinema, **The Barn**. The **gardens**, behind the Great Hall, are open year-round dawn to dusk, and free of charge. Their most notable features are the enormous trees, which have had hundreds of uninterrupted years to grow to maturity, and the lawn terraces which lead to the sunken garden. Sculptures are dotted here and there, including a Henry Moore.

For longer visits, Dartington Hall has 50 comfortable rooms (page 276), and all profits from the accommodation go to the Trust to help their work. The Elmhirsts would be happy to see how their inspiration has lasted.

The Dartington Shops (TQ9 6TQ) is the commercial wing of Dartington, but all profits go to furthering the Trust's aims, and the spirit is very much Dartington, with an emphasis on art, craft and organic produce. Notable among them is The Food Shop, which sells a huge range of local, mostly organic produce. Not cheap, but that's not the point. There's also a café and restaurant. A branch of the Totnes Bookshop is here, and the crafts on offer include a wide range of high-quality glass, pottery and jewellery. For those inspired to have a go themselves, **Crazy about Clay** allows you to try your hand at pottery or sculpture, including use of the wheel (crazyaboutclay.com).

Dartington Hall and The Shops are easily reached on foot via a leafy riverside walk from Totnes or Staverton, from where you can catch a South Devon Railway steam or diesel train to Buckfastleigh or Totnes. The Croydecycle Totnes map shows numerous walking possibilities. Bus 165 runs every two hours from Totnes to Dartington Hall.

⚍ FOOD & DRINK

The Almond Thief Unit 3/4 Webber's Yard, Dartington village, TQ9 6JY ✎ 01803 411290
◷ 08.00–15.00 Tue–Sat. This deserves the cliché of 'best-kept secret'. You're not going
to find this terrific bakery by accident. In the corner of an industrial estate, marked by a
few shabby outside tables crammed with people tucking into breakfast, brunch or lunch,
or chatting over 'the best coffee in South Devon', the Almond Thief sells sourdough bread,
pastries and the fullest of full English breakfasts as well as lunch. Take the road towards
Plymouth at the Dartington roundabout; Webber's Yard is on the left, just beyond the
Dartington Stores and Texaco garage.

The Cott Inn Cott Lane, Dartington TQ9 6HE ✎ 01803 863777. One of the oldest (1320) and
most beautiful thatched inns in the county – perhaps the country – and the place to go for a
special treat. They are famous for their meals, with a varied menu and beautifully presented
dishes emphasising local produce. See also *Accommodation*, page 275.

The Green Table Dartington ◷ summer 09.00–20.00. Located near the car parks, with
outdoor seating, this newish restaurant specialises in vegetarian food (though it also
has meat dishes), especially salads. There's always a choice of two soups, a frittata and a
selection of paninis. A children's menu is offered at half price for a half-portion (and you
don't have to be a child).

White Hart Bar & Restaurant ✎ 01803 847111 ◷ noon–15.00 & 17.30–21.00 daily.
Located adjacent to Dartington's Great Hall, this friendly pub serves classy food, beautifully
presented, at reasonable prices.

LITTLEHEMPSTON

Å Hemsford Yurt Camp (page 276)

Across the river from Dartington Hall and tucked into rural surroundings
only a five-minute drive from the bustle of Totnes, Littlehempston is no
run-of-the-mill village. First, one of its pubs, the **Tally Ho** (TQ9 6LY
✎ 01803 862316 ◷ Tue–Sun plus Bank Holidays), is South Devon's first
community-owned pub, rescued by the villagers from conversion to a
private home and opened in April 2014. The Grade-II listed building is
thought to date from the 17th century or earlier, and to have been built
originally as a church house. By 1841 it was already an inn. Funds for
its purchase were raised largely by the sale of shares, so shareholders
(many of whom also run it, cook its very good food, pull pints at
the bar, scrub its floors and tend its gardens) can truly feel that it is
'theirs'. In 2017 it was Runner Up as South Devon's Pub of the Year and
Rural Pub of the Year. Littlehempston's other pub, the **Pig & Whistle**
(✎ 01803 863733), is also highly praised for its food and offers B&B.

Next-door to the Tally Ho, an innovation in the 15th-century **St John the Baptist Church** could well be copied by any ancient churches seeking to maintain their historic charm while meeting their communities' practical and social needs. Enter the church and all seems traditional: a fine screen, a well-preserved wagon roof, a seven-sided Norman font, stone effigies dozing on the windowsills and carved Victorian pews. It's the pews that hold the secret: they've been mounted on castors, so that they can be pushed aside or repositioned for local concerts, social events and suchlike without permanently damaging the church's appearance and atmosphere.

The Mare & Foal Sanctuary

TQ9 6LW ✆ 01803 866615 ⬧ mareandfoal.org ○ Apr–Oct 10.00–16.00

Between Littlehempston and Berry Pomeroy (pages 94–6) is Coombe Park, the visitor centre for this busy charity which rescues, retrains and rehomes horses and ponies. A visit here is bliss for horsey types. During the morning there are tours of the yard and horses waiting for adoption, plus a café, a gift shop and a secondhand tack shop.

3 STAVERTON

⌂ **The Sea Trout Inn** (page 275)

The village has a good pub but its main attractions are the railway station and the ancient packhorse bridge nearby. The bridge, built in the early 15th century, is considered the best medieval bridge in the county and is unusual in that cars are allowed to cross it – provided they are no wider than 6ft 6in. Two metal posts, decorated by scrapes of multicoloured car paint, act as a gauge. Staverton means 'the village by the stony ford', which suggests that the village existed before the bridge.

"Two metal posts, decorated by scrapes of multicoloured car paint, act as a gauge."

The **South Devon Railway** between Buckfastleigh and Totnes stops at this delightfully vintage station. It is how people like to remember the 1950s, although I doubt the busy station in those days had so many flowers. It is cared for by volunteers from the Staverton Preservation Group, and there is also a wagon repair workshop here to keep the rolling stock on the rails.

Trains run frequently enough for you to alight here and take the riverside footpath to the Sea Trout (nearly a mile away), or take a longer, but lovely walk along the river to Dartington and thence to Totnes (the Croydecycle map, *Totnes*, gives you plenty of options). Alternatively, if you are having a day out with the children, there's a lovely safe swimming pool in the river (page 81).

ⵏⵏ FOOD & DRINK

Ben's Farm Shop TQ9 6AF ☏ 01803 762851 ○ 09.00–18.00. Just off the A384 and formerly Riverford Farm Shop, you'll find seasonal and mostly organic fruit and vegetables, plants, and a large variety and choice of groceries. There's a very good deli, bakery, butchers, a café with outdoor seating, and a picnic area.

Riverford Field Kitchen Wash Barn, TQ11 0JU ☏ 01803 762074 ⌂ riverford.co.uk. Emphatically more than just a restaurant, this is part of the pioneering organic farm that first introduced the concept of veg boxes, where seasonal vegetables are delivered to local homes as well as hotels and restaurants. A tour of the farm is an optional part of the 'field to plate' experience. Lunch or dinner consists of a fixed menu of three courses, with various salads and savouries for starters, five vegetable dishes and one meat or fish dish for the main course, and a choice of around five yummy deserts. Diners sit together at large tables so a desire to be convivial should accompany a good appetite (you help yourself from the communal dishes). Dining here is a unique experience and gastronomically very rewarding. Advance booking is mandatory and there is only one sitting.

The Sea Trout Staverton TQ9 6PA ☏ 01803 762274 ○ noon–14.00 (14.30 Sat) & 18.00–21.00. A friendly 15th-century pub which won Gold in the 2016 Taste of the West awards. The restaurant makes tasty use of fresh local foods, with an emphasis on fish and seafood; look out for daily specials on the blackboard. You have the choice of eating in the smart restaurant or more relaxedly in the dog-friendly Stag Bar. The menu is a mixture of classy dishes and traditional comfort food such as spotted dick. The inn has good en-suite accommodation.

4 BERRY POMEROY

The tiny village – just a few cottages, a school and a church – lies only a mile from Totnes, with the castle a further mile away, so although there is free parking at the castle it's rewarding to walk there, using part of the area's long-distance footpath, the **John Musgrave Heritage Trail**, and the ancient paths through woodland leading to the castle. If you start from Littlehempston there's a lovely walk along Gatcombe Brook to the castle (shown on the Croydecycle *Totnes* map). You can return to Totnes by the twice-daily bus number 149 from the village. If you drive you will pass close to the Mare & Foal Sanctuary (page 93), well worth a visit for horse lovers.

Berry Pomeroy has been in the possession of only two families since the Norman Conquest, the Pomeroys and Seymours, who came over with William the Conqueror. Ralf or Ralph Pomeroy was given the baronial estate by William I, and his family owned it until 1548 when his fortunes collapsed and he was forced to sell it to Edward Seymour, Duke of Somerset.

"The Pomeroys built a defensive castle in the late 15th century, ideally situated in a deer park so hunting could be enjoyed."

The Pomeroys built a defensive castle in the late 15th century, ideally situated in a deer park so hunting could be enjoyed as well as a lifestyle appropriate to their station. The Seymours considered themselves even more elevated, not without reason, since the Duke of Somerset was the brother of Jane Seymour, the third wife of Henry VIII, and the only one of six wives to bear him a son, the future Edward VI, who ascended the throne when he was only nine. The Duke, his uncle, was appointed Protector until the boy reached maturity but Edward died at the age of 15, so being king in all but name, the Duke was a man of immense power and wealth. However, his rise in fortune was followed by an abrupt fall: he was overthrown as Protector by political enemies in 1549 and beheaded two years later.

His son, also Edward, made Berry Pomeroy his home and set about building the finest mansion in Devon within the walls of the original castle. The work was continued by a son and grandson, so four generations of Edward Seymours have left their mark on the village, its church and its castle.

Royalists like the Seymours had a difficult time in the Civil War but their fortunes were restored, along with the monarchy, and the 6th Duke welcomed William, Prince of Orange, to Berry Castle after he had landed at Brixham in 1688.

The church, **St Mary's**, stands on its own, overlooking a glorious view. The first thing you notice is the vaulted porch, with some interesting faces carved on the bosses. Inside, the exposed brickwork is unusual, and the finely carved gilded screen stretching the full width of the nave catches the eye. The saints painted on the panels have been defaced, presumably at the time of the Reformation, leaving their eloquent hands to do the talking.

There's a memorial stone to the Reverend John Prince, author of *The Worthies of Devon* (see box, page 97), but the glory of the church is its Seymour chapel with the memorial to Lord Edward Seymour, son of the Protector, and his son (another Edward) with his wife Elizabeth Champernowne, who was not known for her chastity. John Prince referred to her disapprovingly as 'a frolic lady'. All are lying on their sides, propped on an elbow. Elizabeth looks particularly uncomfortable, but is sustained by a prayer book clutched in her hand. She has two of her 11 children with her: a baby in a cradle at her head and at her feet a little girl, described in the information sheet as 'an imbecile child', sitting in a chair. Lined up below are the kneeling figures of the nine surviving children.

Berry Pomeroy Castle

TQ9 6LJ ✆ 01803 866618 ○ Apr–Nov & winter weekends 10.00–18.00; English Heritage

This romantic ruin had earlier writers in rhapsodies. At the end of the 18th century, W G Maton wrote '… the principal remains of the building … are so finely overhung with the branches of trees and shrubs that grow close to the walls, so beautifully mantled with ivy, and so richly encrusted with moss, that they constitute the most picturesque objects that can be imagined.' S P B Mais, in the mid 1920s, refers to the 'exquisite' ruin with ivy covering every inch of the walls, confirmed by an accompanying photo, and W G Hoskins (1954) describes it as 'one of the most romantically beautiful ruins in Devon, almost buried in deep woods on the edge of a cliff.' It is still romantically beautiful and still almost buried in deep woods, but the ivy has now been removed and quite a bit of clearance must have been done by English Heritage to bring the castle to its present rather austere state. It's worth

"Give your imagination full rein and visualise the castle in its heyday, when a succession of Sir Edward Seymours were striving to make it the grandest mansion in Devon."

taking the time to explore properly, with the audio guide, to give your imagination full rein and visualise the castle in its heyday, when a succession of Sir Edward Seymours were striving to make it the grandest mansion in Devon before running out of money, or enthusiasm, and abandoning it to the elements and nesting swallows. Berry Pomeroy is also famed as being one of the most haunted castles in Britain, and almost yearly there are reports of someone seeing a ghost here, usually the White Lady. For some first-hand accounts check out ✆ ghost-story. co.uk. The **café** at the castle serves very good snacks.

WORTHY OF BEING A WORTHY OF DEVON

John Prince was vicar of Berry Pomeroy from 1681 to 1723, during which time he researched the history of Devon's noble families. His book *The Worthies of Devon* was published in 1701 and makes delightful reading – for the language as much as the content. Here are some extracts from his description of the life of the third Sir Edward Seymour.

The occasion of his being born there [in the Vicarage] … was that Berry Castle … was then a rebuilding: and his Lady-Mother, not likeing the Musick of Axes and Hammers (this Gentlemans great delight afterward) chose to lay down, this her burthen in that lowly place.

He had no sooner passed the care and inspection of the Noursery, but that he was put abroad to School (it enervates youth to keep it too long at home under the fondling of a Mother) … [At Sherborne] he met with a severe Master, tho a good Teacher: the Memory of whom, would often disturb his sleep long after he was a Man.

… it pleased almighty God, in just Punishment of a Nation whose sins had made it ripe for Vengeance, to let loose upon it, a most dreadfull Civil War. A War founded upon the glorious pretences of Liberty, Property, and Religion … And when matters brake out into open violence between the King and Parliament, this Gentlemans native Principles of Loyalty soon instructed him which side to take.

[Sir Edward, then a colonel, was taken prisoner at Modbury before making his escape] by fileing Off the Bars of the Window, and leaping down, upon the back of the Centinel that stood under; who being astonished by so unexpected a rancounter, the Colonel wrested his Musket out of his hand, and gave him such a sound Rebuke as hindered him, for the present, from following after him, or making any Discovery of him.

By the entrance to the car park and the footpath leading to Gatcombe Brook is a pollarded beech tree, its roots reaching down to the eroded path below. This is what used to be the **Wishing Tree**. I first visited the castle with a friend who, in the late 1960s, used to take her children there to make a special wish. 'We had to walk backwards – very tricky with three little children in wellies. They kept falling over. One year we made a special journey [from Guildford] because all three were about to take exams.' There is now no sign indicating the magical powers of this sadly diminished beech, but I found this description in a 1963 Devon guide: 'According to local tradition, to walk backwards round this tree three times will bring the fulfilment of any desire … [but] as the earth has fallen away from the far side, the slope is now too steep to admit of perambulation round the tree – either backwards or forwards.' You can still do a half-perambulation and make a half-wish.

THE MIDDLE & LOWER RIVER DART

The claim that the Dart is the loveliest river in England is not misplaced. Ancient oak forests line the banks (the name Dart is derived from the Old English for Oak, which is probably why there are two river Darts in Devon; the other one joins the Exe at Bickleigh), drooping their gnarled trunks towards the water. Where the trees end the hills begin, chequerboard fields of red earth and green pasture rising steeply up to the horizon. Sometimes the river widens so it feels more like a lake, and at other times it's so narrow you could throw a stone to the other side. Small villages of whitewashed cottages hide along the arms of creeks, and splendid mansions are just visible through the trees. Clusters of sailing boats lie moored at Dittisham and Stoke Gabriel, and a variety of passenger-carrying vessels use the river as a highway.

Perhaps the perfect way to get to know the river is to walk the 17-mile Dart Valley Trail from Totnes to Dartmouth, and take the river ferry for the journey back.

ON (& IN) THE RIVER DART
FOR TRANSPORT OR PLEASURE

The line between a pleasure cruise and transport is blurred on this river. Price is the main difference. The most elegant and expensive way of travelling between Dartmouth and Totnes is by the **paddle steamer** *Kingswear Castle* (⌀ 01803 555872 ⌀ paddlesteamerkc.co.uk – and see box, pages 108–9), but there's an assortment of cheaper boats. The **Dartmouth Steam Railway and River Company** (⌀ 01803 555872 ⌀ dartmouthrailriver.co.uk) are the leaders, with a good commentary and the option of including the steam train to Paignton and bus back to Totnes. Whichever boat you catch, the hour-long trip most delightfully combines getting from Dartmouth to Totnes, or vice versa, with an overview of the sights along the river. You'll see a reasonable amount of birdlife, including cormorants and herons, and if there's a commentary, you'll hear about the wildlife and history of the houses and villages en route. All River Dart boats can only operate within a few hours of high tide, so timetables vary.

For shorter journeys the good-value **Greenway Ferry** (⌀ 01803 882811 ⌀ greenwayferry.co.uk) runs between Dartmouth and Dittisham (pages 105–6).

THE DART VALLEY TRAIL

This walkers' trail links Dartmouth to Totnes, and Greenway to Kingswear. In total it's 17 miles, but is linked to buses, ferries and the steam train so is easy to do in sections. With some planning, you can take in all that is typical of the area: river views (of course), small villages with impossibly narrow streets (you'll be glad you're on foot) and ancient oak woods. The main options are: the lower Dart from Dartmouth to Dittisham and across the river to Greenway, then back to Kingswear (nine miles); ferry from Dartmouth to Dittisham and walk back on either side of the river (about five miles); Totnes to Dittisham, taking in the villages of Ashprington, Cornworthy and Tuckenhay, and take the ferry back (about nine miles). If these seem too long, the river taxi (see below) can drop you off or pick you up at any point along the river providing you plan for the tides.

For your own **river taxi** contact Tim Burke ($\mathscr{O}$ 07814 954869) who has two boats, the *River Rat* (capacity ten people) and the *Otter* (up to a dozen), which he operates as taxis, taking you wherever you want to go on the river for a reasonable price. His main business is transporting people from the steam train station in Totnes to Vire Island and Totnes Town Bridge. However, he will pick you up at any of the riverside places described in this chapter, depending on the tides.

If you're a keen **swimmer**, you can sign up to the Outdoor Swimming Society's **Dart 10k** in September, from Totnes to Dittisham.

Paddling or sailing the Dart

What better way of getting to know this wonderfully unspoilt river than on a hired kayak or dinghy? There is a good choice of companies offering everything from sit-on-top kayaks to stand-up paddle boarding, and from sailing dinghies to cabin cruisers. Operators offering kayaks and canoes are based in the small villages on the upper river, where there is a selection of pubs to visit (always an important consideration!) as well as the best scenery and quietest water. Six hours is generally considered a full day's hire.

⚓ BOAT HIRE

Canoe Adventures $\mathscr{O}$ 07706 343744 $\mathscr{O}$ canoeadventures.co.uk. Guided tours exploring the Dart aboard Voyager 12-seat canoes starting from Tuckenhay and Stoke Gabriel.
Dartmouth Boat Hire Centre $\mathscr{O}$ 07850 118920 $\mathscr{O}$ dartmouth-boat-hire.co.uk. Boat hire for experienced sailors, from cabin cruisers to sailing boats.

Dittisham Boats ✎ 07711 177124 ⌕ dittishamboats.co.uk. Motor boats, sailing boats, kayaks & stand-up paddle boards from Dittisham.

Kayaking in Dartmouth ✎ 01803 832663 ⌕ dyc.org.uk. Tim, who operates this enterprise as an offshoot of Dartmouth Yacht Club, runs taster sessions that introduce visitors to kayaking.

Totnes Kayaks ✎ 07799 403788 ⌕ totneskayaks.co.uk. Operate from Stoke Gabriel. The kayak specialists, with sit-on-top kayaks. You do not need to be experienced to hire one of these for an hour or the day.

RIVERSIDE VILLAGES

Although all these villages are accessible by road, approaching them from the river or on foot gives a unique perspective of their evolution before the age of the motor car.

5 STOKE GABRIEL

⛺ **Broadleigh Farm Park** (page 276), 🏠 **Sandridge Boathouse** (page 276)

A village of confusingly winding lanes funnels traffic down to the riverside car park, where the salmon fishermen used to mend their nets and where boat-hire people now ply their trade. **The Rivershack**, right on the quay, serves good local food and there is excellent crabbing for children from the dam at low tide.

The village itself is contained in one steep, narrow street with the post office and general store the hub. Indeed, this is the only shop, although there's a craft gallery and two pubs, the **Castle Inn**, a crenellated Victorian folly, and Church House Inn.

"The yew tree is feeling its age. It stands hunched and droopy, with every limb supported on a pillar or draped across a tombstone."

The church is large and, for Devon, relatively uninteresting apart from the striking wooden pulpit which is partly painted in green and gilt, and the rood screen with its intricately carved leaf design. The glory of the church is the **yew tree** that stands – or rather sprawls – in the graveyard. It is reckoned to be between 800 and 1,300 years old and is feeling its age. It stands hunched and droopy, with every limb supported on a pillar or draped across a tombstone.

The village is not on the Dart Valley Trail so driving is the easiest way of getting here. It's served by bus number 125 from Paignton.

CAPTAIN PHILEMON POWNALL

Philemon Pownall (or Pownoll, or Pownell) was born in 1734 in Plymouth, the son of a master shipwright, so he naturally went to sea to seek his fortune. At the age of only 28 Philemon struck gold – literally. War between Britain and Spain broke out in January 1762 and His Majesty's sloop *Favourite*, to which he had recently been promoted captain, was one of several warships despatched to guard Cape St Vincent. On 15 May, *Favourite* and the frigate *Active* spotted the Spanish man-of-war *Hermione* returning home to Cadiz from Lima; she responded aggressively to their challenge so they let loose their guns and took her. It then emerged that *Hermione* was no simple warship: she also carried bags of dollars, gold coins, ingots of gold, silver and tin – and, more prosaically, a large stock of cocoa.

The prize money from this capture was massive: in total over £500,000, of which Pownall's share was £64,872. Even the ordinary seamen from the two ships received around £480 each, a sum they would have taken over 30 years to earn. More than 20 wagons were needed to carry all the booty to London.

Pownall and his fellow captain from the *Active*, Herbert Sawyer, had earlier been courting the two daughters of a merchant from Exeter, who had refused their suits because of their inadequate financial status. Now the men rapidly married their sweethearts and even settled an annuity on the merchant.

Pownall spent his money lavishly. He had his portrait painted by Sir Joshua Reynolds, and started building his manor at Sharpham. The house was laid out in the Adams style with gardens designed by a follower of Capability Brown. The estate has a river frontage of nearly three miles. It was his daughter Jane who married the unfortunately named Edmund Bastard (page 102). They had no sons, so the Bastard line ended there.

Pownall remained in the navy, and in 1780 was killed by cannon fire while engaging a French privateer. Admiral John Jervis wrote in tribute that he was 'the best officer, & most excellent kind-hearted man in the Profession'.

6 ASHPRINGTON & THE SHARPHAM ESTATE

The picturesque village of **Ashprington** sits at the top of a hill, the tall, slender tower of its church dominating the scene and its pub, The Durant Arms, a welcome sight for those who've walked or cycled the three miles from Totnes.

The church of St David was thoroughly done over in the 19th century, but still retains some interesting features. Even before entering the graveyard I was struck by the lychgate which has a resting slab for the coffin – often considered to be a medieval feature, although this one dates from the 19th century. The tower, too, is unusual. Probably dating from the 13th century, it is constructed in four sections, each slightly smaller than the last, giving it a tapering appearance, and there's an external staircase to the belfry. On entering, the first thing you notice is the wooden pulpit. This is by the noted Devon woodcarver Herbert Read (or his son, also called Herbert), and is intricately carved with all manner of flora and fauna: vines, birds and even a snail, as well as the Virgin Mary and other biblical Marys (it was given in memory of Mary Coltam Carwithen of Ashprington House).

The monuments are particularly eye-catching. Three generations of Bastards are commemorated without shame: it was the surname of the family that inherited Sharpham Estate in the 19th century, following the death of Captain Philemon Pownall, whose monument is in the church (see box, page 101).

Sharpham House, Captain Pownall's former estate, enfolded in a loop of the river, was purchased in 1961 by Maurice and Ruth Ash. She was the daughter of Dartington Hall founders, the Elmhirsts, so it is no surprise that development of the estate took a spiritual and sustainable path, with quality food production just part of their work. It is now owned by the **Sharpham Trust**, which runs weekly **retreats** at The Barn (⊘ sharphamtrust.org). There could not be a better place to experience the inner stillness that the Slow concept is all about.

Sharpham Vineyard (⊘ 01803 732203 ⊘ sharpham.com ⊘ Apr–Oct 10.00–17.00 daily; check website for winter opening) produces top-quality wine and their own cheeses and offers a variety of tours in addition to a café and shop selling their produce. The estate is not generally open to the public so this is one way of taking a proper look at the glorious landscape. Tours range from a self-guided walk round the vineyards followed by an 'instructed' wine tasting to a full-blown half-day Sharpham Wine Experience. You can also partake in a cheese flight (three cheeses) or a wine flight (four wines) to get your taste buds going. Particularly popular is the 'Trek & Taste' which gives you entrance to the vineyard, plus a tasting of three wines and two cheeses.

The views over the Dart from the long, steep lane down from Ashprington are such that drivers will need real concentration to stay on the road. Both the Dart Valley Trail and NCR2 pass the entrance to Sharpham Estate before reaching Ashprington, and walkers can call the river taxi operated by Tim Burke (page 99) when they're too full to move after a splendid Sharpham lunch.

🍴 FOOD & DRINK

The Durant Arms Ashprington TQ9 7UP ☏ 01803 732240 ⌀ durantarms.co.uk. Hearty pub fare in a typical village inn; walker-, dog- and cyclist-friendly, with a log fire in the winter, and three en-suite guest rooms.

The Vineyard Café Sharpham Estate TQ9 7UT ☏ 01803 732178 ⌀ thevineyardcafe.co.uk. Serves light, high-quality meals in this delightful setting using produce from the Sharpham Estate, mostly free-range and organic. It is very popular so in the holiday season booking is essential.

7 TUCKENHAY & CORNWORTHY

🏠 **Tuckenhay Mill** (page 276) & **Duck Cottage** (page 276)

The tiny, elongated village of **Tuckenhay**, squeezed between the River Wash, Bow Creek and a steep hillside, makes an agreeable and peaceful base for exploring the middle section of the river. It's hard to believe that until 1970 this was an important industrial centre, with the paper mill providing local employment, and ships plying the river to transport its high-quality paper throughout the realm. It was used, among other things, to make banknotes. During wartime, when the raw materials were hard to get, local people were asked to save their rags and printed paper for the factory. They had to divide them into three bags: wool, cotton and paper – an early version of today's coloured bins. The mill and its outbuildings have been converted into luxury self-catering accommodation.

An enjoyable circular walk from Tuckenhay takes you along Bow Creek, past benches for the weary and picnic places for the hungry. You return via **Cornworthy**, which has a pub and the ruined Augustinian priory of St Mary, reportedly founded for seven religious women. It was a victim of the Dissolution of the Monasteries and abandoned in 1539. Nothing much remains except the gatehouse with its rather splendid arch, large enough to allow the passage of horse-drawn carriages, framing Cornworthy in the valley below. Nearby is a humbler doorway for pedestrians. The Croydecycle *Dittisham & Cornworthy* map shows this walk.

🍴 FOOD & DRINK

Maltster's Arms Tuckenhay TQ9 7EH ☏ 01803 732350 ⌀ tuckenhay.com. *The* riverside pub and deservedly popular. The food is excellent and the setting sublime. If possible arrive by river, rather than tackling the nervewrackingly narrow lanes by car. Booking advisable.

Waterman's Arms Bow Bridge (between Ashprington & Tuckenhay) TQ9 7EG ✆ 01803 732214 🖱 thewatermansarms.net. A hotel and restaurant with tranquil outdoor seating next to the Harbourne River. The food is standard pub grub, but I loved the signs such as 'Hiding from the wife bar rates' and 'Nope, not here, just missed him'.

8 DITTISHAM & GREENWAY

The river is at its narrowest between these two places, a delightful village and Agatha Christie's holiday home, with a motorboat acting as a ferry from one to the other. There's no particular schedule, you just ring a large bell when you're ready to cross and by and by the boatman will appear.

Dittisham

🏠 **Gurrow Point Cottage** & **Buzzard Cedar Yurt** (page 276)

Pronounced locally as 'Ditsum', this sailing centre is reminiscent of Cornwall, with a hillside of tightly packed, steeply stacked white cottages

AGATHA CHRISTIE

Dame Agatha Christie – born Agatha Miller in Barton Road, Torquay, in September 1890 – is the best-selling novelist of all time. Sales of her work top two billion, in more than 60 languages, surpassed only by Shakespeare, the Bible and the Koran. Her play *The Mousetrap*, which opened in London in 1952, has by now become the longest-running theatre play in history.

The play came about because the BBC asked the late Queen Mary how they might best celebrate her 80th birthday on radio. She requested something by Agatha Christie – who obligingly wrote a short sketch, *Three Blind Mice*, broadcast in 1947, which she then adapted for the stage as *The Mousetrap*.

On Christmas Eve in 1914, as World War I was breaking, Agatha Miller married Captain Archibald Christie of the Royal Flying Corps;

they honeymooned in Torquay's Grand Hotel. During the war Torquay Town Hall served as a hospital and she worked there, picking up useful details about poisons and meeting Belgian refugees, the blueprints for Hercule Poirot. The Christie Gallery in Torquay Museum (pages 58–9) and the Agatha Christie Town Trail commemorate her connections there. The marriage was not happy, and in December 1926 Britain's newspapers were buzzing with the news that she had 'disappeared'; amid murmurs of foul play a massive search was mounted, with rewards offered for information leading to her return. Ten days later she was spotted: it turned out she had travelled by train to Yorkshire and checked in to a hotel in Harrogate, using the surname (Neele) of her husband's current mistress. She with slate roofs. If you arrive here by car, avoid heading straight down to the quay – there's no parking and your car may end up in the pub or the river. Look for the car park in the upper town (the Ham) which overlooks the river. This is just below the church which is worth a look for its colourful and unusual pulpit carved of stone rather than wood. It dates from the 15th century and is intricately carved, gilded and painted, entwined with fruit and foliage, with some very gloomy saints or apostles in the niches. From the car park you can walk through the park and then along the shore (at low tide) to the quay.

"The pulpit is intricately carved and painted, with some very gloomy saints in the niches."

Sightseeing as such may be limited but there is plenty to enjoy. Dittisham is said to be the best place on the Dart for crabbing (off the pontoon) or just pottering. Most visitors seem to spend their time sprawled happily with a pint of beer in their hand in front of the **Ferry Boat Inn** (✆ 01803 722368), a wonderfully traditional pub which

claimed amnesia, but more probably had been reacting to her husband's affair. They divorced two years later.

In 1930 Christie married archaeologist Max Mallowan, and *Murder on the Orient Express* was inspired by one of her rail trips with him to his excavations in the Middle East. Asked what marriage to an archaeologist was like, she is said to have replied 'Wonderful – the older you get, the more interested he is in you'. In 1938 they bought the Greenway estate on the River Dart.

Burgh Island Hotel in Bigbury Bay (pages 144–5) is the setting for her best-selling novel (and the world's best-selling mystery), written in 1939 as *Ten Little Niggers*, but later renamed *Ten Little Indians* and/or *And Then There Were None*. The 'writer's hut', reputedly built for her there in the 1930s, was rebuilt in 2007; now called 'The Beach House', it's one of the hotel's luxury bedrooms. Kents Cavern in Torquay appears as Hempsley Cavern in her novel *The Man in a Brown Suit*: her father helped to finance excavations there and was an enthusiastic volunteer on the dig.

Christie died in 1976, but constantly gains more fans through the many new adaptations of her work; while the annual International Agatha Christie Festival (⌖ iacf-uk.org) in Torquay attracts ever-larger audiences.

Poet and novelist Sophie Hannah has been chosen by the Christie estate to continue her legacy by writing new stories featuring Hercule Poirot: two are already pleasing her fans and two more are due in 2018 and 2020. Like *The Mousetrap*, the 'Queen of Crime' is still a very long way indeed from reaching her final curtain.

invites lingering. As does the excellent **Anchorstone Café** (✆ 01803 722365), more of a licensed restaurant than a traditional café, serving delicious food on a terrace overlooking the river.

North of the village is the blunt peninsula, Gurrow Point, which you can walk right round (with some difficulty) at low tide.

Greenway

Galmpton TQ5 0ES ✆ 01803 842382 ○ Mar–Dec, varies seasonally – see website; National Trust

The Georgian house was built in the late 18th century, but its predecessor, Greenway Court, was the home of Sir Humphrey Gilbert, half-brother to Sir Walter Raleigh and owner of Compton Castle (page 70). The young Walter spent holidays there as a boy, and as an adult allegedly sat by the river smoking his silver pipe with the first tobacco seen in England. Understandably, this act was misinterpreted by a servant who, seeing his master apparently on fire, threw a jug of ale (or maybe water) over him.

Agatha Christie bought the house in 1938 for £6,000. She took a break from writing while on holiday here, but the sloping grounds, with glimpses of the river through the trees, provided settings for some of her murder mysteries. If you are an Agatha Christie fan you'll love your visit to the house, marvelling that you are looking at the actual Steinway piano she played, and appreciating the papier-mâché tables that she collected. In fact the place is stuffed with Agatha Christie memorabilia, not all of which were here originally. You can listen to an interesting recording of a radio interview with Dame Agatha where she describes the process of writing her books. If your interest is more towards archaeology than murder mysteries, you'll enjoy the collections from Christie's second husband, Sir Max Mallowan, who organised digs in Iraq and other Middle Eastern sites. My lasting impression was of coupledom. The Mallowans clearly loved doing things together and Agatha was an enthusiastic helpmate on Max's archaeological trips. And it would be hard not to be happy in such a setting. The garden is lovely, well worth a visit for its peacefulness and some unusual plants.

Plonked in the river opposite Greenway's boathouse is the Anchor Stone, which doubled as the site of a ducking stool for disobedient wives.

Visitors are encouraged to come to Greenway a green way if possible: on foot, bike, bus, steam train or boat. Car parking has to be booked in advance and is strictly limited. This is no great hardship when a large part of the house's attraction is its position overlooking the river and gorgeous surrounding scenery. The three-mile walk here from Kingswear is particularly rewarding, passing as it does through the oaks of Longwood. Alternatively you can take the steam train (it doesn't always stop at Greenway but you can walk from Churston), the Greenway Ferry (⊘ greenwayferry.co.uk) from Dartmouth or park in Dittisham and cross the river. In fact, you're spoilt for choice.

DARTMOUTH & AROUND

It is rare for a town to combine a rich and interesting history with present-day beauty. Usually the accidents of geography that gave it strategic importance a few hundred years ago also caused its later industrialisation. Dartmouth and Kingswear (page 116), placed either side of the steep-sided estuary, have escaped this fate, probably because the planned-for railway never happened. The writer W G Maton, although sometimes given to hyperbole, describes his arrival in the late 1700s in words that could still be used today:

> We were in some measure prepared for the enchanting scene which our passage across the Dart opened to us ... On our left appeared the castle, which stands at the mouth of the river, surrounded by a rich mass of oak, and the steeple of an adjoining church just peeps above the branches. Opposite to us was the town, situated on the declivity of a craggy hill, and extending, embosomed in trees, almost a mile along the water's edge ... The rocks on either side are composed of a glossy purple slate, and their summits fringed with a number of ornamental plants and shrubs. Enraptured with so lovely a scene, we arrived insensibly at the quay of Dartmouth.

A couple of centuries later, S P B Mais, arriving at night, wrote: 'As you step onto the cobbled quay and dimly glimpse the medieval, richly carved, gabled houses bending courteously to greet you, you feel that you have been transported not merely to another land but to another century.'

Kingswear is equally attractive in a smaller way, and the walk from here to **Coleton Fishacre**, or to Brixham if you can manage the 11 miles, is one of the best on Devon's South West Coast Path.

9 DARTMOUTH

🏠 **Anzac Street Bistro** (page 275)

Tourist information: The Engine House, Mayors Av ✆ 01803 834224 ⊗ discoverdartmouth. com. Very helpful, with a good selection of leaflets & printed matter for sale.

Present-day visitors should endeavour to arrive, as Maton and Mais did, by water, or via the coastal path or steam train to Kingswear, for the enchanting view across the Dart. Arrival by car, in the summer, may only result in frustration and the inevitable backtracking to the park-and-ride car park which may be the only place you can leave your car for longer than four hours. If you do drive into the centre of town, ignore your satnav or you could find yourself wedged in one of those impossibly steep, narrow, and oh-so-picturesque approach lanes. Off-season parking is easier: free along the riverfront and there's a short-stay car park near the little inner harbour. One time you definitely don't want to drive into Dartmouth is during the annual August Bank Holiday **Regatta**.

Seen across the river the view is much as Maton describes it, with the castle at the furthest point of the cliff, and white houses set into the hillside among dark trees contrasting with the terraces of multicoloured

THE SLOW WAY TO SEE THE RIVER DART & AREA

Take a tip from us. Leave your car in Totnes or Torbay and spend a heavenly day enjoying some of Devon's best scenery rather than trying to find that elusive Dartmouth car park. The Round Robin ticket gives you the river, rail and bus journey between Totnes, Dartmouth and Paignton in one day, but the even more relaxing Jubilee Pass lets you take five days over it – and indulge in multiple journeys on all this company's sea, river and rail transport. Contact the Dartmouth Steam Railway and River Boat Company (✆ 01803 555872 ⊗ dartmouthrailriver.co.uk).

In 2013 the paddle steamer *Kingswear Castle* (⊗ paddlesteamerkc.co.uk) was welcomed back to her original home, having spent time in the Isle of Wight and the Medway. Built in 1924, she spent the first decade or so of her life carrying up to 500 passengers between Dartmouth and Totnes, before the more efficient propeller boats took over. The *Kingswear Castle* is now the last remaining coal-fired paddle steamer in operation in the UK. All polished brass and wood, with sleekly pumping pistons keeping the wheels turning ('Nigel's down there shovelling coal,' said the commentator), this is the best-looking boat on the river. Even the loo is gorgeous: almost a throne (raised on a platform, at any rate) with the white ceramic bowl and cistern decorated homes arranged along the waterfront. On a sunny day it is one of the loveliest sights in Devon. And on a wet day you can happily fill a couple of hours under cover.

At the time of the Domesday Book (1086) the River Dart was under the control of the Lord of Totnes, Dartmouth coming into its own only with the arrival of decked sailing ships. The Second and Third Crusades sailed from here in 1147 and 1190, and, for the 300 years that Bordeaux was under English rule, trade was brisk between the two countries, with wine the main import, and wool, carried down the river from Totnes, the export. John Hawley (see box, page 112) built up his business through this two-way trade. Royal favour was guaranteed to this maritime town when privateers could fight the King's battles for him and enrich both themselves and their monarch. Richard II, a weak, effete king if we are to believe Shakespeare, seems to have been particularly grateful for the services of Hawley and his followers to protect the shores from French invasion. In the 15th century the town was kept safe from invaders by a chain which was raised across the harbour mouth during the night, from Gommerock, south of Kingswear where the hole can still be seen, to Dartmouth Castle where remnants of the hoist still exist.

with blue flowers. We took the hour-long river cruise, which starts by doing a circle round the river mouth. Our guide pointed out the sights, including the two castles from where the great chain was stretched across the river in the 15th century to thwart invaders. Then up the river for a look at Greenway and Dittisham before heading back to Dartmouth. Although Danny the dolphin hasn't been seen for a while, we did watch an indolent Atlantic grey seal.

The steam train complements the river trip perfectly. The brass is polished to mirror-shininess, and the trains wear their names with pride. Ours was Hercules. Most trains go via Greenway, over the Brunel viaduct, giving you a chance to visit Agatha Christie's former home (pages 106–7). If you want to see the river views sit on the left, but for a real *wow!* experience find a seat on the right where you steam and toot past Longwood, with its sessile oaks, and on to Churston. It is shortly after this station that the train rounds a corner and, suddenly, there is Torbay. On the sunny October day that we did the trip, the sea was a Mediterranean blue and Broadsands Beach, contained within a semicircle of red cliffs, looked irresistible. Then on to Paignton and the option of taking double-decker bus number 100 back to Totnes.

After England lost Bordeaux in 1453, Dartmouth's prosperity declined, but the great explorers of the Elizabethan era revived it, and from 1580 it profited from the cod fishery in Newfoundland. The Civil War took its toll, and the town sank into relative obscurity until the building of the Royal Naval College in 1899–1905. Its strategic importance during World War II ensured that it was extensively bombed; the town sent 485 ships to Normandy for D-Day. The planned railway never reached Dartmouth so industrialisation also passed it by. We can be thankful for that.

"The planned railway never reached Dartmouth so industrialisation also passed it by. We can be thankful for that."

Much of the Dartmouth you see today is on reclaimed land. Even before John Hawley's time the industrious inhabitants were harnessing the tides to provide power to their mill. Sea water ran into an inlet known as the Mill Pool through an artificially narrow entrance. Then at high tide a sluice gate was dropped, diverting the receding water to turn the mill wheel. The former Mill Pool now provides the only flat land in town.

Dartmouth was the birthplace of **Thomas Newcomen** (1663–1727), whose Atmospheric Engine was one of the forerunners of the Industrial Revolution. It was used to remove water from flooded mines, which hitherto had been hauled out by teams of horses. Take a look at the reconstructed engine by the tourist office. And if you really want to understand how it worked, look at the neat animation on ⌀ animatedengines.com.

Car ferries connect Dartmouth and Kingswear. You can take the Lower Ferry or the Higher Ferry less than a mile upriver, designed to carry cars from the A3122 to the A379, its continuation on the Kingswear side. Both ferries carry cycles and foot passengers as well as cars. River cruises around the harbour or to Totnes, Dittisham or to the castle are booked at one of the several kiosks along the quay.

Exploring the town

Most people arrive en masse on the quay, disgorged either from a river ferry or a bus, so the riverfront (North Embankment) is always crowded. The wise visitor heads uphill to the pedestrianised streets to look at some of the specialist **shops** and have a snack in the market, before going to the museum and the church to be immersed in Dartmouth's rich history.

In Foss Street you'll find the Canvas Factory (⊘ canvas-factory. co.uk) with a great range of old-fashioned holdalls, and you can smell Roly's Fudge Pantry from a block away; you might as well give way to temptation. Next door is the Dartmouth Bookseller, a good independent bookshop, and further along is Simon Drew's gallery (⊘ simondrew. co.uk), full of his distinctive, quirky political caricatures and cards.

Opposite the Visitor Centre is the **Dartmouth Museum** (⊘ 01803 832923 ⊘ dartmouthmuseum.org ⊙ Easter–Oct 10.00–16.00, Nov– Easter 13.00–16.00) housed in the timber-framed Butterwalk, dating from 1635. Dartmouth lost some of its finest medieval buildings in a road-widening scheme in the 1800s, but this house is still there, bending courteously towards visitors, and rich with enigmatic carvings. The museum is well worth a visit. Staffed, as are many Devon museums, by volunteers, it contains a variety of exhibits. Model ships illustrate the maritime history of Dartmouth from the wine trade to Drake's *Golden Hind* and the *Mayflower*, which put in for repairs here before taking the Pilgrim Fathers to America. Look out for the amazing man-of-war carved from bone by Frenchmen incarcerated in Dartmoor Prison during the Napoleonic Wars. There is also an extensive collection of ships in bottles, and some hands-on exhibits for younger visitors, including those in the reconstructed studio of naturalist William Henley.

If you do no other sightseeing in Dartmouth, go to **St Saviour's Church** and look at the door inside the south entrance. It's thought to have been made in 1372 but the vigour and artistry of the ironwork would be amazing even for 1972. Two slinky lions leap through leafy branches, claws out, eyes bulging, mouths snarling. Equally impressive and dramatic are the huge brasses near the altar, sometimes hidden under the carpet but often on display. A print taken from a brass rubbing is on the west wall, so you can examine them as a whole. They commemorate John Hawley and his two wives. He is in full armour, with his feet on a feisty lion, chastely holding the hand of one wife (he outlived them both). Often church brasses and memorials are of people whose deeds have been forgotten, but not so John Hawley. Privateer, pirate, MP and 14 times mayor of Dartmouth, he shaped the history of the town (see box, page 112) and paid for 'his' end of the church.

> *"Two slinky lions leap through leafy branches, claws out, eyes bulging, mouths snarling."*

JOHN HAWLEY, A 'SCHIPMAN OF DERTEMOUTHE'

John Hawley was one of those hugely successful entrepreneurs who shaped the history of England and ensured that their name lived on in brass. Born around 1340 into a prosperous Dartmouth family, Hawley built up his ship-owning business until he had about 30 vessels. This asset came to the attention of Edward III, who was involved in the interminable wars with France which later became known as the Hundred Years' War.

Hawley was granted a privateer's licence by the king in 1379. This meant that he could attack enemy ships, which might just happen to be carrying valuable cargo, and share the proceeds with the king. The arrangement worked well on both sides, and Hawley clearly gained the respect of his fellow citizens, since he was elected mayor of Dartmouth a total of 14 times, and also served twice as the town's MP.

Of course sometimes the line between 'enemy' and 'valuable' became a bit blurred and, as the description of Hawley in St Saviour's notes, 'There seems little doubt that he was also a pirate'.

Hawley is believed to be the inspiration for Chaucer's 'schipman of Dertemouthe', a somewhat shady character. He will have met Chaucer when the latter was customs officer for Edward III. Any illegal business of Hawley's was far outweighed by the benefits he brought to Dartmouth, however, during his tenures as mayor. He successfully kept the strategic port safe from enemy attack by building fortresses on each side of the mouth of the Dart and stretching a huge chain across the harbour to repel enemy ships.

The story goes that after a particularly successful sortie into French waters, from which he returned laden with booty, he declined to accept any personal reward, asking that the King's generosity be visited on his native town instead. Hence Dartmouth has a particularly charming coat of arms: Edward III, flanked by two lions, all perched precariously on a very small boat.

Hawley died in 1408, in his late 60s. His elaborate memorial brass in St Saviour's is not excessive given his larger-than-life contribution to the town's prosperity and status. And anyway, he built the chancel.

Other notable features are the splendid screen, with its fan vaulting, painted in muted gold and charcoal grey, and the early 16th-century painted Devonshire carved stone pulpit, similar to the one in Dittisham, covered with bold clumps of foliage. The figures of saints were hacked off during the Reformation, to be replaced by secular emblems of the Kingdom: England, Scotland, Ireland and Wales.

On the southern outskirts of town, beyond a cobbled quay with benches for gazing at the view or just hanging out, is **Bayard's Cove**, a ruined fortress built to protect the town from pirates and other enemy ships, which has proved too sturdy to demolish to make way for development. **Dartmouth Castle** (⊙ Apr–Sep 10.00–18.00 daily & winter weekends) is a further mile away. Now owned by English Heritage, it was built in 1488 on the site of one of John Hawley's fortifications to guard the narrow opening to the estuary. The church of St Petrock is incorporated within the castle grounds. The Castle Ferry from the centre of town provides an alternative to walking.

A town landmark if approaching from the river or Kingswear is the imposing **Britannia Royal Naval College** (✆ 01803 677565 ⟂ britanniaassociation.org.uk) set high on the hillside. Completed in 1905, this is now the only naval college in the country, training naval cadets from all over the world. Visitors can pre-book a walking tour taking just over two hours. In 1939 the 13-year-old Princess Elizabeth was shown round the college by one of the cadets, Prince Philip. So who knows who you will meet?

FOOD & DRINK

Alf Resco's Lower St, in the southern part of town ✆ 01803 835880 ⊙ 07.00–14.00. Famous for its breakfasts and brunches. Very popular so can get busy in the holiday season.

Anzac Street Bistro Anzac St, off Victoria Rd ✆ 01803 835515 ⊙ 18.00–22.00 Tue–Sat. The menu is small with around five main dishes and a couple of specials, some with a Polish twist; all are all hearty and unusual including vegan and imaginative vegetarian options. They also have three rooms (page 275).

Cherub Inn 13 Higher St ✆ 01803 832571. The oldest building in Dartmouth, dating from 1380, all black timbers, old oak beams and hanging baskets, and just oozing history (it was once a merchant's house). The food is good, with daily specials and proper English desserts such as bread and butter pudding.

Dartmouth Food Festival ⟂ dartmouthfoodfestival.co.uk ⊙ October. Celebrates the best of the southwest with tastings, workshops, seminars and over 120 exhibitors. No entry charge.

Dartmouth Ice Cream Company The Good Intent, 30 Lower St ✆ 01803 832157. Scrumptious ice creams and sorbets made on the premises. Also fudge and clotted cream.

Dart to Mouth Deli The Old Market ✆ 01803 839377 ⊙ 08.00–16.00. An unassuming place at the top of the market that comes as a delightful surprise. Outside seating. Most food is cooked on the premises; daily specials include soups, quiches and salads. Author D Townshend in *The Devon Cream Teaser* claims their cream tea is the best in Devon. The friendliness of the staff felt absolutely genuine, and the owner, Rayne, assured me that customers are kept warm and cosy in winter under patio heaters.

Rockfish 8 South Embankment ℰ 01803 832800 ⊙ noon–21.30. One of six Rockfish restaurants in Devon, its motto is 'Tomorrow's fish is in the sea'. Serves a great range of fish dishes but its fish and chips are famous. There's a separate takeaway outlet.

Seahorse Restaurant 5 South Embankment ℰ 01803 835147. Founded by Mitch Tonks, the Seahorse is famous for its terrific seafood in classy surroundings. Come here for that special treat, and book ahead.

Singing Kettle Tea Shoppe 6 Smith St ℰ 01803 906068. Seriously good cream teas, and lunches too, in a traditional Dartmouth building.

SOUTH OF DARTMOUTH

The South West Coast Path lures you away from the town to the castle, and then along the cliffs to a pretty little shingle beach, **Compass Cove**, where you can swim. Continue round the cliffs or take the short cut via Little Dartmouth, until you pass the delightfully named cluster of rocks, the Dancing Beggars. **Stoke Fleming** is the next village. It has an interesting church whose tall tower used to be an aid to guide ships into Dartmouth harbour, and which has one of the oldest brasses in Devon, dated 1361. The great grandfather of Dartmouth's Thomas Newcomen was rector here in the 17th century. Beyond the village is the surprisingly named beach of Blackpool Sands, scene of John Hawley's last battle.

The walk here from Dartmouth is about six miles – but only three by road. Bus number 93 runs hourly back to Dartmouth.

10 Blackpool Sands & Gardens

TQ6 0RG ℰ 01803 770606 ⊘ blackpoolsands.co.uk

Blackpool Sands is a deservedly popular privately-owned beach. Like Slapton, the 'sands' are actually fine shingle so no good for sandcastles, but there is a sandpit for children with the real stuff. The bay is exceptionally beautiful, framed in a semicircle of woods, cliffs and green pasture. There are no junk-food outlets here, just the **Venus Beach Café**, which serves high-quality organic food and wine. There's an area under cover, an outdoor terrace, and a takeaway hatch so you can eat your picnic on the beach. Toilets, showers, shop, watersports, lifeguards … this is firmly geared towards upmarket holidaymakers, and does it very well. No dogs are allowed in the holiday season.

Above the beach, on the opposite side of the main road, is a subtropical **garden** (⊙ Apr–Sep 10.00–16.00) of the type that grows so well on Devon's south-sloping shores. Sir Geoffrey Newman, owner of Blackpool

Sands, understands the allure of a secret garden: you enter through a green door, overhung with fuchsia. Trees and plants from the southern hemisphere thrive in this sheltered place, as does native vegetation. Informative labels tell you what you're looking at, and if you are after some peace after the bustle of Dartmouth and the beach, you'll find it here on the gentle, shaded walkways. A ticket should be purchased from the car-park attendant.

Blackpool Sands is easily accessible by the hourly number 3 bus from Dartmouth. The bus stop is on the hill on the approach to the Sands; easy to miss.

Fast Rabbit Farm Gardens

TQ6 0NB ✆ 07813 504490 🖉 fastrabbitfarm.co.uk

I know I'm not the first to assume from the name that this was some sort of attraction for children. When I located the owner, Alan Mort, hoeing a terraced flower bed in the evening sun, he told me a coach had once drawn up in the car park and a heavily accented voice had asked 'Excuse me, can I see the fast rabbits?' In fact the name derives from the need to teach an ageing collie that 'Look, there's a hare!' was as exciting as the familiar 'Rabbit!'. 'When told it was a "fast rabbit" both the puzzlement and the collie vanished.'

"The farm's 43 acres are as good as it gets for lovers of beautiful views."

The farm's 43 acres are as good as it gets for lovers of beautiful views, flowers and walking (you can easily cover a mile here without noticing), and parts are also accessible for those of more limited mobility. Every month has something special: daffodils, bluebells, primroses, camellias and rhododendrons. The grounds are laid out with broad paths running through meadows and woodland, and alongside streams, lakes and ponds. There's also a more formal Mediterranean garden. Among regular events are wildlife walks (check the website) and 'clothing optional' days for an Adam and Eve experience. I've lost count of the number of times a place has described itself as 'Devon's best kept secret' but Fast Rabbit Farm really does qualify. It took me five years to find it.

Locals come here for the huge range of plants for sale, with several large polytunnels to browse through. It is manned between 11.00 and 16.00 with an honesty box for out-of-hours sales and help-yourself refreshments. The entrance fee of £5 can also be paid here.

KINGSWEAR &
THE COAST TOWARD BRIXHAM

🏰 **Kingswear Castle** (page 276)

Kingswear, directly across the water from Dartmouth, is little more than the ferry terminal, a steam train station, a pub, a village shop, and a car park (at the Kingswear Marina, up the steep hill towards Paignton). Like Dartmouth, it has multicoloured terraced houses backed by green cliffs up which the road towards Brixham climbs in a series of hairpin bends. It is also the starting point for a particularly worthwhile, though strenuous, stretch of the coast path. When I did it in April the cliffs were splashed with purple and yellow from violets, primroses and gorse, and newborn lambs were gambolling in the fields. But any time of year it would be lovely if you're fortunate with the weather. It's 11 miles to Brixham with opportunities to stop off for refreshment but no public transport until you reach Brixham. It's such a lovely walk it would be worth taking a taxi (Devon Taxis ✆ 01803 833778) from Kingswear to Coleton Fishacre, enjoying the house, garden and tea, and then walking back to Kingswear. It's less than four miles and you'll be bowled over by the view of Dartmouth as it gradually appears through the trees, particularly if the sun is shining on those multicoloured houses.

12 COLETON FISHACRE

Brownstone Rd, TQ6 0EQ ✆ 01803 842382 ○ summer 10.30–17.00 daily, check website for off-season opening; National Trust

The National Trust acquired this house and garden in 1982, initially to link the unconnected sections of the South West Coast Path which now runs through the lower garden. It was built in the 1920s as a holiday home for Sir Rupert D'Oyly Carte, the son of Richard D'Oyly Carte who struck up such a lucrative friendship with the lyricist W S Gilbert and the composer Arthur Sullivan. The contrasting personalities of the barrister Gilbert and the young composer meant that if the partnership were to survive, they needed a manager of great diplomacy. Richard D'Oyly Carte was that man, encouraging them to follow their one-act operetta *Trial by Jury* with others which combined witty words, outrageous plots and catchy tunes, and founding the D'Oyly Carte Opera Company in 1878. Richard moved from one successful enterprise to another, building the Savoy Theatre (specifically for the eagerly awaited Gilbert and Sullivan productions) and the Savoy Hotel.

Richard D'Oyly Carte died in 1901 a very wealthy man, and that inheritance allowed his son Rupert, who took over the business, to continue to make money – and to build Coleton Fishacre. His architect Oswald Milne, formerly assistant to Sir Edwin Lutyens, was influenced by the Arts and Crafts movement which, at the turn of the century, highlighted the skill of individual craftsmen as an antidote to mass production.

You need to be something of a connoisseur to fully appreciate the inside of the house. Only the built-in features are original; Bridget D'Oyly Carte, who inherited the house from her father and sold it in 1949, left very little furniture. It's worth taking time to read about the fixtures that remain from the original house – like the Art Deco Lalique uplighters in the dining room, the tide-indicator in the hall, and the splendid Hoffman painting of Coleton with an accompanying wind-dial in the library. The polished limestone fire surround in the sitting room is also fascinating: the stone comes from Derbyshire and is impregnated with fossils. I was also intrigued by the 1930s map of the Great Western Railway network in the butler's pantry: it would be the job of a gentleman's gentleman to look up the guests' trains.

"I was intrigued by the 1930s map of the Great Western Railway network in the butler's pantry: it would be the job of a gentleman's gentleman to look up the guests' trains."

The **garden** of Coleton Fishacre is absolutely gorgeous. It slopes steeply down in a series of terraces to Pudcombe Cove, where the D'Oyly Cartes had their private bathing pool and jetty. Stone was quarried from the grounds to use in the building of the house, allowing for the dramatic use of level areas and steep descents. Lady Dorothy was a keen gardener and plant enthusiast, and the grounds are an appealing mixture of native, untended vegetation and exotics such as tree ferns and the Persian ironwood. A stream runs down to the sea, providing a natural water feature. A local artist and frequent visitor says: 'I can't be the only person who wants to roll the whole garden up like a magic carpet and take it home!'

THE SOUTH HAMS
& DEVON'S FAR SOUTH

4

THE SOUTH HAMS & DEVON'S FAR SOUTH

The extreme south of Devon has its roots planted firmly in the sea; the coast and all it can offer is the magnet for visitors here, with **Salcombe** its epicentre. From here you can hire a boat and putter around the estuary, select some of the most scenic stretches of the South West Coast Path, or spend the day on one of the sandy beaches. This is an enduringly favourite family destination.

Coming from Dartmouth in the east, the first place of special interest is **Slapton**, with its long beach that stood in for Normandy in practices for the D-Day landings (see box, pages 124–5). But hereafter visitors gravitate south, below the A379. Here, in the South Hams, Devon points two knuckles towards Brittany, bifurcated by the estuary up which a weekly steamer used to carry merchandise to and from Kingsbridge. The name **South Hams** probably derived from the Saxon *hamm*, which meant peninsula but also a homestead or village. Some take it literally, and there are plenty of piggy references in the coastal landscape here: Pig's Nose, Ham Stone, Gammon Head.

Among a clutch of likeable and highly photogenic villages on the west coast are **Thurlestone** and the enchantingly named **Inner** and **Outer Hope**. Cross the River Avon, with its trick pronunciation (pages 142–5), to reach **Bigbury-on-Sea** and walk or take the sea tractor at high tide to **Burgh Island**.

The sea isn't the only attraction in the region, however. If you're heading south from Dartmoor and the A38, you'll pass through **Loddiswell**, little known but with plenty to see and do.

 WET-WEATHER ACTIVITIES

Paint your own pottery in Kingsbridge (page 132)
The South Devon Chilli Farm (page 127)
Overbeck's Museum (pages 138–9)

GETTING THERE & AROUND

There is really only one main road in the region, the A379 from Dartmouth to Kingsbridge and on to Plymouth, connecting with the A381 to Malborough and Salcombe. The narrow lanes that link the villages south of this line evolved through foot and hoof traffic and are not designed to transport holidaymakers. If you are visiting the area in July and August you would do well to leave your **car** at home, or at least drive as little as possible. You can access the area by public transport by taking the **train** to Totnes or Plymouth and then **bus** 164 from Totnes to Kingsbridge, the 'capital' of the region, or the hourly number 3 from Plymouth to Kingsbridge or Slapton. From Kingsbridge there are regular buses to Salcombe, and much of the western part of its peninsula. The most satisfying mechanised way of arriving in Salcombe is by **ferry** from Kingsbridge – if it's running. It was temporarily suspended in 2017. Normally the *Rivermaid* runs several times a day from June to October, dependent on the tides (⌔ 01548 853607).

Once you get into the South Hams, however, you'll find that buses rarely venture south of the A379. When they do, they are utterly delightful, and can be used for bus-assisted walks as well as just the pleasure of riding in them. A few favourite walks are described in this chapter but you can easily devise your own. The bus timetable for the area is *South Hams*, or use the excellent interactive map on ⌔ traveldevon.info.

SELF-POWERED TRAVEL

A maze of small lanes meander up and down the relentlessly hilly, switchback South Hams, and the gradients can make it tough and slow-going for **cycling**. The National Cycle Network's Route 28 runs from Yealmpton to Totnes, taking in the most scenic places; from Totnes you can continue on the NCN 2 to Plymouth. You can take your bicycle on the passenger ferry between East Portlemouth and Salcombe (on the NCN 28), giving you a chance to explore the East Portlemouth prong, and a bicycle is also ideal for touring the other southern lumps and bumps which are isolated between river estuaries connected only by bicycle-carrying passenger ferries.

Most **walkers** will head for the South West Coast Path and this southern stretch is certainly one of the very finest, being far from a main road yet with enough accessible refreshments to keep body and soul together, and enough beaches, some sandy, to encourage you to carry your swimsuit. The coast path between Thurlestone and Hope Cove is broad and pushchair-friendly, while sections by Bolt Head, Soar Mill Cove and around Prawle have significant ups and downs. Fewer walkers do the more isolated rugged stretch of the coast path west from Thurlestone, partly because of the lack of public transport. There are no buses until you reach Newton Ferrers, a tough 13 miles or so away with a tricky river crossing. This is the additional challenge on this part of the path: working out the timing so that you cross the rivers when the ferries are running (if they're running) or, in the case of the Erme, at low tide when you can usually wade across. Carry a tide table.

In contrast to the coast, there are some beautiful riverside walks through woodland along the Avon, particularly recommended in the springtime.

Walking maps, guides, information & websites

The two-sided OS Explorer map OL20, scale 1:25,000, covers all this region. However, by far the best maps for walkers and cyclists are the Croydecycle maps (⊘ croydecycle.co.uk) produced by Mike Harrison at a scale of 1:12,500 (five inches to a mile). They cover most of the South Hams and are widely available in shops and TICs. Not only is every geographical detail marked in, but so are helpful footpath notes for walkers, such as 'can be muddy' or 'grassy and rutted'. For those walking the coastal path, by far the best guide is *Dorset and South Devon Coast Path* (Trailblazer) which describes and maps the trail in great detail, as well as listing places to eat and stay. Also useful is *Shortish Walks: the South Devon Coast* (Bossiney Books). The excellent website for South Devon's Area of Outstanding National Beauty, ⊘ southdevonaonb.org. uk, also describes good walks, with clear directions, information on access and maps.

BEACHES

Devon's south coast is ringed with beaches, varying from powdery yellow to coarse grey sand, and shingle. Some are accessible only to walkers but others are family beaches with car parking and facilities. With the South West Coast Path linking all of these, and a (mostly) fairly decent bus service, you can spend a day walking the cliffs and pausing for a dip at a variety of beaches and coves. Heaven!

THE SLAPTON AREA

The first view of Start Bay is of a spectacular stretch of coarse sand/ fine shingle on one side of a scrub-bordered road and a lagoon on the other, both places of current and historical interest. **Slapton Ley**, one of Devon's most prized nature reserves, and **Slapton Sands** played a pivotal role in World War II (see box, pages 124–5).

John Leland, travelling in the mid 16th century, described Slapton as having 'a very large Poole 2 Miles in length. Ther is but a Barre of Sand betwixt the Se and this Poole; the fresch Water drenith into the Se thorough the Sandy Bank, but the Waite of the Fresch Water and Rage of the Se brekith sumtime this Sandy Bank.' And so it is today. The A379 runs along a narrow spit of land between the 'large Poole' and the sea, and is breached from time to time despite modern engineering providing an outlet for the lake water. In 2001 a severe storm destroyed the road, and isolated the village of Torcross and its neighbours for four months. Now Natural England, which shares responsibility for the area with local councils, says that next time may be the last; it's just too expensive to repair.

1 SLAPTON LEY & SLAPTON

A hundred years or so ago the Ley was of commercial and sporting interest, providing reeds for thatching, and waterfowl and fish for shooting and angling. When it looked as though it was going the way of so much of Devon's coastal landscape, with holiday development taking precedence over scenery and wildlife, it was bought by the conservationist Herbert Whitley, founder of Paignton Zoo, as a wildlife sanctuary. The Ley, the largest freshwater lake in Devon, is now leased to the Field Studies Council by the Whitley Trust.

The nature reserve is well known among birdwatchers for its rare species. The checklist produced by the FSC, and available from TICs, lists 107 species. There are two bird hides looking out over the reed beds, with information on the species most commonly seen as well as a checklist of recent sightings. For those who like to spot their wildlife while on the move, a trail runs through the reserve, sometimes along boardwalks, with a choice of exit points so you can decide on your preferred length. The maximum, if you want to include Slapton on the route, is about three miles.

Starting at the car park at Slapton Bridge, the path runs round the northern shore of the lake, then gives you a choice of two short routes to Slapton or a longer one via Deer Bridge. Watch out for the intricately carved handrail on the wooden viewing platform during the early part of the walk. The Field Centre runs a variety of guided walks, courses and events (⬙ slnnr.org.uk).

You will enjoy **Slapton** itself far more if you walk into it, rather than try to drive; the narrow road forms a fearsome bottleneck in the summer. It's an attractive village and both its pubs offer a warm welcome. The Chantry Tower dates back to the religious foundation set up in 1372 by Sir Guy de Brian who bore the standard of Edward III at the siege of Calais. The foundation was dissolved in the Reformation, and the stone of the associated chapel was used to build the house, also known as The Chantry, in whose garden the tower stands. You can't visit the tower, but can see it from outside the Tower Inn. It is home to a noisy congregation of jackdaws and herring gulls.

At Stokeley Barton, a few miles away, is the excellent **Stokeley Farmshop** (TQ7 2SE ⬙ 01548 581605 ⬙ stokeleyfarmshop.co.uk), which has a restaurant, deli and butchery as well as lots of fruit and veg and, in season, PYO strawberries. They also brew their own beer.

FOOD & DRINK

The Strete village pub is for sale at the time of writing but there's talk of running **The Kings Arms** as a community pub, so keep an eye on the Strete Facebook page.

Queen's Arms Slapton ⬙ 01548 580800 ⬙ queensarmsslapton.co.uk. Good, honest pub food including fish and chips and special curry nights. It has an intimate walled garden, plus the ultimate prize in Slapton, a car park.

Start Bay Inn Torcross ⬙ 01548 580553. A 14th-century beachside tavern serving outstanding fish and chips. Generous portions. Very busy in the summer.

The Laughing Monk Strete ⬙ 01803 770639 ⬙ thelaughingmonkdevon.co.uk. An upmarket restaurant in Strete with very good seafood. It's not cheap but great for a special evening out.

Torcross Boathouse Torcross ⬙ 01548 580747. Family-friendly, in nautical surroundings. A local resident told me 'Forget fine dining – my favourite dinner in Devon is nipping to Torcross Boathouse on a summer's evening, getting takeaway fish and chips or the yummiest beanburger I have ever tasted, and sitting on the beach watching the boats sail past and the sun set'.

Tower Inn Slapton ✆ 01548 580216 ⬦ thetowerinn.com. Has a garden overlooked by the Chantry Tower and a rooftop view of Slapton. The 14th-century flower-bedecked building has low beamed rooms and flagstones, and gourmet food. Parking is awkward.

2 SLAPTON SANDS

The 'sands' are not that inviting, being fine shingle so not the sort of stuff you can build sandcastles from. Swimming is 'bloody cold' according to a resident, because the shore shelves steeply so you are quickly out of your depth and the sun has little effect (however, these two aspects make swimming here particularly attractive to keen 'wild swimmers').

EXERCISE TIGER

In November 1943 the inhabitants of nine villages in the Torcross area were ordered to leave their homes for an indeterminate period. Slapton Sands was similar to a beach in Normandy, codenamed Utah Beach, which would be used for the D-Day landings, and the American troops needed to practise. The locals, however, were told only that the area was needed for 'military purposes'. Just imagine what was being asked of these 3,000 villagers: Torcross, Slapton, Stokenham, Chillington, Frogmore, Sherford, Blackawton, East Allington and Strete were farming communities, their winter and spring crops had been planted, winter fodder was stored in the barns, and their ration of coal in the shed. They had to decide what to do with their cattle or sheep, and how to move heavy farm machinery. Then there were the churches to worry about. The little village church has always been at the heart of the rural English community, and in those days most villagers will have been churchgoers. Church valuables, including the carved wooden screens, were dismantled and removed to a place of safety, those that couldn't be removed were sandbagged, and in each church was pinned the following notice:

> To our Allies of the USA. This church has stood here for several hundred years. Around it has grown a community, which has lived in these houses and tilled these fields ever since there was a church. This church, this churchyard in which their loved ones lie at rest, these homes, these fields are as dear to those who have left them as are the homes and graves and fields which you, our Allies, have left behind you. They hope to return one day, as you hope to return to yours, to find them waiting to welcome them home. They entrust them to your care meanwhile and pray that God's blessing may rest upon us all.
>
> Charles, Bishop of Exeter.

For families it's perfect browsing territory for beach pebbles, with plenty of flat stones for skimming. The northern part of the Sands is popular with naturists.

Near the middle car park is a monument presented to the people of South Hams by the US army as a thank you to the 3,000 villagers who vacated their homes to allow for the military exercises that led up to D-Day (see box, below). The Sherman tank at the Torcross end is a memorial to the American troops killed during Exercise Tiger. Through the enthusiasm and financing of a local hotelier, Ken Small, it was retrieved from the sea in 1984.

Various exercises were held from March to April, all involving heavy bombardment of the beach area. To replicate the Normandy landings as closely as possible, live ammunition was used. Exercise Tiger took place between 26 and 29 April 1944, as a full rehearsal for Operation Overlord planned for June. The first exercise went without a hitch, but during a routine patrol of the English Channel German E-boats discovered the vessels preparing for the second assault and fired on two ships with torpedoes, setting fire to one with the loss of at least 749 lives. The radio message that could have summoned help in time to save some of them was delayed because a typing error gave the wrong frequency. Accounts suggest that around a thousand Americans were killed during the months of exercises, some through 'friendly fire'.

Everyone involved in Exercise Tiger was sworn to secrecy; Operation Overlord was imminent and proved to be the beginning of the end of the war. The villagers started to trickle back to their damaged and rat-infested homes a few months later. Some never returned.

An annual memorial service is held at the Sherman tank in April to commemorate those who lost their lives in Exercise Tiger.

Further reading

The American Forces at Salcombe and Slapton during World War Two Muriel March (Orchard Publications)

Exercise Tiger: the D-Day Practice Landings Tragedies Uncovered Richard T Bass (Tommies Guides)

The Forgotten Dead Ken Small (Bloomsbury)

The Invasion before Normandy: Secret Battle of Slapton Sands Edwin P Hoyt (Scarborough House)

The Land Changed its Face: the Evacuation of the South Hams 1943–44 Grace Bradbeer (Harbour Books)

3 FROM TORCROSS TO BEESANDS VIA THE CLIFF PATH

🏠 **Cricket Inn** (page 276)

This short but varied and scenic walk takes you over the cliffs with good views of Start Point lighthouse, through some woods, and on to the long shingle beach at Beesands. The beach is beloved of mackerel fishers, families seeking seclusion, and also foodies, for the wonderful fresh fish at the unassuming **Britannia@ The Beach** café.

"The beach is beloved of mackerel fishers, families seeking seclusion, and also foodies."

Charles Harper, writing at the beginning of the 20th century, described the villagers keeping chickens in upturned decaying boats. 'They are the most trustful cocks and hens in the world, and follow the fishermen into the inn and cottages like dogs.' He goes on to describe the Newfoundland dogs of Beesands, and neighbouring Hall Sands, which were trained to swim out through the surf to meet the incoming fishing boats. The dogs would grab the end of the rope and bring it to the beach so the boats could be hauled on shore.

Cyclists and drivers can reach **Beesands** (TQ7 2EN) via a network of narrow lanes; it has a large car park.

🍴 FOOD & DRINK

Beesands has an excellent pub, the **Cricket Inn** (✆ 01548 580215), with exceptionally good food, but it is the **Britannia** (✆ 01548 581168 🖱 britanniaatthebeach.co.uk), now rebranded as Britannia @ The Beach, that has fish enthusiasts jostling for a table. It was previously described as 'the shack' but at the time of writing the owners are seeking planning permission for larger premises. With the same team in place, the food – a freshly caught selection of seafood dishes – should be as good as ever, but serving more customers. Reservations will still be essential.

APPROACHING THE SOUTH HAMS FROM DARTMOOR

Heading south from South Brent (pages 179–80) along the B3196, you'll pass several rewarding places to stop before reaching your probable destination of Kingsbridge or Salcombe. The area around **Loddiswell** is worth exploring and makes a good base away from the summer crowds at the beach resorts.

4 BLACKDOWN RINGS

This Iron Age hill fort is worth a visit for the views, the bluebells in the spring, and the interest of a well-preserved prehistoric site which dates from around 400BC. In addition to the fort there are the remains of a more recent medieval castle, built in the motte and bailey style. There is no record of who built it or why. Good explanation boards are dotted around the place, with illustrations of how it probably looked over a millennium ago.

The access lane to Blackdown Rings is easily missed. It's signposted on the left, shortly after California Cross if heading south. The large car park tells you you've arrived.

THE SOUTH DEVON CHILLI FARM

Wigford Cross, Loddiswell, Devon TQ7 4DX ✆ 01548 550782 🖵 sdcf.co.uk
🕐 10.00–16.30 daily

From the small beginnings of a few rented acres in 2003, this unique farm now has around 200 varieties of chilli on a ten-acre site, producing around ten tonnes of chillies in large polytunnels. Visitors are welcome to visit the show tunnel during the summer months and see the different varieties, and a video in the farm shop shows how the sauces and chocolates are made. Here you can buy a huge range of chilli products including chilli chocolate, made on the premises, which is addictive after the initial shock – cautious buyers can taste a sample first. Seeds, seedlings and plants are available by mail order as well as on the premises. The plants are labelled in detail: where they come from, what they look like when mature (so the decorative side) and – most important – the degree of hotness. The very hottest is Carolina Reaper at around two million Scoville heat units, but there are plenty of milder ones too.

The café serves a good range of food, for all tastes, with indoor and outdoor seating. There are activities and a play area for children (including a chilli-themed play tractor).

The best months to visit are July to October, when the chillies are ripening and at their most colourful.

5 LODDISWELL & AREA

🏠 **Avon Mill** Loddiswell (page 276) 🛏 **The Signal Box** Loddiswell (page 276)

Loddiswell is a surprisingly large village given the narrow lanes that serve it. It has a post office and general store, a pub, and a large church which

A walk up the River Avon

✤ OS Explorer OL20 or, better, the Croydecycle Kingsbridge & Loddiswell; start: Avon Mill car park; 3 miles; easy

The upper reaches of the river that reaches the sea at Bigbury, pronounce it Avon or Aune, are enchanting, running through woodland pungent with wild garlic in the spring, when I had the thrill of seeing a stoat cross my path. The Avon Valley woods which incorporate Woodleigh Wood are managed by the Woodland Trust; it has provided board walks over excessively muddy stretches (nevertheless, boots are recommended after rain) and steps up steep sections. There's a variety of circular walks including a circuit through the very pretty Watkins Wood, named after the founder of the Woodland Trust, and returning through Woodleigh with its interesting church. The one described here is just a taster.

From Avon Mill, cross the river via the stone bridge and take the footpath to the left to reach the road. Keep left, under the railway bridge, to the old station. Just beyond Station House is a footpath to the left. Then it's just a question of following one of the paths – there's a high one and a low one – to Silveridge Bridge in about a mile. Cross the bridge (note the fine stone and

benefitted from the medieval wealth of white gold: wool. In the 19th century copper was mined locally, but it was the arrival of the railway in 1893 that put the place on the map. Loddiswell was a stop on the branch line between South Brent and the port in Kingsbridge. Known as the Primrose Line because of the profusion of flowers along its embankment, it was beautiful but not profitable so inevitably closed in the Beeching cuts of 1963. Parts of the old station have been restored and the signal box converted to self-catering accommodation (page 276).

Well Street runs steep and narrow down to **Avon Mill**. This is more than just a garden centre. Within the extensive plant nursery is an upmarket café, a gallery and a boutique. It hosts theatre from time to time and craft courses, and provides B&B accommodation (a complete apartment) for two people. This is the perfect place to indulge yourself before or after doing the Avon Valley walk (see box, above).

¶¶ FOOD & DRINK

Avon Mill Café TQ7 4DD ✐ 01548 550338 ⬡ avonmill.com ◯ 09.00–17.00 daily. Terrific brunches served until 11.45, then a small gap before lunch which is available until 15.00 so ideal for walkers. Courtyard with outdoor seating, or glassed-in tables.

brickwork) and take the left-hand footpath initially through a meadow and then beside the river. The path is up and down, but there are steps so it's not difficult, though you may have to duck under fallen tree trunks from time to time. After less than a mile the path veers away from the river and crosses meadows dotted with old oak trees, then over a stream via a plank bridge and along its left-hand side. When you reach the access road to Reads Farm it's an uphill slog to High Butts, and then left down a green lane to Station Road and steep downhill back to Avon Mill and a deserved lunch or cream tea.

Valley View Café Rake Farm TQ7 4DA ✎ 01548 550413 ✐ aunevalleymeat.co.uk ◷ 08.00–17.00 Mon–Sat. Part of the butchery and farm shop run by Aune Valley Meat. Terrific breakfasts and snack lunches overlooking the Aune (Avon) valley.

DEVON'S FAR SOUTH

With the towns of **Kingsbridge** and **Salcombe** dominating, this most southerly part of Devon is the honeypot of the South Hams. It has all the attractions that holidaymakers need: sandy beaches, boats, fishing, walking, and the mildest climate in Devon. There is also the small pocket of little-known South Hams, north of Kingsbridge, where the village of **Goveton**, with its thatched cottages, **Buckland Tout Saints**, and, to the east, **Sherford** lie tucked into folds of the hills.

6 THE EXTREME SOUTH: HALLSANDS TO START POINT & PRAWLE POINT

For cliff-path walkers, the first place for a rest stop along this stretch after Beesands is **Hallsands**, which is also accessible by road. Charles Harper describes the village which, when he visited (probably 1905), was beginning the process of falling into the sea. Half of the only inn had already gone 'while the landlady was making tea' and it was only a matter of time before the rest of the village met the same fate. This entirely preventable disaster was caused by the commercial dredging of shingle for the construction industry (Plymouth breakwater), with the result that the beach was about 12 feet lower by the time they stopped in 1902. Without their natural defences, the cottages were exposed to every storm and on 26 January 1917, during a particularly ferocious storm, they had almost all gone; the destruction was completed two days later during the spring tide. Only one cottage remained inhabitable. *The Kingsbridge Gazette* headline stated: 'The beach went to Devonport and the cottages went to the sea'. Amazingly, there were no casualties, but perhaps less surprisingly there has never been any compensation despite the villagers' efforts. In 2017, to mark the centenary of the disaster, a plaque was erected near the coast path. A look-out platform over the former village provides detailed information on this sad history.

Continuing along the coast path you'll reach **Start Point**, about four miles from Torcross. The name comes from the Saxon 'steort' which means tail, as for example in redstart. It's a dramatic, rocky little peninsula topped by a lighthouse which sometimes offers tours (✆ 01803 771803 for information). There is no public transport in this area, so walkers either continue to Salcombe Harbour or take the easy option, leave their car at Start Point's car park and make a circular walk to the point and back.

7 EAST PRAWLE

🏠 **Coastguard Cottages** (page 276)

This is the southernmost village in Devon, far from anywhere and approached by miles of narrow lanes, through rather desolate scenery (though cyclists will find it mercifully flat). Prawle Point is a significant corner on the coast where there is a daily watch on shipping and a good visitors' centre. The village is perched some 370 feet above sea level, and six paths radiate like spokes to different parts of the coast offering a great selection of short or long circular walks. Within a short range you can explore soaring cliffs, ragged rocky headlands, secluded coves and picture-perfect small sandy beaches, conveniently facing south. From Prawle Point car park try Gammon Head with adjacent Maceley Cove (low tide best) or walk further to other beaches.

East Prawle village also offers useful facilities: the quirky **Pig's Nose** pub, an excellent shop/café, parking, toilets and basic camping. There is the charm of old buildings and a slow-changing history with a real sense of community. However, before making the pilgrimage be warned that the magnificent views are only achieved by walking. It's rarely level and of course the rain often lashes in from the ocean. Authentic Devon, in other words.

Walkers and cyclists will continue to **East Portlemouth** (pages 136–7) and thence by ferry to Salcombe. Drivers will take the road to Kingsbridge.

¶¶ FOOD & DRINK

The Pig's Nose East Prawle TQ7 2BY ✆ 01548 511209 🖉 pigsnoseinn.co.uk. An idiosyncratic place as popular with locals as visitors. Every corner is crammed with stuff – on the windowsill by my table was Barbie riding a stuffed pheasant. Walkers and cyclists can have a shower here, there are 'books to go,' and board games if you're stuck in a rainstorm and looking for entertainment. And it's decidedly dog friendly; there were seven there when I visited. The pub is famous throughout the region for its live music.

8 KINGSBRIDGE

Tourist information: The Quay ✆ 01548 853195 🖉 kingsbridgeinfo.co.uk. Exceptionally helpful; they publish a comprehensive (& free) guide to the area.

These days the only shipping that calls here is the *Rivermaid*, which plies the estuary between Kingsbridge and Salcombe, but in the early 20th century a 'market packet' steamer ran between Kingsbridge and Plymouth, calling at Salcombe on the way. Limestone was brought by ship from Plymouth, and its by-product, quicklime, was produced in the limekilns that are still to be found between Kingsbridge and the sea.

Kingsbridge retains a lot of charm, its steep Fore Street the very antithesis of Clone Town Britain with varied and interesting shops. There's also a museum, a cinema, and regular happenings throughout the year. The **Cookworthy Museum** is a restored 17th-century grammar school, still in use in the early 1900s, which gives insights into what life was like in Kingsbridge and area over the centuries. It's named after William Cookworthy, who discovered china clay in Cornwall and went on to develop porcelain manufacturing in England.

An artist friend who lives in Kingsbridge extols the town's virtues. 'For me the absolute focus has always been **Harbour House**, a wonderful centre set up as a charitable trust for the benefit of the town. It is an important centre of the Arts, with a fantastic exhibition area. There's an art studio at the top of the building which is used by anyone who wants to paint, draw or experiment in any media. It has rooms where any group can hold meetings, practice yoga, sing songs, exercise the mind or the body, write poetry, or solve crossword puzzles. And it has a lovely garden and a vegetarian café. There's even a Friday morning drop-in art group with a model for life drawing.'

Also for creative types, the **Art Café Ceramic Studio** in Fore Street (⌀ 01548 852802 ⌀ theartcafekingsbridge.co.uk) allows you to choose a piece of unfired pottery (mug, bowl, plate etc) and paint it with your own design; it will then be fired and ready for collection a few days later or can be posted to your home. To feed your inspiration there's a range of hot and cold drinks, toasted sandwiches, toasted teacakes, cream teas etc.

Kingsbridge and Salcombe are linked by the enjoyable *Rivermaid* ferry which takes 35 minutes.

FOOD & DRINK

A farmers' market is held on The Quay on the first and third Saturday of the month.

Crabshell Inn Embankment Rd, Kingsbridge ⌀ 01548 852345 ⌀ thecrabshellinn.com ⌀ daily for lunch and dinner. A lovely place with very good, mostly crab-based, food and the newly opened Zest restaurant for outdoor dining with a Moroccan slant. Great views overlooking the creek (they have mooring as well as parking); stand-up paddle boards can be hired here (⌀ 07908 193632).

Harbour House Café Harbour House, Promenade ⌀ 01548 855666 ⌀ harbourhouse.org. uk ⌀ 10.00–16.00 Mon–Sat. A tasty range of vegetarian and vegan lunches and snacks in this centre of creativity.

The Old Bakery Kingsbridge centre ⌀ 01548 855777 ⌀ 18.15–late Tue–Sat, plus 09.00–14.00 Fri & Sat. Great brunches and evening tapas and sharing dishes with a Mediterranean and Persian twist.

9 CHARLETON MARSH

A couple of miles southeast of Kingsbridge is the village of **West Charleton**. It has a pub, the Ashburton Arms, opposite which Marsh Lane leads down to a birdwatcher's delight, a hide looking out over reed beds and the Kingsbridge Estuary. There is parking at the bottom of Marsh Lane if you only want to go to the hide about half a mile away, but there are a couple of options for making this a very enjoyable longer walk.

The route to the hide is across private land where the farmer works with conservationists to preserve wildlife. Dung beetles are encouraged to flourish and these, in turn, provide food for greater horseshoe bats. You'll spot birds as you walk towards the estuary: mallards, shelduck, and maybe a heron or two. The Chris Rogers Memorial Hide is round to the right (no dogs allowed). It is both comfortable (cushions!) and full of information, with a logbook describing recent sightings. Cirl buntings are quite often seen here, as well as reed buntings, sedge and reed warblers.

"Dung beetles are encouraged to flourish and these, in turn, provide food for greater horseshoe bats."

To make a longer walk, and spot more wildlife, cross the stile at the end of the field to the edge of the estuary. It's usually possible to walk around Wareham Point (avoid high tide) to pick up the footpath that runs to **East Charleton** or Frogmore (the Croydecycle map *Kingsbridge & Loddiswell* shows this clearly). From East Charleton there's a choice of steep lanes and tracks giving wonderful views over the estuary to bring you back to West Charleton, or you can continue to **Frogmore** with its pub and excellent bakery and catch the hourly bus (number 3) back to your car. The circular walk is about five miles.

10 BUCKLAND TOUT SAINTS, GOVETON & SHERFORD

🏠 **Keynedon Mill** Sherford (page 276)

The linguistically odd name of Buckland Tout Saints apparently comes from the Toutsaint family who owned the land in 1238. It seems that it had nothing to do with saints but rather with health: *sain* as in the French 'sain' meaning healthy, so something like 'all-healthy'. **St Peter's Church**, its chunky little silhouette on a hilltop easily visible as you approach from Kingsbridge or Goveton, was rebuilt on its present site in 1778 to serve the family and staff of Buckland Manor House and surrounding villages. Although it has no single feature of particular historic interest, this is a much-loved and tranquil little church. A fine tapestry kneeler in front of the altar portrays the life of the parish, and there is a wild-flower area in the churchyard.

The 17th-century **Buckland Manor** was substantially remodelled in the late 19th century and is now a luxury hotel.

The village of **Goveton** is worth seeking out for its exceptionally pretty thatched cottages. **Sherford** caught my eye with its brown sign advertising a 14th-century church. It's a lovely place and the church of St Martin is indeed interesting. A worm-eaten door lets you into a light interior where the recently restored screen, financed by a lottery grant, is the main focal point. Painted in the 16th century, in the Flemish Renaissance style, the saints now glow in their original colours.

"A worm-eaten door lets you into a light interior where the recently restored screen is the main focal point."

Don't be put off this village by news items about the new town, Sherford: it's being built on the eastern outskirts of Plymouth, and understandably the residents of Sherford village tried to get the name changed.

MALBOROUGH

▲ **Karrageen Caravan & Camping Park** Bolberry (page 276)

This must be one of the most frequently misspelled village names in Devon. It's an attractive village with a good number of thatched cottages, and at least two pubs. The large church, with its spire, dominates the view from miles around and makes a handy landmark for walkers. I found it too austere for my taste, but there are some nice touches inside such as the floor-stone in memory of William Clark with a misspelling and some letters seemingly inserted as an afterthought.

Malborough's post office sells OS maps and a leaflet, *Footpaths in Malborough Parish*, which details all the car parks in the area as well as a selection of footpaths connecting to the most glorious section of the South West Coast Path between Bolt Head and Bolt Tail. Thus car drivers can avoid the hassle of parking in Salcombe.

11 SALCOMBE

Tourist information: Market St, TQ8 8DE ☏ 01548 843927 ⌖ salcombeinformation.co.uk. Very helpful, with a good selection of books, maps & free brochures. They also publish a map of a self-guided walk around town.

Salcombe is boats. The town has always looked seawards, building its prosperity from fishing and maritime trade and, in recent times,

SALCOMBE GIN

salcombegin.com

If you thought that gin had something vaguely to do with juniper berries but mostly to do with tonic, think again. Two chaps in Salcombe have come up with a recipe for gin which is wowing connoisseurs around the world. Angus and Howard describe Salcombe Gin as 'the perfect balance of aromas and flavours between the heady, earthy and resinous pine notes of the finest Macedonian juniper … combined with the warming spiced citrus notes from English coriander seeds grown by one of our suppliers and fresh citrus peels, peeled by us immediately prior to distillation.' Goodness. This is clearly no ordinary gin, and its quality has been internationally recognised with a clutch of major awards. First came Gold at the World Drinks Award in 2016, where it won World's Best Gin in two Design sub-categories. Then, at the San Francisco World Spirit Competition in 2017 they were awarded a Double Gold. Not bad for a company that only began trading in 2016.

You can taste and of course buy the gin at the Gin Bar at The Boathouse on Island Street or, for that special treat, you can sign up for a day at Gin School to produce your own bottle of gin.

from hobby sailors. Most people who come here regularly love messing about in boats, and just about everyone will take an estuary cruise or at least one of the ferries, to either Kingsbridge, East Portlemouth or South Sands. Do-it-yourself sailors can hire a sailing boat, a self-drive motor boat, or a kayak. As befits this book, there is a speed limit in the estuary, so forget about hiring a speedboat. And it's actually not a *real* estuary since there's no river; it's a flooded valley, or 'ria', hence the name which derives from Salt Valley.

Estuary cruises are good for wildlife spotting. With a knowledgeable guide you will see ducks and waders, and also learn what lies under the water – huge fan mussels, for instance, and even sea horses. Their relatives, pipe fish, are sometimes found in rock pools, along with cushion stars, brittle stars and anemones.

The town itself is a maze of little streets, alleys and independent shops, and has a two-room **Maritime Museum** (⊙ summer only) with a display of shipwrecks around the Salcombe coast. This and the Overbeck's Museum (pages 138–9) have photos of the old sailing ships built in the 19th century in Kingsbridge and Salcombe. The Salcombe Fruiters were schooners, designed for speed, which carried citrus fruit from the Azores and Mediterranean for the markets in London. Later, larger, safer vessels carried pineapples from the Bahamas and other foods from wider afield. There is also a **Lifeboat Museum** on Union Street with intricate scale models. Boat building still takes place in Salcombe, with Mike Atfield carrying on the tradition of building the Salcombe yawl in his yard in Island Street. An easy walk south from Salcombe takes you to **North Sands**, a pleasant beach with its Winking Prawn restaurant, and beyond it is **South Sands** and Bo's Café, best reached from Salcombe by the half-hourly ferry (✆ 01548 561035).

North of the town is **Snapes Point**, a National Trust-owned peninsula which juts into Salcombe Harbour. A footpath runs round the peninsula with lovely views at every step. The full circuit from the car park is about two miles.

Salcombe's popularity and narrow streets make driving here something of a nightmare. Use Park & Ride at Batson Cross off the A381.

⚓ BOAT HIRE

Salcombe Boat Hire 11 Clifton Place, Salcombe ✆ 01548 844475 ⌖ salcombeboathire. co.uk. Salcombe estuary cruises.

Salcombe Dinghy Sailing ✆ 07809 556457 ⌖ salcombedinghysailing.co.uk. Sailing courses and tuition, dinghies for hire.

Sea Kayaks Salcombe South Sands ✆ 01548 843451 ⌖ seakayaksalcombe.co.uk. Kayak tours and rentals, paddleboards.

Singing Paddles Kingsbridge & Salcombe ✆ 0775 442 6633 ⌖ singingpaddles.co.uk. Canoes for hire.

Whitestrand Boat Hire 1 Strand Court, Salcombe ✆ 01548 843818
⌖ whitestrandboathire.co.uk. A variety of power boats for hire, also mackerel fishing trips.

12 EAST PORTLEMOUTH & MILL BAY

🏠 **Gara Rock** East Portlemouth (page 276) 🏠 **The Old Rectory** East Portlemouth (page 276)

A passenger ferry (✆ 01548 842061) plies the estuary between Salcombe and **East Portlemouth**, where there are some particularly inviting sandy coves. Most of the sand is covered at high tide so a tide table is handy if you want to spend time here with the family building sandcastles. An easy and scenic walk of five miles or so can be done by following the coast path to Gara Rock, where the Gara Rock restaurant provides the ultimate in indulgence and views (page 138).

You can return via the less scenic 'high path'. We did this walk on Boxing Day, revelling in the lack of crowds and clear views. A variation, possible only at low spring tides in the early afternoon, is to walk along the foreshore all the way to a sand bar called

Hipples at the harbour's entrance. It is only exposed for a couple of hours. If the tide is not quite low enough there is access from the cliff path.

On the way you will cross **Mill Bay**, where the Americans were based during World War II, bringing a sparkle to the eyes of local girls. During the preparations for D-Day, in 1944, the estuary was full of American ships, with landing craft concealed under the trees along the shores of the estuary. Over in Salcombe, Normandy Way and the Normandy Pontoon are named to commemorate their embarkation.

Back at the ferry, a cannonball was recently discovered in the foundations of a wall. It is now proudly on display in the Village Hall.

When arriving by ferry, pause at the **Venus Café** for some energy-boosting calories before climbing the 138 steps to the village. As you go through the five-barred gate at the top of the path, look to your left and enjoy one of the most spectacular views the region has to offer. The estuary lies below you, right up to Kingsbridge. On a clear day the southern fringe of Dartmoor can be seen. Pass the cottages on your right and, at the top of the hill, you will find the 12th-century **Church of St Winwaloe** (St Guénolé), whose followers came over from the Abbey at Landévennec in Brittany. He is also patron saint of at least six churches in Cornwall. The medieval screen, with its panels of saints and fine carving, was restored in the 1930s.

"The estuary lies below you, and on a clear day the southern fringe of Dartmoor can be seen."

¶¶ FOOD & DRINK

Dick and Wills Fore St ✐ 01548 843408 ⌕ dickandwills.co.uk. A favourite with discriminating locals, this waterside brasserie serves very good food, with seating inside or in a glassed-in outdoor area (great for views).

Gara Rock East Portlemouth ✐ 01548 845945 ⊙ 09.30–18.00 daily & until 21.00 Fri & Sat (but check in the winter). Wonderful food and the best clifftop view in the South Hams! Walk here for the full impact, but you can also drive. Dogs and children welcome.

Millbrook Inn South Pool TQ7 2RW ✐ 01548 531581 ⌕ millbrookinnsouthpool.co.uk. Under new ownership (2017) but reportedly as good as ever. Accessible at high tide by boat, otherwise by car down narrow lanes.

Sailor V, Ice Cream Parlour & Café Fore St ✐ 01548 843927. Next to the ferry to East Portlemouth, with a range of sweet and savoury goodies – a real treat for all ages.

Salcombe Yawl Sandwich Shop & Deli Off Fore St ✐ 01548 842143. Good crab sandwiches and excellent homemade deli treats for a beach picnic.

The Winking Prawn North Sands TQ8 8LD ✐ 01548 842326 ⌕ winkingprawn.co.uk ⊙ 09.30–20.30 daily. This beachside café at the cove just south of Salcombe is a relaxed place – a welcome pitstop for coast path walkers.

Victoria Inn Fore St, Salcombe ✐ 01548 842604 ⌕ victoriainn-salcombe.co.uk. A picturesque, central and very popular inn where you can bring your dog to enjoy a special A La Bark menu. All profits from this go to Hearing Dogs for the Deaf. It's an exceptionally cosy place, with a log fire burning on cool days, and several small rooms for dining. Their multi-award-winning meals are traditional pub fare for lunch, with crab a speciality, but gourmet at dinner time, when booking is essential.

13 OVERBECK'S MUSEUM

Sharpitor TW8 8LW ✐ 01548 842893 ⊙ mid-Feb–Nov; National Trust

Otto Overbeck was an eccentric chemist of Dutch ancestry, and an insatiable collector. His former house is full of objects from his travels, a maritime room with model ships, and a mini natural history museum with cases of mounted butterflies, beetles, stuffed animals including an armadillo, and a monitor lizard's foot. And there are cases and cases of birds' eggs. In 2006 the museum received a mysterious parcel. It contained a little bustard's egg, stolen by a teenager in 1963 and returned by the remorseful adult who had rediscovered it when clearing his late parents' home.

Pride of place is given to the Overbeck Rejuvenator, a rather alarming collection of cables, combs and cylinders which passed an electric current from the head to the affected part of the body. It could cure most ills, Overbeck claimed, and its rejuvenation qualities were proved by photographs of the young-looking inventor: 'My age is 64 years, but I feel more like a man of 30'. His book, *Overbeck's Electronic Theory of Life*, was published in 1931.

One room is dominated by a polython, a sort of giant music box, and the predecessor to the gramophone. I requested the 'Hallelujah Chorus' and considering it's all done by mechanically plucking metal struts it sounded pretty impressive.

The subtropical gardens are exceptional, dropping down the hillside in a series of terraces, each with its own character and plants, and with views over the Salcombe estuary. The café, the tourist office assured me, 'has a view to die for'. Which would be a pity since the food is good.

The easiest means of getting here without a car is by the ferry to South Sands, but be warned that it's a steep climb up to the museum.

THE SOUTHERN BEACHES

South Devon is rightly famous for its beaches, and there is something for everyone here, from family-friendly stretches of sand with parking nearby and amenities to more isolated coves which can only be reached on foot. From Hope Cove to Bantham, on the River Avon (Aune), they stretch in a tempting line, linked by the coastal path. And that's the thing – to reach them by car is often a tortuous business, with lots of reversing up single-track lanes. Let the number 162 bus take the strain, and spend the day the slow, relaxing way, swimming and walking.

These beaches are famous for water sports: the best surfing is at Bantham, with South Milton known for windsurfing – and its outstanding beach café.

14 HOPE COVE

Sandwiched between Inner Hope and Outer Hope is one of the most popular beaches in South Devon. Inner Hope, however, has no beach to speak of, which is perhaps its saving grace. The view from the hill where the bus deposits you, and where there's a small car park, will make your spirits soar. There are thatched cottages hugging the curve in the road, and a steep hill down to the shore. Ahead is a forested cliff where the trees have been forced into retreat by the wind, creating a natural amphitheatre, around which the South West Coast Path sets walkers on

Bus-assisted walk: Inner Hope to Salcombe

❈ OS Explorer map OL20 or Croydecycle *Salcombe & Hope*; start: Inner Hope; around 7 miles; plenty of ups & downs but not unduly strenuous.

This walk takes you along some of the most dramatic coastal scenery in South Devon, much of it owned by the National Trust. The bus trip, on the lovely 162 route operated by Tallyho, is as interesting as the walk. It's probably my favourite bus/walk trip in this book.

Park at Kingsbridge or Malborough and take the 162 bus to Inner Hope with a choice of leaving Kingsbridge at 08.50 (Malborough at 09.00) or one at noon which takes the little lanes through the villages of Thurlestone and South Milton before Malborough. It was full of locals when I took it, chatting happily with the driver whom they obviously knew well. He paid scant regard to bus stops, dropping them off at their homes, or in one case the pub.

Once you get off the bus it's simply a case of abandoning Hope (sorry) and following the coastal path to Salcombe, via Bolt Tail where you can admire the view towards Burgh Island. Bolt Head is six miles away past splendid scenery. Around Bolt Head and Sharpitor the landscape really surpasses itself, with craggy rocks high above you and poking out from the sea below. Sailing boats indicate that that you are nearing Salcombe and soon you'll have a spectacular view of the harbour surrounded by wooded hills. Look out for signs to **Overbeck's Museum and garden**, a National Trust property (pages 138–9), which offers a well-earned break in its tea room as well as an eclectic collection and a beautiful garden.

their way to Salcombe. Those who have arrived on foot from Salcombe will find welcome refreshments at the Sun Bay Hotel.

Drivers will head for the large car park at Outer Hope and the cafés, pub (the Hope & Anchor) and shops of this busy little tourist centre. There's a quieter beach, Mouthwell Sand, opposite the car park but Hope Cove proper is particularly attractive, with boats drawn up on to the beach and a concrete causeway to Brandy Rock, popular with fishermen. Overlooking the beach is the enormous Cottage Hotel (anything but a cottage).

15 THURLESTONE & SOUTH MILTON SANDS

It's about a mile by coastal path to the next significant beach, with the iconic Thurlestone Rock posing prettily in the bay – the name Thurlestone comes from this rock (thurled being another word for pierced). South Milton Sands seldom gets crowded, perhaps because it's

From Overbeck's you descend steeply to the South Sands beach from where there is a ferry to Salcombe, with **Bo's Café** by the quay. Or you can walk into town along the road.

Buses back to Kingsbridge via Malborough run hourly until 19.30 or, if the tides are right, you could get the ferry to Kingsbridge.

less sheltered than Hope so can be quite windy. Consequently it's a good beach for wind-surfing.

If arriving from Thurlstone village with its thatched cottages, you'll come to the free car park above **Leas Foot Sand**, a quieter beach than South Milton Sands. The small and unassuming **Beach House Café** at South Milton Sands (TQ7 3JY) has, according to a friend, 'the most amazing seafood you will ever eat', Consequently, booking is essential: ✆ 01548 561144.

16 BANTHAM

Bantham is a rarity – the whole village is privately owned. It was bought from its previous owner in 2014 by Nicholas Johnston. The newly named Bantham Estate declared that it had no intention of changing the character of the village and its beach, but there is plenty of anxiety among residents and some hostility to plans to make a few changes to ensure that the estate is profitable. We'll see. At the time of writing Bantham is a lovely quiet village of whitewashed thatched cottages with a narrow lane funnelling visitors down to the best surfing beach in South Devon. And talking of funnelling, each year the Bantham Swoosh takes place down the River Avon. Promoted by the Outdoor Swimming Society, this is a 6km swim from Aveton Gifford to Bantham, and includes the Swoosh where the river narrows, propelling swimmers towards the sea on the receding tide. And you don't have to wait for the official Swoosh date to do this! Start at the little pink boathouse near the ferry, check that the tide is going out and start swimming.

There's a car park by the beach at Bantham (£6 for all day) where a mobile café, the Gastrobus, provides tasty snacks. But the Gastrobus is the only sort of bus here – there's no public transport, so if you are on foot it's best to take footpaths back to Thurlestone village to catch the number 162. The car park is free after 17.00 so if you are leaving then be warned that the single-track approach road may be clogged up by canny locals arriving for a swim.

Bantham village has an exceptional pub, the recently renovated Sloop Inn (page 144), which serves quality food. If the pub is closed, the Village Stores up the road doubles as a café, serving coffee and snacks until 15.00. The phone box is also a Book Swap: take a book and leave one in its place.

RIVER AVON, BIGBURY-ON-SEA & BURGH ISLAND

It's confusing, to say the least, that this small river that rises in Dartmoor has the same name as the much larger one that flows through Bath and Bristol. A few hundred years ago it was called the Aune,

Awne or Aume, and most local people still pronounce it Awne. When and why it changed its name is open to conjecture. The river is very scenic, with sandy shores, gnarled oaks overhanging eroded banks, plenty of birdlife, and quite a few boats. There's a marked Avon Estuary Walk which, however, mostly follows paths high above the river. It is clearly marked on the Croydecycle map of Bigbury.

If coming from Bantham you will need to cross the river by ferry (✆ 01548561196). This operates in the summer months, on request, so be prepared to stand and wave until the boatman sees you.

BIGBURY-ON-SEA & BURGH ISLAND

The names Bigbury and Burgh both derive from the original name of the island, Borough. This seems to have been in use at least until the early 20th century, perhaps later. Almost as old is the general disapproval of Bigbury-on-Sea by visitors looking for 'unspoilt Devon'. Writing in 1907 the author of *The South Devon Coast*, Charles Harper, describes the estuary thus:

> Wide stretch the sands at ebb, but they are not so wide but that the prints of footsteps have disfigured them pretty thoroughly; for where the land slopes down to the shore in grassy fields, the Plymouth people have built bungalows, and are building more. Burr, or Borough, Island is tethered to the mainland at ebb by this nexus of sand. It is in these circumstances a kind of St Michael's Mount, and like it again in that it once owned a chapel dedicated to St Michael. The chapel disappeared in the lang syne, and when the solitary public-house ceased business, civilisation and Borough Island wholly parted company.

Harper was being unfair. This is a typically family-friendly beach with broad sands where children can safely play and their parents relax. More secluded bays lie a short walk away for those of a more solitary nature. There is a nice café, the Venus, which is open all day. If you decide this is the time to learn how to surf, check out the South Devon Discovery Surf School (✆ 07813 639622 ⌕ discoverysurf.com).

The comment that 'Borough Island' has 'wholly parted company with civilisation' is particularly ironic given that one of Devon's most exclusive hotels is here, along with a pub which is partly open to the numerous visitors who stroll across the sand to the island or take the historic sea tractor there.

⊓ FOOD & DRINK

The Oyster Shack Milburn Orchard Farm, Stakes Hill, Bigbury, TQ7 4BE ⌕ 01548 810876.
Tucked away at the end of the tidal road in Bigbury (the village above Bigbury-on-Sea), the
seafood here is terrific, especially – of course – the oysters. Good wine list too.
Sloop Inn Bantham ⌕ 01548 560489 ⌕ thesloop.co.uk. This characterful pub serves
seriously good food at very reasonable prices. They also have six comfortable rooms.

17 BURGH ISLAND

⌂ **Burgh Island Hotel** (page 276)

A hotel that can cost as much as £680 per night (all inclusive) seems,
at first acquaintance, to be the antithesis of Slow. But once I saw it for
myself I realised that it is as true to the spirit of this book as anywhere
listed because to stay at the Burgh Island Hotel you must step back in
time, to the 1930s, when life was indeed much slower.

First, some history. **The Pilchard Inn** has been serving ale to visitors,
on and off, since 1395. In its smuggling heyday there was supposedly
a tunnel running from a cave on the beach where Tom Crocker, the
king of smugglers, hauled his booty to the pub where it could be
safely stored. Part of the pub is now open to visitors. Apart from a
few fishermen's cottages, the first accommodation on the island was
a wooden summer house built by a famous music-hall artist, George
Chirgwin, who bought the island in the late 19th century as a retreat
from his adoring fans. Known in those non-PC times as 'The white-
eyed Kaffir' he performed in black greasepaint with a white diamond
around one eye. The summer house is still there in the grounds of the
hotel, and is now used as a staff house.

The **hotel** was built in 1929 by Archibald Nettlefold, who commissioned
the architect Matthew Dawson to design him a 'Great White Palace'.
Until the war, the luxurious hotel drew the rich and famous from all over
Britain. Among its visitors were Amy Johnson, Agatha Christie (who
wrote *And Then There Were None* here, pages 104–5), Noël Coward,
Winston Churchill, and royalty: the Mountbattens stayed here, as did
the Prince of Wales with Wallis Simpson. Then came a period of non-
investment so when Deborah Clark and Tony Orchard bought it in 2001
it took years to gradually restore it to its full Art-Deco-style glory. There
is now a controversial plan to build a 'mermaid pool'.

You need to be aware that non-residents are not encouraged to explore
the island. The Pilchard Inn has a small bar which is open to visitors

Dittisham's Manor Street, looking across the Dart to Greenway.

CLIVE HORTON/A

VILLAGE COMMUNITY

Rows of thatched cottages are as typical of Devon as clotted cream. So too is the feeling of community, whether swapping books in the 'library', or showing that Morris dancing is not just for men (they are well looked after in the pub).

TELEPHONE

PULL

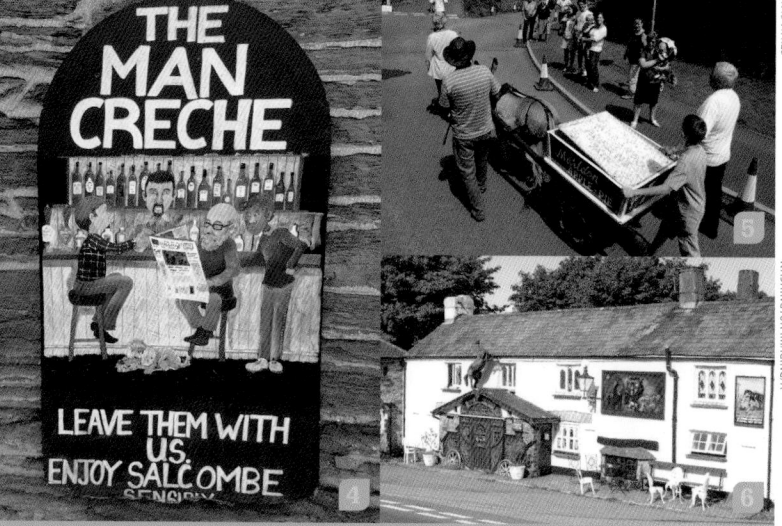

1 Noss Mayo, a world away from the bustle of nearby Plymouth. 2 The library at Kenn — housed in a phone box. 3 Cogs & Wheels Ladies Morris dancers at Sticklepath. 4 A Salcombe solution. 5 The Apple Pie Fair, Marldon. 6 The quirky Highwayman Inn, Sourton. 7 The Orange Race in Totnes. Racers chase the fruit down the steep High Street.

VILLAGE CHURCHES

The county's churches are storerooms of history, with their medieval screens, stained-glass windows and enigmatic carvings. Devon is notable for its carved bench ends, often portraying mythical beasts and bizarre figures.

1 The little church of St Peter at Buckland Tout Saints. 2 The belfry of the tiny chapel in South Zeal.

3 The church at Widecombe-in-the-Moor, often called the Cathedral of the Moor because of its exceptionally high tower. 4 The haunted ruins of Holy Trinity Church, Buckfastleigh. 5 The harelipped devil carving in Doddiscombsleigh church. 6 St Apollonia, patron saint of dentists, proudly holds one of her extracted teeth (Higher Ashton). 7 St Paul, pictured in one of the medieval stained-glass windows at Doddiscombsleigh.

JENNYT/S

SLOW DAYS OUT

The essence of Slow is taking time to enjoy the moment, whatever the weather: watching artisans at work, pottering around a museum or stately home, or strolling peacefully in a secluded garden.

1 Replica of Drake's *Golden Hind*, Brixham. **2** Glass blowing at the House of Marbles, Bovey Tracey. **3** On the Dartmoor Artisan Trail you can try your hand at a variety of crafts. Pictured here, potter Penny Simpson. **4** Agatha Christie's former holiday home at Greenway. **5** Pennywell Farm is famous for its miniature pigs which exhibit considerable agility when racing. **6** Victorian shop in Bygones, St Marychurch.

VICTOR WATTS/A

HOUSES OF THE GREAT & GOOD

Devon's wealthy families built the county's finest castles, and later the imposing manor houses with their meticulously landscaped gardens. Like the village churches, they bring local history to life.

1 The gardens at Dartington Hall, near Totnes. 2 Buckland Abbey, a former home of Sir Francis Drake. 3 Delamore House opens in May for a garden sculpture and art exhibition.

UNIQUE DEVON TOURS

PAUL SELWAY/D

(the rest of the pub is reserved for hotel residents) where you can get a drink and sandwiches but hotel meals, even teas, are rarely available to non-residents so check the website or telephone – don't just turn up and expect a meal.

The hotel, however, is unique. It's not just the place itself that is in the 1930s style, but everything about it is in period. For instance, there are no TVs in the bedrooms (although one has been allowed into the lounge) and the library only has books, mainly Penguin paperbacks with the classic orange and maroon covers, dating from that era. The background music is, of course, 1930s, and guests dress for dinner as they would in its heyday. That means black tie. 'You should never worry that you might be overdressed, as this is simply impossible' states the information leaflet.

AYRMER COVE, WESTCOMBE BEACH & RINGMORE

Flanked by craggy silvery-grey cliffs, **Ayrmer Cove** is nicely secluded, with enticing tide pools. It's owned by the National Trust so is utterly unspoiled and is also only accessible on foot, which keeps the crowds away. To the west, up and over a headland is the steep descent to **Westcombe Beach**. Pronounced Wiscombe, this beach has the same rock pools, grey sand and pebbles as Ayrmer Cove but is even quieter, being further from the car park at Ringmore. Descend to Ayrmer Cove down Smugglers Lane and have a choice of footpaths back to the village (the Croydecycle map *Bigbury, Avon & Erme* shows these).

Apart from the seclusion beloved of Slow travellers, these two beaches give you the opportunity to visit one of the region's prettiest villages, **Ringmore**, and its **Journey's End Inn**. This is a classic Devon village with lots of thatch and tall, crooked chimneys. The church has a funny little spire plonked in the middle of the tower like an afterthought. If the name of the pub sounds familiar to theatre-goers it's not surprising: the playwright R C Sherriff wrote his play in the 1920s while staying there, and the pub was named after it. In its colourful past the inn was thick with smugglers and they say there was a false wall behind which their booty was stashed.

More innocently, the pub hit the headlines by nurturing a piglet called Incredible. Born prematurely just after the war, Incredible's dad was a champion, and the pub's owner was not prepared to let him die like his siblings. During his infancy he consumed three bottles of brandy mixed with glucose and milk, and was kept snug by the Journey's End stove. He flourished but there was, for a while, a downside: he was addicted to alcohol and refused his unfortified feed.

18 AVETON GIFFORD

The pleasant village of Aveton Gifford (officially pronounced Awton Jifford though most locals give up and pronounce it Averton Jifford) with its **Fisherman's Rest** pub ($\mathscr{D}$ 01548 550284) and well-stocked village shop, is a convenient starting point for riverside walks including the 7½-mile Avon Estuary walk described (along with lots of other walks in the area) on $\mathring{\otimes}$ southdevonaonb.org.uk, which uses paths along both banks and the ferry across the river mouth. If it's low tide you can walk along the tidal road from Aveton Gifford which brings you eye to eye with swans, and is slippery with seaweed. If you are beginning the walk here and continuing down the west side of the estuary to Bigbury-on-Sea, keep a keen eye out for a turning where the path leaves the shore and turns right up some concrete steps. At low tide it's possible to walk along the shore but it can be dispiritingly muddy.

MODBURY & AREA

19 MODBURY

🏠 **Weeke Farm** (page 276)

Tourist information: 2 Modbury Court, PL21 0QR $\mathscr{D}$ 01548 830159 $\mathring{\otimes}$ modbury.net. An exceptionally helpful TIC which publishes an annual information guide to the town & region. It has a good selection of books & maps, & advice on the many walking options in the area, as well as a map for the self-guided Heritage Trail – the town was a Royalist stronghold during the English Civil War.

Modbury made a name for itself for being Europe's first plastic-bag-free town in 2007, making a small charge for a bag long before the rest of the country caught up. It's a pleasant town, with a good selection of shops, including the excellent St Luke's Hospice charity shop that specialises in vintage stuff. The town became wealthy through glove making, and the annual May Fair, held during the week beginning with the May Bank Holiday, features a Glove Ceremony among other festivities.

South of Modbury is a network of steep, narrow lanes ambling down to the coast, then turning around because they're blocked by the unbridged

River Erme. This is the attraction for walkers or cyclists. Walkers on the South West Coast Path can wade across the river at low tide (page 148). To the east of the river are **Kingston** and **Ringmore** (described earlier), with paths and lanes running down to meet the coastal path, and on the west side is Holbeton and the lovely private beaches of Mothecombe and Coastguards (page 148).

FOOD & DRINK

Bistro 35 35 Church St ✆ 01548 831273. A French bistro that comes amply recommended for its intimate dinners.

Lazy Cow Café Poundwell St ✆ 01548 831432. A popular coffee shop renowned for its breakfasts and excellent home-baked cakes.

The School House Mothecombe ✆ 01752 830552 ⌨ schoolhouse-devon.com. Near the car park for Mothecombe beach (page 148), this used to be a simple café satisfying the needs of the visitors who arrived on the few days each week that the private beach was open to the public. Now open every day, the restaurant is under the same ownership as the terrific Beach House at South Milton Sands (page 141). It has also been discovered by restaurant critics so booking is likely to be essential in the holiday season. The seafood menu is gourmet, with prices to match. Eating your scallops gratin at one of the outdoor tables with a view of the sea, you won't wish to be anywhere else in the world.

20 HOLBETON

This little village is en route to the lovely beaches belonging to the Flete Estate. It has two pubs and the Village Stores but it is the **church of All Saints** that is special. It appears in Simon Jenkins' *England's Thousand Best Churches*, so any Jenkins devotee will want to see it. What makes it remarkable is that it's an example of Victorian restoration that has enhanced a church rather than spoiled it. The restoration was done by J D Sedding in the 1880s and is typical of the Arts and Crafts movement. The elaborate lychgate, porch and doors give you an idea of what is to come, and the impression on entering is that someone has gone mad with a chisel. Every possible surface of stone or wood is carved. The stone pulpit is dense with apostles, vine leaves, and ears of wheat. The bench ends are a tangle of flora and fauna, and the screen is so intricate that it needs concentration to take it all in. It's admirably done but, to me, lacks the surprises and primitive appeal found in older churches; realism is everywhere, with creatures and plants correct in every detail so leaving little to speculation.

The knight propped up uncomfortably on his elbow has more appeal because of the large number of children he appears to have fathered. In fact three generations of the Hele family are here, all called Thomas. Even so, 22 offspring was not bad going, in between fighting wars and the like. The earliest Thomas died in 1613 and his grandson in 1670. All but the armoured Sir Thomas are kneeling devoutly in prayer.

The church is perched on a hillside overlooking the village, its 120-foot steeple heralding its presence as you descend the suicidally steep hill. The views from the graveyard down to the Erme valley towards Mothecombe are splendid.

21 MOTHECOMBE BEACH & COASTGUARDS BEACH

Part of the Flete Estate, the gorgeous and quiet beach of **Mothecombe** used to be open only on Wednesdays and weekends during the summer. Now open daily, with a great restaurant (page 147), it is likely to become far more popular; it has everything: sand, tide pools, with a backdrop of craggy cliffs and greenery. No dogs are allowed during the summer months.

Coastguards Beach, further up the estuary, is quieter, more spacious (at low tide), and dogs are allowed so it's popular with walkers.

CROSSING THE ERME

At low tide it's usually possible to wade across the river using the old ford. Unless it has been raining heavily this should be only knee deep and more of a paddle than a wade. Heading east, the ford is from Coastguards Beach to Wonwell Beach (pronounced Wonell) where you can meet the coast path for the rugged and very scenic three-mile walk to Ayrmer Cove. Continuing west of the Erme, we move into *Chapter 5*.

SEND US YOUR SNAPS!

We'd love to follow your adventures using our *South Devon and Dartmoor* guide – why not send us your photos and stories via Twitter (@BradtGuides) and Instagram (@bradtguides) using the hashtag #devon. Alternatively, you can upload your photos directly to the gallery on the South Devon and Dartmoor destination page via our website (bradtguides.com/sdevon).

SHIPWRECKS IN BIGBURY BAY

One night in February 1760, the old, 90-gun warship *Ramillies* was sailing from Plymouth to join the English blockade of French ports when a fierce storm arose, carrying her eastward up the Devon coast; waves crashed against her ageing timbers and her captain feared for her survival. Passing a small island in the darkness, he identified it as Rame Head just west of Plymouth, so turned the ship to run for shelter into Plymouth Sound. Too late, he realised the storm had in fact swept him well beyond Rame, and what he had seen was Burgh Island in Bigbury Bay – where there was no shelter from the turmoil, just a line of sheer, forbidding cliffs. The vessel's anchors could not hold her as she pitched and shuddered in the huge seas. She lurched landward and smashed into the cliffs just beyond Bolt Tail.

Her 700-odd men stood little chance in the churning water. Only 26 survived. The *Ramillies* broke up, and one survivor described her as 'drove into such small pieces that it appears like piles of firewood'. As dawn broke, watchers on shore saw Hope Bay littered with bodies, and more drifted in on every tide.

Bounty from the sea was a bonus in a hard existence, and word of the tragedy spread quickly. Looters were soon at work. It's said that several of the old houses in the area still contain timbers and other fittings from the *Ramillies*.

She was by no means the only ship to end her days beneath the waters of Bigbury Bay: the remains of the *Chanteloupe* lie near Thurlestone Rock, where she was wrecked in 1772 with a cargo of rum, Madeira wine, sugar and coffee from the West Indies. There was only one survivor. A sad story tells of a woman washed ashore wearing finery and many jewels, presumably to keep them safe when abandoning ship, who may have reached the beach alive only to be killed there for her riches. Even a century later, it was said that a local woman still had a piece of her fine muslin apron. No murder was ever proved, but villagers had strong suspicions. Earlier, in 1588, during the rout of the Spanish Armada, the *San Pedro el Major* had gone down with the loss of 40 lives. Tin ingots from a wreck uncertainly dated back to the Iron Age have been found in the Erme River estuary, and a wreck from 1671 lies nearby. The 19th and 20th centuries saw more. But it's the *Ramillies*, with her dramatic end and tragic loss of life, that features most strongly in the area's history.

PLYMOUTH, THE TAMAR VALLEY &
SOUTHERN DARTMOOR

5
PLYMOUTH, THE TAMAR VALLEY & SOUTHERN DARTMOOR

Plymouth in the last century was a poor village inhabited by fishermen. It is now so increased in buildings and population, that it may be reckoned among the best cities of England ... This great advantage it derives from the capaciousness and convenience of a large bay, which, extending itself inland between two promontories, not only admits ships to a tranquil and secure sheltering place, but conveys them with the tide, which is here very powerful, into two other bays still further inland, being the spacious channels of two rivers.

Cosmo III, Grand Duke of Tuscany 1669, as recorded by Count L Magalotti

More than 400 years before the Duke's appreciation of Plymouth, one of the 'spacious channels' he mentions, the River Tamar, was carrying tin, lead and silver ores seaward from the mines on and around Dartmoor. Then copper was discovered and, by the 19th century, the Tamar valley was Europe's largest source of copper ore and Morwellham Quay was briefly England's busiest port. Today Morwellham has dwindled into historic tranquillity, whereas Plymouth has 'increased in buildings and population' so much that the Elizabethan seafarers who once knew every nook and cranny would have a hard time finding their way around.

Some of the leafiest lanes and prettiest moorland of Dartmoor National Park lie only a few miles from Plymouth. Dartmoor Zoo is here, the artistic delights of Delamore House, and the gateway villages of Yelverton and Ivybridge, along with one of the region's best hotels. The coastline also has some beautiful bays and beaches.

 WET-WEATHER ACTIVITIES

Plymouth (Aquarium, Art Gallery & others, pages 153–9)
Buckland Abbey (pages 174–5)

GETTING THERE & AROUND

The **A38** links Plymouth and the surrounding area to both Cornwall and Exeter. Plymouth has **rail** connections from most parts of Britain, and regular daytime services from London Paddington. From Exeter, sit on the left-hand side for a wonderfully scenic stretch along the shores of the Exe and Teign estuaries. Locally, the Tamar Valley line covers the 15 miles between Plymouth and Gunnislake. Long-distance buses and National Express **coaches** serve Plymouth, often with a change at Exeter, and there's a good network of local buses.

SELF-POWERED TRAVEL

For cyclists, the Tamar valley offers great possibilities, from moorland on Dartmoor's fringes to the deep lanes near the river. The largely traffic-free **Plym Valley Cycle Trail** has been joined with **Drake's Trail** to provide a scenic cycling route between Plymouth and Tavistock (21 miles). Now generally known just as Drake's Trail (⊘ drakestrail.co.uk), it's one of the best cycle routes in the county. It's the first part of the 99-mile **Devon Coast-to-Coast** Route 27 that runs from Plymouth to Ilfracombe, and officially starts at the Plymouth ferry port; but, to save struggling with city traffic, it's better to start from Marsh Mills at the Coypool Park & Ride (where you can also hire bikes – see opposite). The trail then runs for seven miles along an old railway line. It follows the Plym estuary past Saltram House and through bat-hung tunnels, ferny railway cuttings and shady woodland, then on to Bickleigh Vale and Clearbrook near Yelverton. From there you're ideally placed to explore the Tamar valley and Bere peninsula. Continuing to Tavistock, the trail mostly follows a disused railway line again, with some spectacular views from the new viaduct (Glen Bridge) and then down to this ancient town. **Mountain bikers** can enjoy the wooded acres of the **Tamar Trails**, hugging the river on the western edge of the county. Saturday 5k **parkruns** are held here and in the Plym Valley.

Drake's Trail ends at Tavistock but the Coast-to-Coast Cycle Route continues on-road to Lydford, where it becomes the Granite Way (page 206) until Okehampton and then heads north to Ilfracombe. Don't confuse this cycle route with the Two Moors Way, a 102-mile walking trail from Ivybridge northward to Lynton across Dartmoor and Exmoor (page 230), which also becomes 'coast-to-coast' by adding a further 15 miles from Wembury to Ivybridge. A map of the cycle route is available from Croydecycle or the Sustrans website ⟨ sustrans.org.uk; and for accommodation nearby see ⟨ bedsforcyclists.co.uk.

Bikes can be hired from **Plymouth Bike Hire** (⟨ 07577 279928 ⟨ plymouthbikehire.co.uk) based in the Coypool Park & Ride (PL7 4TB) off the A38 at Plympton junction (bus 200 from the city centre). Their website has advice about trails. If the shop is closed, you can book a bike by smartphone from just outside via the **Donkey Bus** app: see ⟨ donkey.bike. And you're only a stone's throw from the trail.

Of **walking trails**, the most rewarding named one in the area is the **Tamar Valley Discovery Trail**, a 35-mile route from Tamerton Foliot, just north of Plymouth, to Launceston in Cornwall. Its logo, an apple, represents the fruit grown locally. If you follow it as far as Bere Alston, via Lopwell Dam and Bere Ferrers, a train on the scenic Tamar Valley Line will take you back to Plymouth afterwards. There are also fine walks and some spectacular views along the area's coastline.

1 PLYMOUTH

⌂ **Crownhill Fort** (page 277)

Tourist information: 3–5 The Barbican (opposite Mayflower Steps) ⟨ 01752 306330 ⟨ visitplymouth.co.uk ⊙ Apr–Oct daily, Nov–Mar Mon–Sat. Well stocked with information & offers a good range of tourist services. Also contains the Mayflower Museum (page 155).

Cities aren't generally 'Slow', but big, bustling, maritime Plymouth – 'Britain's Ocean City' – holds so much history. At dusk, looking seaward from the Hoe, it's easy to imagine great high-masted ships turning gently at anchor in the bay, their sails curving to some ancient evening breeze. Sir Francis Drake sailed from here, along with Raleigh, Grenville, Hawkins and so many other Elizabethan seafarers; the Pilgrim Fathers finally set off for their 'promised land' from here, and England's battle-fleet of galleons surged from the harbour to defeat the Spanish Armada. Captain James Cook began his voyage around the world here, in 1772, as did Sir Francis Chichester in 1966.

It originated as the 'littel fishe towne' of Sutton, owned by the monks of Plympton Priory until the 15th century, and its deep harbour (still known as Sutton Harbour) offered safe anchorage to the English fleet during the Hundred Years' War. In 1439 Plymouth became the first town in England to receive its charter by Act of Parliament, and it was a prosperous naval and trading centre in Elizabethan times. The Royal Naval Dockyard at next-door Devonport was completed in 1698 and brought further prosperity.

"In 2020, Plymouth celebrates the 400th anniversary of the voyage of the Mayflower."

Severe bombing during World War II destroyed around 20,000 buildings. Massive post-war reconstruction introduced some characterless architecture but also reduced congestion; enough old buildings have survived or been restored, and more of the post-war replacements are listed than in any British city except London. The centre feels spacious, while the historic Barbican area still echoes with its Elizabethan past.

In 2020, Plymouth celebrates the 400th anniversary of the voyage of the *Mayflower*, the little storm-tossed ship that in 1620 sailed into the history books and left so indelible a legacy. A massive international programme of commemorative events is being planned, linking communities, inspiring creativity and culture, and recalling the past. We hope that the many visitors expected from the USA will be using this book! For up-to-date news, check ⊘ mayflower400uk.com.

GETTING AROUND THE CITY

Plymouth has several **car parks** but they get busy. Three **Park and Ride** bus services run from the outskirts to the city centre: Coypool (PL2 3DE) near Marsh Mills roundabout off the A38, the George (PL6 7HB) opposite the George Hotel in Tavistock Road, and Milehouse (PL2 3DE) by Plymouth Argyle Football Club. In Royal Parade they link with the very convenient network of **Citybuses** (⊘ plymouthbus.co.uk). Bus maps are available from the tourist information centre and bus station. There's also a good car park at Ivybridge railway station, just a 15-minute train ride from Plymouth. For a quick chuff on a **heritage steam train**, hop aboard the Plym Valley Railway (Marsh Mills Station, Coypool Rd, PL7 4NW ⊘ plymrail.co.uk), run by volunteers on the rebuilt 1½-mile stretch of line between Marsh Mills (opposite Coypool Park and Ride) and Plym Bridge. Check the website for current times and dates.

Plymouth City Council encourages **cycling** and has produced the leaflet Enjoy Plymouth by Bicycle. A map of cycle routes across the city can be downloaded from ⊘ plymouth.gov.uk (follow 'Cycle Map' links).

Various designated **walks** cover the main places of interest. The tourist office has helpful leaflets, and the steepest hill you'll need to climb is up from the Barbican.

2 THE BARBICAN

The surviving cobbled streets and quaysides of the Barbican were the heart of ancient Plymouth, stamping ground of sea captains, sailors, merchants and even pirates. Now speciality shops, workshops and restaurants jostle together among the old port buildings and alleyways. Pause at a café, and you could be sipping your coffee on the spot where Elizabethan explorers planned their next voyage over a glass or three of fine French brandy.

You'll find everything from secondhand bookshops, a button emporium, a Tuck Box with old-fashioned sweeties, baby clothes, antiques, jewellery, competing varieties of Devon and Cornwall ice cream and galleries displaying local art and crafts, to a huge branch of the Edinburgh Woollen Mill – and lots more. In New Street, the Tudor House, built in 1599, sells Liberty prints; while the Parade Antiques & Curios Museum has rare military memorabilia, antiques of all kinds, and TV relics including a life-sized Dalek.

At 60 Southside Street is the **Black Friars Distillery** (✆ 01752 665292 🌐 plymouthdistillery.com), the working home of Plymouth Gin since 1793 and before that (among other things) a debtors' prison, a non-conformist meeting place and – as you might expect from the name – a monastery. The gin is still made by one man in one Victorian copper still, using natural ingredients such as juniper berries, citrus peel, orris root, cardamom and coriander seeds to create its smooth rich taste. Tours will take you through the process and you can sample it in the striking refectory bar. The distillery is said to be where the Pilgrim Fathers spent their last night in September 1620 before embarking on the *Mayflower*. The **Mayflower Steps** are reputedly close to the spot where they boarded the ship next day to start their voyage, and the **Mayflower Museum** in the tourist information centre opposite the steps tells their story. Most fascinating are facsimile pages from William Bradford's original handwritten journal, *Of Plimoth Plantation*, written between 1630 and 1647; the history of the first 30 years of the colony, it's the single most complete authority for the Pilgrims' story and the original was a great treasure. And if, on the quay nearby, you should spot a giant prawn clinging to the top of a pillar – it's actually a sea monster, representing the Barbican's rich maritime history.

The **National Marine Aquarium** (PL4 0DX ℰ 08448 937938 🖉 national-aquarium.co.uk ○ year-round, 10.00–17.00 daily), across a small footbridge from the Barbican, is the UK's largest public aquarium and the first set up solely for purposes of education, conservation and research. It advised on the BBC's *Blue Planet* TV series, among other productions. The scale is impressive: the Eddystone Reef tank has the UK's largest single-tank viewing panel, while the Atlantic Ocean tank is the deepest in the UK, with 2.5 million litres of water; it contains large nurse sharks, sand tiger sharks, lemon sharks and three species of ray. Zebra sharks are in the Great Barrier Reef tank, and smaller displays include lionfish, clownfish, pufferfish and many other colourful wonders. Then there's the sea life of Plymouth Sound itself, including octopus and yet more sharks. Behind-the-scenes tours (book beforehand) are held at weekends and school holidays, when you can see the technology and sheer hard work that hold the whole enterprise together. The Waves Café provides breakfasts, lunches and (of course) cream teas, using ethically sourced local produce. Ironically, the **Plymouth Fish Market** is only a stone's throw away!

The number 25 bus from Royal Parade stops nearby. By car, follow the brown 'fish' signs. Main parking is in the Harbour Car Park.

AROUND THE CITY

Of other historic attractions, the **Merchant's House** just up from the Barbican is Plymouth's largest and finest 16th-century home, 'modernised' in the early 17th century by seafaring adventurer William Parker, who later became Mayor of Plymouth. **The Elizabethan House**, with its low ceilings and creaky sloping floors, was the home of an Elizabethan sea captain or merchant; the rooms have been atmospherically restored to recreate the conditions of the time. It's closed during part of 2018 to smarten it up for Mayflower 400 (page 154). Nearer to the railway and bus stations, the impressive **City Museum and Art Gallery** (ℰ 01752 304774 ○ Tue–Sat) in Drake Circus covers themes as diverse as Maritime Plymouth (of course!) through porcelain, archaeology, Africa, sculpture, silverware, natural history and 'Artists of St Ives and the South West' including Dame Barbara Hepworth. There's a small tribute wall and occasional exhibitions commemorating Beryl Cook, one of Plymouth's best-loved artists. **The Box**, a dramatic new gallery and cultural centre, will open in 2020 for Mayflower 400; you can follow its progress on ⟨ plymhearts.org/thebox, which includes a webcam view.

Plymouth City Market at Frankfurt Gate (○ closed Sun) has a mass of indoor, family-run stalls selling everything from Devon lamb and locally made cheese to fish, suitcases, clothing and electronics. Streets around it have many small independent shops. A farmers' market is held in Armada Way's Piazza, on the second and fourth Saturdays of the month.

3 ST ANDREW'S CHURCH

This minster church dates in its present form from the 15th century, although a Christian community has been there since the 8th century and the first vicar, Ealphage, was named in 1087. Elizabethan seafarers including Drake, Grenville and Hawkins worshipped there, as did Catherine of Aragon and (it is said) both Charles I and Charles II. War is no respecter of history, however, and two nights of heavy bombing in 1941 left it a burnt-out shell. The next morning, a local schoolmistress placed a wooden board over the north door with the inscription *RESURGAM*, meaning *I will rise again*. For some years it remained a roofless 'garden church' with services held in the open air, but then was indeed rebuilt, with stained-glass windows in gloriously rich colours designed by John Piper. On the feast day of St Andrew in 1957 a moving service of reconsecration was held, attended by around 2,000 people. Behind St Andrew's is the **Prysten House**, dating from 1498; it was built by Thomas Yogg or Yogge, a wealthy merchant involved in the French wine trade. It's not regularly open; ask in the church about seeing inside. Next to the church in Royal Parade, the impressive Guildhall with its tall, landmark tower is a relative newcomer: completed in 1874 and then restored after bomb damage. If you like neo-Gothic carvings, it has them aplenty.

4 PLYMOUTH HOE

Plymouth's must-visit attraction is of course the historic **Hoe** (the name comes from a Saxon word meaning high place), where Sir Francis Drake is said to have been playing bowls when told of the approaching Spanish Armada. Nowadays people stroll there, fly kites, putt, picnic, walk their dogs, and gaze out across Plymouth Sound from helpfully placed benches. The large island in the bay, Drake's Island, isn't open to the public, but various harbour cruises (pages 162–3) will take you past and tell you its history.

The **Royal Citadel** at the Hoe's eastern end, with massive 70-foot walls, was built in 1665 by Charles II and remained England's most important coastal defence for around a hundred years. Today it's used by the military but bookable tours are available (✆ 07876 402728 ⊙ Apr–Sep 14.30–16.30 Sun–Tue & Thu). **Smeaton's Tower**, 72 feet high, was built in 1759 as the Eddystone lighthouse, but all but its base was moved from the Eddystone rock to the Hoe in the 1880s because of sea erosion. From 1937 until decimalisation, its image appeared behind Britannia on the English penny coin. The interior has been restored and is open to visitors year-round (⊙ 10.00–17.00 daily), its Lantern Room giving fantastic panoramic views over the bay.

"The Royal Citadel was England's most important coastal defence for around a hundred years."

The Hoe has various **war memorials**: the large naval memorial, in Portland stone, contains dozens of plain, neatly lettered bronze panels recording the names of the 22,443 (yes, that many) men and women of the Commonwealth navies who lost their lives at sea during both World Wars. In the autumn of 2017 it was movingly decorated with a massive wave of ceramic poppies, the creation by Paul Cummins and Tom Piper seen earlier at the Tower of London.

At the seaward side of the Hoe thrusting out into Plymouth Sound is the huge Art Deco lido, the **Tinside Pool** (✆ 01752 261915 ⊙ May–Sep). It's a wonderful place to swim, in natural salt water surrounded by harbour views.

5 ROYAL WILLIAM YARD

This fascinating area towards the western end of the waterfront was formerly the old Royal Naval victualling yard, built to supply the Navy with everything from gunpowder to rum and ship's biscuits. It would have been named the Royal George Yard, but George IV died of dropsy and cirrhosis in 1830 five years before its completion and was succeeded by his brother William IV. In olden times it was a strictly secret area, its storehouses and manufacturing areas closed to the public eye. Then, up to 100 bullocks could be killed in a day at the slaughterhouse to provide the naval rations of salt beef; the Mills Bakery with its 12 giant ovens and heavy millstones could produce 20,000 loaves of bread daily and the brewhouse 137,000 litres of beer. Now the majestic old buildings have been opened for development; cafés, galleries, boutiques, offices and other enterprises fill their rooms, and diners spill out colourfully on to the once silent quaysides. In the old cooperage, where barrels for storing the mass of food and drink on board ship were once built, a £3.2-million makeover has created Ocean Studios, with working space for up to 100 artists and craftspeople and where regular exhibitions are held. An open-air food market is held on The Green on the first Sunday of the month in summer, involving many local producers.

About a 20-minute walk from Royal Parade, Royal William Yard is served by Citybus 34 and has a central parking area. In season, the Royal William Yard Ferry (page 163) runs there regularly from near the Mayflower Steps.

ANNUAL EVENTS

These include a half-marathon and Lord Mayor's Day in May, the spectacular British Firework Championships in August and 'Meet the Navy' days in September. Also in May there's a lively Pirate Extravaganza weekend in the Barbican; last time I visited I unexpectedly found myself surrounded by swashbucklers large and small. Major national sporting events are streamed to the big screen in the Piazza.

FOOD & DRINK

Plymouth (and particularly its waterside areas) has no shortage of bars, cafés and restaurants. We mention a very few; you'll certainly find others.

Barbican & Hoe

Starting on the Hoe, the **Marco Pierre White** Steakhouse Bar & Grill on the top floor of the Holiday Inn Crowne Plaza (Armada Way ✆ 01752 639937) offers the quality and standards that you would expect, with a top-class menu and pleasant, professional staff. The view over the bay is superb – as is that from the window tables of the smaller Dome waterfront bistro & cocktail bar nearby (Hoe Road ✆ 01752 266600): a stylish place on the cliff just below Smeaton's Tower, with competitive prices and inventive menus.

Of the many eateries down in the Barbican, four in Southside Street are particularly worth a mention. Starting with the furthest inland, at No 60 is the **Barbican Kitchen Brasserie** (✆ 01752 604448) in the Black Friars Distillery, run by celebrity TV chefs James and Chris

Tanner. Their consistently good food is focused on local ingredients, some collected for them by their forager. It's upstairs, but there's a lift for the less mobile. At No 38, family-run **Jacka's Bakery** (℘ 01752 262187 ◷ 09.00–16.00 Wed–Mon) has wonderful bread (particularly sourdough) and other baking, tasty breakfasts and light lunches, and good coffee. The oldest working commercial baked goods in the UK, it's small and very popular, so tables get crowded. At No 33, **Quay 33** (℘ 01752 229345 ◷ 11.00–15.00 & 17.00–23.00 Mon–Sat) provides tasty homemade food in a cheery atmosphere, while opposite at No 32 The Village Restaurant (℘ 01752 667688 ◷ 11.30–22.15 daily, may be less in winter), one of Plymouth's oldest seafood restaurants, serves a fine selection of fish dishes, as well as good-value local meat, poultry and game with a Grecian twist. Around the corner at No 12 The Barbican is **Platters** (℘ 01752 227262), a deservedly popular, unpretentious,

SIR FRANCIS DRAKE

Born around 1540 in a small leasehold farmstead near Tavistock, the young Francis Drake first 'went to sea' some ten years later when his parents travelled by boat from Plymouth to Kent, and found lodging in one of the old hulks moored in the Medway estuary near Chatham. The youngster was now surrounded by maritime life, from small fishing and cargo vessels to the towering men-o'-war in the naval dockyard. In his teens he was apprenticed to the captain of a small merchant boat, and inherited her some years later when her owner died. His cousin, the wealthy Plymouth ship-owner John Hawkins, had trading links with the New World; Drake thus sold his boat and enlisted in Hawkins' fleet.

Drake's father Edmund, a farmer, was an ardent Protestant lay preacher in turbulent religious times, so the young Francis probably acquired strong anti-Catholic attitudes. He encountered (Catholic) Spaniards on a voyage to the West Indies and the contact wasn't friendly; dislike turned to hatred after a Spanish attack in 1568 destroyed three English ships. Thereafter he sought revenge against Spain.

With the Queen's blessing, he became a thoroughly successful pirate, capturing Spanish vessels and bringing home rich spoils. In 1577 he embarked on his famous circumnavigation of the globe (pausing to raid the Spanish harbours in Cuba and Peru on the way); he then claimed California for England, sealed a treaty with the sultan of the Moluccas for spice trading, sailed home with a glittering amount of treasure – and was knighted. He also became Mayor of Plymouth, bought Buckland Abbey as well as other manors and businesses, and entered parliament as MP for Bossiney in Cornwall.

In 1585 the Queen sent him off to raid Spanish settlements in the Caribbean. The Spaniards prepared to counter-attack, but in 1587 Drake sailed into Cadiz harbour and did immense damage, 'singeing the King of Spain's beard'. Spain retaliated the following year with its Armada, a massive fighting waterfront restaurant known for its very fresh seafood, with 'catch of the day' specials straight from the bay. Great chips, too. Tables can get crowded at peak times so you might want to book.

Royal William Yard

With its various cafés and restaurants and convenient central parking area, this has become a popular place to eat (pages 158–9). A good choice is **Le Bistrot Pierre** (✆ 01752 262318 ◌ noon–16.00 & 17.30–22.00 Mon–Fri, Sat & Sun variable hours including breakfast), part of a small chain but a very classy one, serving restaurant and bar meals. It has quality French-influenced food, a warm, relaxed atmosphere and hard-working, friendly staff. Good value. Another branch is in Torquay (page 63).

---

force of 151 warships and almost 30,000 men. The high-born Lord Thomas Howard was appointed Admiral of the English fleet, the lowlier but more flamboyant Drake a Vice-Admiral. For almost a week fierce battles raged along the English Channel. Finally England outmanoeuvred the Spaniards, 'drummed 'em up the channel' and routed them, to huge popular acclaim.

Drake was lauded in prose and poetry, and souvenir-makers had a field day. However, his star was waning and his final voyage was a failure. He had set off from England to Panama in August 1595, with a fleet of 26 ships, hoping to take Panama City for the Queen; but the Spanish force proved too strong. While retreating, Drake contracted dysentery and died; he was buried at sea, off Panama. It was a sadly inglorious end to a colourful and courageous life.

To the public Drake was a hero; to his peers less so. An arrogant, flamboyant, self-made man of relatively lowly birth, he was looked down on by some of the aristocracy.

A favourite of the Queen, he revelled in his glittering social status, yet one of his main land-based undertakings was the very practical construction of a leat (channel) to bring fresh water to Plymouth from the River Meavy. An old legend tells that he rode off to Dartmoor and located a suitable spring, then turned his horse about, spoke some magic words to the spring, and galloped back to Plymouth with it bubbling along obediently behind him. Such was his popular image.

Queen Elizabeth called him 'my pirate', a Spanish ambassador called him 'the master-thief of the unknown world', and the Elizabethan historian John Stow wrote 'He was more skilful in all points of navigation than any'. Tristram Risdon, writing 20 years or so after Drake's death, went even further: 'Could my pen as ably describe his worth as my heart prompteth to it, I would make this day-star appear at noon day as doth the full moon at midnight.' And reputedly he also played a mean game of bowls.

PLYMOUTH & SURROUNDINGS
FROM THE WATER

Thanks to the various boat trips and ferries available, this is a very pleasant way of spending anything from an hour to a day. The Torpoint Ferry is the only ferry that carries cars.

⚓ FERRIES & CRUISES

Plymouth Boat Trips Commercial Wharf, Barbican (near Mayflower Steps) ✆ 01752 253153 🌐 plymouthboattrips.co.uk. This company offers harbour, wildlife and eco cruises as well as short and longer fishing trips. It also runs Cawsand, Cremyll and Royal William Yard ferries (same contact details). The scenic Calstock Cruise (see box, below) takes you past the Dockyard and Brunel's rail bridge, and up through the leafy Tamar valley to visit Calstock. Dockyard and Warship Cruises show you Plymouth Sound (including Drake's Island) as well as Devonport Naval Dockyard. In summer there are trips up the River Yealm. The Boathouse Café, directly by their Barbican slipway and looking over the water, serves fish freshly caught by their own boats.

Cawsand Ferry ○ Apr–Oct daily. This service, said to have been running for more than 100 years, carries people, prams, bicycles and dogs between the Barbican and the beach beside

THE TAMAR ESTUARY: A GUIDE FOR BIRDERS

Tony Soper

Taking the four-hour Calstock Cruise offered by Plymouth Boat Trips will reveal the astonishing variety of scenery and birdlife on the Tamar estuary. These are general-interest cruises, so if you're a birder don't forget your field guide and, whatever your interest, carry binoculars.

As you pass the imposing Citadel and see the grassy expanse of the Hoe, the sheltered anchorage of Plymouth Sound opens on your port hand. Maybe you'll spot a fleet of racing dinghies or yachts; certainly there will be some naval warships or auxiliaries, for you are about to enter the Hamoaze, the deepwater anchorage that serves the Naval Base. Check the upper rigging of any laid-up vessels, for

cormorants delight in colonising ships that sit here for more than a season or two. This part of the trip showcases the marine industrial history of the city, from its 18th-century slips and dry-docks to the nuclear facility.

The twin suspension bridges mark the beginning of the wildlife-rich middle section of the estuary. As you work up on the rising tide there will be exposed mudflats on either side. Shorebirds with short legs probe the soft mud for lugworms and assorted invertebrates, while those with long legs wade in the shallows and pounce or sweep for shrimps. It's along these wet mudscapes that the elegant avocets show up in early winter.

the quaint old Cornish fishing (and formerly smuggling) villages of Cawsand and Kingsand on the Rame peninsula, where there are enjoyable walks and magnificent scenery. The sturdy little red vessel, the *Weston Maid*, was originally built as a lifeboat for the elegant ocean liner *Canberra*.

Cremyll Ferry ✆ 01752 822105 (office) ◔ year-round. An eight-minute trip between Admiral's Hard (near the Royal William Yard, Citybus 34 from Royal Parade) and Mount Edgcumbe in Cornwall, carrying passengers, bicycles – and walkers on the South West Coast Path. There's thought to have been a ferry here since 1204. Mount Edgcumbe Country Park is open year-round and has plenty to explore. An alternative Mount Edgcumbe ferry, also run by Plymouth Boat Trips, operates from the Barbican on weekends Apr–Sep plus daily in Aug.

Royal William Yard Ferry ◔ daily Apr–end Sep, reduced winter service. This runs between the Barbican (near the Mayflower Steps), Royal William Yard and Mount Edgcumbe, with impressive views of Plymouth's sea frontage. Much nicer than the bus for getting from the Barbican to Royal William Yard.

Torpoint Ferry 2 Ferry St, Torpoint, PL11 2AX ✆ 01752 812233 ◈ tamarcrossings.org.uk. This large car ferry, crossing the Tamar between Plymouth and Torpoint in Cornwall, also takes buses and lorries. It's a regular, 24-hour, daily, all-year service, with ferries only ten minutes apart at peak times. Free for foot passengers.

In early summer parties, of young shelducks hoover their way across the mud, finding sustenance in the uncountable numbers of tiny Hydrobia snails. Herons, jealously guarding the riparian rights to their allotted stretch of foreshore, stand knee-deep in water and wait patiently for the fish to come to them. Cormorants jack-knife to chase an eel or a flatfish on the muddy bottom. As the tide rises and covers the mud, the birds find a safe roosting place ashore until the ebb reveals their hunting grounds again. The herons, solitary fishermen, now enjoy some sociable company. Check the waterside trees as you sail higher into the narrower reaches to find a communal cormorant roost. And at each end of the summer comes the time when an osprey, passing by on migration, may stop for a week or two to plunge for a takeaway mullet.

The upper reaches of the tidal Tamar offer fine reed beds, alive in summer with the chatter of warblers. There will be otters here as well, but you'll be lucky to see one. Devonians call them 'dim articles', a reference to their invisibility not their intelligence. And around the Cotehele bend at last you reach the waterside village of Calstock. There's time to stretch your legs ashore and go for a cream tea before you return down a high-water scene, totally transformed from that of the upward journey.

Incidentally, if you want to be a proper Devonian, be sure to say Tamar as 'tamer'!

SOUTH & SOUTHEAST OF PLYMOUTH

If you're near Plymouth it goes without saying that you're near the water, and this section stretches from the River Plym to coastal Wembury, with its rock pools, walks and wide-reaching seascapes, and the twin waterside villages of Newton Ferrers and Noss Mayo beside the Yealm estuary. The nearby River Erme and its pretty villages of Holbeton and Mothecombe are in *Chapter 4.*

6 SALTRAM

Plympton, near Plymouth PL7 1UH ✆ 01752 333500 ◷ limited hours (house), year-round (park); National Trust

The park around Saltram, perched high above the River Plym on the outskirts of Plymouth, is one of the city's valuable 'green spaces'. Bus 21A from Plymouth will drop you half a mile or so away; cycle path NCN 27 and the West Devon Way run along the bank of the Plym (in the park) from Plymouth's Laira Bridge. There's a spacious car park.

The magnificent Georgian **house** – it played the part of the Dashwoods' home, Norland Park, in the film of *Sense and Sensibility* – has exquisite Robert Adam interiors, original furnishings and fascinating collections of art and memorabilia. It has been the home of the Parker family for 300 years and one-time owner Lord Boringdon was a close friend of Sir Joshua Reynolds, so naturally the latter's paintings are featured.

The striking landscaped **gardens** attached to the house are dotted with follies and a fine array of shrubs and trees, but the real delight is the surrounding **park**: open daily from dawn to dusk and offering a range of walks, cycle rides and gentle strolls, whether inland or along the river. Maps are available from reception or you can follow your nose and the signs. Dogs are allowed in the woods and parkland.

The gift shop has local arts and crafts, plants, books (including second-hand) and more; the Chapel Tea Room and the Park Café between them serve snacks, light lunches and traditional afternoon teas.

7 WEMBURY

Wembury's **beach** is the perfect seaside escape. With shale/shingle at high tide and a wide expanse of sand at low tide, it offers safe, clean bathing and paddling as well as surfing. Views are stunning, of sea and cliffs.

Rock pool browsing may reveal sea anemones, starfish, crabs, shrimps, limpets, tiny fish, variously coloured seaweed and more; beach-combing should yield several varieties of shells, including cowries and blue-rayed limpets. By the beach are a café, a small Marine Conservation Centre and public toilets. From Plymouth, bus 48 goes to Wembury village, 10–15 minutes' walk from the beach, or you can follow the South West Coast Path from Bovisand in the west or (via a summer ferry) Newton Ferrers and Noss Mayo in the east. For drivers, there are car parks outside St Werburgh's Church and near the café. The National Trust owns the whole area; Wembury Beach and its surrounding coast and sea are designated a Special Area of Conservation and a Voluntary Marine Conservation Area. It's a short stroll from the beach out to Wembury Point, with spectacular views across the bay and coastline to the historic Mewstone, a tiny triangular island that is now a bird sanctuary but in times gone by was a haunt of local smugglers and a prison.

The **Marine Conservation Centre** (Church Rd ⌀ 01752 862538 ⌀ wemburymarinecentre.org ⌀ roughly Easter–Oct) has good, family-friendly explanations of flora and fauna, illustrations of local sea life, hands-on exhibits, quizzes and leaflets about nearby attractions. Regular rock pool rambles are held in the summer; other events and talks are listed on the user-friendly website.

St Werburgh's Church stands above Wembury bay looking out towards the Eddystone lighthouse. It's believed there was a Saxon church on the site in the 9th century; the present one is described as 14th century on a Norman foundation. The oldest item is the Norman stoup (12th century) inside the north door; there is also a great deal of carved oak, probably 16th century. Among interesting memorials, one chattily commemorates 'a most vertuous Pious Charitable Religious Sweet & lovinge Lady Mightily afflicted with a cough & Bigge with child'.

Wembury does have some attractive old buildings but also a lot of new homes. The website (⌀ wemburyhistory.org.uk) of the active **Wembury Local History Society** is strong on – naturally! – its history, and has an ancestry section that is helpful for visitors wanting to trace their roots. The society has also set up a series of geocaches in the area.

Although the original **Two Moors Way** (page 230) starts in Ivybridge, walkers wanting to do it as a coast-to-coast route can add an extra 15 miles by starting in Wembury; making a total of 117 miles via Dartmoor and Exmoor to Lynmouth on the north Devon coast.

¶¶ FOOD & DRINK

Old Mill Café Wembury beach ✐ 01752 863280 ⏚ oldmillwembury.co.uk ⏰ Apr–Oct 10.30–16.00 plus winter weekends 11.00–16.00 (may close in bad weather). In a centuries-old stone mill-house by the beach, with large grindstones as outdoor table tops and wide-reaching seaward views, this friendly place offers hot and cold snacks, light meals, good baking and the usual range of drinks. A small shop sells beachy things including beach shoes suitable for rock-pooling.

The Odd Wheel Inn Knighton Road ✐ 01752 863052 ⏚ theoddwheel.co.uk ⏰ until midnight daily, food served noon–14.30 & 17.00–21.00 Mon–Fri, noon–20.30 Sat & Sun. A cosy pub at the northern entrance to the village, with a wide selection of local beers, a good-value traditional menu and a changing selection of 'specials'. Popular Sunday roasts.

8 THE YEALM ESTUARY

YEALMPTON

This small town – attractive once you escape from the A379 that runs through – contains Mother Hubbard's Cottage, the former home of the woman who inspired the Mother Hubbard rhyme written in 1805. Its parish **church** of St Bartholomew, which John Betjeman called 'the most amazing Victorian church in Devon', was largely rebuilt in 1849–51 (with a great deal of marble and ornateness) to plans prepared by renowned Victorian architect William Butterfield. It contains the basin of a Saxon font, and rather improbably the old town stocks. In the churchyard is a chunk of Cornish granite with the rough inscription TOREUS or GOREUS. It's thought to be a memorial to a British chieftain who embraced Christianity some 1,500 years ago. There are similar (but slightly later and better carved) stones in Lustleigh and Tavistock; see box, page 248. The first mention of an earlier church is in a charter of 1225, but there's likely to have been one in situ at the time of the Domesday Book, where Yealmpton is mentioned as Elintona. Just outside town on the A379 from Plymouth is **Ben's Farm Shop** (✐ 01752 880925), with a café and a good array of local produce.

NEWTON FERRERS & NOSS MAYO

These two pretty waterside villages face each other across a small and sheltered creek branching off the Yealm, Newton Creek, and are linked by a bridge a little way upstream. It's also possible to cross from one to the other over the bed of the creek, when the tide is low enough.

White houses are dotted amid greenery on the steep banks and it's a popular mooring for visiting yachts, buzzing with watery activity in summer. The twice-daily bus from Plymouth (Target Travel No 94) squeezes its way there along twisting narrow lanes.

Small places can have big histories, and this one is well covered on ⊘ newtonnoss.co.uk. Newton Ferrers was mentioned as Newton in the Domesday Book, and by 1160 had been acquired by the Ferrers family who came over with William the Conqueror. Noss Mayo crops up in 1198 as part of the manor of Stoke, which in 1287 was given by Edward I to one Mathew Fitzjohn, hence the village was named Noss Mayo or 'Mathew's nose'. So they say. Its church of **St Peter the Poor Fisherman**, now a semi-ruin looked after by the Churches' Conservation Trust, was built in 1226 on the cliffs above Stoke Bay: a lovely cove, good for swimming, where you can sometimes spot dolphins and seals. St Peter's remained in use until 1840, when it was badly damaged by a storm. It's a peaceful, atmospheric little place, hidden among trees, with some beautiful stone carving and a hint of monastery about it. Meanwhile Newton's Holy Cross Church was built in the 13th century and, after many alterations, is still in use, across the estuary from the new (19th-century) St Peter's Church in Noss Mayo.

"It's a peaceful place, hidden among trees, with a hint of monastery about it."

Slow visitors will appreciate the lack of brash entertainments: walk in beautiful coastal scenery or ancient woodland, relax over a meal in one of the waterside eateries below (they're all open daily) or just watch the comings and goings in the creek. Newton Ferrers Equus (⊘ 01752 872808 ◷ 10.00–17.00 Wed–Sun) offers hacks in woodland or with views of distant Dartmoor. In summer, a local water taxi or ferry carries visitors across the various creeks and to Warren Point, from where it's possible to walk to Wembury (pages 164–5) via a stone-based track across fields or (better) along the coastal path.

⍨ FOOD & DRINK

The Dolphin Inn (Newton Ferrers ⊘ 01752 872007), **The Ship Inn** (Noss Mayo ⊘ 01752 872387) and **The Swan Inn** (Pillory Hill, Noss Mayo ⊘ 01752 872333) are friendly, traditional pubs with good menus and tremendous views across the water. The Dolphin and The Ship are on the waterside so you can have a paddle while waiting for your meal.

THE TAMAR VALLEY

🏠 & ⛺ **Woodovis Camping & Caravan Park** (page 277)

> For the fruit markets, cherries, pears, and walnuts are raised in great abundance; especially in the township of Beer Ferrers; which is said to send out of it a thousand pounds worth of fruit (including strawberries) annually.
>
> The Rural Economy of the West of England by William Marshall, 1796.

Bere means spit of land, and this peninsula, locked between the Tamar and the Tavy, is less accessible today than it was two hundred or so years ago when ships regularly carried cargoes of fruit down the river to Plymouth. The railway provides the only direct connection between Bere Ferrers, the village near the apex of the triangle, and Plymouth; for car drivers it's a cul-de-sac and they must make a wide detour to Denham Bridge, near Buckland Monachorum, to reach the city, a journey of about 20 miles. This enforced peacefulness means that the walker or cyclist can stroll or pedal the lanes with little danger from cars. It's deservedly one of Devon's Areas of Outstanding Natural Beauty (⌁ tamarvalley.org.uk).

"The Bere peninsula is still a major fruit producer, and walkers will see apple orchards galore."

The Bere peninsula is still a major fruit producer, and walkers will see apple orchards galore, as well as the ever-present river views with clusters of sailing boats. A few centuries back this land between the rivers became valuable for its silver mines; when the silver ran out, lead was discovered. Then, in 1890, the railway arrived and visitors poured in. It is probably quieter now than at any time in its history.

Bere Ferrers has an exceptionally interesting church, a 'Heritage' railway station with displays of memorabilia, and a friendly pub with a beer garden overlooking the Tavy. **Bere Alston** is larger and less picturesque, though it's made an effort with its multicoloured terrace houses. You can buy provisions here and there's a good pub.

Continuing north, the Tamar remains unbridged, save for the railway, until Gunnislake in Cornwall. Once-bustling **Morwellham Quay** is now an intriguing open-air museum. The Tavy's first bridge, Denham, opens up the western fringe of Dartmoor and the picturesque village with the grand name, **Buckland Monachorum**. To its south is **Buckland Abbey**.

THE TAMAR VALLEY LINE

This delightful railway, from Plymouth to Gunnislake, is a commuter service with its roots firmly in yesteryear. On its flower-bedecked and old-fashioned stations you must hail the oncoming train by raising your hand; yet it rescues the residents of Bere Ferrers and its surroundings from a long detour by road to reach workplaces in the city.

The Tamar Valley Line (℘ 01752 584777) is only 15 miles long, but the changing scenery from viaduct to fruit orchards to rivers is always diverting. The summer service is two-hourly and the line even has a **Rail Ale Trail** (℘ railaletrail.com) for the terminally thirsty, with information about distinctive pubs all within walking distance of the stations.

9 BERE FERRERS

🏠 & 🏠 **Tamar Belle** (page 277)

The Ferrers were a leading family at the time of the Norman Conquest and Henry de Ferrers was chairman of the Domesday Commission. When he received the Bere estate from Henry II it would have been prime land, situated so close to the river and Plymouth harbour. Now it is cherished by those seeking tranquillity. Standing on the platform here waiting for a train gives you an *Adlestrop* moment: complete silence save for all the birds of Devon and Cornwall.

The Tamar Belle Heritage Centre (℘ www.tamarbelle.co.uk) has a boxy-looking blue locomotive, the *Earl of Mount Edgcombe*; various old artefacts; a display of old photos and documents in a revamped 1950s sleeping carriage; and vintage carriages converted into accommodation. From the station it's about a mile downhill to the **Olde Plough Inn** (℘ 01822 840358 ℘ theoldeploughinn.co.uk), a nicely sited pub with a sunny beer garden overlooking the river. It has log fires in winter, local guest ales, and occasional live music in the evenings. Next to the pub is the church, so the two provide a pleasant way to spend the hour before the train returns to Plymouth. The **Church of St Andrew** was built – or rather rebuilt, since the tower is earlier – by Sir William de Ferrers, who died in 1280. His monument is one of its treasures. He lies, with his wife Isolda de Cardinham, next to the altar, dressed in chainmail, his legs crossed (though he has lost his feet) and a shield at his side. Both hands are on his sword, ready to draw. His wife wears a simple robe and on one shoulder is a small, disembodied hand, said to be that of a child, although it's hard to see where the arm or body could have been.

And the fingers are too long for a child; a mystery. The stone canopy is decorated with strange carved heads, perhaps male and female.

The memorial to his father, Sir Reginald, who died in 1194, lies next to the altar and seems to have been carved by the same sculptor. This gentleman lies with his body half-turned, his shield over his hands which are also poised to draw his sword. His knee raised, he appears ready to leap from his tomb and defend his honour. Sadly both lower legs are missing, as is the lion on which his feet rested, although the paws and curly tail remain.

Another notable feature of the church is the stained glass in the east window, claimed – rightly or wrongly – to be the oldest in the county apart from some in Exeter Cathedral. The window was a gift of William de Ferrers, and one of the lights shows him – or one of his family – holding a model of the church.

Elsewhere St Andrew's has Tudor carved bench ends, the design echoing the shape of the windows, and a Tudor fireplace to keep the gentry warm in the winter. The screen has gone, as have the saints in the panels, scraped off at the time of the Reformation.

In the graveyard is a sad little tombstone which has no name, just the inscription 'Cholera 1849'.

10 MORWELLHAM QUAY
Nr Tavistock PL19 8JL   ✐ 01822 832766   ⊘ morwellham-quay.co.uk

Morwellham Quay is on the River Tamar, four miles west of Tavistock. Its nearest rail stations are Gunnislake (three miles away) and Calstock. By car it's just off the A390 between Tavistock and Gunnislake, and there's masses of free parking space. Or you can cycle.

Looking at the beauty and tranquillity of Morwellham Quay today, it's hard to believe that in Victorian times it was known as 'the richest copper port in the Queen's Empire'. Originally built in the 10th to 11th century by the Cistercian monks of Tavistock Abbey as a means to transport goods and themselves to and from Plymouth, it quickly developed; by the late 12th century ships came to load up with locally mined tin, lead and silver ores. Later, the Industrial Revolution caused a huge demand for metals of all kinds; the hills of west Devon and east Cornwall were rich in tin, lead, copper, arsenic and manganese, and these were shipped via Morwellham to north Wales, with its substantial coal supplies, for smelting. It was said that Morwellham's quayside sometimes held

THE BERE FERRERS RAIL ACCIDENT

In 1917 ten servicemen from New Zealand were mown down by an express train at Bere Ferrers. The men (aged 20 to 36) had disembarked from their troopship in Plymouth and were on their way to Salisbury Plain for training. They had been told that when the train made its first stop, at Exeter, two men from each carriage should alight and go to the back of the train to distribute rations. When the train made an unscheduled stop at Bere Ferrers they jumped on to the line and were struck by the Waterloo–Plymouth express. They are commemorated by a new centenary shelter and rose garden at the station, unveiled by the New Zealand High Commissioner, and also on a brass plaque in the church accompanied by the New Zealand flag. Their names have been added to the village war memorial, and a special memorial ceremony was held in 2017.

enough arsenic to poison the entire world! A canal was laboriously dug from Tavistock, to facilitate transport.

In 1844, Europe's largest known copper lode was discovered just four miles from the quay, and Morwellham became a busier port than even Liverpool. Vessels from Europe and further afield came to collect their precious loads of ore. But then the copper began to run out. Eventually the company running the mine was forced to close, with huge loss of employment. The Great Western Railway's arrival at Tavistock superseded river transport; the great quays gradually fell silent, machinery rusted and the waterways silted up. After 1,000 years of activity, Morwellham Quay slept. In 1933 the canal was bought by the West Devon Electric Supply Company, and the hydroelectric plant they built there still provides power to the National Grid.

Restoration began in 1970 and UNESCO designated the quay a World Heritage Site in 2006. Nowadays, costumed staff show off the quay's exhibits and help to recreate its 19th-century heyday. A riverside tramway carries visitors deep into the heart of the old George and Charlotte copper mine; children can dress up in period costume and join in with period activities; various traditional crafts (pottery, blacksmithing, etc) are demonstrated and the old cottages have been reopened, showing the furnishings of earlier times. The old Assayer's Workshop is there, and the Cooper's Workshop, and the Victorian village school. The 100-year-old ketch *Garlandstone*, built on the Tamar, is moored at the quayside. Echoes of the past are everywhere and staff work hard to bring it alive for visitors. Despite all the displays and demonstrations, it's hard to imagine the hectic buzz and clatter of earlier days when the great machines were turning; there's an enveloping sleepiness about the place. But it's still one of Devon's most unusual, atmospheric and historic sites.

EAST OF THE TAVY

Probably best known for Buckland Abbey, this area has plenty of other treasures. Dartmoor's heather and spacious views are only a mile or so away, but it's still an area of woodland and deep valleys, impregnated with the name of Drake.

11 YELVERTON

🏠 **Barnabas House** (page 276)

This busy little village, a useful access hub for the surrounding area, is thoroughly geared towards passing traffic, with its petrol station, supermarket, pub (the Rock Inn), deli, post office and ATMs, but retains a lot of charm. A handy cycle hire/repair place is Rockin Bikes (Harrowbeer Mews 🖉 01822 258022). The website 🖉 barnabas-house. co.uk has good information on the local area. Frequent buses pass through to either Plymouth or Tavistock. Close by, as you take the main turning towards Buckland Abbey from the A386, you pass the old **RAF Harrowbeer Airfield** (🖉 rafharrowbeer.co.uk), now grassed over and scenic with some chunky, Dartmoor-style outcrops of rock. Harrowbeer became operational in 1941 and was an important wartime RAF base; shops in Yelverton's main street had to have their upper storeys removed because of low-flying aircraft. Commemorative events are held annually, and there's an explanatory board at the site. In 1960 there was talk of it becoming Plymouth's airport, but there was strong local opposition and it was eventually demolished.

A few miles northeast of Yelverton on the Princetown road is **Burrator Reservoir**, a multi-terrain area with walks, cycle rides or drives around the lake's perimeter, a dam, an arboretum, a lively interactive discovery centre and a network of footpaths, bridleways and off-road trails in the surrounding area. This is the very edge of Dartmoor, as the ponies ambling around it will remind you; you can enjoy open moorland or climb nearby Sheepstor, one of Dartmoor's most spectacular. I came across a pony suckling her very small and spindly foal. There are birds (robins, nuthatches, great tits …) along the wooded trails, as well as bluebells and primroses in season. You could spend as much of a day as you wanted here, just wandering across the different terrains. It's looked after by the South West Lakes Trust (✆ 01566 771930 ⬦ swlakestrust. org.uk) as is Lopwell Dam (pages 175–6), and there's news of current activities on their website.

2 BUCKLAND MONACHORUM & AREA

The approach street of this village is so narrow that you proceed at your peril, but it broadens out at the church and the grand Lady Modyford's School, which she endowed in 1702 with an annual allowance for the schoolmaster of £7.10s.

The church of St Andrew is, at first glance, plain inside with a simple barrel roof, but then you notice the angels. They hang on the horizontal beams, wings half open, merrily playing a range of musical instruments. There's a Saxon font, looking like a cottage loaf, and the rather alarming Drake Chapel (not Sir Francis, but descendants of his brother Thomas) to the south of the nave. The huge Gibraltar Memorial to General Elliot, who successfully defended The Rock against Spain in 1779–83, is thickly planted with dead bodies and heroic words. There's no question which side God was on. The general married into the Drake family.

WILD SWIMMING IN THE TAVY & WALKHAM RIVERS

Joanna Griffin

About two miles due north of Buckland Monachorum is Double Waters, where the River Walkham meets the Tavy. It's a lovely mile-and-a-half walk along the Walkham from Grenofen Bridge, through oak and birch woodlands, passing the chimney of the ruined West Down Mine. The river is shallow and fast-flowing and tumbles its way towards the Tavy in a series of rapids with some calm stretches in between. It is too shallow for swimming but it is possible to wallow in the shallows for a natural jacuzzi on warm day.

There are better swimming areas around the confluence itself. As the Tavy curves round to meet the Walkham, there is a short calm stretch near the bank but the current can be strong in parts and sweep you downstream if you're not careful. A wooden bridge takes you almost all of the way across the Walkham just before the rivers meet – it doesn't reach the other side so you'll have to paddle – and downstream there's a calmer stretch for swimming.

From here you can walk up on to West Down for far-reaching views, or to avoid a steep climb simply retrace your steps.

Close to Buckland Monachorum is **The Garden House** (PL20 7LQ ✆ 01822 854769 ⊘ end Mar–Oct 10.00–17.00), with a gorgeous mixture of formal and informal gardens. The colours are superb. Its ten acres include an arboretum, a wildflower meadow, a two-acre walled garden with smaller gardens inside, lawns, wonderful wisteria and a glade of acers which blaze red in the autumn. Perfect for strolling. The head gardener, Nick Haworth, was previously head gardener at Greenway, Agatha Christie's old home on the River Dart (pages 106–7). There's a **tea room** (⊘ 10.30–16.30) serving light lunches, sumptuous cream teas and good home baking, or you can just sip a glass of wine and enjoy the view from the terrace. The house itself is the elegant former home of the vicars of Buckland Monachorum, built in the early 19th century.

13 BUCKLAND ABBEY

Yelverton PL20 6EY ✆ 01822 853607 ⊘ opening times vary seasonally; National Trust

'The outside looks like a church but the inside feels like a home' says one of the introductory displays, and a home is indeed what Buckland Abbey became in the hands of Sir Richard Grenville of *Revenge* fame (pages 176–7). His grandfather (also Richard) had bought the 270-year-old abbey plus 570 acres of land from Henry VIII in 1541, but did little to it.

The estate passed to three-year-old Richard in 1545 when his father Roger, captain of the *Mary Rose*, drowned when she sank. In the 1570s he began developing it, and decided to make his home in the church itself. He demolished cloisters and monastic buildings, inserted fireplaces and added a new kitchen wing, as well as dividing the interior into three floors and creating the well-proportioned rooms.

"Sir Francis Drake paid for the house with spoils from his capture of a Spanish galleon."

The great hall, with its fine plasterwork ceiling and decoration, was completed around 1576. Then in 1581 his money ran out and he sold the whole property – reluctantly, by all accounts – to Sir Francis Drake, who paid for it with spoils from his capture of the Spanish galleon *Nuestra Señora de la Concepción* in 1579. Drake also owned around 40 other properties and, although he lived there on and off for some 14 years, made no particular mark on it; but it remained in the Drake family (although with periods of disuse) until 1940 when it was presented to the National Trust.

On the way to the house you pass the Great Barn, a relic of the original Cistercian monastery that was founded here in 1278. 'Great' is inadequate: it's truly massive, with an amazing beamed roof and a huge cider press at one end. The spirit of the old monastery is evoked most strongly in this building; cowled monks could well be padding on soft sandalled feet through the shadows, their robes swishing in the dust.

"Cowled monks could well be padding on soft sandalled feet through the shadows, their robes swishing in the dust."

Inside the house, there are paintings, documents, fine furniture, objets d'art, maps, weapons, ornaments – and of course Drake's drum, which, according to legend, will summon the old swashbuckler back to fight for England if his country ever needs his help. One of the paintings shows the surrender of the *Nuestra Señora del Rosario* (pages 60–1).

The cavernous old kitchen gives some idea of the scale of the feasting, with space enough for cooks to handle whole carcases of meat. The Ox Yard Restaurant in the courtyard uses somewhat more modern equipment! Outside there are also craft workshops, a second-hand book store and even a Letterboxing Trail.

There's a full, year-round programme of events, including several for children, from bluebell and woodland walks to charcoal making, weaving, storytelling, concerts, a bug trail and historical re-enactments. Buckland Abbey is a place for all seasons – and for all weathers too, since you'll be well sheltered inside the house on a rainy day.

If you don't want to visit the house itself, for a reduced entrance fee you can just park and stroll around the grounds: meadows, orchards, and four woodland walks along the River Tavy. There's a large car park. Trampers (mobility scooters) are available for hire. From Plymouth there's a bus, the 48, on Sunday only; on weekdays you'll need the 55 from Yelverton, which you can reach by bus from Plymouth or Tavistock.

MILTON COMBE & LOPWELL DAM

About a mile south of the abbey is the almost inaccessible little village of **Milton Combe**, folded into a ravine like a pressed flower. The white cottages find a footing where they can, a stream runs through it, and the pub stands in the square ready to reward your efforts to get here. It's called the Who'd Have Thought It.

SIR RICHARD GRENVILLE & THE REVENGE

As a young man Richard studied at London's Inner Temple, then (aged 24) joined a brief 'crusade' against the Turks who had invaded Hungary. Next he bought land in Ireland and became involved in organising settlements there. He comes across as a somewhat obstinate and domineering character but a loyal and courageous leader, respected by his peers, although lacking Drake's easy charm.

Unlike his cousins Humphrey Gilbert and Walter Raleigh, he was not (apart from his father) from a particularly seafaring family, but he yearned for adventure, and in 1574 sought the Queen's permission to seek new lands and treasure south of the equator. However, she did not grant it. He owned ships and financed voyages but spent little

time at sea, until in 1585 he was offered command of a voyage carrying 100 settlers to today's North Carolina, newly acquired for the crown by Raleigh. He embraced this new maritime career, for 'the pleasure of God on the seas', but it proved short-lived, as other commitments then kept him at home for several years. He became a commissioner for the coastal defences of Devon and Cornwall.

Finally, in 1591, came his finest hour. Captaining the *Revenge*, he was second-in-command to Lord Thomas Howard of a small squadron sent to tackle Spanish treasure ships off the Azores. The superior Spanish fleet caught them by surprise when they were at anchor; Howard ordered his ships to flee to safety but Grenville lagged behind to

Lopwell Dam & Nature Reserve (☎ 01566 771930 🖥 swlakestrust. org.uk) is also signposted from the A386. The superb river views (salt water meets fresh water here) make it worth the detour. It's also good for birdwatching, and is a designated Site of Special Scientific Interest. The old pumphouse has been converted into a café whose outdoor terrace has a stunning view over the water, and a visitor centre with displays and information. You may spot grey seals or otters, and it's one of the best areas in Devon for kingfishers. Across the river via a causeway is the five-hectare local nature reserve, an important habitat for a variety of saltmarsh species, with a woodland and marsh-side nature trail. The impressive mineshaft of Wheal Maristow dates back to the 13th century, as does Lopwell's history of lead and silver mining.

The small snag is that the causeway is above water for only two hours each side of low tide, so you'll need to check the tide table beforehand and get the timing right. If you're a bit too early, just relax in the café. You can also pick up the Tamar Valley Discovery Trail (page 153) from here, going either northward (via the causeway) towards Bere Alston or else southward towards Tamerton Foliot and Plymouth.

pick up crew who were ashore ('waiting to recover the men that were upon the Island that had otherwise bene lost', wrote Raleigh later in his *Report of the Trueth of the fight about the Isles of the Açores*). He then tried to run the *Revenge* forward through the 15 advancing Spaniards but the great ships blocked his way and his wind. Still he could have escaped by turning tail but 'Sir Richard utterly refused to turne from the enemie, alleaging that hee would rather choose to die, than to dishonour himselfe, his countrey, and her Majesties shippe'. An astonishing 15-hour battle then raged, the little *Revenge* firing fiercely into the Spanish galleons and fighting their men hand-to-hand when they swarmed aboard. By dawn next day her masts and rigging had been shot away and she was badly holed. Sir Richard, grievously wounded, called on his gunner to sink her rather than let her fall into Spanish hands; but his seamen struck a bargain with the Spaniards, deserted their captain and surrendered. Sir Richard was taken to the Spanish flagship San Pablo, where he later died.

As the *Revenge* – a considerable prize – was being towed back to Spain, 'the water began to heave and the weather to moan' and a fearful storm arose. The *Revenge* was smashed on to rocks and broke apart, and many Spanish ships and men were also lost. Confrontation had turned to tragedy, Spain had suffered a grievous blow, and Sir Richard Grenville passed into heroic history.

SOUTHERN DARTMOOR

Head south from Yelverton and you'll quickly find yourself in a maze of high-banked narrow lanes which plunge down to river valleys and across gorse-bright moorland. There are some enjoyable walks in the area, perhaps the best being near **Shaugh Prior**, where the River Plym meanders its way eastward. The village itself has a pub and St Edward's Church is worth a look for its unusual carved wooden font cover.

The best walk in the area is through the **Dewerstone Wood**, a Site of Special Scientific Interest. Nearby, to the east, is Dewerston Rock, the remains of an iron-age fort. It's popular with rock climbers though they should bear in mind that the Devil (dewer is one of his ancient names) is said to have a particularly jolly time around here, galloping about on a black horse with his equally dusky hounds, looking for hapless souls to chase over the rock to their deaths.

Continuing south by car or bike towards **Wotter** you'll pass through a lovely area of moorland, which in May was stunning in its gorse yellowness and scent.

14 DARTMOOR ZOO

PL7 5DG ✆ 01753 837645 ⬦ dartmoorzoo.org.uk ◷ winter 10.00–16.00, summer 10.00–18.00

This zoo is only five miles from Plymouth near the village of Sparkwell, via a turning off the A38. It was the subject of the book *We Bought a Zoo* by Benjamin Mee, subsequently turned into a Hollywood film starring Matt Damon and Scarlett Johansson. It's a pleasantly laid-back place, and the helpful staff are happy to talk to visitors about the animals – which seem relaxed and well-cared-for.

Quite a bit of walking is involved as the enclosures are well spaced out; it's also a stiffish uphill walk from the car park, although the compensation is a good view of a family group of happy capybaras when you're halfway up. Notices pointing out how long it would take a cheetah or a frog to make the distance will either encourage or discourage you. There's disabled parking at the top. As well as the smaller animals (including meerkats and several reptiles and amphibians) there are most of the big cats – lion, tiger, cheetah – plus bears, lynx, wolves, tapirs, reindeer and ostriches. Regular events are held each day (feeding time, talks, close encounters and so on) and are listed on a board at the entrance. There's generally plenty for children to enjoy. The Jaguar Restaurant serves hot and cold meals and snacks.

Bus Target 59 from Plymouth's Royal Parade runs to the zoo but not frequently; check times with Target Travel (✆ 01752 242000 ⬦ targettravel.co.uk). Beware: the return bus sometimes leaves a bit earlier than scheduled.

15 CORNWOOD & DELAMORE HOUSE

A few miles east of the zoo is the little village of Cornwood, a delightful place with an interesting church and a pub, and nearby is Delamore House and gardens, open only in May, and worth travelling across the county to see if you love gardens and art. Here there is the perfect combination.

First, **Cornwood**. The village has a Raleigh connection; Sir Walter's grandfather lived in Fardel Manor and probably worshipped in the 13th-century **church** of St Michael and All Angels, which was looking particularly lovely when I visited, with the flower ladies out in force preparing for the biennial mid-May flower festival. There's plenty of interest, from the driftwood cross at the altar to the intricately carved

Jacobean pulpit: more flowers, but this time Tudor roses. Worshippers are watched over by a heavenly host of gilded angels on the ceiling and in a side chapel is the very touching effigy of a child, John Savery, who died in 1696. Part of the inscription reads: 'That he has taught us by his hasting hence/ That the earth's too vile for soe much innocence/ Reader relent since thou noe more shall see/This matchless childe but in his effigie.' Opposite little John is an Elizabethan couple, wearing ruffs.

Delamore House (PL21 9QT ◈ 01752 837236 ◈ www.delamore-art. co.uk ○ May 10.30–16.30), built in 1859 from Dartmoor granite, was designed by James Piers St Aubyn, who was best known as a church architect, which explains the somewhat ecclesiastical feel of the house. For one month each year it plays host to local, national and international artists whose work is on display in both the house and gardens, where sculptures vie for attention with the magnificent azaleas and rhododendrons, and lurk beside woodland paths. All the work is for sale at very reasonable prices, and the proceeds go to charity. The former servants' kitchen serves as a **café** with soup, sandwiches, and a delicious selection of home baking.

If you're not able to come in May, the house and gardens are open to visitors a couple of times a year through ◈ invitationtoview.co.uk.

16 IVYBRIDGE & SOUTH BRENT

While they may lack the charm and interest of the region's other small towns, these two do their job as gateways to Dartmoor, with convenient shops and pubs.

Ivybridge

Å Harford Bunkhouse & Camping (page 277)

Tourist information: The Watermark, Leonards Rd, Ivybridge PL21 0SZ ◈ 01752 879035 ○ 09.15–17.00 Mon–Fri, 09.15–13.00 Sat. (It's a desk inside the public library, with leaflets & helpful staff.)

Ivybridge is well served by trains and buses and beautifully located, right on the edge of Dartmoor. It's the starting point of the original Two Moors Way (page 230), and is also on NCN 2. The River Erme runs through the town and the original stone Ivy Bridge, dating back to 1250 and painted by Turner in 1813, is still in situ. The paper mill built in 1787 produces fine paper, and the viaduct in Longtimber Woods on the edge of the town was designed and built by Isambard Kingdom Brunel.

Its railway station has ample parking space and is an unofficial 'park & ride' site for Plymouth, just 15 minutes along the line. **Rochelle's River Café,** overlooking the Erme, is a friendly place serving breakfasts and lunches; it shuts at 16.00 in winter, later in summer.

South Brent

🏠 **Glazebrook House Hotel** (page 276)

Described in The King's England as 'a grey little town', South Brent, around five miles north of Ivybridge along the A38, has brightened up considerably since the 1960s with some gaily painted houses and shops. The **church of St Petroc** contains interesting items: St Petroc himself is shown in a carving near the choir, accompanied by his faithful dog (or tame wolf), and there are some good modern carvings. A set of stocks stands in the porch.

Half a mile north of the town, on the edge of Dartmoor, is an exceptionally pretty ancient packhorse bridge, **Lydia Bridge**, which spans the River Avon, with its tangled overhanging greenery and splashy waterfalls.

West of South Brent is the splendid and unique **Glazebrook House Hotel** (TQ10 9JE ✆ 01364 73322 ♲ glazebrookhouse.com). The restaurant here is open to non-residents, and if you've never had a 'five-course taster with wine flight' here's your chance for a very special treat.

A short walk from the Glazebrook is **Lady Wood**, managed by the Devon Wildlife Trust particularly for the conservation of dormice. Enter it under the impressive Brunel viaduct, a twin to the one in Ivybridge, for a peaceful stroll. The bluebells here provide a wonderful display in the spring although, I'm sorry to say, they are hybrid.

FOLLOW US

Use #devon to share your adventures using this guide with us – we'd love to hear from you.

☐ Bradt Travel Guides   ☐ @BradtGuides & @hilarybradt (#devon)

☐ @bradtguides (#devon)   ☐ pinterest.com/bradtguides

GREATER HORSESHOE BATS

My thanks to Geoff Billington of Greena Ecological Consultancy for information.

In Britain, this bat is found only in the southwest of England and in Wales. The colony at the Buckfastleigh Caves (pages 199–201) is the largest in the UK, and particularly important since this species is in decline. It's a strange-looking animal with its large mobile ears and fleshy 'noseleaf' (looking like a horseshoe, hence its name) which amplifies the bat's calls; it makes these through its nose with its mouth closed, so that it can judge the distance of its prey. These bats have small eyes, but the expression 'blind as a bat' has little truth as bats can see fairly well, although only in black and white. However, in complete darkness they have to rely mainly on their echolocation 'sonar'.

Greater horseshoe bats are among the largest European species of bats, and can live for 30 years. They mate during the autumn but delay fertilisation until they have emerged from hibernation in the spring. Their impressive wingspan is about 16 inches and, as with all bats, their wings are versatile.

Apart from enabling them to fly – bats are the only mammals that have evolved this way – the wings act as a cooling system in flight, since they contain innumerable blood vessels, and are a means of finding underground sites by detecting temperature changes from draughts emerging from entrances. Dozing bats wrap their wings right round their bodies. And when it comes to birth, the wings are more like an open umbrella, allowing the newborn baby to drop from its upside-down mother into safety. At times the baby hangs from a false nipple, positioned at the lower end of the abdomen, while the real nipples are near the armpit (or wingpit). The mother can fly with her infant thus attached, though she also parks it in the roost, hanging upside down, while she goes hunting. The young can fly and catch insects from about three weeks.

Bats emerge from their roosts about half an hour after sunset. Sit quietly and watch them, but do not disturb this protected species.

THE EASTERN FRINGE
OF DARTMOOR

6

THE EASTERN FRINGE OF DARTMOOR

The River Teign turns south at Dunsford, and gives map-makers the eastern border of Dartmoor National Park before its final journey to Kingsteignton and Teignmouth. Although technically some of the towns and villages in this section lie within Dartmoor National Park, their gentler, leafier character fits better here. Despite their relative proximity to Exeter and particularly to Newton Abbot, it's surprising how remote some of them feel.

Along the river are some of the prettiest wooded areas of Dartmoor, splashed by waterfalls, and networked by footpaths and narrow lanes. England's highest waterfall, Canonteign Falls, is here, as are Stover Park with its inspirational Ted Hughes Poetry Trail and nearby the unique Orchid Paradise in Burnham Nurseries. Then there's popular Buckfastleigh, whose attractions include the South Devon Steam Railway, Buckfast Abbey, the Valiant Soldier (known as 'The pub where time was never called') and the enchanting miniature pigs at Pennywell Farm. The 14th-century stannary town of Ashburton offers intriguing glimpses of its past, while Ipplepen and Torbryan have exceptional churches. And you may more than once catch a passing echo of Conan Doyle's great detective himself, deerstalker at the ready and John Watson hot on his heels.

WET-WEATHER ACTIVITIES

Hannahs (page 189)
Orchid Paradise (pages 191–2)
Ashburton Museum (page 193)
Otters and Butterflies (pages 198–9)
Buckfastleigh Caves (pages 199–201)
Buckfast Abbey (pages 201–2)
Pennywell Farm, where the piglet area and some of the pens are covered (pages 202–3)

GETTING THERE & AROUND

Drivers will find this one of the most easily accessible regions, with all the places described lying near the A38 from Exeter. It's once you leave that dual carriageway to track down the little villages that you're in trouble without a satnav.

Buses from Exeter serve Newton Abbot, Ashburton and Buckfastleigh and pass near Stover Country Park; others call at Ipplepen, Landscove and Doddiscombsleigh; but reaching some attractions involves a bit of walking too. You need the Teignbridge bus timetable or the interactive map on ◊ traveldevon.info.

Newton Abbot is on the direct railway line from Exeter to Plymouth, but the cream of the getting-there options in terms of charm is the steam train run by the South Devon Railway between Totnes and Buckfastleigh (pages 196–8).

SELF-POWERED TRAVEL

For walkers and cyclists this region's lanes are typically hilly and narrow, but with strong legs you could see all its major sights in a day. The Stover Trail is a flat, traffic-free, 3½-mile multi-use route which connects Newton Abbot to Bovey Tracey, crossing the busy A38 via a new bridge. Created as part of the Granite and Gears project, it passes alongside Stover County Park and will eventually extend towards Lustleigh and Moretonhampstead. Otherwise, there's not as much scope as in some other areas, but more good possibilities can be devised using the Teignbridge bus timetable and Ordnance Survey Explorer map OL110 (for the north of the region) along with Explorer map OL28. None of the excellent Croydecycle maps cover this region. Access to Haytor on Dartmoor is achieved via the Templer Way (page 253), which runs through this region including Stover Country Park.

THE NORTHERN TEIGN VALLEY

🏠 **Cridford Inn** Trusham (page 277), **Nobody Inn** Doddiscombsleigh (page 277)
🏚 **Rydon** Trusham (page 277)

Hidden in the hills of the east side of the Teign, Doddiscombsleigh and Higher Ashton have exceptional churches, while Canonteign Falls provide a dramatic cascade of water in cool, ferny woodland.

1 DODDISCOMBSLEIGH

This little hidden village attracts both church crawlers and pub crawlers. 'Everybody knows the Nobody' they say, and indeed the Nobody Inn (page 188) has been there for centuries, although prior to the mid 18th century it was a cottage. The name evolved from The New Inn to The No Body Inn 'with reference to an unfortunate episode concerning a dead landlord'.

St Michael's Church has been providing spiritual refreshment for even longer: it has the finest medieval stained-glass windows in the county, and the original church probably predates the Norman Conquest. It's built from an aesthetically pleasing mixture of local stone of various colours, including granite from nearby Dartmoor. Inside it's curiously square, with two aisles, and the famous windows can be observed at eye level since they and the wagon roof are exceptionally low. This makes it easy for the visitor to appreciate their craftsmanship and imagination, and brings a feeling of intimacy. To quote the Shell Guide, 'the artist has looked at men without romanticising but with much charity.'

Indeed. I loved the tired face of St Paul, shielding his right eye with one hand. And also St George's cute little horse, which looks more like a sheep. Then there's St Michael, weighing souls. A little demon is trying to tip the balance but the good are apparently heavy enough to defeat his efforts. The complicated seven sacraments window at the east end of the aisle is more difficult to see, but there's a good description of it in the church booklet, and photos on the wall showing the detail.

THE DEVIL'S BITE

Carved at the top of one of the stone capitals in St Michael's Church is a face. It's not a green man, nor a saint or angel. It has funny pointed ears, unusual foliage, and something strange about its mouth. Dr Michael Tisdall is a medical doctor with a passion for the unusual in Devon churches, so he has teased out the (probable) truth here. This carving is at the west end of the church, often called the Devil's End (indeed, some old churches have a little opening through which the Devil can escape during services), and he has a hare lip. As a young doctor studying children's diseases, Dr Tisdall came across the expression 'Devil's bite' to describe a hare lip. And the foliage isn't the usual rose leaves, it's *Succisa pratensis*, or Devil's bit scabious. So there we have it. A medieval carver portrayed the Devil in an instantly recognisable form – to the villagers of his day – but for us it takes the detective work of a knowledgeable enthusiast to get to the truth.

The capitals at the top of the columns are finely carved with foliage; the two that are partially set into the walls at each end of the north aisle are worth studying. At the altar end is a frowning green man, and at the west end, near the organ, is the very intriguing harelipped Devil which would escape anyone's notice if it hadn't been pointed out by Dr Michael Tisdall (see box, page 185).

Surprisingly, given the remoteness of this little village, the 360 bus from Exeter runs here five times a day (Monday to Saturday), so you can view the church and have lunch at the inn without the worry of either finding the place or parking.

2 HIGHER ASHTON

About 1½ miles south of Doddiscombsleigh, Higher Ashton is a pretty village of thatched, whitewashed houses set on a steep hill. The church of St John the Baptist is renowned for its medieval rood screen, intricately carved to set off the 32 panels with their painted saints. The church leaflet is helpful in explaining who's who. You'll easily identify well-known saints such as St Sebastian with his arrows (although he is headless), and a baby-faced St George in full armour killing a tiny dragon. This seems a particularly unfair contest since the dragon is depicted with a dog's body and looks as though it's just been woken from a nap. Among the more obscure ones is St Apollonia (see box, opposite) looking speculatively at a huge tooth held in the blacksmith's pincers. There is a wall monument to smug Sir George Chudleigh (1657) who fathered nine sons and nine daughters, and a fascinating commemorative stone embedded in the floor, crudely carved, with September and October written as 7ber and 8ber – the first time I have seen this abbreviation. By the entrance is a list of rectors from 1249 to 1996.

There's nowhere to park near the church; leave your car in the village car park.

3 CANONTEIGN FALLS

EX6 7RH ℘ 01647 252617 ♂ canonteignfalls.co.uk

This is one of Devon's superlatives, the highest waterfall in England (220 feet), but it's also man-made, which takes the gloss off a bit. Nevertheless it's popular with families who relish the challenge of climbing the 90 steps to the top of the falls. And hats off to the enterprise of the ten generations of Lords of the Manor who have played their part in

ST APOLLONIA & ST BARBARA

It's not clear to me why a woman who had all her teeth smashed with giant tongs becomes the patron saint of dentists. However, she appears on so many Devon rood screens that it's worth knowing something about her.

Apollonia lived in Alexandria in the 3rd century AD. She led an exemplary life, preaching the gospel during a time when this held considerable risks. Emperor Philip was none too keen on Christians, especially those like Apollonia who gave succour to his political prisoners. In AD249 she was arrested and, inevitably, tortured to persuade her to renounce her faith. All her teeth were smashed and then pulled out with iron pincers. When this had no effect her torturers piled up firewood, intending to burn her to death, but she leapt into the flames all by herself, thus presenting the church with something of a dilemma: did she commit suicide (a sin) or was she a true martyr, dying for her faith? They chose the latter and sanctification.

Devon has 14 depictions of St Apollonia holding her torturer's pincers (the kind used by blacksmiths, so not really suitable for dentistry). These are usually on painted rood screens or stained glass but one of those, in Stokeinteignhead is carved into a stone capital.

If explosives are your thing, then St Barbara is your patron saint. Possessed of exceptional beauty and intelligence, she was kept locked in a tower by her father who had a rich suitor in mind. Here she converted to Christianity and managed to escape, only to fall into the hands of a shepherd. Before he could have his wicked way with her, divine punishment turned his sheep into beetles. Her father then contrived that she should be paraded naked throughout the region, but God supplied her with a robe. Frustrated, Dad then got fed up and killed her with his sword, whereupon he was struck dead by a thunderbolt. So St Barbara is now the patron saint of artillerymen and their like, also 'those in danger of sudden death'.

creating this tourist attraction. The house is on the site of a monastery owned by the canons of St Mary du Val in Normandy, hence the name Canonteign. After the dissolution of the monasteries it was converted into a manor house which was eventually bought by Admiral Edward Pellew, later Lord Exmouth. His descendants enjoyed a period of prosperity in the 19th century through the nearby lead and silver mines, respectively Frank Mills (named after its owner, a banker) and Wheal Exmouth. In the 1880s the mines fell into decline and the miners found themselves out of a job. But then the third Lady Exmouth stepped in with the idea of putting them to work again by diverting the leat that formerly serviced the mine to create a waterfall tumbling over natural rocks for the enjoyment of family and friends. It, and the nearby paths, fell into disrepair after World War II and it was not until 1985 that the tenth Lord Exmouth rediscovered the walk and decided to open it to the public.

In the grounds are a couple of lakes with resident waterfowl, and some gentle paths for those unwilling to tackle the climb up to the falls. Helpful labels tell you what you're looking at, and there's a recreation of a Victorian fern garden complete with tree ferns.

On leaving, if you turn left at the road you'll see the tall chimneys of the former Wheal Exmouth lead mine adjacent to the engine house, now a thoughtfully converted three-storey private home. There are two chimneys, one circular with finely worked corbels, and the other octagonal, topless, and with trees billowing out of its ragged opening instead of smoke. The whole complex is both scenic and historic, spanning the commercial history of the area from mining to 'grand design' conversion.

FOOD & DRINK

Cridford Inn Trusham TQ13 0NR 📞 01626 853694 ○ from 11.00 daily; food served noon–14.30 & 18.00–21.00. The village (just south of Lower and Upper Ashton) has some thatched cottages and this charming pub (also thatched, and a former longhouse). It claims to be one of the oldest inns in the country and contains what is thought to be Britain's oldest domestic window. Its restaurant (with a mural dating back to 1081AD) serves seriously good food, and its bar offers own-label beer and over 100 gins. It also has B&B rooms and holiday cottages (page 277). Worth a detour.

Nobody Inn Doddiscombsleigh 📞 01647 252394 ○ daily; food served noon–14.30 & 18.00–21.00. Winner of the Good Hotel Guide's 'Inn of the Year' award in 2017. The food at this curiously named place (page 185) is terrific and has also won many awards. Served in the cosy pub, with an open fire in winter, a beer garden in the summer, cheery staff and happy locals, it competes with the nearby Cridford for a gastronomic treat. And an alcoholic one: the pub can offer you around 300 different whiskies (!) and quite a few gins. If you can't bring yourself to leave, there's a 'games menu' including Monopoly, so (as it also offers B&B) you could be here for days.

NEWTON ABBOT & AREA

Attractions in this area are easily reached from either Newton Abbot or Ashburton, and include butterflies, railway museums, Sherlock Holmes and Roman remains.

4 NEWTON ABBOT

🏠 **Hannah's** (page 277)

Tourist information: 6 Indoor Market, Market St 🖉 01626 215667 ⊙ 09.00–13.30 & 14.00–16.00 Mon–Sat

Although this busy town is a bit hectic for Slow visitors, it's the starting point for the Haytor Hoppa (page 228), there's a big outdoor market on Wednesdays, and the **Town and Great Western Railway Museum** is worth a visit (St Paul's Rd 🖉 01626 201121 𝒶 museum-newtonabbot. org.uk ⊙ Apr–Oct 10.00–16.00 Mon–Thu, 10.00–noon Fri & some Sats). It has exhibits relating to (among many other 'notable Newtonians') Isambard Kingdom Brunel and the 18th-century wreck-salvage pioneer and inventor John Lethbridge. Its GWR room has a working signal box and an original section of Brunel's atmospheric railway, together with a model of the atmospheric system. Newton Abbot's railway history began in 1846, when Brunel and South Devon Railway board agreed to open Newton Station the following year, and developed so energetically that the town became known as the 'Swindon of the West' because of all its workshops and sheds.

Cider lovers should head for **Ye Olde Cider Bar** in East Street (𝒶 01626 354221), a basic traditional pub with lots of atmosphere and a huge array of ciders from local independent producers, which in both 2011 and 2017 was named the Campaign for Real Ale's UK 'Cider Pub of the Year'.

Along a lane off the A383 about three miles west of Newton Abbot is **Hannahs** (𝒶 01626 325800 𝒶 discoverhannahs.org). The massive main house in extensive grounds, Seale-Hayne, was built as an agricultural college in 1912–14. The college closed in 2005 and today it's owned by the Dame Hannah Rogers Charity, which for 250 years has been working with disadvantaged children, young people and adults with a range of disabilities. Now there are art galleries, music studios, a gift shop, the old library (with fascinating vintage books on rural history and agriculture), a pleasant all-day bistro, and a Health & Wellbeing Centre. Art exhibitions and other events are held regularly. There is also an accommodation annex and two safari tents (page 277), and all activities (including the accommodation) are geared for less mobile visitors. It's an unexpected place to find in the middle of the Devon countryside, and worth checking to see what events may be on while you're in the area.

5 IPPLEPEN & TORBRYAN

These two villages, only a few miles apart, are remarkable for their churches, which give us so much superb carving in such a small area, yet their medieval congregations probably considered each other to be far away.

Ipplepen

🏠 **Bulleigh Barton Manor** (page 277)

St Andrew's Church is huge; it has a particularly magnificent rood screen, with inset saints and fan vaulting, and a 15th-century carved and painted pulpit resting on an old millstone. Sir Arthur Conan Doyle visited the village before writing his well-known *Hound of the Baskervilles*; living there at the time were his friend Bertram Fletcher Robinson, who lent Doyle his coachman Henry Baskerville to drive him around; and the Reverend Robert Duins Cooke (1859–1939), who regaled him with tales and information about Dartmoor. Robinson's home at Park Hill House and Baskerville's at 2 Wesley Terrace both still exist, and the gravestones of Cooke and Robinson can be seen in the churchyard. See also the box on pages 268–9 by Cooke's great-grandson, Alex Graeme.

Ipplepen is also helping to rewrite Roman history. It was previously thought that Roman influence in Devon had not extended far south of Exeter. However, a series of archaeological excavations, prompted by the discovery (by metal detectors) of many Roman coins in Ipplepen in 2009, have so far unearthed traces of a Roman road (possibly heading towards the Totnes area), and early remnants of bowls and amphorae from France and the Mediterranean that once held wine and olive oil. An early Christian cemetery (mid 7th century) beside the road indicates continued occupation of the site. The dig, a collaboration between Exeter University, the Portable Antiquities Scheme, Devon County Council and Cotswold Archaeology, continues each summer, so by the time you read this there should be news of more discoveries.

Torbryan

🏠 **Old Church House Inn** Torbryan (page 277)

This tiny hamlet was described by Hoskins in 1954 as having 'perhaps the most uniformly attractive village church in Devon'. Unusually, it was built in a single span of 20 years, from 1450 to 1470, making the resulting structure far more unified than one completed over a longer period. Also unusually, workmen would still have been young enough to finish the work that they started. What makes Holy Trinity Church exceptional, however, is that there has been no architectural messing around with its interior since it was built in the 15th century. It has the lime-washed exterior characteristic of Devon, and clear glass windows that let in plenty of light to set off the carved, polychromed oak screen, said to have been among the best-preserved medieval rood screens in Britain. But in 2013 two of its painted panels – representing St Victor of Marseilles and St Margaret of Antioch – were

"In 2013 two of its painted panels were hacked out roughly by thieves, leaving a gaping hole."

hacked out roughly by thieves, leaving a gaping hole. Two years later a sharp-eyed art collector spotted them in an online sale and alerted the police; in 2016, after £7,000-worth of repairs (to woodworm as well as damage from the theft) they were replaced, to great local delight. Together with many other panel paintings of saints in Devon churches they are reproduced in *A Cloud of Witnesses* by Diane Wilks (page 18). Holy Trinity is now cared for by the Churches Conservation Trust.

The old church house, dating from the 14th century or earlier, is now the Old Church House Inn (✆ 01803 812372 🖰 oldchurchhouseinn.co.uk), and is deservedly popular. The meat served here comes from nearby farms, the fish from Brixham and the vegetables from local growers. Retaining a host of old features, it's said to be one of the most haunted pubs in the south west. It has one of England's oldest bread ovens, and panelling retrieved from a ship of the Spanish Armada. It also does B&B (page 277) – for those who don't mind ghosts!

6 ORCHID PARADISE

Burnham Nurseries, Forches Cross TQ12 6PZ ✆ 01626 352233 🖰 orchids.uk.com ⏲ year-round except winter bank holidays, 10.00–16.00 daily

Anyone who loves the variety and beauty of orchids should be extremely happy here. Burnham Nurseries has a 'growing area' of interconnecting greenhouses containing orchids that are for sale, with careful instructions as to what conditions they prefer; while Orchid Paradise itself, in a smaller area, is crammed with delights: a private collection of rare (and sometimes amazing) plants accumulated over many years. It includes specimens from around the globe, many of which are nowhere else to be seen in the UK. Apart from the colours, the aroma is astonishing: a mixture of sweet, earthy and indefinable.

A family business since 1949 and twenty times gold-medal-winners at the Chelsea Flower Show, they have also contributed to the survival of orchids, propagating many rare species threatened with extinction. Arthur the Nursery Manager told me proudly that he has been working there for 41 years, and his boss is the third generation of her family to run it.

Masterclasses in orchid-keeping are held, plus orchid clinics. If you fall in love with a plant (and they are so seductive!) but can't take it with you on holiday, ask about mail order. The light and airy café, Café Vanilla, has good home baking and snacks, and also sells a selection of locally produced goods together with vanilla items (of course, since vanilla is an orchid …) from Little Pod near Exeter (⊘ littlepod.co.uk).

7 STOVER COUNTRY PARK

TQ12 6QG ⊘ 01626 835236 ⊘ devon.gov.uk/stover_country_park

Whoever thought up the idea of linking poetry with nature in this country park deserves an award. Stover is one of those agreeable places which has 'nothing to see' yet everything to observe. Within its 114 acres it brings you over heathland thick with gorse and heather, through deciduous trees and coniferous forests, along the banks of a river, adjacent to a tumbling stream and around a lake where herons stand sentinel among the reeds. A 100-yard, wheelchair-accessible aerial walkway overlooks ponds and woodland. The interpretation boards and the visitor centre are informative, and the place is child-friendly in the right way – for example, they have their own brass-rubbing trail, ten plaques with creatures on them hidden around the lake. No coloured plastic, just an attention-grabbing introduction to the wonders of nature. And then there's the Ted Hughes Poetry Trail. You may not have thought that you liked his poems (indeed many of them are pretty gloomy) but the 16 chosen here – about birds, fish and animals, and the natural world in general – are accessible and perfect for the surroundings. Sadly, for copyright reasons, they haven't been published in a booklet so you need to read them carefully in situ. It's a wonderfully Slow and peaceful occupation that takes about two hours. The park is 300 yards south of the Drumbridges roundabout on the A382 and bus 39 (Exeter to Newton Abbot) passes by. Cycle routes link it to Bovey Tracey and Newton Abbot: the 3½-mile Stover Trail (page 184) runs alongside, and Stover's 4½-mile circular Heritage Trail (waymarked from near the visitor centre) links up with the Templer Way (page 253).

8 ASHBURTON

Tourist information: North St (behind Town Hall) ✎ 01364 653426 ⬦ ashburton.org
◯ 09.30–16.30 Mon–Sat (closes earlier in winter)

One of Devon's four 14th-century stannary towns (page 226), along with Tavistock, Chagford and Plympton, Ashburton manages to combine its historic past with some energetic modern bustle. It's 'Slow' only if you're trying to ease your car through its busy streets – but there are some attractive old buildings, a good scattering of unusual independent shops and a warm sense of community. The small **Ashburton Museum** (✎ 01364 652539 ◯ May–Sep 14.00–16.00 Tue, Thu, Fri & 10.00–14.00 Sat), housed in a former brush factory in the centre of town, has a collection of miscellaneous local memorabilia and – rather surprisingly – North American artefacts. The 13th-century **Chapel of St Lawrence** in St Lawrence Lane, one of Ashburton's oldest buildings, started life as the private chapel of the Bishop of Exeter, then for more than 600 years was the town's grammar school. Some of the detail on its 18th-century decorative plasterwork is among the most impressive in any public building in Devon. It's now a heritage centre, open for a couple of hours four days a week from May to September, also for talks and concerts (⬦ stlawrencechapel.org.uk). Henry Baskerville, the coachman who drove Sir Arthur Conan Doyle around Dartmoor (pages 268–9), lived in Ashburton and is buried in the churchyard of St Andrew's.

The mixture of shops includes just about everything, from a guitar maker to a shop dedicated to graphic novels, with some good-quality clothing, crafts and house furnishings. It's also becoming consciously quite a foodie town (the Food Festival in September is a big and colourful affair), in the sense that excellent local meat, fish, delicatessen and vegetables are available. A great treat (or temptation) is **Moor Chocolate** at 18 East Street, with its array of traditional and newer sweets and chocolate, and if you value really good baking do buy homemade breads and cakes from **Ella Artisan Baker** (9 West St), but get there early – she sells out. All the banks have closed, but the post office on St Lawrence Lane provides what banking facilities it can (including an ATM) and also houses the public library.

There are art galleries, including a small one (12 East St) with work by sculptor Heather Jansch (pages 16–17), who creates amazing life-sized horse sculptures from driftwood. Art of an unexpected kind is the

ALE TASTERS, SCAVENGERS & PIG DROVERS

Ashburton is one of only a handful of towns in Britain to have retained the old Saxon office of Portreeve, dating back to 820AD and meaning the 'reeve' or supervisory official of a 'port' or trading centre. In those days the portreeve was often the only person in the community who could read and write, and his chief duty was to represent the king in legal transactions. Today Ashburton's portreeve may have rather less need to represent Her Majesty but is still elected annually, in November, along with his bailiff, bread weighers, ale tasters and other lesser officers such as Viewers of the Market, Viewers of Water Courses, Tree Inspector, Searcher and Sealer of Leather, Scavengers and Pig Drovers. You'll understand how vital these are for the smooth running of any 21st-century town.

Before Magna Carta there was no official check on the quality of ale or bread, and the first Ale Connors were appointed in London in 1276. Soon afterwards, there are records of brewers in Ashburton being fined for selling substandard ale. The tradition is renewed annually with a bread-weighing and ale-tasting ceremony in July, followed by a colourful medieval fair. One woman told me: 'As soon as there's a celebration of any kind, everyone pitches in and we have a right knees-up.'

For more on this, see ⬧ ashburton.org.

trompe l'oeil of Sir Walter Raleigh apparently leaning out of an upper window and smoking a cigarette, next to the Exeter Inn in West Street. It was painted by artist Emily Smith, and there's another one (of two chefs) on the left as you go up East Street, roughly opposite the Dartmoor Butcher. Sir Walter (apparently a regular drinker at the Inn, as allegedly was Sir Francis Drake) was arrested there in 1603 before being taken to the Tower, accused of plotting against King James I.

9 LANDSCOVE

🏠 & 🏚 **Anrán** (page 277)

Between Ashburton and Buckfastleigh and four miles or so from each, this small village is home to **Hill House Nursery** (TQ13 7LY ✐ 01803 762273 ☉ Mar–Oct daily), which has been described as being 'awash with treasures and temptations' in the several greenhouses and well-tended nursery. It also has pleasant gardens – you may spot a magnolia that came from Dame Agatha Christie's garden at Greenway (pages 106–7). The Nursery is tucked away behind the village church of St Matthew; in fact Hill House (which is not open to the public) used to be the church's vicarage. The network of lanes leading to Landscove are a bit of a tangle and some signs are hard to spot; if you miss the turning from the A38 southwest of Ashburton, then from Buckfastleigh follow the A384 towards Totnes and about quarter of a mile after the Dartbridge Inn take the first turning left, signposted Landscove and Hill House. If you find yourself at the church – its steeple is easily seen from afar – you can leave your car in the car park opposite and walk through the graveyard to the gardens.

Lunch at the Nursery Café (⊙ summer only 11.00–17.00) is a treat, with outdoor tables and a terrific selection of salads, sandwiches and scrumptious cakes as well as cream teas. To drink there are organic fruit juices and a good variety of wine and cider.

⟨⟩ FOOD & DRINK

Ashburton Cookery School Old Exeter Rd TQ13 7LG ✎ 01364 652784
✑ ashburtoncookeryschool.co.uk. The school runs a variety of cookery courses, from half a day to a week or weekend. B&B accommodation is available too, and the receptionist told me that some couples split their holidays so that one partner cooks by day while the other – the cookery widow or widower – follows some alternative pursuit. Courses cover a huge range: sweet, savoury, baking, patisserie, seafood, pasta and much more. Several of the chefs whose food you will taste around Devon were trained or refreshed here.

Hill House Nursery Café Landscove. See above.

Tea at Taylors 5 North St, Ashburton ✎ 01364 652631 ⊙ Mon–Sat, hours vary.
A welcoming, traditional English tearoom renowned for its delicious selection of homemade cakes. The carrot cake is so good that Mary Berry, who tried some when she was passing through Ashburton, asked for the recipe and included it in her next cookery book. Also cream teas and light savoury dishes.

The Old Library Restaurant North St, Ashburton ✎ 01364 652896 ⊙ 08.00–14.00 & 18.00–20.30, closed Sun evening & all day Tue. Attractively designed to give a light and airy feel to a smallish space, this is run by a couple who really care about food and add innovative touches to their European-influenced dishes. Vegetarian friendly. At busy times book ahead for dinner.

BUCKFASTLEIGH & AREA

Tourist information: 80 Fore St, Buckfastleigh ✎ 01364 644522 ✑ buckfastleigh.gov.uk
Here we have attractions ranging from otters, caves and miniature pigs, through a pub in a time warp and a vintage steam railway to leaf-cutter ants and prehistoric bones. No shortage of variety!

10 BUCKFASTLEIGH

Buckfastleigh is a tourist hub which deserves its popularity. Its name – buck-fast – indicates a stronghold, traditionally where deer were kept. Today it's a pleasant and somewhat sleepy town, but with many attractions within easy reach, and is the terminus/start of the steam train that runs between here and Totnes. This tranquillity contrasts with its earlier life as a buzzing industrial centre, with woollen mills, corn and paper mills and a tannery: in 1838 it had 700 looms in action, more than any other town in Devon.

The tourist information centre is conveniently next to **The Valiant Soldier** (⌀ 01364 644522), the town's most unusual attraction and well worth a browse. It's known as 'The pub where time was never called'. When the brewery withdrew its licence in 1965 it seems that the landlords, Mr and Mrs Roberts who'd run the pub for 27 years, simply said 'sod this', locked up, and walked away. They continued to live upstairs, but left the pub area as untouched as if their last customers had only just stepped out into the street. It was only after Alice Roberts, then widowed, sold the property in the mid 1990s that anyone realised what had happened, and Teignbridge council stepped in and bought the premises. It now offers the older generation a burst of nostalgia; the pub area is still as it was more than 50 years ago, when Bass was 1/2½ (less than 6p) a bottle. The only nostalgia you can't indulge in is an actual pint. Upstairs, the rooms have been turned into surprisingly touching representations of village rooms of that period, with personal and household items – clothing, toiletries, a vintage radio playing old tunes, an old Singer sewing machine, framed family photos – that those of us of a certain age remember so well. There's also a good World War I memorial room, again with touchingly personal items, whose display changes each year; and descriptions of the town's past from prehistoric times onwards.

THE SOUTH DEVON RAILWAY

⌀ 0843 3571420 ⌀ southdevonrailway.co.uk

Continuing the nostalgia theme, the South Devon Railway has it in dollops. Just a peep through the carriage windows at the compartments brings back a flood of memories to oldies, as do the acrid smell of the steam and the breathy toot of the whistle. The scenic branch line of the Great Western Railway running alongside the River Dart, built in 1872, was axed by Dr Beeching in 1958, but only 11 years later it was reopened – ironically by Dr Beeching himself – and this service between Buckfastleigh and Totnes is now run by a charitable trust and operated by volunteers.

Buckfastleigh's vintage railway station is a delight, with its evocative advertisements and memorabilia. A venerable old engine named *Lady Angela*, built in 1926, was parked there when I visited, with a notice

SQUIRE RICHARD CABELL & THE HOLY TRINITY CHURCH

Buckfastleigh's Holy Trinity Church is now an evocative ruin, though its spire can be seen for miles around as a reminder of the devilish forces at work on Dartmoor. The church was burned down beyond repair in 1992 when an intruder lit a fire beneath the altar. Was this the work of Satanists? Read on ...

In the graveyard is what looks like a summerhouse with a grille over the window. This is the burial chamber of the Cabell family. Richard Cabell was lord of the manor in the 17th century. He married a local heiress whom he is said subsequently to have hunted to her death with a pack of ferocious black hounds. Another version is that he had his throat torn out by his wife's loyal hound as he stabbed her to death. They say that he is buried in the family tomb, weighed down with a large stone to prevent him from getting out – not that this worked, since his headless ghost still haunts the moor. Sir Arthur Conan Doyle heard the stories when he was staying with a friend in Ipplepen (see box, pages 268–9), whose coachman then drove him to the church – and the coachman's name was Henry Baskerville! No prizes for guessing which Sherlock Holmes story the visit inspired.

That's the stuff of legends, but the reality is that this clearly unpleasant man, who took his wife's money and probably drove her to her death even if he didn't actually kill her, interred her in the tomb with the inscription: 'Here lies Susannah, wife of Richard Cabell, who was buried in linen'. Linen was the fabric of the nobility. The lower orders were required to wrap their corpses in wool to keep the local industry going, so Richard was openly flouting this rule. The tomb's iron grille was left in place, at the pleading of the villagers, during World War II when the government was requisitioning all iron railings; the parishioners of the Holy Trinity Church were taking no chances with their local villain. And when the church burnt down some local people said that it was the curse of Richard Cabell and the floor of the tomb was strewn with home-made 'Palm Sunday' crosses.

These days youngsters dare each other to come up to the tomb after dark, walk round it thirteen times (or maybe seven, accounts vary) in an anticlockwise direction, and then put their hand through the bars to see whether Squire Cabell (or the Devil) bites their fingers off.

saying that she was 'in the queue for a full boiler overhaul'. I felt a surge of sympathy. There's also a spacious refreshment room, a shop and the recently refurbished Railway Museum (✆ 0843 3571420 ⏱ year-round). Well-presented displays here include *Ashley*, a steam engine built in 1942, which shows children – and adults – how a steam train works. The only surviving broad-gauge locomotive, *Tiny*, is also here; the line was later converted to standard gauge. There are descriptions of the stations on the line and their history, and of Brunel's literally 'atmospheric' railway which used air pressure to drive the train (pages 32–3).

"*Ashley, a steam engine built in 1942, shows children – and adults – how a steam train works.*"

Steam locomotives make the round trip (via Staverton station, which appeared in a BBC adaptation of *The Hound of the Baskervilles*) four to nine times a day from April to October, and on Sundays and the odd weekday during other months; the occasional diesel loco also operates. Schedules may change on days when there are special events: a comprehensive timetable is on the website and you can book tickets online.

A perfect day out is to leave your car at Buckfastleigh's free car park by the station, and buy a 'triple ticket'. This gives you the 30-minute train ride to Totnes plus a visit to Otters & Butterflies (next to Buckfastleigh station, below) and/or the Totnes Rare Breeds Farm (by Totnes station, pages 88–9). Both animal places are small and owner-run. It doesn't work as well in reverse, because parking in Totnes is more limited, expensive and some way from the station.

11 DARTMOOR OTTERS & BUCKFAST BUTTERFLIES (OTTERS & BUTTERFLIES)

TQ11 0DZ ✆ 01364 642916 ⏱ ottersandbutterflies.co.uk ⏱ Apr–end Oct 10.00–17.00. It's signposted from the station & is just off the A38, about 1 mile from Buckfastleigh. Satnavs may take you past the turning so watch for signs.

The butterfly centre was founded in 1984 by David and Sue Field, who added the otter part in 1988 because of the proximity of the river Dart. 'It seemed an obvious thing to use this in some way. Originally we wanted to divert a stream to run through the grounds to create otter pools but this wasn't permitted, so the water is pumped out and in each day so they are swimming in river water.'

Completely protected from the elements by their thick, waterproof fur, the otters are particularly lively before feeding times: 11.30, 14.00 and 16.00. The three species here are North American, Asian short-clawed and British, all displaying different characteristics. The large North American river otters, for instance, are particularly adept at balancing upright, meerkat-style. 'That's Toronto,' said Tim, the keeper. 'He's nicknamed Kenwood because he's such an efficient food processor and never gets full.'

If you wear glasses, they'll steam up in cool weather when you move from the otters to the butterfly house. Even on a gloomy autumn day there were plenty of eye-catching butterflies in evidence, but Sue said that they are far more active on bright, warm days. More easily studied are the rows of chrysalises attached to bamboos, showing the range of colours and sizes of these pre-butterflies. As you watch them, one or another may start to twitch, and it's a huge temptation to stay until they hatch.

Equally enthralling is the colony of Costa Rican leaf-cutter ants in the reception area, holding their leaves aloft like tiny sails as they file unswervingly along the walkway to their fungus garden. Apart from leaves, they apparently like fruit cake, Rice Crispies, used teabags and cooked ham or chicken, which must make for pretty exotic fungus. There's also a small display of rescued reptiles in reception, together with stick insects and an axolotl.

BUCKFASTLEIGH CAVES

William Pengelly Cave Studies Trust, Russets Lane, Buckfastleigh TQ11 0DY ℰ 01752 775195 ℰ pengellytrust.org

A visit to the little-known Pengelly Centre is a serious but highly rewarding undertaking. There is no attempt here to provide entertainment – the newly-refurbished museum with its informative displays and the 1½- to 2-hour tours are aimed at adults and bright children who want to know about local history, geology and palaeontology.

Most of the work here is scientific, and volunteers from the William Pengelly Cave Studies Trust are only available to give tours a few times a week, normally Wednesday and Thursday in the summer, so check their website or phone before making plans.

The caves were discovered by local men exploring the disused quarries in the 1930s. On the floor of one cave they found some bones and took them to the museum in Torquay. 'Nothing of importance – just pigs and cows' they were told. Not satisfied by this explanation, they sent them to the Natural History Museum in London. This time the reaction was quite different, and the area was cordoned off until the experts, who had correctly identified the fossilised bones of elephant, hippopotamus and hyena, could take a look. These huge animals, all larger than present-day species, thrived in Devon during the warm period that preceded the last ice age, around 120,000 years ago.

"Elephant, hippopotamus and hyena thrived in Devon during the warm period that preceded the last ice age."

The tour starts with a video explaining the geology of the area and a description of the greater horseshoe bats (see box, page 181) which roost in one of the caves. The nub of the tour is a visit to Joint Mitnor Cave, now easily accessible via a system of boardwalks, where the most exciting finds were made – over 3,000 bones, dug out of the cave floor and walls. A long-ago earthquake opened a hole in the roof of the cavern, and animals fell in.

Herbivores such as bison were followed by their predators, hyenas. These two species provided the majority of bones found, but there were also wild boar, hippopotamus, bear and rhinoceros, as well as four straight-tusked elephants – two adults and two calves.

SOMETHING OLD, SOMETHING NEW ...

In September 2015, thieves broke through the huge steel door to the Joint Mitnor cave and stole some of its precious bones, including an elephant's tooth. They seem to have been professionals, possibly working for a private collector, as it was a slick job and they knew what to take. Despite enquiries throughout the caving and museum communities, no item from their haul has yet been found.

Technology to the rescue! When the cave reopened to the public in August 2017, all seemed to be as it was before the theft; but any paleontologist unknowingly inspecting the bones would have been very startled by their composition. In fact, bones excavated from the same cave in the 1960s had been copied on a 3D photocopier at the University of Birmingham, and the resulting polymer plastic replicas were then cast in gypsum in Cornwall. The elephant's tooth, a far more complex item than the average university 3D photocopier generally encounters, actually broke two machines in the process. London's Natural History Museum, which already had a Joint Mitnor collection, also contributed its expertise and high-tech scanning facilities.

And thus a little scrap of prehistory was re-created by the present day.

The adults, in fact, were too large to fall through the hole but probably became wedged and unable to escape. These elephants were far larger than present-day African elephants, the adults standing at around 15 to 20 feet high. Together with them were found the bones of brown bears and animals familiar in the British countryside today: foxes, voles, badgers, red deer and fallow deer. Quite a few bones have been left to add interest to what is already a fascinating visit. Eventually the cave filled up with animal remains and debris and was no longer a death trap. The last ice age, around 20,000 years ago, probably covered it completely until the 20th-century quarry men opened it.

12 BUCKFAST ABBEY

TQ11 0EE ✆ 01364 645500 ⬦ buckfast.org.uk

The brochure says that Buckfast Abbey, founded in the 11th century and demolished in the 16th following the Dissolution of the Monasteries, is now 'home to a community of Benedictine monks who lead a life of prayer, work and study'. I don't doubt it, but they've also created a thriving commercial enterprise teeming with visitors who happily pay high prices at the well-stocked Monastic Produce Shop and gift shop, and flock to the modern abbey in numbers exceeding those to our great cathedrals. It's utterly commendable in the sense that the profits from tourism undoubtedly sustain the life of prayer. Nevertheless, something about it leaves me feeling a little uncomfortable.

"The abbey church was rebuilt by just a handful of the monks themselves."

That said, entrance to the site is free, as is parking; it's a peaceful setting and there's a wonderfully relaxed feeling about the place, with people strolling contentedly, quietly enjoying all it has to offer without any laid-on entertainment. There's also the extraordinary achievement of the abbey church, rebuilt by just a handful of the monks themselves, starting around a hundred years ago. By hand they cut the great stones to shape, lashed wooden scaffolding together, hauled the stones up on rudimentary pulleys … it took them 32 years, and the imposing St Mary's Church that you see today is the result.

Beekeeping here is also an interesting story, and Brother Adam, who worked with the abbey's bees for over 70 years, is world famous for breeding a new strain which was a high honey producer, relatively gentle, and resistant to disease. Over four decades he travelled some 100,000 miles to isolated areas of Europe, Asia and North Africa, persuading local beekeepers to give him queens from their indigenous strains; these he posted back to Buckfast. The result is known as the Buckfast bee, and its products are sold in the Monastic Shop – along with the famous Buckfast Tonic Wine, which made headlines a few years ago because of its rather incongruous popularity among young and anti-social drinkers. Beekeeping courses are held for both beginners and improvers.

Bees are contented visitors to the lavender garden, which has around 150 species of lavender (when it's in flower, the perfume is wonderful). There are also sensory and physic gardens and spacious lawns, as well as some fine mature trees. Retreats of various lengths are available in the monks' guest accommodation.

The Grange Restaurant, which incorporates the 12th-century arch of the old north gate and whose outdoor patio has a wonderful view of the abbey, provides a good range of food (lunches, teas, snacks) in pleasant surroundings.

Buses serve Buckfast from Newton Abbot, Ashburton and Buckfastleigh. A tourist leaflet on the Abbey can be downloaded from ⊘ tourismleafletsonline.com.

13 PENNYWELL FARM
TQ11 0LT 🕾 01364 642023 ⊘ pennywellfarm.co.uk ⊙ Feb–Oct 10.00–17.00 daily

Forget conservation and endangered species, this hands-on animal place is just that – its aim is to bring humans and animals as close together as possible and as such it offers one of Devon's most rewarding experiences for children. Just look at the expression of a little girl gently stroking a tiny dozing piglet, and you'll see how well it works. Or sometimes doesn't, as disgruntled squeals then make very clear; but whenever a baby cries there are nursemaids – or nursemen – on hand to retrieve it for a soothing word or two.

Pennywell has been selectively breeding miniature pigs since 1992, with the result that a piglet weighs just eight ounces at birth and grows to about the size of a springer spaniel. It's not just the miniature piglets you can hug. The rabbits and older piglets are remarkably tolerant of human attention too, and selected ones are held in pens where visitors can join them for a stroke. As a pig enthusiast I was just as thrilled as the little kids around me when a piglet collapsed on its side in ecstasy as I scratched it under the chin.

PENNYWELL'S MINIATURE PIGS

I talked to the ebullient Chris Murray about his miniature pigs. 'I've always loved pigs. I studied Agriculture at Seale-Hayne and got interested in breeding pigs then. They're ideal animals for selective breeding because they have two litters a year and up to 18 piglets per litter. Of course in those days we were breeding for improved meat, and we wanted our pigs to grow fast. Now it's the opposite – we want small, slow-growing pigs. All sorts of traditional breeds have been used in our breeding programme: Iron Age wild boar, Gloucester old spot and Tamworth for colour, Berkshire, middle white because they're small with smiley faces, kune-kune which have a nice temperament, and English lop, which are docile. We aimed for other small details too – for instance we wanted prick ears rather than lop. But not too small because tiny ears look mean. And we wanted a short snout, because it's more appealing, and the right mouth. It took us 16 years to breed the smile!

Yes, we sell them. As pets, of course. We have some lovely customers here. One lady has a pig that sits on the sofa and watches television with her and there's a man who takes his pig on bike rides.'

Every half hour there is something different happening, such as ferret racing, pig racing (the contestants nonchalantly pause in their canter from time to time for a nibble of grass), bottle feeding or a falconry display, and there are plenty of non-animal activities for children too. A plus on wet days is that many of the pens and activities are under cover.

UPDATES WEBSITE

You can post your comments and recommendations, and read feedback and updates from other readers online at ⊘ bradtupdates.com/sdevon.

**THE NORTHWESTERN
FRINGE OF DARTMOOR**

7

THE NORTHWESTERN FRINGE OF DARTMOOR

This is an area where the ancient underlies the merely old. Medieval thatched cottages, centuries-old inns and much-loved little village churches occupy land where prehistoric monoliths, hut circles and burial cairns once stood, and the footprints of early people stretch back a long, long way. Sheep and red Devon cattle graze in the fields, and crops ripen through deepening shades of green to dusty gold. Between gaps in the trees, the hills and tors of Dartmoor appear as a distant backdrop.

Parts lie away from the tourist routes, allowing the occasional hamlet to be unselfconsciously unadorned. In one tourist information centre the assistant told me: 'The cottages down there are lovely because they haven't been titillated,' leaving me to wonder what a titillated cottage might get up to. Others are in their full thatched and whitewashed finery, with competitive gardens and cats dozing on windowsills.

WET-WEATHER ACTIVITIES
Finch Foundry Sticklepath (page 208)
Okehampton Museum of Dartmoor Life (pages 212–13)

GETTING THERE & AROUND

This area isn't on the regular national **rail network**. However, on Sundays from May to September, the national rail operator for the region (currently the Great Western Railway), together with the Dartmoor Railway (page 207), runs four trains a day from Exeter to Okehampton, calling at Crediton and Sampford Courtenay stations, in connection with Devon County Council's '**Sunday Rover**' initiative. This gives access to a day of travel on both rail and bus services; its routes and timetables are available from local TICs and ⬦ dartmoor-railway-sa.org/sundayrover.

The appropriate bus timetable for the area is West Devon. Okehampton is covered by buses 5A, 6 and 6A from Exeter, 46 from Tavistock and 178 (only twice daily) from Newton Abbot. The 178 also goes to the 'beacon villages' apart from Belstone, which has the 670 from Okehampton (once each way, only on Thursdays). Sampford Courtenay is served by the 5A from Exeter and (three times a week) by the 631 and 648 from Okehampton, as well as – on summer Sundays – by the Dartmoor Railway.

SELF-POWERED TRAVEL

Roads are good throughout the area and it's not excessively hilly. The **Granite Way** is an 11-mile walk/cycle route from Okehampton to Lydford, mostly following the course of the old Southern Region railway line so gradients are gentle; it's part of the Devon Coast-to-Coast cycle route between Ilfracombe and Plymouth (page 152) and National Cycle Network route 27, and much of it lies within Dartmoor National Park. It's relatively easy going, entirely off-road for six miles between Okehampton and Lake Viaduct, and ideal for families and those whose cycling is rusty. See drakestrail.co.uk/pdfs/cycling-leismaps-graniteway.pdf or look for the leaflet in TICs. There are numerous smaller walks, some on lanes and some on footpaths. The relevant OS maps are Landranger 191 and Explorer OL 28 (Dartmoor). It's also shown in adequate detail (and with all pubs marked!) on the handy Croydecycle *South Devon* map (pages 13–14).

For walkers, the 24-mile **Two Castles Trail** links the Norman castles of Okehampton and Launceston, which was the ancient capital of Cornwall. It never strays far from bus or train routes so you can easily break it into sections. Devon County Council's very comprehensive guide is available in TICs or you can download the pdf from devon. gov.uk/two-castles-trail-booklet.pdf. Sampford Courtenay is another pleasant walking area, and historically interesting (pages 215–16), while from nearby Jacobstowe with its 12th-century church the southernmost tip of the Tarka Trail leads south along the bank of the Okement River to Okehampton.

 CYCLE HIRE

Adventure Okehampton Youth Hostel, Klondyke Road, Okehampton EX20 1EW 01837 53916 adventureokehampton.com

Devon Cycle Hire Sourton Down EX20 4HR 01837 861141 devoncyclehire.co.uk

COMBINATION TRAVEL

A happy blend for walkers, cyclists and rail buffs (you could even throw in buses too, by catching one to Okehampton) is offered by the diesel train service operated by the **Dartmoor Railway** from Okehampton (pages 213–14). This normally uses heritage stock lovingly restored by volunteers from the Dartmoor Railway Supporters Association to provide a tourist service to Meldon Viaduct. They run it at weekends in the high season; check times and availability first by phone (✆ 01837 55164) or on the website ⬧ dartmoor-railway-sa.org. One of those volunteers, Dave Clegg, describes the short trip: 'The journey to Meldon Viaduct may take only about 15 minutes but there is plenty to see. You have an unbeatable view of ruined Okehampton Castle (page 213), with its leaning eastern wall, down below in the valley, alongside the West Okement river. The now-closed Meldon Quarry, which used to supply ballast for the whole of the Southern Railway, now uses the sidings to store much of its rolling stock.'

Meldon Viaduct station is currently the end of the line, but the track continues as the Granite Way cycle path to Lydford. And the good news is that a guard's van on the train can carry up to 20 bicycles as well as pushchairs. Walkers can return to Okehampton by train or on foot (downhill!) along the Granite Way, or continue, perhaps, to Sourton to lunch at the extraordinary Highwayman Inn (see box, page 219). But even if you're not a walker, you shouldn't miss the two-minute stroll from the train to the Meldon Viaduct (now a scheduled Ancient Monument), which straddles the West Okement Valley. The views as you walk across the viaduct are magnificent.

THE BEACON VILLAGES

🏠 **Oxenham Arms** South Zeal (page 277), **The Tors Inn** Belstone (page 277)
⚑ **King's Arms** South Zeal (page 277)

The four 'beacon villages' – Sticklepath, South Tawton, South Zeal and Belstone – are so named because they're all located at the base of **Cosdon Beacon**, a broad 1,804ft hill where signal fires were lit in medieval times; it was thought to be the highest point on Dartmoor. Extensive prehistoric remains, including hut circles and cairns, have been found on its slopes; during the 19th century, many were robbed of their stones by villagers seeking free building materials. Roads leading from one beacon village to the other are a bit labyrinthine but the signposting is reasonably clear. Driving or walking between them you'll be playing hide-and-seek with the outline of Dartmoor in its various moods, one minute looming as a backdrop and the next nowhere in sight.

1 STICKLEPATH

Sticklepath has some fine thatched cottages, but its main point of interest is the **Finch Foundry** (⌀ 01837 840046; National Trust; café & gift shop), which isn't actually a foundry at all but the last working water-powered forge in the country. In its heyday it made around 400 tools a day (sickles, scythes, shovels and more) for local farmers and miners. You can watch the machinery in action, and the precision of the great handmade wheels, cogs and other parts is amazing. Tucked away behind the forge is a peaceful little Quaker graveyard, probably dating from soon after 1700. The small thatched arbour there was built by a certain Thomas Pearse (yes, that's the one, and presumably he had a grey mare) who was himself buried in the graveyard, in 1875, aged 81. Sticklepath also has an energetic team of female Morris dancers, **Cogs & Wheels Ladies Morris**, who may be found performing in local venues between May and September.

2 SOUTH TAWTON

South Tawton was a royal manor at the time of the Domesday survey and its fertile land made for successful farming; wealth from the wool trade expanded a smaller, probably 11th-century chapel into the mainly 15th-century granite **church of St Andrew**, a listed building that towers above the village today and has some exceptional medieval carved bosses above the nave and aisles. Unfortunately they're hard to distinguish from below because they're covered with some kind of brown stain (binoculars and a strong torch are helpful), but they've been painstakingly photographed for the Church House website (below).

Beside the church the picturesque thatched **Church House** (⌀ 01837 840418 ⬦ thechurchhouse.org.uk ☉ May–Oct 11.00–17.00 Sun as a heritage visitor centre) was built soon after 1490 as a parish centre where all parishioners could gather to enjoy 'Church ales'. These were parties organised to fundraise for the church's upkeep and to help the poor, in much the same way that churches hold fundraising coffee

DARTMOOR

Dartmoor is one of England's last true wildernesses, where you can wander for hours without seeing a house or road. Its slopes are scattered with remnants of its prehistoric past. But the national park is not all high moorland; around the perimeter are small villages, cultivated fields and tumbling rivers.

1 Brentor, the highest church in England.

HELEN HOTSON/S

2 Dartmoor ponies are an integral part of moor conservation. 3 The moor provides a challenge for mountain bikers. 4 The skylark's soaring song is part of the Dartmoor experience. 5 The Two Moors Way runs for 102 miles between Dartmoor and Exmoor, ending at the north Devon coast.

SANDRA STANDBRIDGE/S

SUE VICCARS/TWOMOORSWAY.ORG

WIG WORLAND/A

6 Hound Tor, the start and end of several walks. The legend has it that when Bowerman the Hunter disturbed a coven of witches on the moor, they turned him and his hounds to stone. The jumble of rocks on this tor are the hounds, with Bowerman himself nearby. **7** Wistman's Wood: 'A green-coated fairyland of gnarled and twisted boughs.'

PLYMOUTH

Big, sprawling, maritime Plymouth – self-styled 'Britain's Ocean City' – was in olden times the haunt of seafarers, smugglers, pirates and world explorers, and traces of its Elizabethan past remain in the Barbican's cobbled alleys. In 2020, it hosts the 400-year celebration of the *Mayflower*'s epic voyage.

1 Royal William Yard – formerly the old Royal Naval victualling yard. 2 Smeaton's Tower on Plymouth Hoe was once the Eddystone lighthouse. 3 The Mayflower Steps, where in 1620 the Pilgrim Fathers began their voyage into history.

mornings today. It was 'ale money' that paid for the roof carvings, in the late 1400s. On the ground floor was the kitchen where ale was brewed and food was cooked in the great fireplace; the feasting hall upstairs with massive roof trusses and a large window could have housed a great deal of medieval jollity. In the 17th century the hall was used as a school, and from 1804 through Victorian times as a poorhouse. During World War II, soldiers were billeted there after Dunkirk.

3 SOUTH ZEAL

In the mid 13th century, the de Tony family who held the manor of South Tawton were granted royal permission to form a borough – a 'new town' – straddling the main route between Exeter and Cornwall: that town became South Zeal. In 1298 it was granted a charter for two annual fairs and a weekly market. The 'strip' layout at right angles to the single broad main street, still visible today, allowed householders street access in front, with a narrow strip of land continuing behind the house where gardens and workshops could be sited. South Zeal also has a number of medieval through-passage and Tudor houses, and the history of the town has been carefully researched; an excellent website is ⊘ south-zeal.eu, and the South Tawton and District Local History Group has produced a booklet *South Zeal: A glimpse at the Village's Past*, on sale in the **Country Store and Tearoom** (itself in a through-passage house, with a splendidly large fireplace). There's a **14th-century market cross** and the appealing little **St Mary's Chapel** with its unusual 15th-century bell turret, as well as two pubs. In August the annual Dartmoor Folk Festival (⊘ dartmoorfolkfestival.org.uk) erupts into the village, as it has done since 1981, filling it with music and activity.

FOOD & DRINK

Country Store & Tea Room ⊘ 01837 840318. Sharing the ground floor of a medieval cottage in the main street, the store stocks various necessities including local vegetables and baking, while the tea room has a massive fireplace, comfy chairs and extremely good cakes. The village computer is also here, making it South Zeal's very own medieval cybercafé.

King's Arms ⊘ 01837 840300 ⊖ noon–23.00 daily. This cheery place with friendly staff dates back to the 16th century but is very involved in today's village activities: you may find local folk groups playing here, or seasonal themed evenings. Their cider is made at a farm less than 20 miles away. Hearty pub food is available noon–14.30 and 16.00–21.00. There's also a simple campsite (toilets are available but no showers) with a good view of the moor.

Oxenham Arms ✐ 01837 840244 ⊙ 11.00–23.00 daily. The oldest heritage inn in Devon and Cornwall and probably originally a monastery, it is thought to have been built by 12th-century lay monks – and they incorporated a 5,000-year-old standing stone into one of its inner walls. Another room has a similar menhir supporting the ceiling. It's a rambling place, visibly full of history. Lunches are available noon–14.30, evening meals 18.00–21.00, and cream teas all afternoon. There's also luxury B&B in beautifully furnished period rooms, some with four-posters (page 277).

4 BELSTONE

This peaceful, charming, leafy village right on the edge of Dartmoor is mentioned as Bellestan or Bellestam in the Domesday Book. It's full of history and moorland atmosphere, with some traditional old stone and thatched cottages, grazing ponies, dramatic Dartmoor views, a Norman church and an incised granite ring-cross dated to the 7th to 9th centuries, suggesting a much earlier place of worship. Similar crosses have been found and dated in south Wales and early Christian sites in the southwest of Ireland. Unusually for village churches, in the 19th century men and women were separated during services here, with men on the south side of the nave and women on the north. The history of the village and area is most painstakingly recorded in *The Book of Belstone* by Chris and Marion Walpole (2002). It's full of anecdotes and personal touches: look for it secondhand on Amazon or in the village café.

The old stocks (now a Grade II-listed monument) still sit on the village green – slats of wood between two granite pillars – as if awaiting some lingering medieval miscreant, and one house still has its old iron pump outside. Belstone is popular with walkers, out on a moorland ramble and heading through to visit a nearby prehistoric stone circle, the somewhat unimaginatively named **Nine Stones** (I counted 21), which is actually a prehistoric cairn: a burial place within a circle of stones. Or, it's a circle of maidens who were turned to stone for dancing on the Sabbath. Your choice. According to one story you'll always count a different number, as one or other skips outside the circle when your back is turned. It's marked on OS Explorer map 28. Once you're through the gate at the end of the road, follow the track to the end of the stone wall, then head uphill and you'll see it.

'The cakes are just arriving,' a man called out cheerily, as he bustled past me with a large box. I was standing by the village green outside the **Old School Tearoom** (✐ 01837 52762), waiting for it to open.

His box's contents were on the counter by the time I went in: some lovely fresh, sticky home baking. On shelves and dressers along the walls were rows of differently sized teapots wearing colourful knitted tea cosies (I couldn't resist one shaped like a sheep), with various other bits of vintage china. Vases of bluebells brightened the tables, and wooden benches were softened by cushions. Jars of homemade jam and chutney were for sale. I loved it! My pot of tea (vintage china, of course) was hot and strong, and my slice of fruit cake was delicious. Opening hours, posted outside on a blackboard, may vary seasonally; when I visited they were 14.00–17.30, Friday to Monday. Check ⊘ theoldschooltearoom.moorsites.com.

For something a bit stronger than tea, the **Tors Inn** (⊘ 01837 840689) is a friendly, unpretentious, traditional Dartmoor pub, popular with locals and walkers. Meals are freshly cooked and generous, and it also does B&B (page 277).

THE REVEREND SABINE BARING-GOULD (1834–1924)

Squire, parson, scholar, antiquarian, novelist, hymn-writer, collector of folk songs … and Sabine Baring-Gould's father had hoped he would be just a mathematician. When he was 34 he married Grace, the 18-year-old daughter of a Yorkshire mill-hand; in the next 21 years they had 15 children and their marriage lasted 48 years. He had carved on her tombstone *Dimidium Animae Meae*, meaning 'half my soul'. In 1872 when he was rector of East Mersea in Essex his father died, and he inherited the Lewtrenchard family estates. The manor house at the time was only one room wide; Sabine extended it, filled it with artistic treasures and created today's stately Lewtrenchard Manor (page 277). As squire, he could appoint himself parson of the parish – and did so; he called himself a squarson. He wrote numerous articles and papers on subjects as diverse as Icelandic folklore and candle-snuffers. He was also a prolific novelist (some tales were quite racy for a clergyman, with a fair bit of bosom-heaving and moustache-twirling), wrote the words of the hymns *Onward Christian Soldiers* and *Now the Day is Over*, and painstakingly tracked down and transcribed old English folksongs that he feared might otherwise be forgotten. His huge collection, one of the most significant West Country collections of the Victorian era, has now been digitised; for details see ⊘ sbgsongs.org.

He lovingly restored St Peter's Church on the estate, adding art and beauty to it in his own unrestrained style, and is buried in its churchyard; the parishioners installed electricity in his memory. He would no doubt be satisfied that it's now listed in Todd Gray's *Devon's Fifty Best Churches*.

OKEHAMPTON & AROUND

The past plays a big role in this section, what with the Dartmoor Railway's beautifully recreated heritage railway station and trains, the Museum of Dartmoor Life in Okehampton, echoes of the Prayer Book Rebellion at Sampford Courtney and the dramatic ruin of 11th-century Okehampton Castle. So prepare for some gentle nostalgia!

5 OKEHAMPTON

🏠 **Betty Cottles Inn** (page 277)

Tourist information: The Okehampton TIC has closed, but the Museum of Dartmoor Life (3 West St ✆ 01837 52295 ○ Apr–Oct 10.00–15.00 Mon–Fri & 10.00–13.00 Sat) has information & a good website: ⊘ museumofdartmoorlife.org.uk

This is one of only two market towns mentioned in the 1086 Domesday Survey of Devon, and in medieval times was an important centre. Its surprisingly wide main street was once the old London Road to Cornwall and held a third row of buildings, which included an ancient guildhall and a 17th-century covered market. These were demolished in 1850. The 15th-century St James's Chapel is the oldest building, and one of only five in England that is strictly non-denominational. Pigs were once used to hoover up the garbage in the streets and were housed near the chapel; the pig-shaped cycle-stands nearby are a reminder of this.

Economically the town is struggling and some high-street shops have closed; but several small independent shops and boutiques down side alleys are flourishing, particularly those offering fresh local produce: baked goods, meat, vegetables, fruit, etc. There's also good-quality country clothing, and the **Red Lion Yard Retail Village** has a pleasantly boutiquey feel. Its Dovecote Tearoom & Bar was impressively full when we checked at lunchtime, there's very good coffee at Grants, and the Red Lion Bakery (you can smell its bread as you approach) has sweet and savoury baking plus hot drinks and sandwiches. A nearby small shopping arcade that's a miniature version of London's Burlington Arcade is an extra treat.

The **Museum of Dartmoor Life** (see *Tourist Information*, above) is well worth a visit. It's housed in an old mill (dated 1811) with a restored waterwheel, tucked away down an alley with cobbles down the middle and mosaics on the sides, roughly opposite Lloyds Bank. Its three floors of exhibits cover around 5,000 years from prehistoric times to the present day. You'll find Bronze Age, Roman and Saxon collections, historic Dartmoor trades and industries, transport, and the military – with quirky personal links bringing history to life.

Perched on a hillside about a mile from the centre of town is 11th-century **Okehampton Castle** (✆ 01837 52844 ⊙ Apr–Nov; English Heritage), an atmospheric and allegedly haunted ruin that is said to have been Devon's largest castle. Built soon after the Norman Conquest and originally a motte-and-bailey construction with a stone keep, in the 14th century it was converted into a private residence by the Earl of Devon. In the 16th century, after his descendant fell into dispute with Henry VIII and was beheaded, it was left to decay. The walls are feeling their age now and you can explore the interior only when the site is open, but the view of its ancient stonework silhouetted against the sky is dramatic at any time, and there are attractive woodland and riverside walks nearby. When I approached in February the grass below its walls looked frosty, until I realised that the 'frost' was a mass of snowdrops.

"When I approached in February the grass below its walls looked frosty, until I realised that the 'frost' was a mass of snowdrops."

An unusual and popular annual event in Okehampton is the **Baring-Gould Folk Weekend** (⌂ wrenmusic.co.uk) in October, inspired by Sabine Baring-Gould (see box, page 211). His was the first systematic attempt to collect the traditional songs of English country folk, particularly in west Devon.

Okehampton Station & Meldon Viaduct

The beautifully restored **Okehampton Station** (✆ 01837 52762 ⌂ dartmoorrailway.com), a ten-minute walk from the centre of town, is open daily throughout the year (except over Christmas when special events take place) and its loving period refurbishment and displays of railway memorabilia will stir the heart of anyone over a certain age: you're transported straight back to the days of chatty ticket officers, wooden luggage trolleys piled high with trunks and leather suitcases, old railway posters and baskets of flowers. The **Old Station Tea Room** (⊙ 10.00–17.00 Mon–Fri, longer at w/ends) is a friendly and pleasant place with all-day breakfasts, light lunches, fish and chips, pasties, afternoon teas, good baking and a comfortably nostalgic atmosphere. There is also a **railway museum**, and a (weekend) shop aimed at the

WILD SWIMMING IN MELDON LAKE

Joanna Griffin

Not to be confused with the nearby Meldon Reservoir, where swimming is not permitted, Meldon Lake (known locally as Meldon Pond) is an old limestone quarry, south of Okehampton. Follow signs to Meldon Quarry which will take you to a car park from where you will be able to see the lake between the trees. It is a five-to-ten-minute walk down to the water from here. At one end of the lake is a striking rock face with long trails of overhanging ivy. The water, which turns a dazzling shade of green in the sun, is deep and much warmer than the rivers, and it is possible to have a good long swim here. It's a bit of scramble down a short, steep well-worn part of the bank among a tangle of hawthorn ragwort and other shrubs, but it is well worth it.

enthusiast market. The team of volunteers are kept busy, as Dave Clegg (page 207) explained: 'There are so many aspects to running a railway – train crews, catering, station maintenance, tending flower beds, refurbishing the rolling stock and engines, running tombolas to raise funds, and so on. Volunteers are involved in all of these activities and, speaking as a "regular", I can say how heart-warming it is when the public give positive feedback about what we are achieving.'

Plans currently being discussed by Devon County Council and other involved local councils may possibly see a return to regular train services between Okehampton and Exeter in the next few years, once GWR electrification releases sufficient diesel trains. A new Okehampton Parkway station is also proposed, to attract traffic from the adjacent A30. Thankfully this will not replace the existing gem, but both initiatives would give a great boost to Okehampton's prosperity.

Nearby **Meldon Viaduct**, a scheduled ancient monument with spectacular views, is a dramatic example of Victorian engineering: one of only two examples in Britain of a wrought-iron truss-girder viaduct. Spanning the deep, steep river gorge required a strong but flexible structure; the wrought-iron and cast-iron frame consisted of six 90-foot warren trusses on five wrought-iron lattice trestles, riveted together. It was built in 1874 for the main line between Waterloo and Plymouth, then doubled in width (to allow a second track) in 1878 and finally closed to trains in the late 1960s. Now it's a part of the Granite Way (pages 206–7 and 228). **Meldon Reservoir**, accessible by road and via a diversion from the Granite Way, is 900 feet above sea level;

it was created in 1972 by a dam across the West Okement River, and offers fine views over the moors and to the viaduct. It's managed by the South West Lakes Trust (⊘ swlakestrust.org.uk). **Black-a-Tor Copse National Nature Reserve**, on the bank of the West Okement as it flows into the reservoir, is one of Britain's best examples of high-altitude oak woodland, nationally important for the great variety of lichens on its trees and rocks. The only comparable one in Devon is Wistman's Wood (pages 269–70).

6 SAMPFORD COURTENAY

This village five miles or so north of Okehampton is known mainly for its involvement in the Prayer Book Rebellion of 1549 (see box, below). It's also a stop on the Dartmoor Railway's summer Sunday service from Exeter (page 205) so is accustomed to visitors and presents itself well, having 70 or so listed buildings and monuments. As Arthur Mee wrote 70-odd years ago: 'It is charming, with white cottages and thatched roofs

THE PRAYER BOOK REBELLION

As part of the Protestant reforms instigated under the boy king Edward VI, the familiar prayer book in Latin was declared illegal and, from Whit Sunday 1549, churches in England were required to adopt the new *Book of Common Prayer* in English and to adapt their traditional rituals. Resistance to this was particularly strong among the villagers of Devon and Cornwall, as people saw their traditional methods of worship under threat. At Sampford Courtenay they likened the English prayer book to a 'Christmas game', something like a Nativity play without true substance; initially their priest obeyed orders, removed his robes and conducted the 'new' Sunday service, but vocal parishioners quickly forced him to revert to the Latin form. Others dissented, a fracas developed, and in the melée a local man was stabbed with a pitchfork on the steps of the Church House and then hacked to death.

Villagers in their thousands, armed with no more than farm implements and staves, then rose in support and marched to Exeter, laying siege to the city and demanding the withdrawal of the English version. The siege lasted six weeks, but in the end the rebels were no match for the well-armed military force sent to quell them: more than 3,500 died in skirmishes in Devon, including 1,300 in a final stand at Sampford Courtenay. The militia continued into Cornwall and, by the time the rebels were crushed, some 4,000 from both counties had died – and to little eventual purpose, as when Edward's half-sister Mary, who was a devout Catholic, succeeded him in 1553 she re-legalised the Latin version anyway.

and a lofty pinnacled tower. Old crosses keep watch by the road, and another guards the 15th-century church.' That church, **St Andrew's**, rebuilt from an earlier building in 1450 and mentioned in Simon Jenkins's *England's Thousand Best Churches*, has some fine bosses in its wagon roof, including a sow suckling seven rather elongated piglets, and a permanent descriptive display about the Prayer Book Rebellion. There's also a venerable old oak chest, made from a single block of wood, and a rare walnut pulpit.

The Church House nearby, which will have been used, like South Tawton's, for communal feasting and 'Church Ales', probably dates to around 1500.

You can shop for a local treat at the **Sampford Courtenay Cider Company** at Solland Farm (EX20 3QT ✆ 01837 851638 ◈ devoncider. com ◷ from 10.00 Tue–Sun). Their ciders are handmade, using only apples grown in their own orchard. And they have stories behind them! For example *Grenville's Revenge* refers to Sir Richard Grenville's ship (see box, pages 176–7), while *War Horse* commemorates a bay pony from the farm, named Olive, that was requisitioned by the army and taken to France in 1914.

LYDFORD & AROUND

🏠 **Lewtrenchard Manor** (page 277), 🛏 **Twelve Penny Barn** Lewdown (page 277)

From photogenic country houses to a folly, a gorge and a 12th-century tor-top church, this is an area of contrasts, and of gentle meandering lanes once you leave the main roads.

7 THE TRENCHARDS

It's unusual to find two such perfect, traditional country houses, set in extensive and typically English gardens with lawns and terraces, only a ten-minute walk from each other; both have intriguing histories and contain som impressive period art and furnishings. With sun on their classic stone frontages and flowers splashing their borders with colour, they're an artist's or photographer's delight. The main difference is that while Coombe Trenchard was built in 1906, Lewtrenchard is around three centuries older. Although wonderfully secluded they're actually only a few miles from the A30, and also lie fairly close to the Two Castles Trail (page 206).

Lewtrenchard Manor

Lewdown, nr Okehampton EX20 4PN ✆ 01566 783222 ⏣ lewtrenchard.co.uk

The Domesday Book mentions a royal manor here, but the core of the present house seems to have been started around five centuries later. It was a simple oblong building, only the width of a single room, until Sabine Baring-Gould (page 211) in the 19th century began transforming it into this colourful, imposing and graceful building, now a family-run hotel. Inside it's opulent; Baring-Gould was a great collector, and brought treasures from far and wide: oak and leather, gilt and carvings, knick-knacks and heavy period furniture. It's a delight just to walk from one well-proportioned room to another.

In the gardens, beyond the palm trees and colourful flowerbeds, is little **St Peter's Church**, originally St Petrock's but dedicated to St Peter when it was rebuilt in 1261. Barely a trace of that old church remains; the present one dates from 1520 and again Baring-Gould brought additions from far and wide to embellish it: a medieval tryptych and 15th-century brass chandelier from Belgium, the lectern from France, the altar painting from Switzerland, the east window from Germany and so on. On his tombstone is carved *Paravi Luvernam Christo Mew* or 'I have prepared a lantern for my Christ' – and indeed it burned brightly.

Lewtrenchard Manor has an excellent restaurant, open to non-residents for lunch, afternoon tea (including cream teas) and dinner. It's top-class cuisine; the chef works closely with local producers, and vegetables mostly come from the hotel's own walled garden. Menus change frequently to make use of whatever is freshly available. For an extra treat, you can arrange a private dinner with the kitchen's activities relayed to you on a large flatscreen TV, giving you the opportunity to interact with the head chef and his team. The place is popular locally, and booking is strongly recommended.

Coombe Trenchard

Lewdown, nr Okehampton EX20 4PW ✆ 01566 783179 ⏣ coombetrenchard.co.uk

Friends of Sabine Baring-Gould had been renting the old rectory on the Lewtrenchard estate, while he lived next door in Lewtrenchard Manor. Sabine then offered them that portion of the land and they bought it, demolished the rectory and in 1906 began building this elegant Arts-and-Crafts house, using architect Walter Sarel and Devon church builders Dart & Francis.

The interior (only accessible by arrangement, see below) has fine oak panelling, ornate ceilings, gracious rooms and period furnishings – and somewhat surprisingly an ingenious disappearing wall, thought to be unique, which can be slid down to the basement, rather in the manner of a sash window, to make space for large gatherings. When the current owners bought the property in 2007 the large gardens, originally designed and laid out by Walter Sarel, were badly neglected; now, after a huge amount of work, the forgotten paths, glades, woodland garden, terraces, steps and other structures are back in view.

The **gardens** can be visited through the annual National Gardens Scheme (page 16). Otherwise they are not regularly open to the public but private group visits to the gardens and some rooms in the house can be arranged by request. They're also accessible through **Invitation to View** (✆ 01284 827087 ⬧ invitationtoview.co.uk), a company that organises visits to stately homes.

8 LYDFORD GORGE & LYDFORD

⌂ **The Dartmoor Inn** (page 277)

Hidden away on a feeder road off the A386, this is one of those happy places with plenty to see and a regular bus service, the number 46 between Okehampton and Tavistock. People have always loved waterfalls, and **Lydford Gorge** (EX20 4BH ✆ 01822 820320 ○ ticket office 10.00–17.00, trails close Dec–Feb & in bad weather; National Trust) has been enticing visitors to its White Lady Waterfall for around 300 years, although it was the arrival of the railway in 1865 that put it within reach of holidaymakers. Now owned by the National Trust, the 1½-mile stretch of river deserves its popularity – it really does live up to expectations.

The gorge walk is designed as a circular route, and follows a one-way system – necessary because the paths are narrow – so from the main entrance you walk in a clockwise direction, above the river and through the woods to the waterfall, returning close to the river. The three-mile walk has some steep sections so you need to be fit enough, and have the time (allow two hours) to do the whole thing. There are alternatives, however. On my last visit I parked at the waterfall entrance and walked the lovely river section to the main entrance. The number 46 runs every two hours so if you get your timing right you can enjoy the facilities of the tearoom and take the bus back. It stops outside each entrance.

THE HIGHWAYMAN INN & COBWEB HALL

Philip Knowling

Highwayman Inn Sourton EX20 4HN ✆ 01837 861243 ♂ thehighwaymaninn.net
⊙ noon–14.30 & 18.00–22.30. Ales, meals & snacks in its Aladdin's cave of artefacts & curios. Also B&B & a self-catering cottage.

Putting the lie to the idea that follies are useless is the Highwayman Inn at Sourton, on the bleak west side of Dartmoor. Sourton is the sort of place you could pass through without noticing if it weren't for the hard work, imagination and enthusiasm of the late John 'Buster' Jones, who over a 40-year period transformed two of its key buildings into fabulous, fascinating and accessible architectural wonders.

What makes this pub a folly? Well, it's the most lavishly and imaginatively decorated inn you could ever visit. Inside and out there's wit and whimsy, imagination and inspiration – plus a little macabre kitsch. The Highwayman is a fantasy blend of pirate ship, church, museum, junk shop and fairytale.

In 1959 Buster Jones moved his family to Devon and took over Sourton's New Inn – a small, run-down pub in a 13th-century building. He and his wife Rita changed the name to the Highwayman Inn and, to promote it, Buster acquired the old Okehampton–Launceston stage coach and set it up as a lobby at the front door of the pub.

He hauled pieces of bog oak off the moor and used them as bar tops; the dartboard is fixed to a tree stump set into the wall. There are bits of ship (a carved door from an old whaling ship called *Diana*) and pieces of church (from Plymouth).

One room has a nautical theme – it's below decks on an 18th-century sailing ship cum bric-a-brac shop with bar facilities. Elsewhere, there's an indoor grotto full of stuffed animals (an inventive use of roadkill). Cartwheels and lanterns and sewing machines also feature.

Buster also turned the former Sourton village hall, just across the road, into a fairytale Gothic cottage orné – despite a certain amount of conflict with the planning authorities. Today Cobweb Hall is a unique holiday let, standing on the edge of rising moorland.

The two buildings are now in the good care of Buster's daughter, Sally. The Highwayman is world-renowned – and rightly so. If you visit it, you'll never see your own local in quite the same way again.

There are also short circular walks at each end, the most dramatic being the Devil's Cauldron accessed from the main entrance. Here the river is forced through a narrow space between rocks, with the path pinned against the steep fern-clad rock face so you look down on the churning white water. Even after a dry period it's impressive, and breathtaking (and slippery) after rain.

The other end, with the **White Lady Waterfall**, is drier and less ferny than the eastern section, and the descent to the falls is down a long flight of steps, although there is a longer, 'easy' path as an alternative. The waterfall is just that – a waterfall – not spectacular but very pretty in its wooded environment. However, the Reverend Stebbing Shaw, who visited Lydford in 1788, was moved to paroxysms of delight. ' … You are presented with the finest milky streams imaginable, neither too perpendicular to be one confused heap, nor too much divided to be ungraceful; but one continued silvery chain of 200 feet [actually it's 90 feet]; towards the bottom the rock projects so favourably as to fill the air with aqueous particles, and to imitate the effect of a real fountain, softly falling in a silver shower . . '

The paths between the two entrances have a variety of trees and flowers, including swathes of bluebells and pungent wild garlic in May, and allow you to see the different moods of the river, from quiet pools to mini-waterfalls. Dippers and grey wagtails are frequent visitors and, if you're lucky, you may see a flash of blue as a kingfisher whizzes by. It's a lovely, varied walk and well worth doing the whole stretch, whether assisted by the bus or in both directions.

Lydford Gorge attracts large crowds so, if you can, avoid the busy summer months. Early spring is a perfect time to visit, when the water is high and the woods are touched with green. Autumn, with its yellows and russets, is equally appealing.

Lydford is more than just the gorge. The village has the remains of a Norman fort (now visible only as a grassy mound) and a little square Norman 'castle' that looks as if it were built by a young child out of Lego bricks. This was used as a stannary court and jail, infamous for the harsh judgements meted out in the 17th century, possibly by Judge Jeffries. Lydford's position between two ravines gave it a natural defence so the village has prospered since before the Norman Conquest when it had its own mint, producing silver 'Lydford pennies' from 973. The tin boom at the end of the 12th century turned it into a stannary town (page 226). It was also Dartmoor's biggest parish, so decaying corpses had to be transported across Dartmoor, from as far afield as Bellever, to be buried at its St Petrock's Church. **The Lych Way**, running from Powder Mills (between Postbridge and Two Bridges) to Lydford, is the ancient route that they used to take. St. Petrock's is early Norman, but it's thought that and earlier, possibly 7th-century building preceeded it.

FOOD & DRINK

Castle Inn ✆ 01822 820241 ⏲ noon−15.00 & 18.00−21.00 daily. Lydford's pub in the centre of the village has plenty of unforced charm as well as two exceptionally fine stained-glass panels. I wasn't able to find out their history, but possibly they came from a church since one shows a green man, and another the 'tinners' rabbits' or 'three hares' which feature in most stannary town churches (page 226).

The Dartmoor Inn ✆ 01822 820221 ⏲ noon−15.00 & 18.00−23.00 Tue−Sat, noon−15.00 Sun. A classy inn with B&B accommodation as well as seriously special meals for non-residents. Grilled locally-sourced meat is the speciality here, including enormous ribeye steaks. The chef proudly lists the Devon or Cornish farm that raises the beef cattle. Dining areas are exceptionally cosy with a warming log fire burning on cold days.

9 BRENTOR (BRENT TOR)

The conical hill topped with its proud little church is a landmark throughout western Dartmoor, and the view from the top is, as you'd expect from the highest church in England, magnificent. On a clear day you can see Bodmin Moor and Plymouth Sound. The church is old – some say it was finished in 1130 – and stands at an altitude of 1,130 feet, but that sounds a little too neat. There are many legends about why it was built at such a height. One explains that the original intention was to build the church at the base of the tor nearer to the village. However, the Devil feared this might encourage the villagers to go regularly to worship, so he sent his imps to move the foundation stones to the top of the hill each night after work had finished. At first the builders rolled the stones back to the bottom again, but soon got fed up with this and decided to let the Devil have his way. They named the church after St Michael, who is patron saint of grocers, mariners, the police and other emergency services, paratroopers (that must surprise him) and the sick. The saint came to visit his newest church, and took great exception to the fact that the Devil had engineered its position outside the village. St Michael then engaged in a fearsome battle with the Devil, finally hurling a great boulder at him and knocking him head over heels to the base of the tor. The boulder still lies there today, as a reminder of this saintly victory.

It's only a ten-minute climb to the church for a fit person, up a rough path lined with foxgloves, through cow-grazed pasture, dodging cowpats. The church itself is tiny and utterly simple inside. It's the location that makes it so special; and the fact that it celebrates evensong every Sunday in the summer and holds a Christmas carol service.

DARTMOOR
NATIONAL PARK

8
DARTMOOR NATIONAL PARK

Look at any map of Devon and you'll see the largely roadless blob that is Dartmoor. Literature and imagination give it an air of menace: *The Hound of the Baskervilles*, a bleak prison where the surrounding moor is the best security, and craggy tors emerging from heavy, disorientating mists. This national park is high – the highest land in England south of the Pennines – leaving the visitor exposed to raw winds sweeping in from the Atlantic. But there's a softer side to Dartmoor: sheltered, wooded valleys which feel a world away from the typical moor. So if you want Dartmoor bleakness you can find it. Once you cross a cattle grid the hedges disappear, sheep and ponies raise their heads to watch you pass, and the wind catches your hair as you reach for a sweater. You can walk for hours without seeing a road – or a tree. And everywhere you see granite: rocks as large as cars scattered randomly or piled on top of hills to form the tors that define Dartmoor, quarried and dressed in the walls of the ancient village churches, or rough-hewn and arranged in circles or rows by the first humans to make the moor their home.

The low-lying perimeter is another world, however, networked by deep narrow lanes. Footpaths meander through gentle, flower-filled meadows or dark woodland, or along the banks of rivers. The Tavy, Teign and Dart dominate, but all have tributaries and you are never far from a brook. Hidden in the valleys are small villages, their church towers poking through the trees, and welcoming pubs. But no one visiting here would stay only in the valleys; Dartmoor is the high moor. You may regret venturing up there in mist and rain, but on a sunny day its wildness is alluring. It's aptly called England's last wilderness, and the feeling of space and silence, broken only by the trilling of skylarks and the scrunching of boots on stones, is intoxicating.

Dartmoor also has, uniquely, its visible prehistory in the monuments such as hut circles and stone rows that litter the moor. A newcomer might assume the tors are also the work of prehistoric people. The word comes from the Celtic *twr*, or tower, but these are the work of nature – erosion – not of man. And in an area that has blessedly few 'tourist attractions' nature has provided children with some rewarding scrambles and adults with hills to test their stamina, as well as giving Dartmoor its unmistakable horizon.

☂ WET-WEATHER ACTIVITIES

Castle Drogo (pages 239–41)
Dartmoor Artisan Trail (page 229)
Bovey Tracey Devon Guild of Craftsmen and House of Marbles (pages 250–1)
Tavistock Museum and Pannier Market (pages 264–5)
Princetown Dartmoor Prison Museum and High Moorland Visitor Centre (pages 270–1)

DARTMOOR: THE HAND OF MAN

There are more prehistoric sites here than anywhere in Europe, and Dartmoor is one of the easiest places in Britain to view the march of history, from Neolithic circles to the neo-medieval Castle Drogo. Most archaeologists believe that the earliest remains on Dartmoor are **Neolithic**, from around 4000BC, and that as true settlers these people had the most profound effect on the landscape by domesticating animals and cultivating crops. Then the Beaker people in the early Bronze Age, around 2200BC, built the Grimspound enclosed village (page 256) and some 2,000 other 'hut circles' on the moor. Bronze is an alloy of tin and copper so tin-rich Dartmoor was an obvious place to settle, the metal being easily extracted from rivers and surface deposits. Later, still a few centuries BC, came the **Iron Age**, whose most tangible heritage is the plethora of hill forts that are found in other parts of Devon, but not Dartmoor; and finally the two centuries of Christianity and its enduring symbol, the English country church, its fortunes tied to those of the tinners who continued to extract the valuable metal from Dartmoor until the mid 20th century. Wealthy tin merchants who endowed a church in a stannery ('tin-workers') town were ensured a shortcut to heaven.

Visiting Dartmoor today, you may find it puzzling that Neolithic and Bronze-Age people chose to settle in such an inhospitable region. Probably, in an age where finding enough to eat was the main preoccupation, the attraction was the abundance of game in the woodlands that at that time covered low-lying parts of the moor, and the good grazing for both wild and domestic animals in the higher areas. The climate was milder then, and the soil less acid; thousands of years of slash-and-burn agriculture impoverished the land and helped create the moor that we see today. The availability of granite for constructing durable, weather-proof homes and the mysterious stone circles and monoliths will have helped the inhabitants but frustrates archaeologists, since granite cannot be carbon dated. But that is part of the attraction: we just don't know what a lot of these structures were used for, nor even when they were built. We can simply enjoy them for what they are.

It's thrilling to come across the signs of early human habitation on the moor, particularly when we really don't know why these people, living up to 4,000 years ago in a warm, forested place which provided for all their basic needs, went to the trouble of moving huge hunks of granite into geometric patterns. It is also a sobering reminder of the effect of deforestation and climate change on a once green and fertile land. Some of the most striking sites are the chambered tomb known as Spinsters' Rock (page 242), the easily reached Nine Stones stone circle at Belstone (page 210), the stone rows at Merrivale (pages 267–9), the Bronze-Age pound of Grimspound (page 256), and the cluster of prehistoric features on Shovel Down (pages 237–8).

Moving forward to our known history, the **Norman Conquest** in 1066 resulted in tracts of land being set aside for the new King to indulge his enthusiasm for hunting. These areas, rich in game, were called '**forests**' although this did not mean woodland; the moorland of Dartmoor was a royal forest. In those times deer, wolves and wild boar were all plentiful. All have gone now, including most of the red deer.

THE TINNERS' RABBITS

In several places on Dartmoor you can see depictions of three rabbits or hares, so designed that they appear to have two ears each while actually sharing the second ear with their neighbour. No one really knows their significance. Some say they are a symbol of the Holy Trinity, others that they are a secular symbol of the three elements of the tin trade: tin, market, wealth. One thing is certain: they are not unique to Dartmoor, a similar design being found in Iran, Mongolia and along the Silk Route. So this curious emblem has been favoured by Muslims and Buddhists as well as Christians.

Penalties for harming animals in the royal forests were severe, and in the 12th century King John yielded to pressure and 'deforested' all of Devon apart from Dartmoor and Exmoor. In 1337 Edward III gave the Forest of Dartmoor to his son, the Prince of Wales and Duke of Cornwall. It remains the property of the Duchy of Cornwall – and the current Prince of Wales – to this day.

DARTMOOR TIN &
THE STANNARY TOWNS

Dartmoor, with Cornwall, was the first known source of tin. Some 4,000 years ago, metal workers discovered that by mixing tin (10%) with copper (90%) they created a stronger but easily worked material: bronze. Because tin doesn't rust it is also used to coat other metals. Minerals containing tin are almost always associated with granite, hence tin's abundance on Dartmoor. The ore was originally collected from the streams and rivers, through the simple process of panning or 'streaming'. Once these deposits were exhausted – and streaming continued into the 17th century – the ore was extracted from the ground using pick and shovel, sometimes with the help of leats, or diverted streams, to wash away the debris. Millstones were used to crush the ore and extract the metal, which was then smelted. Dartmoor is littered with evidence of these primitive mines, from the remains of mining cottages to deep pits, protected by guard rails, amid the gorse and bracken. Two smeltings generally took place, one at the site and the second, to produce pure tin, in one of the **stannary towns**. The Latin for tin is *stannum*, hence the term stannary.

Stannary towns in Dartmoor were mining centres where refined tin was collected, weighed and stamped. When sold, the proceeds were passed to the Duchy of Cornwall. In 1305 Edward I established Tavistock, Ashburton and Chagford as Devon's first stannary towns, with the right to organise their own political affairs through the Stannary Parliament and Stannary Courts. Other stannary towns were established later as mining became more organised. Stannary laws were the first legal code of England, affording the miners considerable power – providing they were honest. Legend has it that any tinner convicted of mixing impurities with his metal was to have three spoonfuls of it poured down his throat in a molten state.

GETTING THERE & AROUND

If there were a better bus service in Dartmoor we'd recommend leaving your car at home rather than tackling the single-track lanes – in the summer months you can spend as much time in reverse as going forward. Car drivers should be aware that although the national park authorities have been generous with the provision of parking areas, and only charge a fee for the most popular car parks, they are tough on those who park at the roadside; if there's a risk of blocking access for emergency vehicles your vehicle will be towed away. And note: there are no petrol stations within the National Park, so fill up in one of the large gateway towns.

CAR-FREE ACCESS TO DARTMOOR

If you're willing to use taxis from time to time you can just about enjoy a car-free holiday on Dartmoor, especially if you're a walker. The nearest mainline **railway station** is Ivybridge (pages 179–80), at the southern end of the national park and handy for the Two Moors Way. Newton Abbot is a little further from the moor, but convenient for the eastern section. From Exeter you can catch the hourly X38 express bus to Ashburton, or, if you're basing yourself in the north of Dartmoor, take bus 173 to Moretonhampstead or Chagford.

TAVISTOCK COUNTRY BUSES

In the last edition I wrote about 'Britain's rarest bus', which went across Dartmoor on the fifth Saturday of the month, summer only. Which meant that it ran about three times a year. Sadly, it is now extinct, but there are several other equally scenic and enjoyable routes to choose from. The Tavistock Community Transport Association was founded in 1981 to provide transport to areas not serviced by commercial bus companies. It is run entirely by volunteers, and the buses are a joy to ride on for the routes they take and the friendliness of the passengers and drivers.

These buses mostly only run once a week and all start in Tavistock, taking between 30 and 90 minutes for their journey. Most are round-trip (just one, the 113, crosses Dartmoor to go to the shopping centre of Trago Mills where it waits for passengers to have a wander around the shops and relax over lunch before returning). The routes are varied; some take you round the edge of Dartmoor or venture over the county border into Cornwall. Timetables are available at TICs or online at ⬧ tavistockcountrybus.co.uk; alternatively phone ☏ 07580 260683.

A perfect car-free day in Dartmoor can be achieved on summer Saturdays by using the delightful **Haytor Hoppa** bus (details on the ⌖ dartmoor.gov.uk website). This follows a circular route through some of Dartmoor's most popular eastern places, including Haytor, Widecombe, Hound Tor and Becky Falls. With four departures a day from Newton Abbot train station (or Bovey Tracey) you can relax and enjoy the moor. The Haytor Hoppa runs from the end of May to mid September – and dogs are allowed on board. Other once-a-week offerings are equally rewarding but need more organisation. Spend some time on the handy interactive map on ⌖ traveldevon.info or get creative with the two relevant bus timetables: Teignbridge and West Devon.

SELF-POWERED TRAVEL
Cycling

Cyclists may find the lanes around the moor too steep and narrow for enjoyable riding (but take heart: electric bicycles are increasingly available), but those with mountain bikes are well served: there are few restrictions to cycling off-road as long as you stick to bridleways and designated cycle tracks. Many of these follow dismantled railway lines with easy gradients. The national park authority has comprehensive cycling information and maps on ⌖ dartmoor.gov.uk.

Among the several dedicated cycle paths is the **Dartmoor Way**, a 95-mile circuit around the perimeter of the national park, some of it along abandoned sections of railway. Clearly signposted, it is strenuous in parts, but always on hard ground so perfectly manageable for an ordinary cyclist. There are plenty of pubs and B&Bs throughout the route so you can do it in two or even three days, using Luggage Transfers (page 12) or taxis to transport your bags. The old Princetown railway track is also a popular route for mountain bikers. Easiest of all is the four-mile circuit round **Burrator Reservoir** in western Dartmoor (pages 172–3).

There are several good bike-hire places. **Devon Cycle Hire** (Bridestowe, Okehampton ⌖ 01837 861141) is popular since it's at the start of The Granite Way and hires out electric as well as pedal bikes. At the other end of the moor, **Fox Tor Café** in Princetown (page 271) has bikes for hire, and **Tavistock Cycles** (⌖ 01822 617630) is handy for Drake's Trail but quite a pedal from the moor. **Let's Go Biking** (⌖ letsgobiking.com) will do a holiday package that includes luggage transfer.

If you like cycling but look at Dartmoor's hills in dismay, consider a guided tour with **Dartmoor Electric Bicycles** (✆ 07914 184220 ✎ dartmoorelectricbicycles.co.uk) near Poundsgate, which do the hard work for you. They also hire out electric bikes if you prefer to go solo.

Walking & backpacking

Until I came to live in Devon I avoided walking on Dartmoor, imagining waist-deep bogs negotiated in driving rain, and being lost for days in landmark-obscuring mists. So I've been excessively pleased by the reality – strolls along tumbling brooks, walks through bluebell woods, striding out along a disused railway with the knowledge that it won't

DARTMOOR ARTISAN TRAIL

Dartmoor has always attracted creative people; perhaps it's to do with all that space and wildness. The Dartmoor Artisan Trail was established in 2017 to bring together a group of 20 or so of the most interesting artisans, artists and food producers to create an in-depth experience for visitors. Blacksmiths and beekeepers, potters and painters, woodturners and weavers, farmers and brewers – they're all there, and more. The trail gives you the chance to meet these people, see them at work, and perhaps try your hand at creating something yourself. You'll also be able to buy products directly from the makers.

The Artisan Trail is the brainchild of writer and photographer Suzy Bennett, who has sought out the most talented and innovative people on Dartmoor. She is continually adding to the list, and this endeavour won the award for the Best UK Tourism Project by the British Guild of Travel Writers in 2017.

The trail is self-guided: you choose the artisans that most interest you and, if you want to participate in a workshop, book ahead through the website ✎ dartmoor-artisan-trail.co.uk. There is no set route for car drivers but cycling is encouraged, with two suggested routes and bike hire information.

Suzy explained what inspired her to set up the trail: 'There is a resurgence of interest in traditional skills and crafts across the UK, and Dartmoor is one of the creative hubs of this new energy. In a world of mass production, it's wonderful to see that things are still being made by hand, with passion, honesty and integrity.' I spent an inspiring day visiting workshops in Moretonhampstead, one of the hubs with a variety of artisans (pages 244–5) and Chagford (page 235) before heading southwest to meet Jane Deane to learn about natural dyes and spinning at Huckerby Bridge (see box, page 267).

Even if you're not a creative type, the chance to see so many of these traditional crafts within reach of each other and amid a lovely landscape is surely unique.

suddenly take me up an energy-draining hill, and grassy paths up to tors with a 360-degree view.

That said, walkers should take the challenges of Dartmoor seriously. On the moor itself there is no shelter from lashing rain, mist can descend suddenly, leaving you with no idea where you are, and to cap it all there's a Dartmoor speciality, 'featherbeds', which are bogs covered by a firm-looking layer of moss. Step on them and you'll feel as though you're balancing on jelly – until you sink in. So stick to well defined paths and check the weather forecast.

Die-hard hikers can get their teeth into the real thing by tackling the 102-mile **Two Moors Way** (⬧ twomoorsway.org), which runs from Ivybridge on the southern edge of Dartmoor (accessible by train) and across the roadless area of the southern moor, before revisiting civilisation at New Bridge and continuing north to Exmoor. Walkers wanting to do it as a coast-to-coast route, which is how it's sometimes described, can add a further 15 miles from Wembury (pages 164–6) to Ivybridge. (Don't confuse this with another route also described as 'Devon Coast-to-Coast' – the 99-mile cycle trail between Plymouth and Ilfracombe (page 152).) The first stretch from Ivybridge is around 12 miles of moorland with no escape, so a serious undertaking, but the feeling of being utterly alone in one of the most densely populated countries in the world makes it worth the effort. You will also be walking through Dartmoor's history, crossing an ancient clapper bridge on the old **Abbots Way** between Buckfast and Tavistock abbeys, and pass **Huntingdon Cross**, a 16th-century boundary marker and one of the stone crosses that are such a feature of the moor. After Holne the path frequently crosses roads so can be walked as part of a circular route if you are not planning to continue across Mid Devon and on to Exmoor. The easy option for transporting your luggage is to use **Luggage Transfers** (8 luggagetransfers.co.uk) who can also arrange accommodation, or choose the cheaper option of arranging for taxis to carry your luggage between B&Bs.

The **West Devon Way** runs for 37 miles between Okehampton and Plymouth, skirting the western edge of the moor, while the **Templer Way** (see box, page 253), from Teignmouth to Haytor, is only 18 miles long and accessible in many places by public transport.

Some **bus-assisted walks** which allow you to go from A to B without returning to your starting point are described in this chapter, and there are others on the Haytor Hoppa website.

Dartmoor is one of the few places in England where true **backpacking** – carrying all your needs for a few days in the wilderness – is both possible and sensible. Camping is permitted almost everywhere, providing you avoid farmland, prehistoric sites and enclosed areas. If you'd prefer not to carry your own tent there are a dozen youth hostels and bunk houses scattered around the moor. However, to my mind once you've experienced the freedom of wild camping, and if you're strong and fit enough to carry a pack, there's no contest between it and dormitory accommodation. See ⊘ dartmoor.gov.uk for more information on where you can and can't camp.

Guided walks

The National Park runs these throughout the year, varying in length from two to eight miles and covering every area and aspect of the moor. Led by knowledgeable and enthusiastic guides, they are a great way of getting under the skin of Dartmoor. If you prefer a smaller group (maximum 10), Keith Lambeth, **Out there on Dartmoor**, is your man (✉ outthereondartmoor@gmail.com; see ad, 4th colour section). He is a team leader for Dartmoor's Search and Rescue team, and his knowledge of the moor is encyclopaedic. Keith has devised a variety of walks, choosing the most suitable when he has gauged participants' interests and abilities, and also with the weather in mind. Specialities are full-moon night walks and circular walks around Dartmoor's historic sites. Afterwards he emails you the route with GPS points, mileage and summaries of what you've seen.

Llama Walks, based near Widecombe-in-the-Moor (✆ 01364 631481 ⊘ dartmoorllamawalks.co.uk), offers guided walks where your luggage and picnic are carried by llamas or alpacas, and custom-made guided tours are offered by **Dartmoor Walks and Rides this Way** (✆ 01364 654471 ⊘ dartmoorwalksthisway.co.uk), which organises walks or e-bike rides specifically to suit your interests and ability. Finally there's the **Dartmoor Walking Festival** (⊘ dartmoorwalkingfestival.co.uk) in late August to early September with a choice of around 70 guided walks, short and long, to choose from.

Walking & cycling maps & guides

Although there are no large-scale Croydecycle maps for Dartmoor, the *South Devon* one (pages 13–14) at a scale of 1:100,000 is perfect for cyclists (and drivers), giving an overview of the moor and its roads and lanes, plus the main sights and pubs. It costs a fraction of the other Dartmoor maps. There's a good choice of more detailed maps for walkers, with the double-sided OS Explorer map OL28 the most popular. However, we call it 'the tablecloth' because of its size, and find it too unwieldy; there are more user-friendly alternatives available in the visitor centres at Haytor and Princetown. These include the OL28 (1:25,000) in a booklet: **Dartmoor A-Z**, and the **Yellow River Maps** (scale 1:16,000) for various popular areas in Dartmoor using OS cartography. Other excellent maps for walkers are Harvey's **Dartmoor** (separate maps for north and south) at 1:25,000, and Harvey's **British Mountain Map: Dartmoor**.

DARTMOOR PONIES

In contrast to Exmoor, where all ponies on the moor are similar in appearance (as you would expect of a distinct breed), Dartmoor's ponies are much more varied. There are few true Dartmoor ponies left now, the result of generations of cross-breeding, there being no rules on which ponies may graze Dartmoor common land as long as the stallions do not exceed 12.2 hands (4 feet 2 inches) and are believed by a vet to be fit for surviving the often harsh conditions found on Dartmoor.

Since no pony is truly wild, and many will be sold on at some point, there are commercial considerations. 'Coloured' (piebald or skewbald) ponies attract higher prices than bay or brown, the original Dartmoor pony colour, so they are replacing the less strikingly coloured animals.

Pony drifts, when the animals are rounded up and marked for ownership before being sold on, take place once a year in the autumn. The pony markets are held at Tavistock on the first Friday in October and Chagford the second Thursday in October.

The Dartmoor Pony Heritage Trust (DPHT) was set up to preserve the unregistered Dartmoor pony gene pool, and to maintain traditional native herds on Dartmoor. It aims to increase the value of the annual foal crop by handling, castrating colts not suitable for breeding and promoting the good temperament and versatility of these moor-bred ponies. Every year the DPHT, supported by the Dartmoor Pony Society, assesses the quality and conformation of the foals and awards the cream of the crop Heritage status.

One of the Trust's most successful strategies for highlighting these ponies' exceptional temperament is through its 'Ponies Inspiring People' programmes aimed at young people with physical, emotional, behavioural and learning disabilities. The Trust's **Visitor and Education Centre** is in the Parke Estate near Bovey Tracey (TQ13 9JQ ✐ 01626 833234 ⌾ dpht.co.uk ⊝ Apr–Oct 13.30–16.00 Sun) where they run a 'meet the ponies' afternoon. It's run by volunteers, so check they're open when planning a special visit.

The scale is 1:40,000 but there's enough detail for a variety of walks. By the same publisher and at the same scale is *Dartmoor for Cyclists*. It's double-sided, with one side showing routes for cycle touring and the other for mountain biking. Several walking guides with clear maps are available. Recommended ones include the Bossiney guide, *Shortish Walks on Dartmoor*, and Pathfinder's *Dartmoor: Outstanding Circular Walks*, but there are several others for specific areas.

RIDING

Several specialist companies offer riding holidays on Dartmoor, varying from a weekend to a full week. Liberty Trails ($\mathcal{O}$ 01822 851463) do luxury weekends on quality horses, but if you fancy trying something really different you can release your inner cowboy at Meldon Farm Riding Holidays ($\mathcal{O}$ 07966 522363) whose western-style holidays on American quarter horses include a seven-day ride around the moor and cattle drives.

Climbing Dartmoor's hills on someone else's legs has an obvious attraction, and a couple of hours on horseback, riding through such a varied landscape, is far superior to a normal hack along rural bridleways. The riding stables listed below offer a variety of rides ranging from one hour to all day. When booking, riders need to be honest about their abilities. I was told that riders who could count themselves experienced at home were sometimes unprepared for a hack in such rugged terrain so it's better to underestimate your proficiency. Complete beginners are welcome at most places – the ride will be tailored accordingly. If you are fit an all-day ride is superb, allowing you to experience varied countryside and have a good pub lunch. Something really different, for experienced riders, are the Clydesdales kept at Brimpts Farm (pages 259–61).

Most stables offer similar rides at a similar cost, about £25 for an hour, and do half-day pub rides.

RIDING STABLES

Adventure Clydesdale Brimpts Farm, Dartmeet $\mathcal{O}$ 07901 943038 $\mathcal{O}$ adventureclydesdale.com
Babeny Farm Riding Stables Poundsgate $\mathcal{O}$ 01364 631296
Cholwell Riding Stables Mary Tavy $\mathcal{O}$ 01822 810526
Shilstone Rocks Riding Centre Widecombe-in-the-Moor $\mathcal{O}$ 01364 621281 $\mathcal{O}$ www.dartmoorstables.com

CHAGFORD, CASTLE DROGO & THE NORTH

This is one of the prettiest areas of Dartmoor, with more than its share of river gorges, tors and prehistoric ruins, as well as the delightful Stone Lane Gardens, which are close to **Spinsters' Rock**. Chagford makes a perfect base for exploring the region, as it has a reasonable bus service: the number 173 from Exeter and the 178 from Okehampton or Newton Abbot.

1 CHAGFORD

🏠 **Gidleigh Park** (page 278) 🏠 **Mill End Hotel** (page 278)
Tourist information: No office but the Courtyard Café has some leaflets & a notice board; also see ⌂ visitchagford.com

Chagford can strike one as almost too perfect. It sits in an ideal location, sandwiched between the River Teign and Chagford Common, which is cluttered with prehistoric remains, and the village has a satisfactory shape with a defined centre dominated by the 16th-century 'Pepper Pot' market house in The Square. The shops are varied and concentrate on local produce, such as the **Devonshire Dairy** which sells cheese, honey and Dartmoor-bred lamb, and **Black's**, the very good deli, but the town

LETTERBOXING & GEOCACHING ON DARTMOOR

In 1854, a Dartmoor guide named James Perrott placed an empty glass pickle jar by Cranmere Pool. He told hikers and other guides about it, and encouraged them – if they reached it – to put some record of their visit inside. People began to leave postcards and letters, addressed either to themselves or to others, which the next visitor would take and post: the Dartmoor equivalent of throwing a bottle into the sea containing an address. By the early 1900s the Cranmere pickle jar had been replaced by a tin box containing a more formal visitors' book, and in 1937 a granite box was erected there.

Gradually letterboxes were placed in other parts of the moor, each with a notebook and appropriate rubber stamp. Letterboxers now 'collect' these when they find them by marking the stamp into their own notebooks; when their total reaches 100 they can join the '100 Club'. Letterboxes today range from solid structures to jars and tins to plastic sandwich boxes, generally well concealed. There are strict guidelines about their maintenance, choosing sites considerately and not damaging the landscape; make sure to read them on ⌂ letterboxingondartmoor.co.uk before placing a box of your own.

is dominated by an enormous hardware shop, James Bowden, where DIY enthusiasts can disappear for hours. Notable among the many arty shops is **The Artisan** (✆ 01647 432414 ⌖ www.leafleather.co.uk), part of the Dartmoor Artisan Trail (page 229), where Martin Brady has his leather workshop. You can watch Martin at work or make a small item yourself (pre-book for this) as well as browse the other local crafts such as ceramics. Two more Chagford participants in the Artisan Trail are Linda Lemieux and Ed Hamer. Linda gathers her own rushes and willow for basket weaving and rush chair seating; she runs courses and day workshops on her craft (✆ 01647 231330 ⌖ woodandrush.net). Ed is a community farmer supplying local villages with his organic produce: members pay an annual fee and receive a regular supply of vegetables. Sort of like having an allotment but without the work. You can have a tour of the farm or volunteer for the day in return for a free lunch and veg box: ✆ 07858 381539 ⌖ chagfood.org.uk.

This was a stannary town and shows its former tin wealth in its church, which has some 'tinners' rabbits' on one of the bosses adorning the splendid wagon roof. Although much restored, with some very modern additions, the church has great appeal; its features include a 400-year-old stone carving of an archangelic St Michael with luxuriant locks, slaying a 'nasty little demon'. This has been placed just inside the door. The list of

Remember, too, that a box placed in winter may be hidden by vegetation when you return to check it in the summer. A friend described how the growing bracken swallowed up not only the box but her smallest grandchild who was hunting for it: they found him when a little voice piped up from deep in the fronds 'Grandad, where are you?' Children love the challenge of letterboxing, and another friend told me that her three would be seriously grumpy in the car on the way home if they hadn't managed to find a box.

From Dartmoor, letterboxing has spread to several other parts of Britain. It caught on in the United States in 1998 then reached New Zealand and various European countries. A new and more technological version called **geocaching**, using GPS co-ordinates, started in the US in 2000 (⌖ geocaching. com) and now has well over six million participants worldwide. The Geocaching Association of Great Britain was established in 2003; its website ⌖ gagb.org.uk is full of useful information.

So, if you spot an unexpected container on the moor, you may have taken the first step towards becoming a fully-fledged Dartmoor letterboxer or geocacher!

benefactors is interesting; it ends with one pound seven shillings worth of bread to be delivered to the poor every Good Friday 'to be continued for ever'. Look out, too, for the painstakingly done needlework hanging in the south aisle; showing the history of the region, this was made by the Chagford Women's Institute.

Chagford has the largest **outdoor swimming pool** in Devon (⚭ chagfordpool.co.uk ⊙ May–Sep 14.00–17.45). Fed by the River Teign, heated by solar power to 24 degrees, this is something special!

On the approach road to Chagford from the north you'll pass **Proper Job** (TQ13 8DR ✆ 01647 432985 ⚭ proper-job.org) on your left. This wonderful not-for-profit recycling place is absolutely crammed with goodies. There's a room stacked full of books, another with good antiques, and three rooms of quality clothing plus furniture, curtains, tools, toys and much more. If you're a natural scavenger you'll love it.

🍴 FOOD & DRINK

Courtyard Café The Square (down the hill to the left of the Pepper Pot) ✆ 01647 432571. A small, relaxed and friendly café specialising in wholefoods, with a pleasant outdoor seating area. It's open for coffee, cakes and light lunches. Tourist information is available here – useful in the absence of a TIC.

TO BOLDLY GO ...

If this chapter tempts you to explore Dartmoor, beware! It holds many and fearsome hazards. Take the pixies, for a start. They're friendly little beings on the whole, but if you mock or disbelieve in them they turn distinctly nasty. Visitors who are 'pixie-led' can lose all sense of direction and wander alone for days through the mist or be drawn to their death in marshes. Be particularly careful not to trample foxgloves or stitchwort, as these are their special flowers, and avoid their cave on Sheepstor. If you do feel threatened, quickly turn your jacket inside out (or your pockets, if you're not wearing a jacket) as this will appease them.

Then there's the Devil. Despite its many churches, Dartmoor is one of his favourite haunts. He and his Wisht hounds, huge and fearsome black creatures with eyes like glowing coals, hunt at dead of night by Dewerstone and Hound Tor, and you may hear their ghostly baying in the darkness. His frying pan is near Mis Tor, so if you catch an appetising whiff of crispy bacon don't be tempted to investigate; he'll be cooking up his breakfast.

Witches are another risk. To mix her potions, the Witch of Sheepstor uses the water from Crazywell Pool, and Bowerman the Hunter was turned to stone (Bowerman's Nose) because

Gidleigh Park nr Chagford TQ13 8HH ✆ 01647 432367 ⌂ gidleigh.co.uk. Set in its own 45 acres, yet near Chagford, this is a seriously posh hotel with a two-star Michelin restaurant. Come here for that very special treat when you don't care how much you spend. Or maybe come for their afternoon tea, which gives you that glimpse of luxury without going the whole hog.

Globe Inn ✆ 01647 433485. A relaxed and good-value inn by the church in Chagford, popular with the locals, offering accommodation as well as meals.

The Birdcage The Square, Chagford ✆ 01647 433883 ⊙ all day until 23.30. A lovely little café/restaurant which is a popular choice for coffee as well as meals.

Three Crowns High St, Chagford ✆ 01647 433444 ⌂ threecrowns-chagford.co.uk. A fine thatched inn in the centre of town with excellent food. Pricey, but it's a lovely place for a bit of a treat.

2 SHOVEL DOWN & FERNWORTHY RESERVOIR

For a total immersion in prehistoric sites, have a walk on to **Shovel Down** near Scorhill, at the end of tiny lanes west of Chagford. It has bits of everything, but you need to follow the OS map carefully to locate them – a clapper bridge (Teign-e-ver Bridge), Scorhill stone circle, several stone rows, a standing stone aptly known as the Long Stone, and Round Pound (an Iron-Age animal enclosure). Park near Scorhill Farm

he and his hounds disturbed a witches' coven. In fact, being turned to stone isn't unusual, so watch your step, particularly on Sundays: it happened to the Nine Maidens at Belstone Tor and The Dancers near Cornwood because they danced on the sabbath.

If you're driving or cycling along the moor's roads, beware the Hairy Hands: they'll grab the steering wheel or handlebars and try to force you off the road. Mostly they frequent the B3212 near Postbridge, although they've also appeared near Exeter. Making the sign of the cross is said to discourage them. UFO encounters have been reported on Dartmoor too, so watch out for aliens.

Ghosts can appear anywhere. A headless coachman drives Lady Mary Howard across the moor from Okehampton at midnight, in a coach made of the bones of her four husbands, and the infamous Judge Jeffries haunts Lydford Castle in the form of a black pig. On Merripit Hill, little ghostly piglets trot sadly to and fro in search of food. Finally, be careful in Ashburton: the malevolent red-eyed water-sprite Cutty Dyer, who lives by King's Bridge, accosts drunks and other undesirables and throws them in the river. Normally he tolerates tourists, but one never knows …

And you'll find many other Dartmoor legends on ⌂ legendarydartmoor.co.uk.

(SX661877), walk southwest past the stone circle, then southeast over the clapper bridge to Batworthy Corner and the Long Stone, then head northeast up Kes Tor for a splendid view over the whole area.

About four miles southwest of Chagford, on a good road, is **Fernworthy Reservoir**, looked after by the South West Lakes Trust (swlakestrust.org.uk). Although an artificial lake and surrounded by introduced conifers, it is a beautiful, peaceful place for a walk and some birdwatching (there's a bird hide), with much to see including an impressive double stone row. When the water level is very low, submerged clapper bridges are visible. The reservoir can also be accessed from the car park just north of Warren House Inn where you can pick up the Two Moors Trail which takes you close by. I joined one of Keith Lambert's walks (page 231) which took our little group here via hut circles and other prehistoric curiosities which I would never have found myself. The highlight was **Assycombe stone row** in a clearing in the woods, but walking back to the inn along a faint path bright with heather was equally rewarding.

Warren House Inn (PL20 6TA 01822 880208 warrenhouseinn. co.uk 11.00–20.00 daily) is a curiosity in its own right. The most isolated inn in Dartmoor, one of the highest in southern England, and with so much history and legend that there is a book about it. It's famous for having a fire which is alleged to have burned continuously since 1845 (despite, it must be said, patrons' occasional efforts to dowse it by readjusting their fluid intake and output). And there's the legend about the corpse. The story goes that, sometime in the 18th century, a traveller was caught in a snowstorm and asked for a room in the inn. There was only one available, sparsely furnished, but with a large wooden box at one end. Curious, the traveller lifted the lid and saw, to his horror, a well-preserved corpse. Next day he got his answer from the landlady's son: 'Tis only fayther! The snaw being so thick, and making the roads so cledgey-like, when old fayther died, two weeks agon, we couldn't carry un to Tavistock to bury un; so mother put un in the old box, and salted un in: mother's a fine hand at salting un in.' Another version has it that 'We'd just killed the pig and we was saltin' 'un down, so mother, 'er put father in too.'

Warren House Inn is a welcome sight for walkers looking for warmth and food. It serves a great rabbit pie, appropriately, given that its name comes from the commercial rabbit warren nearby.

3 CASTLE DROGO

Castle Drogo EX6 6PB ✐ 01647 433306 ☉ early Mar–end Oct & winter w/ends;
National Trust

I overheard a visitor liken the castle to a Stalinist gulag, and indeed, some find it hard to warm to this monument to 20th-century extravagance and megalomania. But warm I did, and I think it's worth the effort, although at the time of writing the building is hidden behind scaffolding and many of the rooms are closed while major repairs take place because the roof leaks. It's always leaked. It leaks because Mr Drewe specified that there should be a flat roof and no windowsills or guttering. Asphalt was used, and it cracks. The work is scheduled to finish in 2019 but meanwhile you'll be looking at items rather than finished rooms.

Drogo was conceived by Julius Drewe, who made his money as founder of the Home and Colonial Stores which he and his partner sold in 1889 for £3.5 million pounds – around £193 million today. Retired at the age of 33 and needing a way to use up his money he decided, without any evidence, that he was descended from the Norman Baron Drogo de Teign who had given his name to Drewsteignton. Now he needed an ancestral home; so he bought the Drogo estate in 1910 and employed Edwin Lutyens to make his dreams reality. Not a bad commission, even for the most renowned architect of the 20th century. Drewe wanted a castle of 'heroic size', which must have made Lutyens very, very happy.

SIR EDWIN LUTYENS 1869–1944

The home-schooled architect of Castle Drogo was uncomfortable with his wealthy public-school-educated patrons, preferring to sketch ideas for mansions on napkins when seated next to their wives at dinner parties. The commissions that followed were traditional in style but always demonstrated some unique features; Lutyens was as involved in the interiors as with the buildings themselves, including designing furniture. Budgets held little interest for him, and he made it almost a point of honour to exceed them. In 1897 he married Lady Emily Bulwer-Lytton, the daughter of a former Viceroy of India, which must surely have helped him secure his greatest commission: to design the new administrative centre in New Delhi, a task which took him nearly 20 years.

Among Lutyens's best-known designs are the Cenotaph in London and Liverpool Cathedral, but perhaps his most appealing was Queen Mary's Dolls' House which is on permanent display in Windsor Castle and was created as a showcase for the craftsmen of the time.

He was knighted in 1918.

Fingle Bridge & the Teign Gorge

✺ OS Explorer map OL28; start: Fingle Bridge, ♀ SX743899; 3½ miles; easy

One of the most popular walks on Dartmoor, this 'circular' (oblong really) walk takes you from the picturesque Fingle Bridge, south of Drewsteignton, along the Fisherman's Path which hugs the north side of the River Teign, passing through deciduous woodland and mossy rocks, and returning along the higher Hunter's Path beneath Castle Drogo.

Joanna Griffin, wild swimming enthusiast, recommends places where you can swim in the deep pools of the river. Just upstream from Fingle Bridge, there is a small deep pool above Fingle Weir which is great for a quick dip. A mile and a half upstream from here is a long, calm, shady (and rather bracing) stretch of water above Drogo Weir, just downstream from an iron bridge and the Hunter's Path which will take you on the long wind up to the Castle Drogo Estate. Just below the weir is a series of pools – Salmon Leaps – built by castle Drogo's original owner, Julius Drewe, to assist the upward migration of salmon, which doubles as a natural whirlpool for wild swimmers.

The return along the Hunter's Path takes you through open moorland with gorse, heather and stands of silver birch. There are opportunities to access the Castle Drogo estate at the western end of the circuit, and the walk can begin from the Castle's car park instead of Fingle Bridge (where the parking is limited); here you can pick up the National Trust's booklet *Walks in the Teign Valley and Castle Drogo Estate*. Variations of the walk can be done by taking bus 173 to Drewsteignton and catching it again at Castle Drogo.

I never thought that granite could look identical to concrete, but that's the impression given by the precisely cut blocks of stone. Inside, the plasterless walls are the same austere grey and even the garden is all right angles. The feeling of incarceration is not helped by the muted light. But as you make your way through the house, whether before or after the renovation is finished, you'll start to appreciate what you're seeing. The view from the drawing room, for instance, with windows on three sides allowing you to appreciate the castle's magnificent location: ahead lies craggy Dartmoor and to the side is the Teign Valley. Make use of the enthusiasm and knowledge of the National Trust volunteers: they really know their stuff. The human side of this story is what makes a visit to the castle ultimately rewarding: the children's toys, eye-popping in their extravagance; look out for the horse-drawn carriage which could be pushed like a pram. There's a beautiful dolls' house too, though it was explained to me that what we call dolls' houses were not for children to play with, but rather used as decorative objects and to teach household management. The most poignant memorabilia are for Adrian Drewe, the first-born son who died in 1917 at Ypres, at the age of 26, having been married for just one year. As the oldest boy he had been involved in the planning of Castle Drogo from the beginning. It's clear from the lovingly displayed items how deeply missed he was, and one imagines that his father's enthusiasm for the great castle died along with his son; the reduction of the original plan by two-thirds could not have been purely for financial reasons. Tired visitors might be relieved to see the model of the house as planned compared with the one actually built.

Castle Drogo is served by **bus** 173 between Exeter and Moretonhampstead (⊙ weekdays).

▌ FOOD & DRINK

Drewe Arms Drewsteignton EX6 6QN ✆ 01647 281224. This 17th-century thatched pub, right next to the church, serves good food and local ales in an assortment of small rooms, and has a history tied to Castle Drogo. It was Drewe (who else?) who persuaded the landlord to change its name from The Druid Arms and provided his coat of arms for the inn sign. The Mudge family took over in 1919 and Mabel Mudge was reputedly the oldest landlady on record, retiring in 1994 at the age of 99, having run the pub for 75 years. She was 101 when she died.

Fingle Bridge Inn Fingle Bridge, Drewsteignton EX6 6PW ✆ 01647 281287. The verdant location by the river is the main draw here.

4 SPINSTERS' ROCK & STONE LANE GARDEN/ SCULPTURE EXHIBITION

The carved stones in these two sites may span 5,000 years, but in their own way they are equally mysterious and appealing. How convenient that they are within walking distance of each other (less than two miles), and accessible by the 173 bus, although of course most people will drive.

Spinsters' Rock (♀ SX701907) is a Neolithic burial chamber which stands nonchalantly in a meadow full of buttercups and, occasionally, cows. This chambered tomb or cromlech would once have been visible only as a mound of earth which has either eroded away or been removed to reveal the 'chamber' (now more like a shelter) comprising three upright stones forming a tripod, capped by a huge domed piece of granite. The sign tells us that it was allegedly built by three spinsters one morning before breakfast. Take the A382 off the A30, pass the sign to Venton on the left, and at the next crossroads you'll see it signposted. The gate leading to the site is opposite the yard of Shilstone Farm (a shilstone is the 'lid' of a cromlech). If coming by bus you will need to ask the driver to let you off at the turnoff, half a mile beyond Venton, from where it's a very pleasant walk up the hill to Shilstone Farm.

Stone Lane Gardens (TQ13 8JU ✆ 01647 231311 ✆ stonelanegardens. com ☉ year round; sculpture exhibition May–Oct) is home to the National Collection of Birch and Alder, collected by the late Kenneth Ashburner from around the world. There are over a thousand trees with 47 species of birch including *Betula ashburneri*, named in memory of Ken, and 33 of alder. Their white trunks give the five acres of woodland and water an ethereal appearance. The gardens are a joy to stroll in at any time of year but the surprise and pleasure of the summer **Mythic Garden Sculpture Exhibition** makes this the best season for a visit.

To reach the garden on foot or car from Spinsters' Rock, carry on up the lane to the

T-junction and turn right, then either continue to the car park from where there's a short cut to Stone Farm or, if on foot, turn right again down the lane to the Gardens. There are some parking places in the Stone Farm yard for disabled visitors. An 'honesty box' collects your £6 fee, there are maps to guide you round the woodland paths and a printed list of the sculptures, and you're on your own to enjoy this perfect blend of the work of man and nature.

THE EAST

At each end of the oblong formed by the northern apex of the A382 and the B3212 are two of the gateway towns to the high moor, Moretonhampstead and Bovey Tracey, contrasting with some of the most remote-feeling yet accessible valleys in Dartmoor and two of its prettiest villages. Here also are a couple of Dartmoor's few paying attractions, the Miniature Pony Centre and Becky Falls.

5 MORETONHAMPSTEAD

Tourist information: New St ℰ 01647 440043 (○ summer 09.30–17.00 daily, winter 10.00–16.00 w/ends). Staffed by enthusiastic volunteers who love their town, it has a comprehensive stock of local information.

This small town sits right in the centre of Devon, surrounded by some wonderful countryside and with the moor on its doorstep. It has a few attractive old buildings (among them arcaded 17th-century almshouses and a fine 15th-century granite church) but it is as a centre for the arts that it excels. The artist-led arts and heritage centre, **Green Hill Arts** on Fore Street (ℰ 01647 440775 ℰ greenhillarts.

co.uk ○ 10.00–16.00 Tue–Sun) has a changing exhibition of local artists, and art and craft courses.

"It has a few attractive old buildings but it is as a centre for the arts that it excels."

The town is the main hub for the **Dartmoor Artisan Trail** (page 229) with four of their artisans working here: blacksmith, shoemaker, potter, and felting (see box, pages 244–5). All well worth a visit.

For street art, look out for the wrought ironwork outside the Parish Hall opposite the gallery and the sparrowhawk in the central square. The main street has small independent shops with some good local produce – baking, meat, cheeses etc – and cafés.

THE ARTISANS OF MORETONHAMPSTEAD

Mortonhampstead hosts some of the most interesting and diverse participants in the Dartmoor Artisan Trail (⊘ dartmoor-artisan-trail.co.uk). When I asked a passerby for directions to **Bellacouche** where I was to learn felting, I was taken aback when she said 'Oh yes, the coffin lady'. But indeed, that is Yuli Somme's main job: making felt coffins. So while I worked at creating a picture using the technique called needle felting, I chatted to Yuli about death. Scattered around her studio in a beautiful converted chapel are gorgeously decorated sections of white felt. 'It's an updated version of an old tradition' she said 'It used to be the law to bury the dead in a woollen shroud to protect the wool trade'. The felt coffins are supported by a wooden frame with carrying handles, but no conventional coffin is so beautiful. Yuli decorates the top cover with pictures appropriate to the

person being buried. After internment the family can keep the cover or leave it in place over the grave and let it gradually rot down and become part of the earth. 'Thinking outside the box' she calls it, and what a beautiful way to leave this world! Yuli's studio (⊘ 01647 441405 ⊘ bellacouche.com) is in the Unitarian Chapel in Cross Street. She sells a range of felt items, such as tea cosies and slippers, so not just coffins.

After Yuli I visited **Green Shoes** where Alison Hastie was busy doing a final fitting for a woman with green hair and a happy smile. I hadn't planned to buy shoes, but when I saw how meticulously they were made, how mismatched feet of different sizes could be catered for, and the joy of seeing a normally mass-produced item made by hand, I was hooked. My feet have been measured, style and colours chosen,

What struck us most about Moretonhampstead was its friendliness. Certainly some places are prettier, or richer in visible history, or more spectacularly located; but everyone we spoke to was so pleasant and so ready to spend time answering our questions that we continued on our way afterwards with a great feeling of warmth.

The **Motor Museum** on Court Street (TQ13 8LG ⊘ 01647 440636 ⊘ moretonmotormuseum.co.uk ○ school holidays 13.30–16.30 daily; check website for other times) will have classic car enthusiasts purring with happiness. Created and run by Frank Loft and housed in the old bus depot is a collection of 120 vehicles, including such rarities as a D-type Jaguar with a racing speed of 178mph, and a stately 1918 charabanc with a basket for umbrellas on the dashboard. Necessary, I should think, when the rain blew horizontally through the glassless windows. Some bonnets are raised so you can gaze knowledgably at the engine, and the signage is informative and comprehensive.

and the next fitting arranged. Alison showed me what remained of an old pair of shoes, shaped to every bump of the wearer's feet. 'I've finally persuaded her that it's time for a new pair' she said. 'She's had these for 20 years and they've been resoled twice. But she loves them.' Among Alison's employees is Polly, funded by QEST (the Queen Elizabeth Scholarship Trust) which was set up by the Queen Mother to support apprenticeships for aspiring craftspeople. The Prince of Wales is now patron, and these apprenticeships are another example of how heritage crafts are being helped to stay alive. Alison's workshop is also in a lovely converted chapel on Cross Street (26A ☏ 01647 440735 ⌀ greenshoes.co.uk). If you want a fitting it's best to make an appointment, but the shop is usually open ⊙ 09.15–17.15 Monday to Friday for browsing.

Most popular of all on the Artisan Trail for 'having a go' is Greg Abel the blacksmith, also on Cross Street. Working in his old forge full of the implements used by his predecessors, Greg makes a variety of traditional forged items such as gates, railings and firesets. You can drop in and watch him work (check first that he's there), have a demonstration of blacksmithing techniques or, best of all, learn how to make a small item yourself. I know how rewarding this is since I regularly go on blacksmithing courses to make scrap-metal sculpture, so do try it (27 Cross St ☏ 01647 440331 ⌀ moretonforge.co.uk).

At 44a Court Street, on the other side of the village, is Penny Simpson's ceramics studio, full of beautiful ceramic tableware in a variety of colours and designs. Her shop is usually open 10.00–17.00 Monday–Friday and Saturday mornings.

6 THE MINIATURE PONY CENTRE

2 miles west of Moretonhampstead, TQ13 8RG ☏ 01647 432400 ⌀ miniatureponycentre. com ⊙ late Mar–end Nov

This is a perennial favourite within Dartmoor National Park. Although aimed at families there is plenty for adults to enjoy here; just the sight of quite small children towering over these dog-sized ponies in the paddock brings a smile. The place is well organised, with a variety of other creatures as well as the ponies, including a recently introduced display of 'weird and wonderful' animals. In contrast to the tiny ponies there are two massive heavy horses to remind us of the variety in the equine world.

7 MANATON & BECKY FALLS

Manaton was once two villages, Manaton Magna and Manaton Parva, which explains its fragmented nature. Upper Manaton, around the church, is perfection: a spacious green sets off the fine church of St Winifred, dressed in traditional Devon white, with a row of thatched houses behind it. One splendid house, Wingstone Manor, was, for a time, the home of John Galsworthy who wrote *The Forsyte Saga*. The village green was bought in 1928 from its previous owner, Lord Hambledon (who owned a huge swathe of the region in the early 19th century), for £75 collected from parishioners. Last time I visited a game of village cricket was in progress.

"The coffin wagon on display doubles as a handy surface from which to serve tea."

The interior of the church has some rather splendid pillars of Devon granite, carved bench ends (mostly foliage and coats of arms) and a fine wooden screen defaced during the Reformation: every carved saint and angel has had its face chiselled away. The coffin wagon on display doubles as a handy surface from which to serve tea. The view from the churchyard across the moor to Haytor must be one of the best on Dartmoor.

Two saturday walks to Manaton using the Haytor Hoppa

✳ OS Explorer OL28 or Harvey's *Dartmoor* (North); start: Parke or Jay's Grave ♀ SX733799; about 5 miles from Parke or 2 miles from Jay's Grave; some steep bits on both walks but nothing too challenging

I tested out two Haytor Hoppa walks and found the timings spot on. For the first I did the full bus circuit, for the pleasure of it, and got off at **Parke** near Bovey Tracey, to walk through the woods and along quiet lanes to **Lustleigh**, and then up to the beautiful mossy woodland of **Lustleigh Cleave** and down to **Manaton**. There's a particularly memorable bit close to Manaton where you cross the river on the boulder stepping stones known as Horsham Steps in the National Nature Reserve of Bovey Valley Woodlands. It would have been a perfect place for a picnic, surrounded by trees and birdsong, and with water to cool off in. This walk took four hours but I stopped at Lustleigh for a cream tea!

The other, shorter, walk starts from **Jay's Grave**, and takes in the famous landmark of **Bowerman's Nose** (pages 257–8). A footpath runs south of the Nose and brings you out at Manaton. Two hours is sufficient for this walk. For both walks you'll need a detailed map that shows the footpaths.

The local pub, **the Kester Inn** (TQ13 9UF ✐ 01647 221204) is actually in a little hamlet called Water, a half mile outside Manaton. It has views from the conservatory area, and a mix of locals and hikers enjoying the homemade bar food.

A little over a mile to the southeast is **Becky Falls** (TQ13 9UG ✐ 01647 221259 ✐ beckyfalls.com), a good place to bring the family to see the meerkats and owls, and pet the rabbits, pygmy goats and miniature ponies, before visiting the reptile house to squeal over the huge boas and other snakes, and one of my favourite animals, a Madagascar hissing cockroach. The waterfall itself is pleasant rather than dramatic in the summer, but makes a good focal point. There are three walking circuits of varying difficulty, so you can suit your visit to your abilities. It's quite pricey (check their website for the current rate), so it's worth spending half a day here to enjoy the birdwatching (we saw a dipper bobbing about on the rocks) and the mossy quietness (which you won't get during the school holidays). The Haytor Hoppa bus runs to Manaton and Becky Falls on Saturdays (summer only), and the 671 makes a single journey on Wednesdays all year. The timing allows you to explore Becky Falls and Manaton and have a meal at the Kestor Inn before catching the return bus.

LUSTLEIGH & NORTH BOVEY

Here are two classically picturesque villages of thatched cottages, only a few miles from the A382 but cut off from mainstream traffic by the nerve-rackingly narrow approach lanes.

8 Lustleigh

Lustleigh would probably feature in most shortlists of Devon's prettiest villages, sitting at the base of the Lustleigh Cleave escarpment (see opposite) with narrow car-free paths winding around thatched cottages. It has a well-stocked village shop, The Dairy, which sells 'terrific sausage rolls' according to a visitor, and a long May Day tradition. This is celebrated with aplomb on the first Saturday of the month with maypole dancing in The Orchard, which is reached by keeping St John the Baptist's Church on your right and going straight ahead at the (road) T-junction past the old post office. The names of all the May Queens since the 1960s are recorded on a rock in the centre of the Orchard. Carry on to the gate at the far end for the footpath to Lustleigh Cleave.

LIGHT ON THE DARK AGES

Current thinking defines the span of Britain's 'dark ages' as roughly the two centuries following the final departure of the Romans, so around AD400–600, and relatively few artefacts from that period have been found.

In **Yealmpton** churchyard (page 166), a granite slab like a small standing stone, roughly engraved with the word TOREUS or more probably GOREUS, has been dated by past local historians to between the 3rd and 6th century, and described as a memorial to either a Christianised Roman or a converted British chieftain. Holes in its back suggest it was also used as a doorpost or fence post.

A similar but better-engraved stone in **Lustleigh** church, with the inscription DATUIDOCI CONHINOCI FILIUS (of Datuidoc son of Conhinoc), is put at around AD550–600. The names are British but the language is Latin.

In **Tavistock** (on private land) are three more, roughly six feet high, described as 5th–6th century, whose Latin inscriptions translate as *Sabinus son of Maccodechet*, *Nepranus son of Conbevus*, and *Dubunnus the smith son of Enabarrus*. They were retrieved at different times in the 19th century, from Buckland Monachorum, Roborough Down and Tavistock. One had been used as a farm gatepost, one served as a footbridge over a leat and one was lying beside a road, so it's fortunate that they were spotted and taken to safety.

The men they commemorate remain a mystery (what type of smith would merit so important a memorial?), and more undiscovered onces may well exist, so, if you unexpectedly come across a similar slab of granite, do check whether or not it has been inscribed!

The church is well worth a visit for its beautiful wood carvings. The pulpit is by Herbert Read, a fine wood carver who contributed to the beauty of several Devon churches at the end of the 19th century, and the bench-ends are more recent with figurative carvings of various animals including a rather jolly lion and an elephant. The screen is equally finely carved (though the painted panels have been defaced) and it has a modern (1929) rood (crucifix) above it, as would have been the case with all churches before they were removed by Cromwell's henchmen.

Two 13th-century stone effigies of a knight and his lady have been repositioned on their sides, and quite a few centuries later the stonemason (probably) carved a portrait of his gloomy-looking wife above the west window. A piece of granite against the west wall is described by Arthur Mee in 1965 as 'a mysterious stone inscribed with strange characters which have not been deciphered.' More recent research has solved some of the mystery – but created more (see box, above).

¶¶ FOOD & DRINK

Primrose Tea Rooms Lustleigh ✐ 01647 277365. Serves excellent lunches and classic cream teas in its primrose-yellow, thatched cottage.

The Cleave ✐ 01647 277223 ✐ thecleavelustleigh.co.uk. This lovely 15th-century thatched pub in Lustleigh changed owner in 2017 and is reportedly as good as ever, with quality food and a varied menu. In the rear is the renovated old station waiting room which gives access to the garden for summer lunches.

9 North Bovey

Bovey Castle (page 278) **The Chapel** Lettaford (page 278)

With its spacious green surrounded by whitewashed thatched houses and backed by a church, this is a classic English village and exceptionally tranquil. The green is shaded by oak trees of different sizes, each planted to commemorate an event: variously Queen Victoria's Jubilee, George V and Queen Mary's Silver Jubilee, several coronations, and the smallest tree of all – the Millennium. At the edge of the green is a Dartmoor stone cross which was retrieved from Bovey Brook in 1829 by the Rev Pike Jones, known as Bovey Jones, and hauled into position. The famous thatched pub, The **Ring of Bells**, burned down in 2016, but is being restored at the time of writing and is scheduled to reopen by the time you read this. Several medieval features have been discovered and will be retained, and if it serves food anywhere near as good as it used to, it's worth a visit.

The **church** (St John the Baptist) is delightful, with worm-eaten pews and mainly clear glass to let Dartmoor in. There's an elaborate carved pulpit, donated by parishioners in 1910 to commemorate the vicar's 80th birthday and 45 years of service. The intricately carved screen is a few hundred years older, but the painted saints have been removed. The old pews in the centre have carved bench

"The church is delightful, with worm-eaten pews and clear glass to let Dartmoor in."

ends, mostly with architectural designs, but there are two in the south aisle of particular interest. One is carved with the initials WP, which could have been William Pipard, who was Lord of the Manor in the 14th century. The other is described in the church information sheet as 'a bearded Renaissance man with a jaunty feather in his hat.' He appears to have a string of beads emerging from his mouth: one of those enigmatic bench-end carvings the meaning of which we can only guess at.

The floor of the nave is almost covered with crudely lettered memorial stones to parishioners who died in the 1700s, and overhead is a splendid wagon roof with some brightly painted roof bosses; look for the 'tinners' rabbits' (see box, page 225) above the altar rail.

10 BOVEY TRACEY

🏠 **Ilsington Country House Hotel & Spa** Ilsington (page 278)

Tourist information: Station Rd car park ✆ 01626 32047 ⌂ boveytracey.gov.uk
🕙 10.00–16.00 Sun–Fri, 09.30–15.30 Sat. Run by (very helpful) volunteers, so may sometimes be unexpectedly closed.

Bovey (pronounced Buvvy) Tracey is a lovely town to spend time in. If you approach from the A38, you'll be able to park next to the TIC and near the town's outstanding attraction: the **Devon Guild of Craftsmen** (Riverside Mill, TQ13 9AF ✆ 01626 832223 ⌂ crafts.org.uk ⌂ Apr–Nov 10.00–17.30 daily, Dec–Mar Sat only & check website for closures). The displays here are top quality, with a shifting exhibition showcasing the best of Devon's artists and crafts people, from jewellery and stained glass to sculpture, pottery and ceramics, not to mention fabulous clothing. It also holds events and workshops including some aimed at children.

Some of Bovey's shops, too, are aimed at creative visitors. One of the most popular is **Spin a Yarn** (26 Fore St ✆ 01626 836203 ⌂ spinayarndevon.co.uk), which stocks a huge range of wools. This shop is a painter's palette of colours, all softly blending with each other. The yarns come from around the world and the shop attracts visitors from far and wide. Nearer the entrance to the town is **Serendipity** (6 Station Rd ✆ 01626 836246 ⌂ serendipityquilts.co.uk), which focuses on patchwork and quilting. Myriam Van de Pas and her daughter Sunny sell a huge range of fabrics, patterns, buttons and other sewing supplies

DARTMOOR DIALECT

The late Tony Beard, 'the Wag of Widecombe', who was born and bred on Dartmoor, told me some of the local words still used in rural areas. 'There are lots of different words in the Devon dialect, and these can even vary from region to region within the county. For instance, that little creature the woodlouse has several different names; round here it's called *granfer grigg*. A blue tit is an *ackermail* and a wren is a *tit-e-tope*. We call a thistle a *daishel*, and sometimes we swap letters around so a wasp is a *wapse*.'

as well as finished goods, and run courses. While I was in the shop an old fellow came in for two more yards of material. He told us that a heart attack had put an end to his long walks on the moor so he'd taken up sewing instead. 'I've been making some amazing stuff,' he said.

All the delights of Bovey seem to be clustered together near the river at the eastern end of town, but the **House of Marbles** is some way away, near the roundabout on the Newton Abbot road (Pottery Rd, TQ13 9DS ✐ 01626 835285 ⌂ houseofmarbles.com). This is a working glass factory with a large shop selling just about everything, some fine exhibitions of glass, and small museum devoted to marbles. It opens at 09.00, which puts it a step ahead of most attractions, and it's free so is popular with coach parties. There's plenty to enjoy here apart from shopping. You can watch the glass-blowers at work and, best of all, gaze mesmerised at the giant marble run at the top of the stairs. It's the biggest in the world, created to mark the Millennium in 2000, and I could happily have spent an hour watching the giant marbles progress along an intricate maze propelled by nothing more than gravity. There are two smaller marble runs in the museum, equally enjoyable, and an interesting display of marbles from earliest times, when they really were marble, to the present day.

PARKE

TQ13 9JQ ✐ 01626 834748; ⌂ almost year-round, dawn–dusk; National Trust

This peaceful 205-acre estate, about a mile out of town on the B3387, is one of the National Trust's unsung properties. The walled garden is of particular interest, being run jointly by the National Trust and Bovey Climate Action (⌂ boveyclimateaction.org.uk), raising warm-climate produce such as peaches, apricots and almonds, as well as salads; there's a solar-powered pump for irrigation.

People come to Parke to stroll in the gardens or walk in the woods – or for the energetic, to do the Saturday parkrun – and to eat in the excellent café. The Dartmoor Pony Heritage Trust is here, open on Sunday afternoons to visitors, and the Dartmoor National Park Authority has its offices in the old manor house.

⫶ FOOD & DRINK

For a town of its size, Bovey is not blessed with good restaurants serving evening meals. I didn't find one I could recommend for dinner, but lunch is a different matter.

Home Farm Café Parke Estate ✆ 01626 830016 🖱 homefarmcafe.co.uk. This is a bustling and popular place, with freshly cooked meals and snacks using locally sourced and mostly organic fair trade ingredients. Good coffee, too. Open in the daytime plus some weekend evenings.

Inner Light coffee shop ✆ 01626 832394 ⊙ 08.30–17.30. A lovely vegetarian café with a huge selection of teas and juices, and good baking. There are comfy armchairs as well as conventional seating, and a traditional sweet shop attached.

The Terrace Café Devon Guild of Craftsmen (page 250). Delicious homemade food in spacious surroundings, inside or out, and those wonderful exhibits close at hand.

THE HIGH MOOR

My favourite approach to the high moor is from Bovey Tracey. Cyclists toil up the three-mile hill, overtaken by drivers in third gear, but their goal is the same: the sudden view of Haytor and the feeling that you've arrived in the 'real Dartmoor'. With Widecombe-in-the-Moor as its focus, this region has bleak, open moorland, craggy tors and farms. Some of Dartmoor's oldest prehistoric sites are here, including **Grimspound** and well-known landmarks such as **Jay's Grave** and **Bowerman's Nose**.

11 HAYTOR

🏠 **Rock Inn** (page 278) 🏠 **The Secret Holt** (page 278)

Tourist information: Dartmoor National Park Visitor Centre TQ13 9XT ✆ 01364 661520 ⊙ Apr–Oct 10.00–16.30 daily, Nov–March 10.00–15.00 Thu–Sun. Helpful & informative, with an extensive selection of leaflets, maps & books.

Four miles west of Bovey Tracey, Haytor is the best-known of all of Dartmoor's tors. Easily accessible from the road, the 1,499ft summit is almost always topped by the silhouettes of scramblers who have reached the top of this huge granite outcrop. Nearly two centuries ago some steps were cut and a handrail provided (now removed) to make the ascent easier, to the disgust of a local doctor who commented that the steps were 'to enable the enervated and pinguitudinous scions of humanity of this wonderful nineteenth century to gain its summit'. It is no coincidence that the granite tramway (see box, opposite) ran from here; the granite is of exceptionally high quality, although erosion has now reduced Haytor's once single stone to two, with an avenue running between them.

THE TEMPLER WAY: THE GRANITE TRAMWAY

This 18-mile trail is more than just a long-distance footpath from Teignmouth to Haytor, it is an extraordinary example of using a local material – granite – in hitherto unimaginable ways.

James Templer was born in 1722. An orphan, he ran away to sea and made his fortune in India. On returning to England he bought the Stover estate (page 192) and built Stover House.

In the 1820s his grandson, George Templer, bought a granite quarry on Haytor, Dartmoor, and needed to find a way of moving the blocks of stone to a seaport so they could be transported to London at that time

(Dartmoor granite was used for a great many of the capital's buildings and even London paving stones). So he built a granite tramway, using grooved granite instead of metal rails. Even the points and sidings were made out of granite. Teams of up to 19 horses pulled the huge, flat wooden trucks. The braking mechanism for going downhill was primitive, to say the least, but history does not tell us about the accidents that must surely have happened.

The granite tracks are still visible along parts of the Templer Way; on Dartmoor you can see them on a popular walk near Haytor and near Bovey Tracey.

There are some good walks from here, including the popular one to Hound Tor and the Templer Way, and a choice of circuits.

Parke's **Home Farm Café** (see opposite) has a van here in the summer serving hot drinks, snacks and ice cream.

¶¶ FOOD & DRINK

Rock Inn Haytor Vale TQ13 9XP ⌀ 01364 661305 ⌀ rock-inn.co.uk. A 300-year-old inn standing high on Dartmoor. Run by the same family since 1983, it offers convivial surroundings and local produce. Beer garden for fine summer days. See also page 278.

Ullacombe Farm Shop & Café Haytor Rd (between Bovey & Haytor) TQ13 9LL ⌀ 01364 661341 ⊙ 08.30–17.00 daily. A terrific farm shop and butchery selling everything, including their own organic produce. Excellent café.

12 WIDECOMBE-IN-THE-MOOR

To most visitors this village is the capital of Dartmoor, with a cathedral to boot. Its popularity as a tourist honeypot stemmed from the traditional song about Widecombe Fair: it's the one place in Dartmoor everyone's heard of. And once the tourists came they needed to be provided for; Widecombe must, for its size, have more tea rooms and car-parking space than any other village in Dartmoor. Despite the coaches and

WIDECOMBE FAIR

Widecombe Fair (⊘ widecombefair.com), the popular market that enticed Bill Brewer, Jan Stewer, Peter Gurney, Peter Davy, Daniel Whiddon, Harry Hawk, Old Uncle Tom Cobley and all to borrow Tom Pierce's grey mare to transport them from their homes in north Dartmoor to the fun and revelry, is always held on the second Tuesday in September when the village is closed to traffic. Originally a livestock show, it has now evolved into more of a tourist attraction, with exhibitions and a funfair. The recently restored Uncle Tom Cobley model with its working parts, which was last exhibited 50 years ago, made its reappearance in 2009 and is now housed in the church.

crowds its charm is undiminished, making it a good base for exploring the moor and the valleys even without a car. With transport – car or bicycle – all of Dartmoor is within easy reach.

The village sits in a hollow, with the extraordinarily high tower (350 feet) of the **church** visible from the surrounding hills and giving it the popular name of the Cathedral of the Moor. Much of the church dates from the 14th century, but the tower was added later and reputedly paid for by well-to-do tinners. The church is dedicated to St Pancras, who most people associate with a London railway station rather than a child martyr. This orphan was beheaded in AD304 as a 14-year-old for proclaiming his faith, and is patron saint of children; he can also do his bit for headaches and cramp. And for perjury, although I'm not sure how that works … Quite a few of his relics ended up in England, which explains why there are several churches dedicated to him. Widecombe church has two depictions of Abraham and Isaac (relevant to child martyrdom): a painting near the south door and a carved panel displayed at the west end of the church. The sign identifies this as a tester, or bed-head from a four-poster bed, which once belonged in a farmhouse. There's some delightful detail here, with Abraham being stopped from killing his son by a very chubby angel. Nearby is an unattributed model of the church made from matchsticks. Another model, at the opposite end of the church, is Widecombe's *Old Uncle Tom Cobley and All*, made nearly 60 years ago and recently rescued and restored.

With the number of tourists who visit this church, the interior has become as much of a museum as a place of worship. Large display boards tell the history of the church and show the main items of interest, one of which is the carved and coloured bosses on the roof: hard to see by craning your neck so the display showing most of them is convenient and rewarding. They include a green man, a scapegoat and a pelican-in-her-piety, as well as the 'tinners' rabbits' near the altar (see box, page 225).

Mixed up with all the legends of Widecombe is the fact that during a dramatic thunderstorm on 21 October 1638, the church was struck by lightning and four people were killed, and many injured, when the tower crashed through the roof. Very little happened in the 17th century that wasn't the work of God or the Devil. In this case, an innocuous-looking gentleman had popped into a Poundsgate inn for a glass of ale and asked the way to Widecombe. The landlady remembered afterwards that she heard his drink hiss as it went down his throat. In Widecombe the Devil, for it was he, tethered his horse to a pinnacle of the tower while he went about his mischief with some local lads. Some say he was involved in a tussle to gain a soul, others that he simply forgot that his black steed was still tethered, and galloped away, toppling the tower. The pious congregation disregarded the fact that God had, perhaps, selected a time when a service was being held to do a bit of smiting, and the church records their gratitude and praise.

Next to the church is the original **Church House**, which was once an ale house to refresh travellers, and then a poorhouse. It is now the village hall and headquarters of the local National Trust, with a shop and information centre. On the fourth Saturday of every month a **food market** is held here.

On the spacious green is a **Millennium Stone** under which are buried photos of every house and every family in the parish. However, they are on CD/DVD so whether the people who unearth it centuries hence will be illuminated or puzzled remains to be seen.

FOOD & DRINK

Rugglestone Inn ✆ 01364 621327 ⌂ rugglestoneinn.co.uk. Named after a local logan stone (a wobbling stone that has become detached from its base), this small and very popular inn on the outskirts of Widecombe has been a favourite with locals and visitors for many years, and is one of the best on Dartmoor. The listed building is charming, the food excellent and the location sublime. Reservations essential.

The Café on the Green ✆ 01364 621720 ⊙ 10.00–17.00. Indoor and outdoor seating, a very good and varied menu, and fast service make this an excellent choice for lunch or tea.

The Old Inn ✆ 01364 621207. Situated in the centre of the village, it is indeed old (14th century) and has a spacious car park. The food is simple but good, and reasonably priced.

13 HOUND TOR, JAY'S GRAVE & BOWERMAN'S NOSE

Northeast of Widecombe are some of the high moor's most iconic attractions. Park at Swallowton Gate, near Hound Tor, reached from either Widecombe or Bovey Tracey. If you visit on a Saturday, the Haytor Hoppa provides the perfect transport, or if you're a keen walker there's a popular three-mile walk from Haytor to Hound Tor which takes in part of the granite tramway (see box, page 253) and the medieval village (see below). Pick up a walks leaflet from the Haytor Information Centre for a description of the route.

Hound Tor

Hound Tor is a wonderful jumble of rocks, often less busy than Haytor and providing plenty of scrambling for children. It is the starting (or finishing) point of several walks including from Manaton (pages 245–6). It's also the site of a ruined **medieval village**, although this can be so hidden among the vegetation in summer that it's easy to miss. From the car park, walk up the track that runs to the right of the tor and continue to the top of the rise; then as you pass the tor bear slightly left so that you're descending into a valley rather than heading for level moorland. You'll come to the low, broken foundations of around 12 buildings, some showing recognisable features.

Without a plan or some archaeological knowledge they're hard to identify; a helpful booklet by Lesley Chapman, *Grimspound and Hound Tor*, covers both these sites (for Grimspound, see page 258). There's a good description of the village and its history on the English Heritage website (⊘ english-heritage.org).

"It was farmed for a while at least as early as the Bronze Age, then abandoned after a series of cold wet years."

Activity on the land pre dates the ruins: it was farmed for a while at least as early as the Bronze Age, then abandoned after a series of cold wet years when the climate deteriorated. Several centuries later, in about AD500, Saxon farmers on the lookout for good agricultural land began to work it, as it had conveniently been cleared of boulders by its previous inhabitants; they built rough homes of wood and peat, which haven't survived but can be identified archaeologically by post holes. Sometime in the 13th century, these were replaced by more solid stone buildings with wooden doors and thatched roofs. Some were traditional 'longhouses', on a slight slope so that the family could live at the higher end and the animals at the lower; drainage channels from the animals' quarters are still visible. They had barns, gardens, ovens – and the people probably enjoyed a healthy diet from their crops, livestock and nearby game.

The scope of the buildings suggests that it was a comfortable little farming community for a while, but in the 14th century the climate deteriorated again: persistently cold wet weather destroyed crops, leaving both animals and people hungry. Then came the Black Death, sweeping its murderous way across the country. Some families may have struggled on for a time, but almost certainly by the early 15th century the homes were abandoned. Today it's a peaceful place, protecting the memory of moorland farmers from long ago.

Jay's Grave & Bowerman's Nose

From the car park take the left fork to walk to **Jay's Grave**. I first heard about this from my neighbour on the Haytor Hoppa. 'I haven't been there for a while but there always used to be fresh flowers laid there every day.' The grave belongs to Kitty Jay, a girl who took her own life after being seduced by a local lad. As a suicide she was buried outside the parish boundary, but exhumed in 1860 and reburied in a proper grave in its current position at a crossroads. And there are indeed always fresh flowers there, and often other items such as coins. Treat the grave with respect or you may regret it (see some of the comments on ⊘ legendarydartmoor.co.uk).

From here it's a pleasant and easy walk along a footpath to the lane that runs north of Swallowton Gate, and then over a grassy hill to Hayne Down from where you can take a look at **Bowerman's Nose** before returning to your car. Despite the misfortune of having been turned to stone when inadvertently disturbing a coven of witches while out with his hounds, the hunter does not look unhappy. Indeed, he has the expression of a twitcher who has just spotted a rare bird. After all, he has an idyllic view of patchwork fields to look out on for eternity, and his faithful hounds are nearby, also turned to stone, on Hound Tor.

On a Saturday you can continue walking to Manaton and pick up the Haytor Hoppa bus (page 228).

14 Grimspound

About four miles north of Widecombe, and roughly the same distance from Moretonhampstead, is Grimspound, the best-preserved Bronze-Age pound, or walled enclosure, on the moor and only a short, though steep, walk from the road. The rather fanciful speculations that this massive circle of stones was a Druid temple or Phoenician settlement were quashed when excavations in the late 19th century concluded that the large external wall was nothing more exotic than a corral for cattle, and the smaller stone circles within it the remains of huts, some of them dwellings and others food stores. Considering their age, the huts were quite sophisticated: you can still see the stone beds, which were probably covered with bracken or animal skins. Grimspound, in its moorland setting, is incredibly atmospheric. Alex Graeme (page iii) says: 'It's my favourite place on Dartmoor and every guest I bring there loves it. As you look back across the valley you can see lynchets (medieval irrigation systems) on one of the hillsides and the remains of the tin-mining industrial landscape on another hill. So it's a perfect place to see the sweep of Dartmoor's history in one spot.'

"The rather fanciful speculations that this massive circle of stones was a Druid temple or Phoenician settlement were quashed."

A sign on the B3212 points towards the site (♀ SX808697) but a better alternative is to walk there from Widecombe, taking the Two Moors Way; it runs above the site, thus giving you the best view of the circle and huts in this wild and desolate place. Imagine the time it would have taken to haul all those stones into position. Then visualise the hillsides covered in trees, providing cover for wildlife and edible plants, and the cattle safe inside the compound. Maybe it wasn't so harsh a life after all.

15 Postbridge & Bellever Forest

🏠 **Lydgate House Hotel** (page 278)

Heading south along the trans-moor road, the B3212, you come to **Postbridge**, where there's an accessible **clapper bridge**, and one of the few post offices on Dartmoor. There's also a National Park Visitor Centre here providing information, maps etc (PL20 6TH ✆ 01822 88027).

Southeast of Postbridge is **Bellever Forest**, owned by the Forestry Commission so consisting mainly of conifers. Nevertheless, this is a deservedly popular place for families and picnickers, with a good car park (with toilets) and walks along the Dart riverbank with swimming possibilities.

A few hundred yards from the car park, by the path on the opposite side of the river, and marked on the OS map, are the ruins of the **Snaily House** (page 273). It gets its name from the story of two spinster sisters who lived there in (probably) the early 19th century and flourished, so it's said, on a diet of snails and slugs.

SOUTHWEST DARTMOOR

This region of woods and deep river valleys reveals the gentler side of Dartmoor, ideal for a drizzly day when the mists are hanging low over the tors. There are riverside walks with swimming possibilities, as well as the lovely walk to Buckland Beacon for one of the best views on Dartmoor. **Dartmeet**, as you would expect, is where the two branches of the River Dart meet. It lies deep in the woods, with sunlit meadows and wild swimming possibilities nearby. It's a popular picnic place and can get crowded in the holiday season.

The main towns here are **Holne** and **Buckland-in-the-Moor**, both easily accessible from Ashburton or Buckfastleigh.

BRIMPTS FARM

🏠 **Brimpts Farm** (page 278)

Between Two Bridges & Dartmeet, PL20 6SG ✆ 01364 631450 ⌂ brimptsfarm.co.uk

Look at any old map or book about Dartmoor and Brimpts is there. William Crossing (1909) describes it as 'one of the ancient tenements, and in 1307 is referred to as Bremstonte' before charting its progression through several names to the present day. Andy Bradford and his wife Gabrielle now run the farm, which is an example of successful

ST RAPHAEL'S CHURCH & VICTORIAN SCHOOL

St Raphael's church, Huccaby, near Hexworthy PL20 6SB

What a wonderful piece of serendipity to come upon this charming place as I made my way towards Holne from Dartmeet. First I noticed the tall chimney and then the sign on St Raphael's church noticeboard caught my eye: 'It's summer. Son Screen prevents Sin burn!' I ever! It was worth a look. I learned that the simple chapel was built in 1868, initially to provide local farmers with a place of worship, saving them the journey to Lydford, but later a school was opened for their children, thus ensuring that the new building was put to full use.

What makes a visit so worthwhile is that the chapel serves as a little museum. The pews adapted to desks are there, with a quill pen stuck in each inkwell, and slates. The master's desk sits high in a commanding position, and to ensure discipline there is a dunce's cap and a swishy cane. It's altogether delightful.

The church is claimed to be the only Anglican one in the whole of England that is dedicated to St Raphael, and is still used for monthly services.

diversification from way back. Andy's mother got the tenancy of the farm in 1947, but it has provided accommodation since World War I. In 1969 the Bradfords became leaseholders for £1 an acre, to the disapproval of some locals who thought this too high a price. Andy's mother opened the tearoom in 1975; it has retained its popularity ever since. Andy loves green technology ('He's the one with vision,' says Gabrielle, 'I look after the practical side.') One of the fruits of this vision is the biomass boiler and the Dartmoor Wood Co-operative to harvest the woodchips for it; diseased or dead trees such as larch and ash are often used.

"When I attended a literary weekend one participant said firmly that she was 'here for the cakes'."

In the 1990s some barns were converted to accommodation and group spaces for conferences including popular literary weekends (ask Gabrielle about these). Traditionally, however, Brimpts is for beef cattle (South Devon crossed with Limousin). 'Dartmoor wouldn't be Dartmoor without the farms,' said Andy, before the conversation turned to Brexit and his worry about imports from the USA. 'There are uncertain times ahead'.

Brimpts is famous for its baking (when I attended a literary weekend one participant said firmly that she was 'here for the cakes') so a visit to the teashop is recommended, but for a real indulgence book for a Sunday Roast.

The farm is the home of **Adventure Clydesdale** (adventureclydesdale. com) run by Tim Ware and his wife Aileen. Magnificent Clydesdale heavy horses (one is 18hh) take experienced riders over the moor for a unique experience. 'Wonderful!' said the rider I chatted to afterwards. 'Mind you, my hips feel a bit stretched!'

6 HOLNE TO POUNDSGATE

The Barn Scorriton (page 278)

Holne's attraction is its notable feeling of community, a lively place with plenty happening – and a lovely walk there with an option to cool off in the river. Park at **New Bridge** (not very new – it dates from the 15th century) and take the footpath south through National Trust property for about a mile. The track initially follows the River Dart through flower-filled woodland and then meanders uphill, crossing a field or two before emerging near the village. As the main track leaves the river you can take a small path to the swimming area where flat slabs of rock channel the stream into deep, cool pools (page 81).

HIGHER UPPACOTT: A DARTMOOR LONGHOUSE

There are plenty of longhouses on Dartmoor, but none that has preserved its original features as well as Higher Uppacott in **Poundsgate**. The function of a longhouse was to house animals and people in the same building, using the warmth of the animals to provide primitive central heating – a perfect concept in a harsh environment like Dartmoor. These houses were usually built on a slight slope so animal waste could drain out.

Higher Uppacott was probably built in the 14th century and retains the shipon, or animal quarters, as used by the medieval farmers, with the cattle tied up in parallel rows, their backsides over a drain running down the middle of the floor and out on to the dung heap in the adjacent pasture. Hay was stored on racks made from branches and,

since the building was probably running with rodents, an owl window was built to allow these predators in.

Originally the human living quarters were extremely simple, with a fire in the middle of the room, the smoke rising to the thatch above (this open-hearth arrangement can still be seen in Africa, and is effective in killing insects that would otherwise infest the thatch). Later, in the 17th century, an upper storey was created and the fireplace moved to the wall where a chimney stack was built.

Improvements continued to be added in the 18th and 19th centuries, and it was still in use in the 20th.

The house normally opens from time to time for group visits but is currently being renovated. Check dartmoor.gov.uk.

Charles Kingsley, who wrote *The Water Babies* and *Westward Ho!*, was born here. His father was the vicar, and Charles is commemorated in a stained glass window in **St Mary's Church**, which is worth visiting in its own right. A splendid lightning-blasted yew stands in the graveyard, so hollow it resembles scaffolding rather than a solid tree. The church entrance is a little wonky – it seems to lean to the left – but inside all is as it should be. There's a fine wagon roof and a striking rood screen, recently restored, which depicts 40 saints of varying obscurity. A helpful loose-leaf binder explains who's who and what they were patron of, including St John the Apostle who is patron saint of authors, booksellers and typesetters.

"St John the Apostle is patron saint of authors, booksellers and typesetters. I'm sure he'd add publishers if asked nicely."

I'm sure he'd add publishers if asked nicely. The pulpit, richly carved in 1480 from a single block of oak, has recently been restored with its original polychrome.

The village has an excellent community-run **village shop and tea room** (✆ 01364 631135), providing coffee and a good selection of cakes and light lunches as well as tourist information.

Just north of Newbridge is Poundsgate, just a scatter of houses and an inn with a history. **The Tavistock Inn** (✆ 01364 631251 ⌂ tavistockinndartmoor.co.uk) is one of the oldest in the county, and it was here that the Devil had his glass of ale before heading for Widecombe (pages 253–5). Nearby is **Higher Uppacott**, a historic Devon longhouse (see box, page 261), which is owned by the National Park and has kept its original features.

17 BUCKLAND-IN-THE-MOOR & BUCKLAND BEACON

From the high moor the village is approached via single-track lanes so it's quite a relief to see the tower of the famous church and know you've reached your destination (it's easier to access it from Ashburton, three miles away). It's the church clock that is famous – the numerals have been replaced by the words 'MY DEAR MOTHER' in gothic lettering by 19th-century landowner William Whitely (more of him later) who also arranged for the bells to chime a rough version of 'All things bright and beautiful'. But the **Church of St Peter** is much more than the clock and worth visiting in its own right. As one description puts it, 'The church on its sloping site looks as if it were carved from a natural granite outcrop or perhaps risen over time fully formed from the rock of Dartmoor'. Before entering, look for the tomb of a soldier who died 'succouring a foeman'. It's touching how proud the community obviously was of this demonstration of humanity.

Once inside, you can appreciate the contrast between the rough-hewn granite pillars and the intricately carved wooden rood screen showing traces of gilding. Its narrow uprights end in fan vaulting – a characteristic of Devon churches. Some of the painted saints remain in the panels, but half have been scraped off, no doubt in the Puritan era. More recently there's been a strong Royalist tendency. Above the south door is the coat of arms of George II, dated 1745, and along the wall are framed telegrams from the congregation congratulating a series of monarchs on their coronations and jubilees. They are mostly undated but the earliest is probably George V, with later ones to George VI and our Queen Elizabeth.

"The Ten Commandments remind parishioners of God's unchanging laws – and landowner Whitely's influence."

Up on nearby **Buckland Beacon** are two granite slabs on which are carved the **Ten Commandments**. These were provided by the same benefactor as the unique church clock: William Whitely of Buckland Manor. Mr Whitely was one of many Devonians who felt strongly about the attempted introduction of a new prayer book (thought by many to have 'popish trends') in 1928. The proposal was rejected, and the Ten Commandments remind parishioners of God's unchanging laws – and landowner Whitely's influence.

The Beacon is not easily accessed from the village. With a car it is easiest to drive towards Cold East Cross and park just over the cattle grid (♥ SX 739737). A good track runs close to a wall on your left and leads to the rocks which mark the Buckland Beacon (one of many such 'beacon hills', where fires were lit to commemorate the Silver Jubilee of 1935). The walk is level and easy, taking only 15 minutes, and from the top you have one of the choicest views on Dartmoor, a mixture of woods, river and moorland. On a clear day you can see the English Channel. The two slabs of rock inscribed with the Ten Commandments are just below the Beacon, and have recently been restored so that the text is easily read. The combination of easy walking, splendid views, and a focal point makes this one of the best short walks on Dartmoor.

THE WESTERN MOOR

Much of this area, north of the B3357, is used by the Ministry of Defence as a firing range (no doubt under the watchful eye of St Barbara – page 187). If a red flag is flying, you can't go there. This uncertainty restricts the number of visitors, which perhaps gives it extra appeal for those who like to be alone. One of Dartmoor's most interesting and popular ancient sites is here, but outside the 'danger area': the **Merrivale stone rows**. The B3357 leads to **Tavistock**, the gateway town to the region (so described first in this section), and just south of Two Bridges is Princetown, famous for its prison and the headquarters of the National Park.

18 TAVISTOCK

🏠 **The Bedford Hotel** (page 278) ▲ **Langstone Manor Holiday Park** Moortown, Tavistock (page 278)

Tourist information: 4 Abbey Place, near the church & the river bridge, combined with the post office & a food shop.

One's heart lifts on entering this ancient town. There is no urban sprawl, just an arrival over a humped stone bridge with the view of the stately Victorian Gothic of Bedford Square. The first building of significance here was the Benedictine abbey, built about a hundred years before the Norman Conquest on the banks of the River Tavy. *Stoc* is old English for a farm or settlement. The abbey became wealthy, and the town's success was cemented when it was made one of the first stannary towns. Fragments of the abbey wall still remain; some are clustered by the river and one piece is even incorporated into the wall of The Bedford Hotel.

"Fragments of the abbey wall still remain; one piece is even incorporated into the wall of The Bedford Hotel."

On the dissolution of the monasteries the abbey's land and the nearby town were bought by the Russell family, who later became the Dukes of Bedford. The tin ran out, but a burgeoning cloth industry filled the gap before that too failed. However, just when the town seemed destined for oblivion, large deposits of copper were found at Mary Tavy at the end of the 18th century, and the new wealth of Tavistock was assured.

William Marshall, travelling in 1796, thought Tavistock had the potential to 'rank high among the market towns of the kingdom,' adding:

SHEEP ON DARTMOOR

Most visitors to Dartmoor are only vaguely aware of the sheep that graze the moor and wander over the road in front of their cars. A conversation with Jane Deane (see box, page 267), who uses their wool for a variety of crafts – dyeing, spinning and weaving – told me how much they vary in both the quality of their wool and their suitability to moor life. 'Rare breeds are rare for a good reason!' says Jane. For instance, the rare local Devon and Cornwall longwool sheep are reputed to be terrible mothers, giving birth and then relinquishing all responsibility for their offspring.

The best wool comes from blue-faced Leicester sheep which Jane describes as looking 'a bit like Victorian clergymen, with a bare head and Roman nose'. But they are too delicate for the moor. The Dartmoor greyface has been developed to thrive on the moor but their wool is coarse and mainly used for carpets. Even scratchier are the Hardwick sheep from the Lake District which Jane says have wool like Brillo pads.

Most of the sheep that you see on the moor are the hardy Scotch blackface. All sheep must be clearly marked to identify their owner, and the marks registered with the Commoners' Council. Sheep are marked with a splash of paint on their fleece, the position and colour being unique to the owner, and a distinguishing notch in their ear.

'at present, though meanly built, it is a tolerable market town'. His prediction came true. It is now one of the most architecturally homogenous towns in the West Country, thanks to the money lavished on it by the 7th Duke of Bedford.

The Victorian Gothic architecture is most evident in Bedford Square, the centre of the town. Leading from the square is the covered **Pannier Market** (⊙ Tue–Sat), which has been held here since 1105. Though you should forget picturesque visions of shoppers clustered round horses with loaded panniers, this is more than a standard market. There are permanent small shops and temporary stalls selling everything from plastic dinosaurs to organic bread. A busy **farmers' market** is held on the second, fourth and fifth Saturday of the month, but on any day of the week you'll find some fresh produce or plants for sale in Bedford Square. Each year in October the annual **Goose Fair** spreads along Plymouth Road where you can buy just about anything – except, possibly, geese. Historically these markets will have been just as their names suggest. The Reverend Stebbing Shaw, writing in 1788, describes the approach road to Tavistock: 'This being market day we met numbers of the people flocking hither with grain, a few sheep, and an abundance of

Michaelmas geese. The common vehicles in this country are panniers and horses; nor did we meet a single carriage the whole day.'

Tavistock has a fine 15th-century church, dedicated to the converted Roman, St Eustachius. It is full of carved beams and angels, and monuments to the town's historic dignitaries. Most notable is Sir John Glanville, a judge, leaning uncomfortably on his elbow. John Fitz is laid to rest under a carved canopy, having survived being lost on the nearby moor where a carved stone with his initials covers the spring that he drank from to protect him from mischievous pixies who might have misled him further.

"A carved stone with Fitz's initials covers the spring that he drank from to protect him from mischievous pixies."

Sir Francis Drake is said to have been born here in 1542, in the Crowndale area about a mile from the centre; his statue is on Plymouth Road. The little **Tavistock Museum** (Bedford Sq ✆ 01822 611264 ⬥ tavistockmuseum.co.uk) is open from March to October and has changing exhibits on the town's history. The town is mercifully free of large chain stores, and has plenty of small independent shops including a good bookshop, Book Stop, on Market Street.

If you have time to spare in the town, take a stroll along the **canal**. Built to transport copper ore to Morwellham Quay (pages 170–2), it runs for 1½ miles before going underground. You can also walk across the viaduct, which is such a prominent landmark in the town. For a deeper appreciation of the town, join a guided walk led by experienced guides. These take place on Fridays from 14.00 to 15.30; meet outside the museum.

As you would expect for a town of this size, Tavistock is easily reached by **bus** from Plymouth, and also by the 118 and 187 from Okehampton. You can also enjoy the 21-mile scenic cycle ride on the Drake's Trail from Plymouth (page 152).

 FOOD & DRINK

Taylors 22 Market St PL19 0DD ✆ 01822 613045 ⬥ taylorstavistock.co.uk. Exceptional food in a cosy setting in the centre of Tavistock.

The Bedford Hotel Bedford Sq. Bang in the middle of town with a quiet restaurant serving great locally-sourced food whose suppliers are listed on the menu. Evening meals are creative and interesting with a slightly unusual take on traditional dishes. See also *Accommodation*, page 278.

OFF THE B3357

🏠 **The Priory** (page 278) & **Two Bridges Hotel** (page 278)

Between Tavistock and the crossroads at **Two Bridges** there are several places of special interest: a textile artisan, a fairy-tale wood, Merrivale's enigmatic row of stones and Princetown.

19 MERRIVALE STONE ROWS

These are thought to date from between 2500 and 700BC and comprise two double rows of stones, with a third single row at an angle to the others. A standing stone, or *menhir*, marks each end of the rows and there's also a small burial chamber. The second row is just beyond it, running parallel, and the small burial chamber is about halfway along. As with all stone rows, it is assumed that these had a ritual purpose.

To reach the stones you need to park at Merrivale car park (OS Explorer map OL28 ♀ SX553750). Get your bearings from the television mast which supplies Princetown and walk towards it; you should find them.

After viewing the stones you can, of course, just retrace your steps, but this can be part of an interesting four-mile **bus-assisted walk** if you park in Princetown and take the number 98 bus to Merrivale car park. Then you can do a linear walk back to your car, through a satisfyingly chronological slice of Dartmoor's history, from prehistoric times to the 19th century with the option of a dip in a quarry lake en route. Bus 98 currently runs twice a day, at 10.06 and 15.05, but check the timetable.

WOAD & WENSLEYDALES

South of the B3357 near Sampford Spiney, and next to the painfully narrow Huckworthy Bridge over the River Walkham, is Jane Deane's **dyeing, spinning and weaving** workshop (🖥 janedeane.co.uk). Jane is part of the Dartmoor Artisan Trail (see box, page 229); she runs weekend natural dyeing and weaving courses and spinning days on Thursdays. I found it fascinating seeing the plants in her garden which produce the vibrant or subtle colours of the unspun Wensleydale fleece piled up in baskets. I now know what woad looks like (a bit like spinach) and learned that the blue from this plant is a mild antiseptic so that those blue-painted ancient Britons that we learned about at school were just treating their sores and flea-bites. Maybe. Blue is a hard colour to achieve. Most plants, whatever the colour of their flowers, give shades of yellow or brown.

THE HOUND OF THE BASKERVILLES

Alex Graeme

What a story! One of detective fiction's finest, the most popular of the Sherlock Holmes novels, and famous all around the world. And yet the story behind the story is just as intriguing as the tale itself, and stems from this part of Devon. Spending the day visiting all the places that inspired Sir Arthur Conan Doyle when writing his book, with their combination of historic churches, dramatic country views, tranquil old towns and iconic Dartmoor locations, makes for the perfect Slow visit.

First, **Ipplepen** introduces us to some of the real-life characters who contributed to the story. Bertram Fletcher Robinson, a friend of Conan Doyle, lived here, and it was he who told Doyle the legend that inspired the story: that of Squire Richard Cabell III, a 17th-century brute of a man, who lived near Buckfastleigh, supposedly murdered his wife, and terrified the locals while out hunting with his devilish pack of hounds. His coachman, Henry Baskerville, drove Conan Doyle around the area during his visits. Finally, Robert Duins Cooke, the local vicar at Ipplepen from 1897 to 1939, also happened to be an expert on Dartmoor, and suggested which Dartmoor locations Doyle should visit when he came to Devon to do his research. These three were all in Ipplepen while the story was being constructed, and their homes can still be seen. The headstones of Bertram Fletcher Robinson and Robert Duins Cooke are both in the graveyard at St Andrew's Church, as are those of Henry Baskerville's parents and brother.

Baskerville eventually moved to **Ashburton**, where we can still see the red

If heading for Princetown from Merrivale you need to find a standing stone adjacent to a wall, then set your sights on **King's Tor** (and the television tower) to the north. This involves a certain amount of cross-country walking, but the disused railway track circles round it, so you can't really go wrong. After that it's easy – just follow the track to Princetown. You are walking on a nice piece of history here. The **Plymouth and Dartmoor railway** was built in the 1820s to transport granite from the quarries. When this became uneconomical in the 1880s the route was sold to the Great Western Railway. The last passenger service ran in March 1956. The track passes the disused Swell Tor Quarry, and if you have the time and energy it's worth investigation; look for the stone corbels that were cut in 1903 for the widening of London Bridge but never used. You can also take a short detour to Foggintor Quarry, and the possibility of a swim, by taking a left turn towards the somewhat forbidding ruins of the old mining buildings. From here, the quarry is brick house where he lived. His headstone is there in the churchyard of St Andrew's Church, not far from the headstone of a certain James Mortimer, whose name also appears in Doyle's story.

We continue to **Buckfastleigh** to visit the unique Holy Trinity Church, both tragic and fascinating in its history and very different from any other church in Devon. This is where the Hound of the Baskervilles story really began, as you can see in the box on page 197.

Next the mystique of Dartmoor beckons, and it's off to the high ground, passing Brook Manor where the notorious Squire Cabell lived. We come to the extraordinary Bronze Age settlement of **Grimspound** (pages 258–9), which inspired Conan Doyle's reference to 'prehistoric man' in the story, as well as the prehistoric huts that an incognito Sherlock stayed in when he came to the Moors. In **Princetown**, the most central town on Dartmoor and without doubt the bleakest, with its prison and higher-than-average rainfall, what is now the National Park visitor centre was once the Duchy Hotel, where Doyle stayed whilst exploring the Moors. **Fox Tor Mire**, one of Dartmoor's most desolate and atmospheric places, inspired him to create Grimpen Mire, the most evocative of the locations in his story.

I have followed this circuit many times, since a Hound of the Baskervilles Tour is among those that my company offers. After all, the Reverend Robert Duins Cooke was my great grandfather!

Alex Graeme runs Unique Devon Tours (see page iii and the ad in the fourth colour section).

down a short track to the right. Wild swimmers can walk around the left side of the quarry wall and enter the water from there. It's deep in parts but very shallow in others, with large rocks just below the surface. It isn't ideal for anything too enthusiastic but it's great for sheer atmosphere, and offers a different perspective on the imposing faces of the quarry.

20 WISTMAN'S WOOD

'It's straight out of Tolkien,' a friend remarked. 'You wouldn't be surprised to meet a hobbit there.' Concealed on the western side of the B3212, this small grove of stunted oaks is one of the few remaining examples of the forest that once covered much of Dartmoor, and one of the most wonderful sights on the moor. Perhaps I'm biased, having visited it on an intermittently sunny day in April, when the banks of the approach track were covered with primroses and the gorse was in bloom. From the **Two Bridges car park** it's a two-mile walk north to the grove, first up a farm track and then across the moor where you scan the barren hillside ahead for anything resembling a tree. Suddenly there it is, a green-coated fairyland of gnarled and twisted boughs, festooned in epiphytes, ferns, liverwort and moss, the oaks finding footholds between moss-covered boulders. It's as though some fanatical knitter has been at work with miles of green wool. In early spring the low sun gave the leafless green branches an almost golden outline.

21 PRINCETOWN

Tourist information: High Moorland Visitor Centre PL20 6QF ✆ 01822 890414 ⌖ dartmoor. gov.uk ◷ 10.00–16.00 daily. The main TIC for the national park, housed in the old Duchy Hotel where Conan Doyle stayed, has a fund of local information (accommodation, routes, weather conditions, etc) as well as interpretive displays & exhibits, & all the books & maps that you need.

At around 1,340 feet Princetown is the highest settlement on the moor; this and its well-known prison suggest a wild, bleak place with echoes of *Wuthering Heights*, but in fact it's a neat, functional little town geared to the needs of moor walkers and visitors. Rather than chain-gangs and fleeing convicts it has pubs, shops, eating places, B&Bs, its own Dartmoor Brewery (the highest in England) and an excellent, and unusual, museum. At the time of writing, plans to build a whisky distillery are under way.

"Rather than chain-gangs and fleeing convicts it has pubs, its own Dartmoor Brewery and an excellent museum."

The town is not particularly old. In 1785 Sir Thomas Tyrwhitt, secretary to the Prince of Wales, leased a large area of moorland from the Duchy of Cornwall, intending to convert it into profitable farmland. The road from Tavistock was built and a settlement gradually grew, named Princetown after the Prince of Wales. The Plume of Feathers Inn, reputedly Princetown's oldest existing building, dates from around this time. When French prisoners from the Napoleonic wars were too numerous for Plymouth jail, Tyrwhitt suggested that a prison be built in his 'new town' to house them; the French were soon followed by American sailors from the war of 1812. The warders and other prison staff needed accommodation, so that was constructed, and in 1812–15 prisoners built the simple granite **church of St Michael and all Angels**, which is now looked after by the Churches' Conservation Trust (⌖ visitchurches.org.uk). It wasn't until 1850 that the old POW camp was converted into a prison for the most dangerous convicts; before that they were dispatched to Australia. So the small town and its prison have always coexisted, their histories closely linked.

The Dartmoor Prison Museum (PL20 6RR ✐ 01822 322130 ⬢ dartmoor-prison.co.uk ⊙ Feb–Dec 09.30–16.00 daily) is housed in the old prison dairy just past the main prison entrance on the road to Tavistock. Extensively enlarged and refurbished in 2017, exhibits in this exceptionally interesting museum range from items made by French prisoners of war, including a model of Notre Dame cathedral, to the brutal punishment implements from years gone by. These include a flogging frame, last used in 1952, and a 'man-hauling belt', with the aid of which prisoners could pull carts around the prison and village. Old Pathé News clips reporting on 'the toughest prison in the country', riots and escapes contrast with interviews with present-day prisoners describing the modern regime with a positive spin. A description of Moor Trees where prisoners help in reforestation projects reinforces the message of how much the prison has changed.

With its knowledgeable and enthusiastic staff this is an absorbing and different museum – and one that children will love.

There's a cash machine (paying) outside the village store in the main street, and the post office counter inside offers free withdrawal services during normal hours. The Dartmoor Brewery Shop (⊙ 09.00–17.00 Mon–Fri) sells its own Jail Ale, Legend, Dartmoor IPA and Dartmoor Best as well as seasonal 'specials' including Santa's Secret, Dragon's Breath and the very warming Christmas Ale.

Princetown is served year-round (Mon–Sat) by the rather sparse Tavistock/Yelverton bus number 98; the 113 between Tavistock and Newton Abbot only runs (once each way) on the first and third Wednesdays of the month.

Yelverton and the Burrator Reservoir are described in *Chapter 5*.

FOOD & DRINK

All in the town centre are:

Fox Tor Café ✐ 01822 890238 ⬢ foxtorcafe.com ⊙ 09.00–17.00. Snacks, full meals and cream teas; comfy sofas. Indoor and outdoor seating and free Wi-Fi. Also has a bunkhouse and can arrange guided walks, mountain biking and cycle hire.

Old Police Station Café ✐ 01822 890407 ⊙ 09.00–17.00. A friendly café with traditional all-day food (good breakfasts, including vegetarian) and takeaways.

Plume of Feathers ✎ 01822 890240 ⬧ theplumeoffeathersdartmoor.co.uk. A busy and popular pub with good-value food; also runs a year-round campsite and a bunkhouse.
Prince of Wales ✎ 01822 890219 ⬧ princeofwalesbunkhouse.co.uk. Hearty pub meals, generous helpings, friendly company, log fires in winter, bunkhouse and campsite.

FOX TOR MIRE

If you take the minor road south from Princetown you will come, eventually, to Fox Tor Mire, an area so desolate that you can believe all the legends associated with it. Most famous is that it was the inspiration for Grimpen Mire in *The Hound of the Baskervilles* (pages 268–9) and, being probably the most treacherous 'featherbed' bog on Dartmoor, it is the stuff of other legends. One story (from ⬧ legendarydartmoor. co.uk) goes that a fellow was heading home across the moor when he saw a rather splendid top hat sitting on a green patch of featherbed. The lad gingerly approached the mire to retrieve the hat. As he picked it up he was astonished to find that under the hat was a head, which smiled courteously, introduced itself and asked if the lad might, perhaps, try to pull him out of the bog. Regaining his composure the fellow gave it his best effort but to no avail. The gent then offered a suggestion: 'If you wouldn't mind waiting a moment I'll try to take my feet out of the stirrups; I'm still on my horse.'

I was taken here by Alex Graeme, who described it as 'a huge bowl of granite through which the water never really drains away'. One of Dartmoor's stone crosses, marking **Childe's Tomb**, is near here, and the remains of tin-miners' houses and the mining pits all contribute to the feeling of desolation and abandonment.

SOUTH DEVON & DARTMOOR ONLINE

For additional online content, articles, photos and more on South Devon and Dartmoor, why not visit ⬧ bradtguides.com/sdevon.

THE SNAILY HOUSE

Once upon a time, as one version of the story goes, two spinster sisters living near Widecombe existed for many years on a diet of snails. Their small two-storey cottage, named Whiteslade, became known locally as 'the snaily house', and the crumbled lower part of its ruin is still visible today. The surrounding vegetation is tangled now, with gorse and nettles growing up among the stones, but 200 or so years ago it was part of a working farm. The snail legend (which started some time before 1840) possibly referred to the thick black slugs that thrive in damp areas; locally they are sometimes known as snails. They may have been pickled or salted, as was done long ago in the Hebrides to provide food during the bleak Scottish winters. Probably some snails were involved too, perhaps spiced up with the wild garlic that grows nearby.

It is said that the two sisters were negligent farmers and produced poor crops, yet they appeared healthy and well fed even when times were hard; some villagers suspected them of stealing sheep or other livestock, while others whispered furtively of witchcraft. Few visited the isolated cottage. Then one day someone braver (or nosier) than the others sneaked along the muddy track to peer through the window as the sisters were sitting at their meal, and saw with horror what was on their plates. For the story to have survived for almost two centuries and given the cottage its nickname, the discovery must have caused lively local gossip and consternation, and yet there are old records of slugs being eaten in other parts of Dartmoor too when food was short. It's a mystery how legends develop. But there we have the two old women in their isolated cottage, hunched together over their wooden table by the light of a smoky lamp, tucking in to something highly unlikely to feature as an example of fine medieval dining. What happened next? We don't know. One version of the tale says they were so shamed by the discovery that they 'just faded away'; or perhaps good-hearted villagers took their diet in hand. Choose your own ending!

ACCOMMODATION

The places to stay that are listed in this section have been chosen either because of their location, because they are in some way unusual, or because they encapsulate the Slow approach. Since the last edition, glamping has really come into its own, so that is included too. The suggestions below are just a small selection of the many places that we

SELF-CATERING

Blue Chip Holidays ⬦ bluechipholidays. co.uk. Southwest specialists.

Canopy and Stars ⬦ canopyandstars. co.uk. Sawday's glamping selection.

Classic Cottages ⬦ classic.co.uk. West-Country specialists.

Classic Glamping ⬦ classicglamping.co.uk

Coast and Country Cottages ⬦ coastandcountry.co.uk. South-Hams-based self-catering holidays.

Dart Valley Cottages ⬦ dartvalleycottages. co.uk. Focus on the most attractive parts of the River Dart.

Devon Holiday Cottages ⬦ devonholidaycottages.com. Specifically Devon for all budgets. You can book direct with the owner.

Exclusively Dartmoor ⬦ exclusivelydartmoor. co.uk. Not just accommodation but other useful bits of information too.

Helpful Holidays ⬦ helpfulholidays. com. Based in Chagford, Dartmoor, with a huge range of places.

Holiday Cottages ⬦ holidaycottages.co.uk.

Quality Unearthed ⬦ qualityunearthed.co.uk. Glamping.

Quirky Accommodation ⬦ quirkyaccom.com. Self explanatory; includes boats & tree houses.

The Landmark Trust ☏ 01628 825920 ⬦ landmarktrust.org.uk. This charitable organisation is quite different from the other accommodation providers listed here. Their role is to rescue historic buildings in danger of dereliction, restore them, and rent them out to holidaymakers. Furnishing is done with an eye for the history and character of the place, and there are no TVs or telephones.

Salcombe Finest ⬦ salcombefinest.com. As the name suggests, they specialise in luxury holiday lets in & around Salcombe.

Toad Hall Cottages ⬦ toadhallcottages. co.uk. West-Country specialists. See ad, fourth colour section.

Unique Homestays ⬦ uniquehomestays. com. Genuinely unique places at the upper end of the market.

happened to find or hear about as we researched; an internet search will reveal hundreds more.

In Devon by far the most popular accommodation is self-catering, offered by a large number of agencies. We have listed some alphabetically in the box opposite.

Alex Graeme, of Unique Devon Tours, has his own favourite hotels and B&Bs – or rather the places his international clients tell him they love to stay in. His selection – *Alex's picks* – is on page 278.

The hotels and B&Bs featured in this section are indicated by ♠ under the heading for the town or village in which they are located. Self-catering is indicated by 🏠 and campsites by ▲. For complete listings and fuller descriptions, go to ⬧ bradtguides.com/southdevonsleeps.

1 THE EXE & TEIGN ESTUARIES

B&Bs

Church Farm Haccombe ⬧ wildlink.org. Luxury B&B in TV wildlife producer Andrew Cooper's country home. Pages 46–7.

Lammas Park House Dawlish ⬧ lammasparkhouse.co.uk. Super-comfortable B&B & sea views from all rooms.

The Turf Exminster ⬧ turfpub.net. Cosy B&B in a traditional pub beside the Exe estuary. Great views. Page 28.

Self-catering

Brunel Holiday Park Dawlish Warren ⬧ brunelholidaypark.co.uk. Converted railway carriages on quiet site. Page 36.

Camping

The Turf (see *B&Bs*, above). A yurt & basic camping in pub grounds. Breakfast toastie available.

2 THE ENGLISH RIVIERA: TORBAY

Hotels

The Cary Arms & Spa Babbacombe Beach ⬧ caryarms.co.uk. Luxury seaside hotel; includes beach hut accommodation.

Orestone Manor Maidencombe ⬧ orestonemanor.com. Boutique hotel & restaurant north of Torquay. See ad, fourth colour section.

Redcliffe Hotel Torquay ⬧ redcliffehotel.co.uk. A hotel folly by the sea; see box, page 64.

B&B

The 25 Boutique B&B Torquay ⬧ the25.uk. 6 extraordinary rooms. The tops in award-winning quality.

Self-catering

Faithful Brixham. Converted fishing boat in the marina, sleeps 2. Book through several agencies.

Glamping

Brownscombe Tabernacle Marldon ⬧ brownscombe.co.uk. Sleeps 2. One of a range of glamping options.

3 TOTNES & THE RIVER DART

Hotels & pubs

Anzac Street Bistro Dartmouth ⬧ anzacbistro.co.uk. 3 rooms in the centre of town.

Cott Inn Dartington ⬧ cottinn.co.uk. Old, thatched & beautiful. 5 rooms.

The Sea Trout Inn Staverton ⬧ theseatroutinn.co.uk. Lively riverside pub with good restaurant.

B&Bs

Dartington Hall Totnes ⊘ dartingtonhall.com. 50 rooms around the medieval courtyard. Pages 89–91.

Kilbury Manor Between Buckfastleigh & Totnes ⊘ kilburymanor.co.uk. 4 comfortable B&B rooms plus self-catering apartment.

Self-catering

Ashley's Shack Harbertonford, between Totnes & Dartmouth ⊘ classic.co.uk. Rural setting. Sleeps 2.

Broadleigh Farm Park Stoke Gabriel ⊘ broadleighfarm.co.uk. Dog-friendly camping & 85 caravan pitches in a quiet location with easy access to the River Dart.

Duck Cottage Tuckenhay ⊘ dartvalleycottages. co.uk. Waterside cottage, tranquil river views. Sleeps 4.

Gurrow Point Cottage Dittisham ⊘ gurrow.com/gurrow/welcome. Superb location at the tip of Gurrow Point. Sleeps 6.

Kingswear Castle ⊘ landmarktrust.org.uk. Yes, a castle! Sleeps 4.

Sandridge Boathouse Stoke Gabriel ⊘ helpfulholidays.com. Right on the River Dart. Getting there involves a half-mile field-&-woodland walk. Sleeps 4.

Tuckenhay Mill Tuckenhay ⊘ tuckenhaymill. co.uk. Historic paper mill converted to classic cottages in 20 acres of natural landscape. Indoor pools & spa.

Glamping

Buzzard Cedar Yurt Between Dittisham & Dartmouth ⊘ classicglamping.co.uk. Deep in the countryside. Hot tub. Sleeps 5.

Hemsford Yurt Camp Littlehempston ⊘ devon-yurts.co.uk. 4 Mongolian yurts & a shepherd's hut in peaceful surroundings.

4 SOUTH HAMS & DEVON'S FAR SOUTH

Hotel

Burgh Island Hotel ⊘ burghisland.com. Unique accommodation in a unique hotel (pages 144–5).

B&Bs

Avon Mill Loddiswell ⊘ avonmill.com. 2-person apartment in old mill, great views (page 128).

Cricket Inn Beesands ⊘ thecricketinn.com. Waterside pub with good food.

Keynedon Mill Sherford ⊘ keynedonmill.co.uk. Upmarket B&B near attractive village.

The Old Rectory East Portlemouth ⊘ oldrectoryeastportlemouth.com. Luxury B&B with stunning views. 3 rooms.

Weeke Farm Nr Modbury ⊘ weekefarm.co.uk. Working farm deep in the countryside.

Self-catering

Coastguard Cottages Prawle Point ⊘ toadhallcottages.co.uk. Remote, on the SWCP.

Gara Rock East Portlemouth ⊘ bluechipholidays. co.uk. Stunning location, great restaurant.

The Signal Box Loddiswell ⊘ loddiswellstation. co.uk. Quirky restored railway building. Sleeps 4.

Camping

Karrageen Caravan & Camping Park Bolberry, nr Malborough ⊘ karrageen.co.uk. Spacious, with a green philosophy.

5 PLYMOUTH & THE TAMAR VALLEY

Hotel

Glazebrook House Hotel South Brent ⊘ glazebrookhouse.com. Luxurious, unique, with a touch of magic. 9 rooms. See ad, fourth colour section.

B&Bs

Barnabas House Yelverton ⊘ barnabas-house. co.uk. Very comfortable B&B, helpful owners, walks & cycle trails nearby.

Tamar Belle Bere Ferrers ✑ tamarbelle.co.uk. Have your own *Brief Encounter* in a converted railway carriage. Also self-catering.

Self-catering

Crownhill Fort Plymouth ✑ landmarktrust.org. uk. Built in the 1860s. Accommodates 8 in the old Officers' Quarters.

Harford Bunkhouse See *Camping*, below.

Woodovis Camping & Caravan Park Beautifully converted old stable, sleeps 3. See *Camping*, below.

Camping

Harford Bunkhouse & Camping West Combeshead ✑ pitchup.com. On a working farm 1½ miles from Ivybridge. Also pods & bell tents.

Woodovis Camping & Caravan Park Gulworthy PL19 8NY ✑ woodovis.com. Camping, luxury static caravans, glamping pods. Wooded site 4 miles west of Tavistock. Swimming pool.

6 THE EASTERN FRINGE OF DARTMOOR

B&Bs

Anrán Tidwell Farm, Ashburton ✑ anran.co.uk. Luxury boutique B&B in a restored manor house (c1840). Also self-catering.

Bulleigh Barton Manor Ipplepen ✑ bulleighbartonmanor.co.uk. Luxury B&B in a beautifully renovated country house. See ad, fourth colour section.

Cridford Inn Trusham ✑ thecridfordinn.co.uk. Historic thatched longhouse. Also 2 self-catering cottages. Page 188.

Hannah's nr Newton Abbot ✑ discoverhannahs. org. Includes B&B rooms adapted for less mobile visitors, hostel & safari tents. Page 189.

Nobody Inn Doddiscombsleigh ✑ nobodyinn. co.uk. 5 B&B rooms in a historic inn. Page 188.

Old Church House Inn Torbryan ✑ oldchurchhouseinn.co.uk. Double/twin, single & family rooms, including one adapted for less mobile guests. Page 191.

Self-catering

Anrán Ashburton. See *B&Bs*, above.

Rydon Trusham ✑ uniquehomestays.com. A large converted barn; sleeps up to 6. Heated pool (summer).

7 THE NORTHWESTERN FRINGE OF DARTMOOR

Hotel

Lewtrenchard Manor Lewdown, nr Okehampton ✑ lewtrenchard.co.uk. A gracious Jacobean manor in extensive grounds. 13 luxury bedrooms & excellent restaurant. Page 217.

B&Bs

Betty Cottles Inn Okehampton ✑ bettycottles. co.uk. Inexpensive accommodation includes standard en-suite rooms, bunk rooms, log cabins & camping.

Oxenham Arms South Zeal ✑ theoxenhamarms. com. 7 exclusive en-suite rooms with hand-stitched fabrics & antique furniture. Page 210.

The Dartmoor Inn Lydford ✑ www. dartmoorinn.com. 3 rooms, good restaurant, convenient for the Lydford Gorge.

Tors Inn Belstone ✑ thetorsinn.co.uk. Good-value B&B in traditional family-run pub on edge of Dartmoor. Good location for walkers. Page 211.

Self-catering

Twelve Penny Barn Lewdown ✑ uniquehomestays.com. A converted barn in west Dartmoor. Sleeps 2.

Camping

King's Arms South Zeal ✑ thekingsarmssouthzeal.com. Simple campsite (toilets but no showers) with good views of the moor. Page 209.

ALEX'S PICKS

Full descriptions of Alex Graeme's favourites are on the website ✎ bradtguides.com/southdevonsleeps

Anrán Landscove, nr Ashburton
Barnabas House Yelverton
Bulleigh Barton Manor nr Ipplepen
Gidleigh Park nr Chagford
Glazebrook House Hotel nr South Brent

Ilsington Country House Hotel nr Bovey Tracey
Orestone Manor nr Torquay
The 25 Boutique B&B Torquay
The Rock Inn nr Haytor
Two Bridges Hotel Dartmoor

8 DARTMOOR NATIONAL PARK

Hotels

Bovey Castle North Bovey ✎ boveycastle.com. Large luxury hotel ideal for families. Lots of activities.

Gidleigh Park nr Chagford ✎ gidleigh.co.uk. A luxury country-house

Ilsington Country House Hotel & Spa Ilsington (nr Bovey Tracey) ✎ ilsington.co.uk. Upmarket, comfortable & gracious. See ad, fourth colour section.

Lydgate House Hotel Postbridge ✎ lydgatehouse.co.uk. Inexpensive & super location on Two Moors Way.

Mill End Hotel Chagford ✎ millendhotel.com. Dog-friendly country-house hotel on the B3206.

Rock Inn Haytor ✎ rock-inn.co.uk. Long-established inn; lovely location.

The Bedford Hotel Tavistock ✎ bedford-hotel. co.uk. In the centre of Tavistock. Plenty of parking.

Two Bridges Hotel ✎ twobridges.co.uk. Large hotel on the River Dart.

B&Bs

Brimpts Farm Between Two Bridges & Dartmeet ✎ brimptsfarm.co.uk. B&B in a lovely Dartmoor setting. Also self-catering & camping. Page 259–61.

The Barn Scorriton, nr Buckfastleigh ✎ thebarndartmoor.com. 2 rooms in a barn conversion.

The Priory Whitchurch ✎ priorybnbtavistock-dartmoor.co.uk. Historic, arty place convenient for Tavistock.

Self-catering

The Chapel Lettaford, North Bovey ✎ landmarktrust.org.uk. A tiny converted chapel sleeping 1 or 2.

The Secret Holt Haytor ✎ uniquehomestays. com. A wooden chalet off the beaten track. Sleeps 2.

Campsites & holiday parks

For a selection of campsites, bunk houses & hostels see ✎ dartmoor.co.uk. In Princetown the Fox Tor Cafe (✎ foxtorcafe.com), the Plume of Feathers (✎ theplumeoffeathersdartmoor.co.uk) & the Prince of Wales (✎ princeofwalesbunkhouse.co.uk) have bunkhouses & campsites.

Brimpts Farm Informal camping in farm fields. See B&Bs, above.

Langstone Manor Holiday Park Moortown, Tavistock ✎ langstonemanor.co.uk. Camping areas (wooded or meadow) plus wooden pods. 'Green' facilities.

INDEX

Page numbers in **bold** refer to main entries; *italics* refer to maps

A

accommodation 20, **274–8**
animals & wildlife 15–16,
  see also zoos
Anstey's Cove 48, 53, **55**, 57
Aquarium, National Marine,
  Plymouth 156
Artisan Trail, Dartmoor 11,
  229, 235, 243, 244
arts & artisans 16, 40, 132,
  229, 243
Arts and Crafts movement
  117, 147, 217
Ashburton 182, 193–5
Ashprington 78, 80, 99,
  101–3
atmospheric railway **32–3**,
  34, 189, 198
Aveton Gifford 118, 142,
  146
Avocet line (rail) 26
Avon, River 118, 119, 121,
  128–9, **142–3**, 146
Ayrmer Cove *118*, **145–6**,
  148

B

Babbacombe beach *48*,
  52–3
Babbage, Charles **82–3**, 85
backpacking, Dartmoor
  229–231
Bantham *118*, 141–2, 144,
  147–8
Bantham Swoosh (swim)
  142

Baring-Gould Folk
  Weekend 213
Baring-Gould, Rev Sabine
  29, **211**, 217
Baskerville, Henry 190, 193,
  197, 268–9
Baskervilles, Hound of the
  268–9
bats, greater horseshoe 77,
  181, 200
  lesser horseshoe 42
Battery Heritage Centre,
  Brixham 72
beaches 14–15
  south coast 121, 130,
    139–48
  Torbay **54**, 68–9, 71
Beacon Villages, the
  207–10
Beard, Tony 250
Becky Falls 222, 247
beekeeping 201–2
beer, local 123, 271
Beesands 118, 126
bell ringing 20
Bellever Forest 222, 259
Belstone *204*, 207–8,
  210–11
Ben's Farm Shops 87, 94,
  166
Bere Ferrers *150*, 168,
  169–70, 171
Berry Head Nature Reserve
  48, 77
Berry Pomeroy 78, 94–7
Bigbury Bay *118*, 149

Bigbury-on-Sea *118*,
  143–4
Birdwatching 15
  Berry Head 77
  Exe estuary 29
  River Dart 98
  Slapton Ley 122–3
  Tamar estuary 162–3
Black-a-Tor Copse 215
Blackdown Rings *118*, 127
Blackpool Sands *78*,
  114–15
boat hire
  Exe estuary 26–7
  River Dart 99–100
  Salcombe 136
Bovey Tracey 222, 250–2
Bowerman's Nose *222*,
  256–8
Brentor *204*, 221
Brimpts Farm 259–61
Brixham *48*, 72–4
Broadsands beach 48, 54,
  69, 71
Brunel, Isambard Kingdom
  32–3, 34, 66, 179, 189,
  198
Brutus of Troy 86
Buckfast Abbey *182*, 201–2
Buckfastleigh *182*, 195–8
  caves 199–201
  Holy Trinity Church 197,
    269
  railway 196–8
  Valiant Soldier 196
Buckland Abbey *150*,
  174–5

Buckland Beacon *222*, 263
Buckland Monachorum *150*,
173, 248
Buckland Tout Saints *118*,
133–4
Buckland-in-the-Moor *222*,
262–3
Burgh Island *118*, 143–5
Burrator Reservoir *150*,
172–3
buses 11–12, *see also*
public transport
Tavistock Country Buses
227
Bygones, St Marychurch 52

C

Cabell, Squire Richard 197,
268–9
Canonteign Falls *182*,
186–8
Castle Drogo *222*, 239–41
caves 55–58, 199–201
Chagford *222*, 234–6
Charlton Marsh *118*, 132–3
cheese, local 9
Chilli Farm, South Devon,
the *118*, 127
Christie, Agatha 58, **104–5**,
106
churches, exceptional 14
Churston Cove *48*, 71
cider **9–10**, 63, 75, 189,
216
Clegg, Dave 3, 207, 214
Coastguards Beach *118*,
148
Coast-to-Coast (cycle route)
80, 152, 230
coast-to-coast (walking
route) 12, 152, 165, 230
Cobweb Hall, Sourton 218

Cockington *48*, 61–3
Coffin House, Brixham 74
coffins, felt 244
Coleton Fishacre *78*, 116–7
Combeinteignhead 22,
44–5, 47
Compass Cove, Dartmouth
114
Compton Castle *48*, 70–1
Conan Doyle, Sir Arthur 190,
193, 197, 268–9, 270
Cooke, Robert Duins 190,
268–9
Cookery School, Ashburton
195
Cookworthy, William 131
Coombe Trenchard *204*,
216, 217–18
Cornwall, Duchy of 226,
270
Cornwood *150*, 178–9
Cornworthy *118*, 103
Coryton Cove, Dawlish 38
Cosdon Beacon 207
cream, clotted 8–9
Cremyll, Cornwall 162, 163
Crossing, William 259
Cruises
  Dartmouth–Totnes
  108–9
  Exe estuary 26–7
  Plymouth 162–3
  River Dart 98–9
  Salcombe 134–6
  Teignmouth 40
Cutty Dyer 237
cycling & walking 12–14

D

D'Oyly Carte family 116–17
Daddy Hole, Torbay *48*, 57
Dart Valley Trail 99

Dart, River *78*, 79, 98–100,
108–9
Dartington Hall 78, 89–92
Dartmeet *222*, 259
Dartmoor Artisan Trail 11,
229, 235, 243, 244
Dartmoor Folk Festival 209
Dartmoor Prison *see*
Princetown
Dartmoor Railway *204*, 205,
207, 212
Dartmoor Zoo *150*, 78
Dartmouth *78*, 107–14
  castle 113
  museum 111
  Royal Naval College 113
  St Saviour's Church 111
Dartmouth Steam Railway
78, 80, 98, 108
Dawlish *22*, 34–5, 38
Dawlish Warren 22, 34–5
Delamore House *150*,
178–9
Devil, the 177, 185, 197,
236, 255
Devon Guild of Craftsmen
250, 252
Devon Violets perfume 38
Devon Wildlife Trust 15,
180
Dewerstone Wood 177, 236
dialect, Dartmoor 250
Dittisham *78*, 104–6
Doddiscombsleigh 182,
185–6
Dog-friendly Devon, guide
to 16
Drake, Sir Francis 60, 76,
160–1, 174, 194, 266
Drake's Trail (cycle) *150*,
152
Drewe, Julius 239, 240

Drewsteignton *222*, 239, 240
Duncan, Isadora 66
dyeing 267

E

East Portlemouth *118*, 136–8
East Prawle *118*, 130–1
Edgcumbe, Cornwall 163
Elberry Cove *48*, 71
Elmhirst, Leonard & Dorothy 90–1, 102
Erme, River *118*, 148, 179
Exe Estuary Trail 24
Exercise Tiger (Slapton) 124–5
Exeter *22*, 24–5
Exeter Ship Canal 26
Exminster Marshes Nature Reserve *22*, 27–8
Exmouth Local Nature Reserve 22, 29
Exmouth–Starcross ferry 26, 34

F

fairs & festivals 17
Fast Rabbit Farm Gardens *78*, 115
Fernworthy reservoir *222*, 238
ferries and boat trips
  Exe estuary 26–7
  Plymouth 162–3
  River Dart 98–100
  Salcombe 136
  Teign estuary 40
  Torbay
Finch Foundry 208
Fishcombe Cove *48*, 71

Folk Festival, Dartmoor, 209
Folk Weekend, Baring-Gould, 213
food & drink **7–11**, 41, *75*, 102–3, 135, 155, 189, 216, 271
Fox Tor Mire, Dartmoor *222*, 269, 272
Franklin Totnes Trail 80–1

G

Garden House, the 174
geocaching 165, 234–5
gin 9, 135, 155
Golden Hind, the (replica) 75–6
Goveton 133–4
Graeme, Alex 3, 10, 258, 268–9, 275, 278,
Granite Tramway 253
Granite Way *204*, 206
Greenway *78*, 104–7
Grenville, Sir Richard 174, 176–7
Griffin, Joanna 3, 81, 173, 214, 240
Grimspound *222*, 224–5, 256, **258**

H

Haccombe *22*, 45–7
hairy hands, the 237
Hallsands *118*, 129–30
Hannahs, Seale-Hayne 189
Harper, Charles 53, 54, 56, 58, 126, 129, 143
Hawley, John 109, 112
Haytor *222*, 252
Haytor Hoppa 228, 246
High Moorland Visitor Centre 270

Higher Ashton *182*, 186
Higher Uppacott 261
Highwayman Inn, Sourton 218
Hill House Nursery, Landscove *182*, 194–5
Holbeton (church) *118*, 147–8
Holcombe *22*, 37
Holne *222*, 261–2
Homeyard, William Newcombe 42–3
Hope Cove *118*, 139–40
Hope's Nose *48*, 55, 57
Hoskins, W G **18**, 96, 190–1
Hound of the Baskervilles, the 268–9
Hound Tor 222, 256–7
House of Marbles 33, 251

I

Inner Hope *see* Hope Bay
Invitation to View 218
Ipplepen *182*, 190, 197, 268
Ivybridge *150*, 179–80

J

Jacobstowe *204*, 206
Jansch, Heather 16–17, 193
Jay's Grave 256–7
Jenkins, Simon **18**, 20, 52, 65, 147, 216
John Musgrave Heritage Trail *78*, 50, 94
Journey's End, Inn & play 144–5

K

Kenn *22*, 29–30
Kenton *22*, 28–9

Kents Cavern *48*, 55–8
Kingsbridge *118*, 131–2
Kingswear 78, 116
Kingswear Castle, the
  108–9
Knowling, Philip 3, 64,
  67, 219

L
Labrador Bay 37
Landmark Trust 239
Landscove *182*, 194–5
letterboxing 175, 234–5
Lew Trenchard *204*, 216–17
Liqufruta cough remedy
  42–3
Littlehempston *78*, 92
Living Coasts, Torquay *48*,
  59–60
llama walks 231
Loddiswell *118*, 127–9
Lopwell Dam *150*, 153, **176**
Lustleigh 166, *222*, 247–9
Lutyens, Sir Edwin 239
Lydford & Lydford Gorge
  204, 219–21
Lydia Bridge, South Brent
  180

M
Mais, S P B 3, 7, 11, 14, **19**,
  55, 62, 96, 107
Malborough *118*, 134
Manaton 222, 245–7
maps & guides (walking)
  13–14
Mare & Foal Sanctuary, the
  78, 93, 94
Marldon *48*, 69
Martin, Rev W Keble 46
Mary Tavy 164, *222*

Mayflower, the 111, 154,
  155
media (local) 18
medieval village
  (Dartmoor) *222*, 256–7
Mee, Arthur 19, 115–6, 248
Meldon *204*
  Lake 214
  Quarry 207, 214
  Viaduct 207, 214–15
Merrivale stone rows *222*,
  267
Mill Bay 137
Milton Combe *150*, 175
Miniature Pony Centre, the
  222, 245
Modbury *118*, 146–7
Moretonhampstead *222*,
  243–4
Morwellham Quay *150*,
  170–2
Mothecombe beach *118*,
  147, 148
Mythic Sculpture Exhibition
  242

N
National Gardens Scheme
  16–17, 218
nature reserves:
  Berry Head 77
  Dawlish Warren 35–6
  Exe estuary 25–9
  Slapton Lea 122–3
Newcomen, Thomas 33,
  110, 114
Newton Abbot *182*, 189
Newton Ferrers *150*, 166–7
Nine Maidens (stone circle)
  204, 237
North Bovey *222*, 249–50
Noss Mayo *150*, 166–7

O
Oddicombe beach *48*, 53
Okehampton *204*, 207,
  212–14
Old Walls Vineyard 9, 41
Oldway Mansion, Paignton
  66–7
Open Studios fortnight
  16–17
opening times 21
Orchid Paradise *182*, 191–2
Otters & Butterflies *182*,
  198–9
Outer Hope *see* Hope Bay
Overbeck's Museum *118*,
  138–9

P
Paignton *48*, 63–8
  beaches 68–9
  Oldway Mansion 66–7
  Picture House 65
  Pudden' Eaters 66
  Zoo 67–8
Parke (Bovey Tracey) *222*,
  251–2
parkruns 153, 251
pasties 9
Pengelly, William 56–8,
  199
Pennywell Farm *182*,
  202–3
pigs, miniature (Pennywell)
  202–3
Pilgrim Fathers 155
pixies 236
Plant World (gardens)
  22, 47
Plym Valley Cycle Trail 152
Plym Valley Railway 154
Plymouth *150*, 153–163
  Aquarium 156

Plymouth *continued* . . .
  Barbican 155–6
  gin 155
  Hoe 157–8
  Royal William Yard 158–9
Plymouth & Dartmoor
  Railway 268
ponies, Dartmoor 232
Postbridge *222*, 259
pottery, paint your own 52,
  84, 132
Powderham Castle *22*,
  30–3
Powderham Marshes *22*, 27
Pownall, Captain Philemon
  101–2
Prawle Point *118*, 130
Prayer-book rebellion 65,
  215, 216
prehistoric remains **224–5**,
  234, 252
  Blackdown Rings 127
  Cosdon Beacon 207
  Dancers, The 230
  Merrivale Stone Rows 267
  Nine Stones 210
  Shovel Down 237–8
Preston Sands *48*, 68
Prince, John (*Worthies of
  Devon*) 19, 97
Princetown *222*, 270–2
public transport 11–12

R
Radio Devon 18
RAF Harrowbeer 172
rail travel 23–4, 26, 50, 80,
  152, 184, 205
  railways, steam *see*
    steam railways
Raleigh, Sir Walter 70, 106,
  194

Rare Breeds Farm, Totnes
  78, 88–9, 198
Read, Herbert, woodcarver
  102, 248
Redcliffe Hotel 64
Redgate beach 55
Revenge, the 60, 176–7
riding 167, 233
Ringmore *118*, 145–6
Riverford Field Kitchen
  78, 94
RSPB, the 15, 26–7, 29, 37

S
St Apollonia 187
St Barbara 187
St Marychurch *48*, 52–3
  Bygones 52
St Pancras 254
St Raphael's church,
  Huccaby 260
Salcombe *118*, 134–6
Salcombe gin 135
Saltern Cove *48*, 68
Saltram *150*, 164
Sampford Courtenay *204*,
  215–16
sea tractor *see* Burgh Island
Shaldon *22*, 42–3
  Homeyards Botanical
    Gardens 42–3
  Shaldon Wildlife Trust 42
  Teignmouth ferry 40
Sharpham Vineyard 9, *78*,
  102–3
sheep 265
Sherford *118*, 133–4
shipwrecks 39, 135, **149**
Shovel Down *222*, 237–8
single-track roads 13
Slapton *118*, 119, 122–5
  Slapton Ley 122–3

Slapton *continued* . . .
  Slapton Sands 124–5
Slow mindset, the 8
Smith, Colonel Robert 64
smugglers 145
Snaily House, the 259, **273**
Soper, Tony 3, 162–3
Sourton *204*, 218
South Brent *150*, 180
South Devon Chilli Farm
  118, 127
South Devon Railway *78*,
  182, 196–8
South Milton *118*, 140–1
South Tawton *204*, 208–9
South West Coast Path
  (highlights) 13, 37, 51,
  72, 77, 107, 120, 134
South West Lakes Trust
  172–3, 215, 238
South West Sculptors'
  Association 3
South Zeal *204*, 209
Spinsters' Rock *222*, 242
Stabb, John 19
stannary towns 193, **226**,
  264
Starcross *22*, 33–4
Starcross–Exmouth ferry
  26, 34
Start Point *118*, 129–30
Staverton *78*, 93–4
steam railways
  Dartmouth Steam
    Railway *78*, 80, 90,
    108–9
  Plym Valley Railway 154
  South Devon Railway
    196–8
Sticklepath *204*, 208
Stoke Bay 167
Stoke Fleming *78*, 114

Stoke Gabriel *78*, 100
Stokeinteignhead *22*, 44, 47
Stone Lane Gardens *222*, 242
Stover Country Park *182*, 192
Stover Trail 184
Sunday Rover (bus, Dartmoor)
surfing 139, 142, 164
swimming, wild 81, 173, 214, 240, 259

T
Tamar Belle Heritage Centre 169
Tamar Valley Discovery Trail 153, 176
Tamar Valley Line (rail) *150*, 152, 153, **169**
Tamar, river *150*, 151, **162–3**, 168
Tavistock *222*, 227, 264–6
Ted Hughes Poetry Trail 192
Teign, River *22*, 26, 40, 42, 183, 240
Teignmouth *22*, 39–41
   Chapel of St Mary 40–1
   Shaldon ferry 40
   Teign Heritage Centre 39
Templer Way 253
Thurlestone *118*, 140–1
tide tables, use of 15
tin mining 226, 258
tinners' rabbits 221, 225
Torbryan *182*, 190–1
Torquay *48*, 54–61
   Living Coasts 59–60
   Museum 58–9
   Torre Abbey 60–1
Totnes *78*, 79–81, **82–8**, *182*

Totnes *continued* . . .
   markets 85–7
   museums 84–5
Tuckenhay *78*, 103
Turf Inn, Exminster 27, 28
Two Bridges *222*, 267
Two Castles Trail *204*, 206
Two Moors Way *222*, 230

V
Valiant Soldier, the 196
Vineyards 9, 41, 102–3

W
walking & cycling 12–14
Warren House Inn 238
wassailing **10**, 11
Watcombe beach *48*, 52
Ways with Words 91
Wembury *150*, 116, 164–5
West Devon Way 164, 230
Wheal Exmouth *182*, 187, 188
whisky 9, 270
Widecombe-in-the-Moor *222*, 253–5
wild swimming 81, 173, 214, 240, 259
wildlife parks *see* zoos
wildlife reserves *see* nature reserves
William of Orange 73
wind-surfing 139, 141
wine, local **9**, 41, 102–3, 202
Wistman's wood 215, 222, 269–70
wool 128, 196, 208, 244, 250, 265
World War II 110, 122, 124–5, 137, 154, 197, 209

Worthies of Devon, the
19, 97

Y
Yealmpton *150*, **166**, 248
Yelverton *150*, 172

Z
zoos & wildlife parks
   Aquarium, Plymouth 156
   Dartmoor Zoo 178
   Living Coasts 59–60
   Miniature Pony Centre 245
   Otters & Butterflies 198–9
   Paignton Zoo 67–8
   Pennywell Farm 202–3
   Rare Breeds Farm (Totnes) 88–9
   Shaldon Wildlife Trust 42

BYGONES

Bygones is three floors of pure nostalgia for all the family. Go back in time from the end of Queen Victoria's reign, through the war years, to the 1950s/60s. Whether you're into history, railwayana or militaria, immerse yourself in the past!

Fore Street,
Marychurch, Torquay,
Devon, TQ1 4PR

https://bygones.co.uk
Tel: 01803 326108
Email: info@bygones.co.uk

KENTS CAVERN PREHISTORIC CAVES

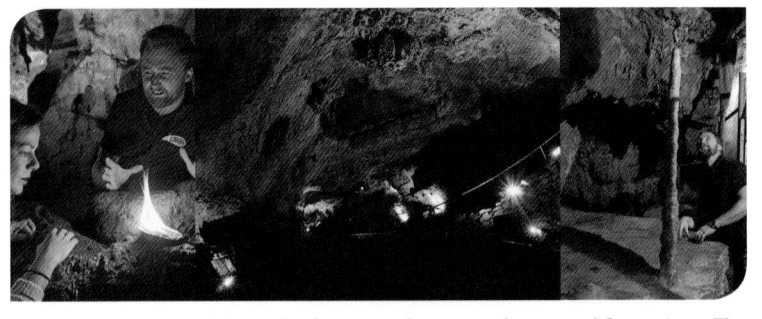

Kents Cavern is a vast labyrinth of caves with spectacular natural formations. The human archaeology discovered here is the most ancient found in Britain. The most significant artefact is a 41,000-year-old human jawbone – Britain's oldest human.

KENTS CAVERN
PREHISTORIC CAVES
UNESCO GLOBAL GEOPARK

Ilsham Road
Torquay
Devon TQ1 2JF

www.kents-cavern.co.uk
Tel: 01803 215136
Email: caves@kents-cavern.co.uk

ake time away."

Hugh Fearnley-Whittingstall

Local, characterful guides to Britain's special places

Bradt

Available from bookshops or www.bradtguides.com